METAPHOR REEXAMINED

Advances in Semiotics
General Editor, Thomas A. Sebeok

METAPHOR REEXAMINED

A Non-Aristotelian Perspective

Liselotte Gumpel

INDIANA UNIVERSITY PRESS
Bloomington

Library of Congress Cataloging in Publication Data

Gumpel, Liselotte.
  Metaphor reexamined.

(Advances in semiotics)
Bibliography: p.
Includes index.
  1. Metaphor.   2. Semiotics.   3. Languages—Philosophy.
I. Title. II. Series.
P99.4.M48G85   1984   401'.41   84-47707
ISBN 0-253-33781-X
1 2 3 4 5 88 87 86 85 84

To Edgar Lohner
and
To my Parents
Victims of the Holocaust

Ψυχῆς ἐστι λόγος
ἑαυτὸν αὔξων

Of the soul is the word
which increases itself.

—Heraclitus

Contents

Preface

Aristotle (384-322 B.C.) opens his *Metaphysics* with the statement that all humans "naturally" desire knowledge. Unfortunately, this proclivity has not brought the investigation of metaphor very far since it originated with him. At my time of writing, barely two decades are left before the second millennium yields to a third. Yet so closely has criticism in this area adhered to Aristotelian ideas that I call the tradition from its ancient beginnings to the present "neo-Aristotelian." In his own time, Aristotle may not have been the first proponent of metaphor, but from the contemporary vantage point he is acknowledged as the major influence of this tradition and has thus become its undisputed progenitor. This very fidelity is startling since Aristotle's principle was never free from problems. The fact that its presentation in the *Poetics* does not match his usual acuity of insight and clarity of approach caused some Classical scholars even to doubt the authorship.

The trouble is that metaphor never made the transition from the fields of rhetoric to semantics, despite the fact that in 1897 the French critic Bréal coined the term *Semantics*, hoping to initiate *Studies in the Science of Meaning*, to cite here from the English translation of his title and subtitle. Both were echoed again in the middle of this century in the titles of a work by Ullmann (1970), but to no avail; metaphor remained a distinctive "problem" of semantics (Weinrich, 1967, p. 3). This curious historical lag parallels the critical neglect: metaphor enjoys a longevity of over two thousand years while meaning as a semantic discipline is barely a century old. Theoretically and historically metaphor was put before meaning—the *semantic* idiosyncrasy arrived before its base.

My theory of "non-Aristotelian" semantics aims to correct these problems. It is "Aristotelian" only in its focus on metaphor in language. To be sure, myth and the visual arts also exude meaning. But broad "Languages of Art," to quote Nelson Goodman (1968), are not at issue. Rather, my interest is narrowed to the type of language a speech community shares through *words*. So the word as bearer of meaning and metaphor is my primary concern, a topic that turns out to be complex enough. Methodologically, I apply a Cartesian reduction by taking absolutely nothing for granted.

I begin with the startling assertion that the traditional metaphor does not exist in language, any more than does solar movement across the sky. Like this movement, metaphor is based on sense impressions. Any lay person regards metaphor as a unique figure of speech, a colorful content, and unfortunately the experts have not advanced much further than that with their detection of metaphor. They, too, react to the presentational immediacy of surface contents, with Bréal himself no exception to the rule, much as one is indebted to his intent of wanting to make a "science" out of semantics. While lay persons can be satisfied with speaking about metaphor when they sense its presence, experts have to isolate its substance and explain why it disappears as fast as it is found.

The scientific nonexistence of the traditional metaphor, along with its swift diappearance or "death," has three major causes: this type of metaphor is based on categories which are not "in" language; it is grounded in functions already owned by its supposed antonym, "literal" meaning, once this has been thoroughly examined; it is denied a genuinely "structural" base which anchors contents to their mode of contextualization. Each problem reduces metaphor ontologically to a hybrid: in the first case, it straddles logic and language, in the second, meaning and metaphor, and in the third, literal and literary use. The first problem erupts repeatedly into an "Ontological Argument for the Existence of Language through Logic." One might as well attribute a divine origin to language than seek anything in meaning by such faulty "divination." The third issue becomes ever more important in an era of the "poetic" sounding commercial jingle and, conversely, of a deliberately "prosaic" literary style whenever "antiart" trends eschew the traditional poetics of an elevated diction by other means than an indulgence in experimental excess (Gumpel, 1976, pp. 49-52).

To rectify the problems, my non-Aristotelian theory begins with the ontological placement, not of metaphor but of language as bearer of meaning, a task achieved with the aid of the phenomenological semantics of Ingarden (1893-1970). After the identification comes the specification, which begins with the semiotic "Picture of Language" based on the sign classes of Peirce (1874-1945). Every sign is followed through systematically from its most "degenerate" foundation to full "Interpretant" generation. Since the presentation is rigorously systematic, readers are asked to follow it closely. They will then see where the traditional metaphor is lodged and why it "dies"; they will glean also the advantages of the non-Aristotelian metaphor, which is the ultimate, positive climax of my theory. "Structurally" grounded in meaning as a semantic idiosyncrasy, this metaphor eludes all destruction, no matter what its surface releases.

After the theory comes its application: three textual analyses check out every criterion empirically while delving into issues of genre, stance, and time that govern authorial inception and reader reception of literary works of art. Moreover, since the topic as a whole is difficult and at times technical, all parts of the study draw on concrete examples obtained from mass media excerpts including cartoons, as well as diagrams. And to give the tradition its due, my theory, pure and applied, is followed by a neo-Aristotelian "adjunct," so called because this part is ancillary to my own thesis yet important for contrasting non-Aristotelian semantics with extant neo-Aristotelian premises.

In sum, non-Aristotelian semantics systematically puts the linguistic before the extralinguistic domain, broad meaning before idiosyncratic metaphor, function before form, and holistic context before content taxonomy. Though partially expository of the above named thinkers, the study rests on a unique thesis. Its primary aim is to grasp metaphor through an exhaustive understanding of meaning in language, the most powerful tool for human communication and perhaps the only acceptable "weapon" which, through the word, may bring peace without violence to the modern world. My theory should be of interest to scholars of philosophy, literary theory (English, classics, comparative literature, and foreign languages), linguistics, and psychology. Philosophy is the basic tool for ontology, but issues of genre determination, syntax, and context as well as language acquisition encompass these other fields.

By its end, my study will have taught readers who followed it consistently how to distinguish phenomena from essence and recognize thresholds separating material from meaning, meaning from metaphor, and everyday from esthetic use. Readers will be able to diagnose clinically semantic "death" in its various phases as they let "die" the traditional principle by knowing why it is a myth--and ontologically not part of that myth which flourished as polytheism at the time of Aristotle. Lastly, readers will be certain that my language here as I write about language is "literal" no matter how "metaphorical" its appearance. The age of a "science of meaning" and a metaphor of substance is at hand!

Now to a few technical matters. Considerations of length (originally covering 900 manuscript pages) encouraged me to follow the recent practice of keeping the annotation in the text, usually directly following the author's name. The dates within the parentheses match those in the bibliography, which is divided into two parts, books and articles. Second, the translations in this study are my own unless otherwise identified.

No work of this magnitude could have been written in the first place without the support of many individuals. Thus I thank those who read the whole or parts of this manuscript: Edward Stankiewicz of Yale University, Eugene Falk of the University of North Carolina at Chapel Hill, Victor Lange of Princeton University, and Jeremiah Reedy of Macalester College, who checked some of my Greek transliterations. Others who expressed interest in the project and or gave me the opportunity to speak on it are Paul deMan, Yale University, Kurt Mueller-Vollmer, Stanford University, Max Bense and Elisbeth Walther, the Institut für Philosophie und Wissenschaftstheorie, Stuttgart University; Helmut Kreuzer of the Gesamthochschule, Siegen, Joachim von der Thüsen of the University of Utrecht, and Käte Hamburger, Stuttgart. I am especially grateful to Warren Shibles of the University of Wisconsin at Whitewater, editor of the annotated bibliography on metaphor, for providing me with material. In addition I thank Girton College, Cambridge, Great Britain, where I completed parts of the original manuscript as Helen Cam Fellow of 1977- 1978.

In the immediate vicinity, I wish to thank the Graduate School of the University of Minnesota for their support as well as the staff of the Minitex Library. The same applies to the entire library staff and to the computer center at the Morris Campus. Individuals who supported me on this campus were Provost John Q. Imholte, Dean Elizabeth S. Blake, and Nathaniel Hart, Chairperson of the Humanities Division. Those generally helpful and or willing to read small parts of the text were: Dwight Purdy and James Gremmels (English), Howard Wettstein (formerly of Philosophy), and Vernard Brown (General Services). Persons who took charge of specific tasks were: Jane Kill, typing and word processing, David Jones, Tim McKenzie, and Randy Guetter, typesetting. Two students, Lisa Pilarski and Debra

Wieland, completed the index and computerized drawings. Lastly, a special thanks to Thomas A. Sebeok, editor of the series, *Advances in Semiotics*, and to the staff of the Indiana University Press, specifically its Senior Sponsoring Editor, Janet Rabinowitch, and to my proofreader, Judith Allensworth. As a final reminder, let me not forget either the two Anglo-Saxon cultures, Great Britain and the United States, that made it possible for me to become a survivor of fascist persecution and thus enabled me to advance knowledge in this important area of study.

Acknowledgments

Acknowledgment is made to the following publishers, authors, and cartoonists:

Agis-Verlag, Baden-Baden, for Max Bense's "thetic" and "symbolic" graphs in *Zeichen und Design*, 1971.

Deutsche Verlags-Anstalt, Stuttgart, 1, for Paul Celan, "Ins Nebelhorn," in *Mohn und Gedächtnis*, 9. Auflage, 1970.

Johnny Hart, for the *Wizard of Id* (5/18/79), by permission of Johnny Hart and Field Enterprises, Inc.

Hank Ketcham, for *Dennis the Menace*; reprinted by courtesy of Hank Ketcham, and copyrighted by Field Enterprises, Inc.

Little, Brown and Company, Boston, for "When Etna basks and purrs." From *The Complete Poems of Emily Dickinson*, edited by Thomas H. Johnson. Copyright 1914, 1942, by Martha Dickinson Bianchi. Reprinted by permission of Little, Brown and Company.

Methuen, Inc., New York, copyright © 1976 by Eyre Methuen Ltd. "1940" by Bertolt Brecht, translated by Liselotte Gumpel by permission of the publisher, Methuen, Inc., by arrangement with Suhrkamp Verlag, Frankfurt 1. All rights reserved. Official U. S. translation available in the collection *Bertolt Brecht Poems 1913-1956*, edited by John Willett and Ralph Mannheim.

Warren Shibles, *Essays on Metaphor*, The Language Press, Whitewater, Wisconsin, 1972 (excerpted from *Metaphor: An Annotated Bibliography and History*, Wisconsin, 1971).

Suhrkamp Verlag, Frankfurt a/M, for Bertolt Brecht, "1940," in *Gedichte 1934-1941*, IV, 1961.

United Feature Syndicate, Inc., © 1979, for *Peanuts*, "ABC."

Tom Wilson, for *Ziggy* (6/15/80). Copyright, 1980, Universal Press Syndicate. Reprinted with permission. All rights reserved.

Introduction: Ringing in the New Millennium
of Non-Aristotelian Semantics

My study, as stated, commences with the non-Aristotelian theory in pure and applied form and concludes with a neo-Aristotelian adjunct that offers the most famous expositions of metaphor through the ages. In this introduction, however, I reverse that organization by starting with neo-Aristotelian problems and concluding with vital aspects governing my own theory. What Crystal (1971, pp. 208-209) had to say about the attitude of Bloomfieldian linguists toward meaning in the early decades of this century is still applicable today, to approaches to metaphor as a supposedly "semantic" principle. Crystal notes that there was "no critical reliance on the idea of 'meaning' in making or formulating grammatical analysis. . . . Meaning was felt to be an 'internal' phenomenon, a mental residue not susceptible to direct investigation . . . ."

Critics of metaphor similarly circumvent "internal" phenomena and settle instead for the most tangible, "external" base a language has to offer in the way of presentational immediacy, and that is the explicit *lexicon*. The lexicon obligingly reflects empirical reality by representing it like a mirror and thus unwittingly leads those who cling to it into an unwarranted *skepticism* by undermining the genuine constitutive powers of language. Such an approach will never lead to the "scientific" semantics Bréal envisaged. To illustrate, I introduce my only comparison from the sciences. In a work dedicated to *Einstein's Universe*, Calder (1979, pp. 9-11, 41-42) discusses movements of objects through space that are designated "blueshift" and "redshift" in physics. Without going into technical detail, I take up the part where Calder emphasizes that, of these two shifts, the former causes an increased and the latter a decreased frequency; what in terms of sensation becomes described in everyday parlance as "cool" blue or "warm" red turns into its "opposite" for the physicist. The senses yield one type of information and the scientific facts another.

Einstein's ancient precursor, Euclid, lived close to the time of Aristotle. But physics has made such strides that it can separate sheer perception from a drastically different unseen condition, while the study of metaphor has yet to realize such distinctions. Scientists are thus cognizant of their separate roles as lay perceivers while experts of semantics still resemble the lay persons who associate

1

a reaction to sensation with valid information about a function of linguistic signation. No expert should be needed to respond to the lexical surface of a language, any more than the public at large has to learn from a physicist why red feels "warm" compared to blue.

Curiously, critics of language possess one added advantage over physicists because, paradoxical as this may seem, the "lay speaker" within them is also a genuine if unconscious expert, as is made explicit by the reference to a "linguistic competence." Perhaps it is also a disadvantage to be so close to the object under investigation as all humans are to their language. Therefore I advocate something like a Fichtean type of "intellectual introspection" (intellektuelle Anschauung): to "watch" oneself using words while articulating them. Persons who like myself are bilingual benefit doubly from this approach and, certainly, I shall draw on it frequently.

A concrete example of what happens to metaphor when sought as single, "odd" content in lexical incompatibility may be witnessed by a case I call the *Ingendahl Experiment*. I name this experiment after Ingendahl, the critic who wrote it up in a German essay (1972) that asked whether the concept metaphor still served any purpose. Since the outcome of the experiment is inconclusive, the answer would have to be in the negative (pp. 268-269). In this experiment, a group of individuals was asked to underline only metaphorical words extracted from a newspaper article on political elections. Out of 58 words, alone two were assessed as metaphors by all of the participants, and Ingendahl rightly laments this lack of consensus. Curious and yet typical is the fact that the experiment was conducted in a seminar devoted to "Poetologie." What does literary language have to do with a feuilletonistic write-up?

No satisfactory answer can be supplied other than to predict that the question will arise in the course of such an experiment. The reason is the evidence of a practice I term "spotsighting." This procedure reifies the localized content taxonomy single words bear, disregarding holistic criteria that bind contents to their mode of contextualization. One hardly needs the German original to conjure up colorful figures in English that similarly permeate the rhetorical oratory of political elections. Who has not heard of the political programs that become "platforms" like the dais candidates mount to present their plans? Who has not listened to the self-pitying complaints of an "underdog" about having to confront an incumbent candidate fortunate enough to possess that coveted "seat" in government? No expert is needed to perceive what the lexicon so conspicuously releases as "metaphorical" excess, but discerning critics would provide a great service if they could explain what keeps these meanings nevertheless "literal" rather than genuinely "poetic."

Such a critic I hope to represent. Thus I diagnose next how the lexical orientation produces the traditional metaphor. *Reference* in meaning is confused with a direct *representation* of the empirical reality, in essence a "pointing at . . ." a this or that. Meanings are thus considered stand-ins for things in the world. When meanings exhibit *arepresentational* pockets of lexical deviance, they are believed to have abrogated their "denoting." Then meanings stand in as "proxies" for one another, at which point they partake of a *transference* yielding metaphor, in keeping with the etymological root of Greek "metaphora." In this transferral, set *analogies* provide the underpinning for surface *anomalies* and thus keep the words bearing these meanings construable. Because this type of transference is based on a barter of semantic proxies, I call it the *proxy-tenet*. The majority of linguists, under the influence of Chomsky (1965, pp. 148-163), seek proxy-tenet transference in *selectional* violation of the lexicon. Current philosophers identify the same phenomenon as the *category-mistake* introduced by Ryle (*Concept of Mind*, 1949/1963, p. 16; "Categories," 1961, Flew, ed., pp. 75-76).

An annotated bibliography on metaphor put out by Shibles (1971) lists a plethora of studies devoted to the Rylean category-mistake, from Baker's "Category Mistakes" (1956) to Cross's "Category Differences" (1959), and from Hillman's "On Grammars and Category-Mistakes" (1963) to Drange's *Type-Crossing* (1966), to name a few. All these titles reflect a "categorician" stance which, ironically, swiftly lapses into an *ontological category-mistake* when the mistaken "categories" are claimed to be mistaken by metaphor. In Rylean terms, these categoricians commit a "cross-sorting" as they "type-trespass" from logic into language on the basis of little more than a deviant surface. Equally ironic is the fact that they would all be right if they were to accept metaphor only at face value as an *ontological* category-mistake. The traditional metaphor is not even "in" language proper; it straddles *two* forms of programming in what I term a momentary "collison" between logic and language, but without any detriment to linguistic competence. That is the only reason why metaphor stays construable, and not because it is based on some compensating analogy. That is also why metaphor so swiftly reverts to meaning when such a sense impression subsides.

My diagnosis of neo-Aristotelian theses, so glibly summarized here, took years of painstaking synthesis. Once isolated, the identifiable problems run like a thread through the neo-Aristotelian expositions. Since the metaphorical characteristics a tradition has pinpointed actually do not exist in language, such a principle remains a mirage. As already indicated, there is no such function as proxy-tenet transference anywhere in the generation of meaning, because the *contents* are selected for their precise purpose by authorial *intent*. The constituents are thus *willed* as chosen by a speaker, creating all "analogies" in the process. I use "author" and "speaker" interchangeably for the present since one term only is adjectival. And insofar as I function as author my illustrations more frequently, but not exclusively, emphasize the *written* word. In any case, to apply that introspective approach advocated, as potential speaker and as an author here, all my sentences consist of selected constituents harboring *my* intent through *their* denominations. Words are vehicles for speech; their primary task is to "name" what it is speakers wish to "say." That is how they acquire their explicit and implicit contents, and for that purpose they become assimilated in the first place, not as neat lexical labels for realities outside of language.

Linguistic activity thus creates and validates norms--in one language at a time. That is the ontogenetic origin of meaning. When semantic redundance is complete, the oddest contents seem "proper" or "literal." Language, and not its lexicon reflecting an extalinguistic domain, thus ordains what is "odd" or acceptable. For example, English has validated gadgets and machines that "work." Speakers of English consider the predicate ordinary because semantic redundance has done its "work," so to speak. Yet in renewed contexts accompanied by punning the predicate may become strange in its connotations of a nine-to-five job, leaving these gadgets "linguistic robots." The same happens in a bilingual cognizance; the equivalent German and French verbs, "arbeiten" and "travailler," apply only to persons in the labor force, not machines. By the same token, machines that function in these languages are made to "go" or, when literalized, even "march," in the respective "gehen" and "marcher," giving rise to other types of robots by assuming the voluntary movement of live beings.

How do these oddities arise? While the full answer will take up a good part of this study, let me say for now that the implicit meaning of explicit contents becomes engendered in the crossfire between *reference* and *transference*. Therefore transference does exist in language, but not as a function based on juggled categories and proxy-barter. Rather, the meanings chosen to engender an authorial intent undergo a *shift* as their explicit denomination releases the implicit connotations relevant to the constitutional unit(y), as in this book's every sentence. Since this processing occurs irrespective of lexical deviance, the traditional metaphor is deprived once more of its being, this time by losing its idiosyncrasy. Not only are its alleged categories not in language, its function when in language, and with some modification, belongs to any meaning. The problem here is not only one of focusing on superficial phenomena like the lexicon, but of relying on a vulnerable method which fails to specify a whole before its parts. To correct such faulty procedure, I introduce an *obverse* and *reverse* order. Drawn from the minting of coins, the adjectives distinguish "right side up" and "underside": obverse meaning comes before reverse metaphor. When thus approached, metaphor will not end up invested with idiosyncrasies already owned by meaning. The full impact of this corrective will materialize in the neo-Aristotelian adjunct where critics are forever attributing to metaphor what meaning, when fully examined first, has already preempted.

My theory of non-Aristotelian semantics thus does not pit transference against reference as the exclusive property of metaphor. Rather, the non-Aristotelian metaphor I develop after a thorough probing of obverse meaning is to be invested with a special mode of transference, still reinforcing the etymological root of "metaphora" without destroying its self-identity by positing violated categories and proxy-tenet substitutions that are not intrinsic to meaning--anywhere. My type of metaphor faces neither "death" nor "destruction" because it remains *structurally* based, meaning that its foundation is functionally and not lexically reinforced; it is *context*-sensitive instead of *content*-sensitive.

To be sure, if methodologically one starts with reverse metaphor as an instance of transference, obverse meaning appropriates this quality and becomes accordingly "metaphor," although the function is the very result of semantic generation, irrespective of content. Certainly, the traditional categoricians leave themselves open to making metaphor so ubiquitous that the principle becomes attenuated. The "nature" of meaning in a "natural" language is indeed very "unnatural" when held up against empirical nature, just because language is a volitional product of human intervention. Linguistic meaning is "metaphysical" insofar as it transcends "physis," the Greek word for "nature." Those familiar with the etymology of "metaphysics" know that the term stems from the arrangement of the Aristotelian volumes, which had the "metaphysics" come "after" and in a sense "beyond" the natural sciences or "physics." I thus trade on this etymology. Critics today nevertheless insist on a "transcendence" unique to metaphor when language as bearer of any meaning partakes of it quite naturally. A principle that is everywhere--ends up being nowhere.

The main problem areas have been cursorily identified. Aristotle initiated them all, as the adjunct will prove. Curiously, despite his early affirmation of the "conventional" base of language, and despite his role in devising logical categories as well as isolating literary genres, Aristotle confused all these distinctions when he analyzed and illustrated metaphor as a linguistic phenomenon in a literary setting. Accordingly he also committed the first ontological category-mistake by imposing erroneous logical categories on alleged lexical deviance as "alienation," the Greek *allotrios*. Since an alien *metaphora* then gives rise to a series of transferrals he calls *epiphoras*, the functions entailed in those shifts have no other recourse but proxy-tenet substitution.

Some of these flaws, coming from so versatile and astute a thinker as Aristotle, disturbed the Classical scholars sufficiently to make them question the possible authorship of this exposition in the *Poetics*, leaving this principle on shaky historical ground as well. But the neo-Aristotelian followers throughout Western civilization, ancient and Christian, have remained strangely unperturbed by the weakness of the original concept. Despite a great proliferation of material, the theories manifest a stagnation in the field. By not correcting the vital flaws, these theories never really advanced from the ancient exposition, whose most immediate link from a present "retrospective" view was Latin rhetoric in the persons of Cicero and Quintilian. The principle, though lacking in the most basic areas indicated, was kept intact by these two rhetoricians and has been handed down that way.

Non-Aristotelian semantics, as stated, breaks with the traditional outlook and is guided by Ingarden's phenomenology as well as Peirce's semiotics. Phenomenology is particularly useful for underscoring semantic entities as "objects" of signitive consciousness, which to Ingarden are not only "pure-intentional" as targets of an "intending" act but also "heteronomous" insofar as they are dependent only on acts of *meaning*. Language is thus the sphere of "ontic heteronomy" whose entities, unlike those of "ontic autonomy," are directly dependent on signitive acts. The contents that meanings own arise with the acts of meaning that use them and thus claim them as their "own" intrinsic products. Since linguistic activity is indigenous to a language, this ownership cannot transcend one language.

Ingarden's phenomenological semantics eradicates the ontological category-mistake which in turn undermines the constitutive prowess of language by basing "categories" on a superficial content taxonomy obtained from the lexicon. Logic is once and for all barred from language although Ingarden, committing none of the defaults that mar the approach to semantics at large, certainly specifies where it has a part in the formation of the so-called proposition or judgment which, as "literal" language, then opposes a genuinely literary use. Again, the difference is functional; "truth," too, rests on a special processing, termed "adequation," through which language attains a reality-nexus irrespective of lexical appearances. This issue will be crucial to the study of metaphor, especially the "Fregean" contingent (after Frege, 1848-1925) among neo-Aristotelians. And, unlike this contingent, Ingarden remained entirely methodical by heeding what I have termed here heuristically the obverse/reverse order. Because he explained first what everyday language is, he could also deal with the literary kind of language which operates without a reality-nexus.

In reliance on the presentational immediacy exuded by the lexicon, critics naively identify deviance at that level with true or false conditions. Since their arepresentational metaphor no longer bears "reference," it depends on the lexicon only long enough to extract incompatibility from it; once found, the lexicon is abandoned and metaphor is said to be "nondenoting." Since their arepresentational metaphor is not first sought in function, it not only straddles logic and language but literal and literary language, a position which leaves it quite literally "use-less." At the same time it is dimly realized that literary use, even when not deviant, possesses no reality-nexus and as a consequence this, too, is often held to be nondenoting. Frege, who was foremost a mathematician, tried his hand at language and, without adequate explanation, contended that the literary kind depended on "sense" only, minus "reference." This dichotomy has been picked up by Fregean critics of metaphor, as enthusiastically as others have adopted the Rylean category-mistake, with several individuals pleading non-existent "Contextualist Dilemmas" precisely because a literary or metaphorical context "means" or "refers to" something when it is falsely assumed to subsist on nondenoting contents.

Non-Aristotelian semantics will remove not only such dilemmas but also the dichotomy underlying them. Just as reference cannot be split from transference, it cannot be separated from sense. When the theory moves from ontological placement to a detailed identification by the means of a semiotic "Picture of Language," readers will be made to see where the ground of language begins with the "Qualisign" and where indigenous "truth" in language becomes anchored through the validating powers of the "Legisign," which figuratively might well be termed a "linguistic copyright"--long before any government agency decrees it authorial rights. Simultaneously, the lexicon is to be relieved of its duplicative role and become reinstated in its rightful function of providing that vital explicit foundation for speaker intent instead of content surrogates for things in the world.

Semiotics is an excellent means for identifying every facet of language, and my theory thus moves methodically through the signs, listed first on the diagram of this so-called Picture. The schema adheres to Peircean nomenclature in reference to his trichotomies and their triadic relation, though utilizing nine of his ten sign classes, with the tenth, "Argument," modified to befit the state of linguistic semantics, ontic heteronomy. The Picture then reveals the difference between the traditional metaphor lodged at the *Icon*--to Peirce the "Hypoicon"--and the non-Aristotelian counterpart, which resides at the level of the *Interpretant*, specifically the Rheme. Since confused notions of "death" cling to the traditional metaphor, this Picture additionally clarifies what demise is in language, at various levels of degeneration. The non-Aristotelian metaphor, structurally secured, remains indestructible unless the entire context were to disintegrate, together with the language itself, in which case not even "meaning" is left. As shown, the semiotic terms are capitalized to signify my use (though Peirce, too, at times followed this practice).

Peirce enabled me to modify Ingarden's phenomenology numerically, since the latter goes mainly by a binary system separating literal from literary use. The end result is, therefore, that I posit *three linguistic structures*, among them *two literary genres*. By "genre" I mean a functional composite and not the numerous historical subcategories based on the literary etiquettes current in one era, although some of even these formats are briefly mentioned in the chapter preceding the textual analysis which deals with issues of inception and reception of literary works of art. This is where temporal aspects also become relevant to literary constructs devoid of a reality-nexus, particlarly during construal in a processing Ingarden terms "concretization."

Three structures, inclusive of just two literary genres, present deliberately a "Cartesian" type of reduction aimed at the bare minimum where nothing any longer is taken for granted. "Post-Aristotelian" followers may then differentiate further subcategories without conflicting with the basic non-Aristotelian divisions. Such possibilities will be indicated. Nor are phenomenological and semiotic approaches in conflict. Ingarden may have looked to Husserl (1859-1938) rather than to Peirce for his phenomenology, but Peirce's very definition in the *Collected Papers* (1960, p. 141, par. 1.284) of his phenomenological concept, the "phaneron," becomes relevant: it constitutes a "collective total of all that is in any way or in any sense present to the mind, quite regardless of whether it corresponds to any real thing or not."

This very "presence to the mind," signitively induced and intersubjectively validated, is the core of linguistic reference. Conversely, positing a representational correspondence between a meaning and any "real thing" reflects as naive a stance as expecting the green and serrated form of a painted leaf, for instance, to ooze chlorophyll or engage in photosynthesis. No ontological measure applies to that relation beyond a loose description of theme, since two different modes of existence are involved, leaving the entities in relation to one another "category-mistakes" and those overriding their bounds the type-trespassers committing the ontological category-mistake. No one would confuse the visual arts this way, but critics of language succumb that naively to the visible lexicon although it subsists on an equally purposive foundation.

Other thinkers besides the two mentioned who aided me in isolating this foundation are, in their order of importance, the following. Ernst Cassirer (1874-1945) did so, specifically through ideas he laid down in his first volume on language comprising the tripartite *Philosophy of Symbolic Forms*, where linguistic and logical concept formations become separated. Although Cassirer is generally considered "neo-Kantian" in affiliation, he really exhibits his *neo-Humboldtian* roots in these discussions. But then the Humboldtian "energetic" tradition will be shown also to have preserved its neo-Kantian or "Critical" roots, as indicated by none other than this neo-Kantian, Cassirer. Certainly, Wilhelm von Humboldt (1767-1835) made a point of stressing that language was the very "Organ" of its own thought; he realized that the "spoken" (das Gesprochene) serves new speaking (1963, pp. 191-192, 223, 426).

Heidegger (1889-1976) a hundred years later reiterates Humboldt's point almost *verbatim* (1959, p. 16). He is relevant to my immediately ensuing discussion that leads to the ontological placement of language because he underscores the "coercive" nature of language which, in the dialectics between availability and acceptance, lets speakers feel "at home" in their language, no matter how transparent the lexical oddities. Part of that discussion is also taken up with Nietzsche (1844-1900) who commented on metaphorical ubiquity as a metaphysical predicament caught in the "extramoral lie." Even empirical reality lapses into a "metaphor" by being tangible only as a *transmitted* sphere, filtered through human capacities. Yet Nietzsche is more an iconoclast of traditional values than a skeptic of human constitutive powers. Thus his thesis ultimately affirms the unique combinatory powers of poetic art, a sphere no more elusive than reality itself. I then extend his idea to cover the unique artifice of language itself which, if it did not possess such vital creativity from the start, could not serve poetry either.

However, no matter how much I am indebted to all these thinkers, I adopt none of their theories slavishly; nearly all require some modification in order to project metaphor as genuine semantic idiosyncrasy. That point applies no less to my emphasis on "structure," a term which signifies a nonlexical orientation rather than a trendy "ism," and despite the fact that I often quote Saussure (1857-1913), who has been tagged a "Structuralist." Though disparaged by transformationalists, Saussure is one of the few linguists who grasped correctly the value of the "arbitrary" nature of language as a volitional medium. His notion of "opposition" combats the narrow deviance cult which would leave the very critics espousing it at such an atavistic state of juvenile competence that they could not even formulate their ideas. Finally, Saussure's distinction between diachronic and synchronic planes enables me to explain why a "dead metaphor" is nothing more than meaning in developmental stages.

Although the ideas of the thinkers cited here have been extant a good many years, none has been appreciated sufficiently; they need to be reread rather than replaced by "modern" views. Ingarden, who had the courage to name the essence and major functions of language, fulfilled the hopes of Bréal by providing a system equal to a "science" of meaning. He really deserves to be called the "Copernicus of Semantics." Unfortunately, postwar Marxists in his native Poland mistook his endeavors of isolating language for purposes of its much needed ontological identification for some form of elitism and were discouraged further by his somewhat abstruse style (Fieguth, ed., 1976, pp. XI, 135 ff.). Certainly Ingarden is not easy to follow but very rewarding when understood.

I end where I actually first intended to begin: this introduction was originally called "propaedeutic" in honor of Kant, employing a term used in the *First Critique* (Cassirer, ed., 1913, III, pp. 49, 562). There, Kant speaks about scrutinizing the "sources" (Quellen) and "bounds" (Grenzen) of the rational faculties, and a similar concern should accompany the investigation of linguistic capacities. Kant will be reinvoked in this study on a few occasions. Peirce rightly refers to Kant as the "King of modern thought" as he deferentially capitalizes to match the name of this monarch of the mind, and he later uses the comical figure of "udders" to convey how Kant influenced him early in life (1960, p. 193, par. 1.369; p. 64, par. 2.113). In addition, Peirce (p. 23, par. 2.36) made a connection between ancient and Enlightenment thought that is directly relevant to my topic; he calls Aristotle and Kant the two great exponents of metaphysical systems. Indeed, both thinkers incorporated logical *categories* in their metaphysical systems, yet with a difference. While in the *First Critique* Kant concedes that he named his logical concepts "Kategorien" after Aristotle, he renders them powerless in his *Third Critique* devoted to a purposive state such as art, an ontological distinction he expresses as being "without concept" or "interest" (Cassirer ed., 1913, III, pp. 98 ff.; 1914, V, pp. 280 ff.).

Language as a parallel autotelic system follows suit by bearing only the categories or "interest" of its own making. Kant, who recognized such an ontological difference that early, thus remains more "enlightened" than many a "modern" thinker. In one essay (1913, trans. 1970), Kant confronted his own age as he sought to provide an answer to what Enlightenment meant. It involves breaking out of a "self-incurred immaturity" which, for his time, pertained to the stern mentorship of the church, especially in its hold over the "fair sex." Kant thus urges his contemporaries to "Sapere aude!"--"Have the courage to use your own understanding!" Two more centuries have passed since then, but because an enlightened theory of metaphor is still lacking, I set myself the laborious task of presenting one, lest the stagnation lapse into an "Age of Endarkenment." Though of that sex Kant mentions--fair or otherwise--I "dared to know," as his Latin imperative reads when condensed, in the hope that the tradition finally leave behind the teenage years in order to move forward into the year two thousand, the twenty-first century, as a new age of majority. For despite their mental residue, meaning and metaphor lie as much within human grasp as the use of language itself.

PART I

The Task of Ontological Placement

The Task of Ontological Placement

The Procreative and Coercive Powers of Language

"The wise poem knows its father/And treats him not amiss;/But language is its mother/To burn where it would rather/Choose that and by-pass this. . . ." These are some of the concluding lines in I. A. Richards's "Lighting Fires in Snow" from his *New and Selected Poems* (1978, p. 12). Together, title and text convey the analogy between lighting a fire in snow and creating a poem, undoubtedly two difficult tasks. Through the image of burning, the two contexts coincide in reference to what fires do automatically when lit and to the way in which language has the power to "brand" consciousness with the contents of its creation. Signitive activity becomes imprinted on the mind and forms a repertoire of semantic availability, if only in one language--here English--which makes the poem come alive.

I heard Richards recite this poem at Cambridge, England, in January of 1978, shortly before this grand old man of letters died. Although Richards's contribution to the theory of metaphor will be treated later, I could not resist commencing with the above lines, much as they are a fragment from a contextual whole. Supporting a critical exposition with a literary sample might seem risky, but the reader will be eased by this means more gently into a difficult topic. Also, the appeal of this quotation lies in the maternal, indeed matriarchal, image of language. In this little family of the poem, language as "mother" overrides the implied role of the author as father where the "progeny" of the poem is concerned.

What can it mean to characterize language as mother? My answer partially foreshadows the Picture of Language and its semiotic signs, of which the sign in most "degenerate" order is the "M-base." This locus turns out to be the form at its most "material" ground; the germinal source of language no speaker can by-pass once language has not chosen to by-pass the content, as the poem has it. The M-base cannot be circumvented because in it is rooted what Ruth N. Anshen (1971, p. 3) has called the "procreative power of language" through which the "corporealization" of a speaker's intent becomes actualized.

Richards, then, is this poem's father who abides by the entities his

Mother--more precisely, mother tongue--saw fit to "choose" for him. With linguistic material, the nature of language in a language commences and remains inescapable for the nativism on which fluency in a mother tongue depends. Native speakers cannot escape from the procreative forces of language. Now, poems in terms of structural entities do not turn up again for quite a while in this study, in detail not until the textual analyses take over in the applied part. For the present, the task is to find the very ground of language, since this is always missed by tradition's immediate focus on the lexicon. In that ground lies also the word "ontology" whose etymological root is Greek "ousia"; it denotes "being, substance, essence" (Fobes, 1966, p. 287). All three readings have relevance for the type of existence language calls its own. Fundamentally, the being of language is entirely functional, is in substance sustained by its own activity, which solidifies into semantic redundancy.

As Heidegger (1959, p. 33) had put it (with reiteration), speakers "converse" while language "coerces" them. My role as translator here certainly let me sense what he means: the inimitable German wordplay between "sprechen" and "entsprechen," denoting "to speak" and "to parallel" or "match," simply could not be conveyed directly without losing the *pointe* in the gist of the sense. Instead, I forged my own alliterative pair in relatively close connotation. A small instance here proves how language in a different tongue also "directs" me differently when attempting to corporealize Heidegger's thought, because another repertoire is involved. Availability, confined to only one language, simply leaves speakers no other choice. Rebellion is hardly possible if speakers desire to continue as members of their speech community. Only language itself in the particular language may pick and choose or by-pass coinages in the way the poem conveys. To be sure, speakers are collectively behind that language but barred from breaking the intersubjective consensus on their own--if they still intend to "own" their language. Together speakers preserve the power of language. How forceful that power is will be seen in the detailed discussion of translation problems as these surface in the textual analyses.

Yet tradition makes much of untranslatability in metaphor, also an emphasis which comes about with the neglect of the obverse and reverse sides my introduction brought up. If meaning is properly understood in all its apparent unruly complexity, problems of translation may arise at any point. No one would call Heidegger's wordplay outright "metaphor" even if his language on the whole is more colorful than the sober writings of most philosophers. Sometimes the most innocuous syntactic vestiges such as the relative pronoun, for instance, may block a translation. The "meta-" prefix, which was seen (in the introduction) to initiate the metaphysical domain, characterizes language with or without metaphor as a substratum existing "beyond" empirical nature (or "physis") through its unique, volitional origin.

A comic figure to pinpoint that origin was used by none other than the eminent Martin Luther as he painstakingly tried to ply the German *vernacular* in his translation of New Testament Greek. The amusing word is "muzzle"--German "Maul"--(Leipzig/Wien, n.d., p. 176). Luther advocated looking into that muzzle in order to get at the German language used by housewives and their offspring romping in the gutters of back streets. The very fact that the German word does not have an English synonym proves further the curious linguistic proclivity of conversing and coercing. "Maul" is a term used only for the buccal orifice of a carnivorous animal. The missing term in English does not mean that creatures in the countries of those speakers have more refined palates, only that this linguistic perspective was not culled from those creatures and validated as a term. An apt coinage for the neglected mouths of common folk in Luther's era, this muzzle comes to life, down to brown teeth and exhalation of a breath less than sweet; one envisions this venerable translator peering into it like a dentist to extract not decayed teeth but vibrant, current lingo.

The muzzle, then, is a type of metonym for an idiolect used collectively among speakers and, essentially, one "place" where language arises. Out of the same muzzle sprang also Luther's own epithet "Esel," meaning "ass" or "donkey," which he liked to hurl at his papal adversaries (ibid.). A metaphor or meaning? Well, considering that "Esel" actually is used as an invective for a human fool more frequently than as a reference to the donkey as animal, it has obviously become literalized. That is, the German language has standardized the donkey as semantic staple for a human fool, and this stabilization takes precedence in frequent contextualization over said animal. In the empirical world, "Mother Nature" keeps human and equine species categorically apart; language, the Mother, has flattened the donkey into natural coinage which thus evolves as a norm to the point of superseding the animal designation.

Urban settings would hardly call for donkeys since these do not roam streets outside of zoos. Many German speakers had an input into the word's normalization as well as its continued transmission through a collective muzzle. Yet once stabilized, the coinage genuinely forces native speakers into acceptance; they cannot escape it without sacrificing linguistic competence. In my own wordplay which takes off loosely from Heidegger, German speakers become "coerced" into being "conversant" with this flattened commonplace if they want to "converse" fluently in what is "common" to their mother tongue.

Accordingly for better or worse, the fool in this German invective is one solidified import which stays present to the mind, to linguistic consciousness of a language, and here I am trading on the formulation cited from Peirce in the introduction. The language may not reflect the traits of the animal accurately, but it has still legitimized this import as part of speaker performance. Participants in something like the Ingendahl Experiment certainly could not achieve a consensus in assessing semantic reference versus metaphorical transference on the basis of the lexicon if they subjected this idiom to simple measures of overt deviance. All they would be guilty of is the ontological category-mistake which looks to logical cross-sorting of classes--between human and equine species here--that have no direct bearing on language. Non-Aristotelian semantics, however, must base all powers of standardizing on language and not logic. Only from linguistic competence can contents be deployed and internalized in their specific contextualization. Most witty puns leave speakers aware of apparent type-trespassing, much as that cognizance comes from nonlinguistic classes. Then the normalizing process weakens momentarily and in this attenuation has other forms of programming intrude, yet never at the genuine expense of the competence needed exclusively for wielding language.

As noted in the introduction, semantic competence is not touched by a mere sensation of lexical incompatibility. Otherwise the language could not even come together. Before, I spoke of this sensation as a "collision" or "conflict" between two forms of programming, and since only one of the two is indigenous to language, the other can have no impact on language. The programming which lets native speakers realize that their "Esel" is odd in reference to humans has no effect on speaker expertise and thus does not touch functionally the semantic entities involved; the programming which has made "Esel" current in that usage alone controls speech in the particular language, creating a commonplace with literally a locus "common" to that inventory.

To be sure, a nice transparency is in evidence here: donkeys are none too bright. Neo-Aristotelians in their own ontological cross-sorting depart from this fact: stupidity becomes the analogy which bridges the anomaly between human and equine beings. Neat! If the transparency is so easy to motivate, then why does English "ass" match the German "Esel" and then split into yet another content with the "donkey?" The semantic divisions thus do not necessarily parallel those of nature's species. Hence absurd consequences might result from this type of motivation, suggesting a more or less "accurate" signation. Approbation or its opposite is then based on an extralinguistic vantage point, here the selection of the most stupid creature on earth, perhaps, in its most uniform and/or transparent designation. From there, one might get into disagreement about such a rating, even after consulting the most expert zoologists. At this point, the controversy has moved far away from the domain of language and its priority, which is plainly the effective manipulation of speech and not the measuring of zoological versus human traits. Fortunately, non-Aristotelian semantics could never get into such difficulties. Linguists assign an asterisk (*) to unmarked meanings, but concentration must always go on what there *is* and thus parallel the need of speakers to deal with the availability language holds out to them as first priority.

The last issue involving the zoo brings me to a crucial distinction that Saussure's *Course* (1966, pp. 79-100) introduced as *diachronic* and *synchronic* planes. Diachronic evolutionary stages are the concern of the etymologist, philologist, and so on; synchronic language states alone govern speaker competence. That is why non-Aristotelian semantics stresses the synchronic plane. Here is a typical case where appropriate introspection into the role of native speakers should help critics distinguish the expertise which goes into the wielding of words from etymological and other such "professional" concerns. Yet the two critics, Bréal and Ullmann, who were cited in the introduction for wanting to establish semantics as a science of meaning, failed in their goal primarily because of an excessive diachronic orientation.

Bréal's interest in diachronics is a subject reserved for the historical adjunct; Ullmann's will be illustrated here. In one of those cases of unfortunate critical regression, Ullmann's chapter on "Transparent and Opaque Words" (1970, pp. 80-115) tries to improve on Saussurean theory through diachronic motivation while intending to prove there are exceptions to "arbitrary" states in language Saussure apparently had overlooked. Saussure was right not to heed such exceptions. To claim otherwise, as Ullmann does, forces the critic into that skepticism mentioned before which justifies everything found in language from without. Since all language is volitional in provenance, its essence *ipso facto* must be arbitrary, even if the term itself suggests somewhat unfortunately a type of contingency like the throwing of dice. Saussure will be shown to have given a perfectly satisfactory explanation of linguistic arbitrariness. But to rectify Ullmann's point first, whether isomorphic fragments reflect contact with an extralinguistic reality is not at issue and indeed remains as superfluous for the solidified states of synchronic planes as lexical deviance for determining the traditional metaphor.

Saussure did better by language than Ullmann, particularly where he asserted in the *Course* (1966, pp. 69, 73) that the linguistic arbitrary state possessed "no natural connection with the signified," adding that arbitrariness "of the sign is really what protects language from any attempt to modify it." The very protection to which Saussure refers makes it obvious that, *qua* language, the arbitrary state has become *absolute*. The natural donkey is out in the empirical world; no one can make or break it. Yet the "Esel" acquires validity only through collective signitive consciousness outside of which there is--nothing, or only that asterisk shown above for the unmarked meaning. Were it otherwise, there would be no point in coining the meaning at all. Human attention endorses signation for authorial intent and simultaneously endows a semantic entity with being. That is also why I keep emphasizing that sense cannot be split from reference. If anything, *that* relation is the "natural" one, to trade on Saussure, though not in accordance with the nature existing in the empirical animal kingdom. Fascinating as diachronic transparencies are, their limits must be recognized, whereas Ullmann makes far too much of them, for a critic purporting to aim at the essence of meaning and not just its origin.

Ultimately, the donkey term could still serve German speakers for designating the human fool if the animal were the wisest on earth and the human so designated the most foolish, leaving the connection (what Ullmann calls) "opaque." Those acquiring a language do not delve into zoology, hanging labels on finished, formed creatures. What they do is to cope with forms their language holds for them in order to express themselves; they find words for their authorial intent and subsequently assimilate this along with the contents wielded. Through that interiorization, the mind becomes signitively indented, a process to be illustrated with the aid of diagrams later in the study. For the present, my point is that undue stress on the stupidity of the donkey as a direct source for the import of "Esel" would have language picture merely that other maternal figure known commonly as "Mother Nature." Instead, language normalizes its creations, here the invective in German "Esel," until speakers remain conscious of this negative value in the animal image. Otherwise they might hurl the word at the wrong person and face serious consequences. Luther, in his own political climate, was obviously more fortunate.

I shall switch now from "donkey" to "dog." These two "English animals" loosely resemble one another in semantic (M) material, enhanced by the "d" alliteration. But my choice was not so much guided by the need to pun. Rather, I am partially recapitulating since the introduction seized on a canine hybrid, and that was the human "underdog" which I brought up while discussing political jargon with the Ingendahl Experiment. Again, the form of the word, sonorous or visual, has language project itself uniquely, since no live canine quadruped could look like the three letters composing English "dog." How unique this form is native speakers of English can be made to realize with this canine's "tail end" (in yet another amusing pun), which goes even beyond the "meta-" nature of natural beings into the supernatural sphere. For English "dog" is--the other side of "god!"

Is this palindrome of sonorous-visual reversal sheer accidence within an arbitrary state of being? No, this curious linkage is also an entity the collective will of the English speech community has opted to keep suspended, if not in deliberate blasphemy. One may thus posit that no isomorphic transparency accounts for the formation of this palindrome. Etymology no doubt caused the origination of "god" as much as "dog" if hardly their planned association. But such roots are a part of a diachronic investigation. At the synchronic level, content is now confined to authorial intent of any possible manipulation which has the "right" to trade on the palindrome just because it is an extant linguistic connection, reinforcing mnemonic ties and, with these, positive-privative relations language has marked in a language for serving speakers. Basically, of course, English remains neutral with respect--to the disrespect, one might pun. That is exactly the point: inadvertently or not, English has created this profanity and the palindrome now awaits the wit of comedians, advertisers, poets, or politicians in a way no other language can match. This palindrome will become something of a mascot for my study, to be reinvoked in certain relevant explanations. Speakers of English, even the greatest religious fanatics, must abide by it if they want to converse effectively. They may not pun with the palindrome directly, or even have it uppermost in their consciousness every waking moment. Yet the palindrome hovers in the background of possible invocation, with full signitive knowledge of what the words mean, how they sound and look when spoken or written, separately and together. There is no escaping that important knowledge, since one such gap would impair the link in the chain of vital positive-privative values which make up the English inventory of vocables in the "semasiological" differentiation of its internalized dictionary. That is the only way in which meanings exist as semantic vehicles bearing reference--not so much in relation to a this or that as to one another. And no other language shares that differentiation equally, even though the contents in one such system expand further from repeated exteriorization among interlocutory partners who are familiar with all their language-bound nuances.

To be sure, an added nuance of respect surfaces with the mandatory English capitalization of "God." Those who understand meaning do not interpret this simply as a blanket rule of spelling but realize simultaneously that a vital signitive value is involved, to what extent my textual analyses will reveal later. Here, the capitalization potentially breaks up the proximity between the reversed forms of the palindrome; the capital letter at the onset of "God" distances the word from "dog," although that may not be the case with a polytheistic or mythological "god"--who in fact will turn up in the Aristotelian exposition of metaphor. Now, German also capitalizes its cognate, "Gott," but this is mandatory for *all* German nouns. Consequently the signitive value of "respect" accorded an English "God" becomes attenuated by the set syntactic rule. Nor does German possess the disrespectful sounding palindrome, redeeming itself on that score (if one must put it that way): its dog is "Hund."

English, of course, also possesses a "hound," which spills over into the verb "(to) hound (someone)" and other potential uses. So again, English meaning diverges into yet another series of synchronic connectives inimitable in any other language. A dog and hound in classification of real beings present a genus-to-species relation, since the hound is a particular breed of dog. Aristotle's "epiphora" as transference in action will make much of such relations in the operation of metaphor. That focus, exactly, constitutes an *ontological* category-mistake, in this case by confusing categories of the real canine with those of language. Speakers of English must know first how to get from the noun "hound" to the identical-looking verb or other such extant homonyms which nevertheless go their own signitive way as they lend meaning to a speaker's meaning. For that exclusive purpose all semantic entities were forged and keep being sustained.

Admittedly, there is a nice transparency which shows off the "underdog" with some insight into diachronic contact: dominance rites among real canines force a lesser dog to submit to the superior one in a humble posture of cowering "under" the dominant one. Humans in disadvantageous situations appear to fall right into a parallel predicament, as in the political context described. But then one may wonder also why cats, often the "underdogs" when it comes to city ordinances not safeguarding their protection, do not deserve the same prefix in similar motivation. Yet "*undercat" remains starred because language has not seen fit to mark the word. Strictly speaking, the word is thus not a vocable of English, although certain punning in contextualization with the "underdog," for instance, may remove the asterisk as a construable neologism for a given context, especially since the individual segments are already validated meanings.

The ultimate point is that even obvious transparencies remain "arbitrary" with respect to their presence in language, particularly in the signitive relations that they form with other such entities of a given language. What matters is not the realism in linguistic contact with extralinguistic realms but only the ability to "know" meanings for their intrinsic semantic values at every level of their being, from sound to written, visual sign. If one must go to motivation, why does the dog frequently become an invective, actually in both English and German, when this creature is called in real life "man's best friend?" The German "Hund" is a mean fellow, and so is the "dog" of a colleague with whom one must work but can barely stand.

From a mass media array selected at random, I present the following examples. The *St. Paul Dispatch* (April 5, 1979) speaks about some solar panels, installed in Washington, D. C., in order to save oil, as an "economic dog" taking "the heat"; they were "under fire," one might add, for producing heat that was insufficient or too costly. Next, the *Minneapolis Tribune* (January 22, 1980) displayed a picture of a Great Dane at a canine exhibition that was so "doggone tired" he (or "it") took a "cat nap." The same paper (July 23, 1980) carried yet another "dog" story of sorts, this one involving a human, a shoe manufacturer in charge of a footwear firm called "Hush Puppies," of which he was the "top dog"--the opposite on the scale of dominance (if one must motivate this transparency) to my former "underdog." In addition to this "dog" riding high, one may add what in black language should come off as "top cat," hence a type of antonym to the "*undercat" above. No one should interfere singly with the asterisk without damaging that very "ordinance" language has created, here in a language like English, whether or not cats by city ordinances are the more fitting "underdogs" than dogs.

As for the inefficient "canine" heating panels above, they were called "dogs" because they did not "work" properly. This paraphrase is intended as a reminder of the example in the introduction, where I indicated how "normal" the idiomatic usage of "work" had become for the context of machines, releasing the curious nine-to-five job adaptation only in the transferral to a foreign language, hence with bilingual insight. The point there was to underscore the vagaries of lexical deviance that tradition foists on language in quest of a "metaphor"; the point here is that what language itself foists on speakers normalizes fast once that imprint (like the "burn" mark in the Richards poem) has been left on the minds of speakers.

Not unjustifiably, Heidegger (1949, p. 5) called language the "house of being" (Haus des Seins) within which speakers of their language reside. Heidegger has thinkers and poets--"die Denkenden und Dichtenden"--become the guards of this dwelling. Exactly how they do so, this philosopher demonstrates simultaneously through the very "D" alliteration of which he avails himself to exhibit the poet within him while expressing himself as thinker. That is to say, the poet and philosopher within him not only feel comfortable in that house but remain keenly aware of the edifice language has built for them at every level of use, determining how what he says emerges. Again, my translation forces me to tamper with the original "how" because the words for English poets and thinkers do not yield Heidegger's alliteration and the planned impact this leaves in the original, derived from the intersubjective validation a collective German "muzzle" upholds.

My next example turns that muzzle into a beak. For critics have noted that the "rooster crows 'cockadoodledoo' in English, 'corico' in French and 'kikeriki' in German." That is how Leo Spitzer (1971, p. 201) put it in his essay, and to these variations may be added the Spanish "coquelico" offered in Roger Brown's work (1958, pp. 117, 134 ff.). The example, no matter in which of these languages, crops up frequently. I gave Spitzer's formulation because in a comical vein the bird seems to be crowing in all these languages as though possessing multilingual skills. Or do English, French, German, and Spanish birds compete in a situation equaling a veritable Tower of Babel?

In a curious way, all and none of the above suggestions apply. Now, to begin this discussion systematically, all the linguistic sounds together exemplify language as *universal* stratum; all cries partake of that linguistic essence which separates them from the real birds and their cries. What these critics find interesting, of course, is the fact that, despite the apparent onomatopoeia, the sounds have evolved so differently. Brown goes somewhat awry in his emphasis on a "representational" motivation, which remains a futile effort, as the very differences in the cries indicate. Still, Brown sees fit to defend the representational inadequacies of the English linguistic sound by contending that it approximates this bird cry better than the "chirp of the robin or the meow of the cat" (ibid., p. 134).

Brown does not realize that his defense is literally "immaterial" to native competence, whose only task is to cope with the material a language has proffered. To be sure, when one stays simultaneously aware of the two cries, the real and the linguistic, the latter comes off as a "metaphor," a poor surrogate of the real thing "transferred" into a particular linguistic sound. Reference, however, begins with cognizance of word material, where this enters the positive-privative network of relations in a language, down to the nouns and verbs which yield meanings from "cock" as well as "doodle." No reader of English here has to be told what these signify; if they did, they would not possess native competence of vital metalinguistic connections which preserve the "nature" of ("Mother") language.

So the "ground" for these words is not the one trodden by the rooster in emitting its sound but instead constitutes the material which composes the *regulative* base of the forms, shown nicely in the standard switch from English, French, or Spanish "c" to German "k." That is to say, language coerces speakers of these languages to adapt sound to visual sign in the manner the particular language ordains for any literate person. Those conditions are far more important than any approximation of the real thing. Language makes that known too in these languages: their alphabetic repertoire of sounds surely could reach closer mimicry of the real bird sound, in which case the words would resemble one another far more readily than they do here. But those concerns are not the ones of language; they are superseded by the sheer importance of validation, since that is the foundation of the linguistic sphere if speakers are to cope with wielding their linguistic repertoire instead of remaining mere bird imitators.

Certainly, linguistic bird sounds are somewhat limited in range of application, but their full value is tied to the network of sounds and signs owned at every level by one language, as already indicated with the English "doodle." To repeat, these are the synchronic connections which, *qua* language, matter before any original contact of diachronic stages, much as the very existence of such a bird sound once justified the subsequent coinage, onomatopoetic or not. Ontologically, I am saying, there is no longer any connection between the real and the linguistic cry or cries illustrated here. The priority goes to all the features that competent speakers must know for the disposition of the words involved because this is where *reference* begins and ends in language. From that availability alone does Heidegger's house of being arise, making speakers feel at home no matter how "unreal" the bird sound is in comparison to the real thing.

By sheer coincidence, I managed to locate a rooster cry in the following cartoon from the *Minneapolis Tribune* (June 15, 1980). Here, then, is the English speaker "at home," in that Heideggerian "house."

The cartoon shows five panels, two of which contain the "Cock-A-Doodle-Do" word, this time hyphenated. This modified spelling seems to contradict what I emphasized before about the strict regulative base of language. Were the word not an onomatopoetic vestige, such an option would not be admissible. For the cartoon, the fact that no normal contextualization is in effect is made plain by the unusual diagonal rendering of this bird cry, in contrast to the standard horizontal sequence of the final message, the response to the crowing, one might say. Ontologically, this onomatopoetic word constitutes the median between the bruitistic elements of the first and third panels and the complete contextualization of contents in the final panel. The bruitistic components also evade any normal sequence; the "Z" letters are vertical in order, resembling in that respect an "Oriental" sequence, while the "AAAARGH" parallels the diagonal dimension of the crowing.

In any case, the bruitism conveys respectively the involuntary noise resulting from gentle snoring during sleep and the voluntary reaction of dismay to the crowing, which in turn suggests the rude awakening of sleep beyond the bird cry. The fact that such a cry is generally associated with early morning remains what is commonly termed "encyclopedic" knowledge, hence information not necessarily intrinsic to linguistic competence. Any competence in language must begin with language in use, and that emanates from construal, here the orthographic and distinct rendering of these sounds carried mutely by the visual sign. Moreover, speaker competence still becomes controlled by wholly *degenerate* semantic stages, such as the "Z" material presents by imitating the real noise of snoring. Thus, had this cartoon been for Germans, the equivalent sound repertoire for the sibilant would have come across visually as an "S" since this language has "Z" pronounced hard (unvoiced), as "/ts/" in a phonetic transcription. Still, these orthographic sounds do not render a validated word as contained by the rooster cry and the final message. That is why these bruitistic elements exemplify linguistic material at the most degenerate material level.

The actual bird, of course, is not drawn in. But even if it appeared (in the message perhaps) as a validated English word, it would not be present in all its glorious feathers, its colors and contours. Skeptics of language see this "abstract" quality a disadvantage. These critics are inclined to lean excessively on the "arbitrary" state of language because they assess its nature in accordance with its representational value for empirical nature, a vantage point I have taken to task already above by citing Saussure. Those cognizant of the power of words, on the other hand, concentrate on these and realize that even if the bird as such is missing in graphic detail, unable to "sound off" in the actual crowing, the distinctive and unique being of language has taken over anyway with the communication of this cartoon wherever any words appear. The concrete situational setting present in graphic detail certainly offers much constitutive support to the verbal meaning here, as would ostensive usage in a real setting. Any linguistic meaning nevertheless becomes construed only from the words. Were the bird drawn in and also included verbally, its two appearances as graphic picture and orthographic sign would have nothing in common. Also, should a word like "rooster" degenerate to the level of the bruitistic letters discussed, all its avian significance would evaporate and leave behind no part of the bird, a condition that is not applicable to a drawing.

Obvious as these conditions are, those seizing on the lexicon for idiosyncrasies of semantic functioning do not pay enough attention to details at the level of form where coercive signation begins with language in a language. To make certain this does not happen here, I offer one more related avian example, namely the "cuckoo," whose regulative German base changes the word to "Kuckuck," again with a phonetic c-for-k transcription and mandatory capitalization of nouns. No native speaker needs to be reminded of what the word designates--yet another bird. However, something peculiar has happened: in both languages this word signifies the animal through the sound it makes. Another onomatopoetic vestige is involved, one these two languages seem to approximate more closely in sound and sight than in the rooster cries that saw German supplant the English back vowels "/o/a/" with the front vowels "/i/e/." Both languages also take equal liberties with the cuckoo by naming the animal through its sound. Is this a transgression in the order of a category-mistake spelling "metaphor" or ordinary "meaning?" I affirm the latter since, beyond this diachronic transparency of the switch from creature to cry, synchronic validation has normalized the word, forcing speakers in either language to accept the switch as commonplace.

How many readers here would have been conscious of this abnormality had I not drawn their attention to the switch from the animal to its sound or brought this out in punning? Only in such instances does the irregularity override momentarily the ingrained sensation of normalcy. However, while the two languages seem to run the same quirky parallel course here, my next example destroys that (always false) belief. In the process, other ramifications of this "cuckoo" surface in the second cartoon from the *Minneapolis Tribune* (May 18, 1979).

Wizard of Id / By Brant Parker and Johnny Hart   Minneapolis Tribune, May 18,1979, P. 6B

First there is the famous cuckoo clock, recognized in graphic shape by speakers of *any* language. Then it chimes in the form of an English sound, and out comes the word "cuckoo"; the boldface projects its semicircular "C," horseshoe contours of "U," and ringed "O" in duplicate. A walking human figure, a king, hears this sound and, none too flattered, delivers his final message in the last panel. In that respect this cartoon concludes in a similar manner to the former cartoon, though the message is addressed at some underling here as interlocutory partner.

What upset the king? Well, any competent native speaker of English gleans the connotation of the inept "fool" in the word "cuckoo," an import not that remote from the German donkey, now encapsulated in this animal image as lexical item. German "Kuckuck," on the other hand, could not penetrate to this implicit level, even if its form looks and sounds so similar to "cuckoo" and matches the basic avian signation. Now, is there any available transparency to trade on? Are cuckoos crazy or stupid, any more so than donkeys? Who cares? In yet another transference from human to animal--though by avian rather than equine species--sound has appropriated bird, and bird the human of a foolish disposition. There is no need to worry about the transparencies or opacities that made or did not make the original contact with the coinage. Priority should go to the cognizance that semantic redundance, residing solely within the normalizing powers of language, has managed to override all apparent jumps of blatant category-mistakes and made these common for English. Those surveyors who forget their expertise as speakers and get stuck in the wrong categories base their alleged jumps on some lexical "metaphor"; those who concentrate on the coercive regulating prowess of language, the Mother, point simply to a normalized meaning as a vocabulary staple.

As native speaker the king in the cartoon does not wonder how the bird got to be verbalized by its sound and from there moved to encompass a human trait. All he hears is the insult in the word, much as the clock communicates it quite unconsciously. Beyond this cartoon figure and his inanimate time-telling object, however, lurks the ultimate interlocutory partnership between the cartoonists named and their reading public, for whose benefit the cartoon was created. So chime and human affront convey their message, not only to the cartoon figure but to the newspaper readers as native competent speakers of English. I put it that way just because a similar sounding and looking German "Kuckuck" would fall flat (with or without wings). This difference stresses once more the point reiterated several times; reference does not pertain to words as stand-ins for things in the world, here this bird. Rather, reference also affirms the signitive connectives of related values one word harbors in relation to the next. No such fool resides in the "Kuckuck," my bilingual competence tells me. Accordingly, despite any possible paraphrasing, the cartoon would lose its sting or *pointe*. Of course, the Germans or, more precisely, the Swiss Germans, first invented the cuckoo clock, in the way of added encyclopedic knowledge. But only English "invented" this invective, and there it is, no longer to be circumvented by any of its fluent speakers.

All the above examples manifest the language-bound nature of meanings: they are really bound to the "wagging" of that mother tongue, from the first bisyllabic gurgles of a young speaker to the full metalinguistic control of the oppositional values that a German donkey-fool versus an English cuckoo-fool exhibits. The real "Mother" of that "tongue" has the human mother pass on its natural foundation to the child; that is what makes language a primordial maternal figure, capable of connecting two interlocutory partners. From the first mnemonic sounds that young speakers emit in self-expression arises a simultaneous need for communicating what they wish to say. All such articulation, furthermore, can be generated only through the reference of a speaker's meaning in the transaction with transference.

My concrete maternal example in terms of mother-child interaction may make it not surprising to learn that the word for "language" in languages with generic *gender* for nonpersons often comes in the feminine: German "die Sprache," French "la langue," and Spanish "la lengua." Certainly, such motivation has its limits, especially since abstract nouns as a whole often appear in the feminine. Indeed, gender is an interesting phenomenon insofar as it straddles diachronic transparency and synchronic opacity. Ernst Cassirer (1972, pp. 273-274), for instance, discusses findings of the great nineteenth-century philologist Jakob Grimm, who proved how rudimentary personification led to gender formation as humans personalized their immediate environment in an effort to interpret its meaningfulness. Cassirer, of course, is equally interested in showing what he calls generally "mimetic" origins, more specifically how any imitative onomatopoeia or direct transparency became superseded by the mediation of active symbolic-semiotic synthesis, about which my next chapter will have more to say. In other words, Cassirer stressed tacitly the synchronic states that originate with language, in this case irrespective of isomorphic sexualization. Indeed, because gender has become so opaque, students of a foreign language have difficulty memorizing it.

If one may sympathize with students of a target language, one should marvel at the intrinsic power of language to uphold norms that seem flagrant irregularities by any other standard. Native speakers feel at home in the synchronic states of their gender system, no matter how odd. They certainly do not motivate gender in accordance with empirical distribution of the sexes in order to make themselves understood. Rather, only the correct use that language has established can lead to any understanding here. Although later chapters deal with poetic texts, let me indicate here briefly what gender may accomplish for literary language. One of my analyses (Gumpel, 1971, pp. 293-294) showed how a nineteenth-century German poem (by Eichendorff) evoked a nocturnal vanishing horizon through the image of a kiss between the masculine sky (or heaven) and the feminine earth. These nouns were cast already in their respective gender which then became resuscitated in esthetic form (see also Stankiewicz, 1961, pp. 21-22).

Gender is thus one of the most important linguistic phenomena to make evident where diachronic and synchronic planes cross and where they should be kept apart. Although my last example may leave the impression that poetic language returns to original diachronic contacts, that assumption would be wrong. All complex exteriorization of language stays grounded in synchronic states that become palpated, in a manner of speaking, for maximal realization by full speaker competence. In the loose determination of traditional semantics, moreover, the above personification of sky and earth could well spell yet another "metaphor" of lexical deviance. What this description *cannot* do is to attach any vital function to mere lexical appearances, since the findings are then left literally "use-less."

Curiously, not only the word for language but also the word for "metaphor" becomes cast consistently in the feminine by modern languages. Thus it came as no surprise to the German side of my bilingual competence to find a German critic (Nieraad, 1977, p. 52) refer to "Lady Metaphor." What amazed him was not the femininity but the survival of this sprightly female, whose existence covers more than two thousand years. What astounded me was the gender, but only on the English side of my bilingual competence. My other side, programmed by German gender, accepts the validity of this personification much as English preserves a neuter "it" for the word. That is a typical case of the power governing legitimation in language, specifically gender, to the point of guiding my awareness even in areas of critical theory.

The critic who had transformed "metaphor" into a female used "Dame" for her, a word which, without the capitalization, exists also as a lexical item of English. But even if my choice of "Lady" in the translation sounds rather quaint--especially in view of the disrepute into which this sexist designation has fallen of late--the English "dame" could not replace it. No competent reader here needs to be told of the current negative connotations in this lexical item. Of course, the British meaning of "Dame" signifies a title that commands respect when capitalized like the German word. But this nuance is not meant in the German critic's use. I have pointed out already on several occasions how tricky translation becomes at every level. This example illustrates once more how explicit contents in two languages may coincide as much as their implicit contents diverge, and the only reason, it will turn out subsequently, is that reference in the transaction of transference has been deployed differently by the speakers who make up that speech community--built on norms Germans have accepted as their Heideggerian "house."

That categorical norms as such do not exist anywhere is the argument presented by Nietzsche, that great iconoclastic German thinker, specifically in an essay on metaphor which deals with "truth" or "lie" in the "extramoral sense." Though the essay is much quoted, its implications seem to get lost. This is evident even in the English translation (in Shibles, 1972) for Nietzsche's "Lüge," a term that clearly refers to a "lie," yet becomes designated as "falsity." Since the lie is extramoral and thus a metaphysical predicament, something like falseness obviously applies. However, that an element of "conspiracy" may lurk behind this very situation is better revealed in the word that Nietzsche himself, after all, had deliberately selected.

The immediate relevance of this essay to my discussion is that it alludes also to metaphor (and not only language) as a "mother" and in an afterthought even calls metaphor the "grandmother" of every concept (Salzburg, n.d., p. 1085). Nietzsche realized only too well that all truth is "anthropomorphic"; reality itself remains a mere transmission or "transference"--"Uebertragung"--filtered through human faculties, since no one grasps a "thing-in-itself" (ibid., pp. 1082, 1084, 1086-1087). Now, this German term for "transference" turns out to be the very word used in Teutonic designations of metaphor, signifying literally a "carry-over." The thing-in-itself, of course, scholars will recognize as the Kantian "Ding an sich" from the *First Critique* (Cassirer ed., 1913, III, pp. 212-224). It is the ontological concept of "noumenal," or transcendentally real proportions that no human within empirical reality, the "phenomenal" or transcendentally ideal sphere, manages to reach. "Ideal" here becomes synonymous with the immanent faculties of the mind, whose "ideas" are nevertheless incapable of penetrating to an extramental state of being as "real reality."

What I am trying to prove with Nietzsche, then, is that everything becomes "metaphor" when gauged from a wrong vantage point. In comparison to such an elusive real world, all of empirical reality undergoes the "shift" of metaphor as a world translated through the mind, whether rationally or not; in comparison to this world, language as a universal stratum becomes the next metaphor in line, since the goals of signation rather than direct perception and cognition produce yet another shift, away from the empirical domain. What neo-Aristotelians thus interpret as lexical deviance within a vast metaphor becomes only yet another metaphor, since every realm here named is deviant or anthropomorphic through a different activity of consciousness. The traditional metaphor then ends up attenuated further. By what metaphorical domain is it to be assessed? No wonder the Ingendahl Experiment dissolved in a lack of consensus. With all these ontological metaphors, one is reminded of the game which consists of boxes within boxes. Metaphor as lexical deviance is the tiny, innermost box; metaphor characterizing all of language presents a shift which separates language from the *extralinguistic*, empirical reality; this reality in turn constitutes a metaphorical shift when compared to an *extramental* state of being, even if no one knows what the transcendent thing-in-itself really is, except that it definitely cannot become an object of knowledge.

Put paradoxically, Nietzsche's extramoral tenet verifies that there is no truth in the world of human experience, and what there is outside of it will never be known. The extramoral lie is all-pervasive, its "metaphorical" base truly inescapable ubiquity. Moreover, despite his seeming pessimism, Nietzsche typically ends on a more positive if defiant note: why not affirm art, which is no more or less a lie than any other part of reality? In a similar vein, I insist that the traditional view of metaphor only makes more conspicuous what is a foregone conclusion, namely that language as a whole, due to its very "meta-physical" being, is metaphor anyway. No wonder the traditional principle is so hard to isolate; the omnipresence of metaphor appears too boundless to dwell on it. Instead, speakers accept as familiar what language the Mother ordains they are to have, even if wordplay and related usage disrupts familiarity with some content momentarily, as may apply to native speakers here being shown how "god" of all things (or divine beings) becomes the tail end of "dog."

Even the astute thinker Nietzsche, however, falls prey to one major neo-Aristotelian default that has been so hard to live down, and that concerns his lack of understanding that there must be an indigenous linguistic, not just a logical, concept of language. Nietzsche uses the German "Begriff" as the only concept and thus treats the term as if it straddled logic and language--exactly what I said should not be done, if the ontological category-mistake is to be eradicated once and for all. Thus Nietzsche says (pp. 1083, 1085 ff.) that language through this "Begriff" effects "equalization of the unequal" (Gleichsetzen des Nichtgleichen). Against the "Begriff" he has pitted the "Bild" or esthetic image which essentially becomes a metonym for poetry and art. This image, he observes (pp. 1086-1088, 1091), does not partake of monolithic equalization but instead manages to combine "the strangest" (das Fremdeste) and to separate "the closest" (das Nächste).

What non-Aristotelian semantics will prove time and again is that language as such, even before it waxes metaphorical or poetic, possesses these "esthetic" capacities Nietzsche attributes only to the image of art. My introduction already touched on this issue; language, like art, is the most basic expressive medium, exteriorizing entities according to autotelic directives whose provenance is the act of meaning. Whimsical from the outside, meanings are vital from the intrinsic vantage point, where they become absolute through intersubjective validation among interlocutory partners. Hence any meaning is the product of both equalizing and unequalizing powers; language severs here what in logic belongs together and combines over there what stays rationally inimical. So even when language equalizes, it does so in accordance with its intrinsic instead of logical goals. The German donkey-fool and the English cuckoo-fool illustrated these powers in part, always reserved for a particular language. Once normalized, words have also become equalized into acceptable commonplaces for all speakers of that language. In thrusting the species together, as shown by these "odd couples," language does indeed combine what Nietzsche called "the strangest," hence the most uncombinable entities in other spheres. So, in Nietzsche's division, the concept of language partakes as much of the esthetic "Bild" as the equalizing "Begriff."

Nietzsche, however, uses the example of a leaf to prove that his "Begriff," the rational concept, subsumes the manifold zigzag concretions of this natural object in empirical reality under one flattened, epistemological qualifier. There is no doubt that this logical concept relies on an abstracting process, as will be pointed out again when I differentiate it from the linguistic concept with the aid of Cassirer. Let me illustrate the synthesizing powers of linguistic concepts in their dynamic breadth with my third cartoon, again from the Minneapolis Tribune (October 3, 1979, p. 8B).

Below (p. 28) is a young speaker whose metalinguistic awareness of English contiguities is about to solidify: his shaping competence of intrinsic semantic associations tells him that a leaf "leaves" and, curiously from any nonlinguistic vantage point, that many leaves "leave." From there, he gleans the possible connections between their seasonal departure and the verb "leave," made explicit in the past tense (or past participle) "left." Every native speaker reading the cartoon will be able to follow the wordplay which surfaces accordingly. The connections reside in language and await cognizance through this type of punning. Behind this child, of course, is the cartoonist. The child looks almost too young for this sophisticated association, although such awareness can be reached, if fitfully, at a relatively early age. Later, I shall discuss in more detail when and how such metalinguistic conceptualization takes root. At this point, the cartoon is presented for the benefit of adult readers--mine or those of the cartoonist--who get the point(e).

DENNIS the MENACE

"THAT'S WHY THEY CALL'EM LEAVES, JOEY....THEY'RE ALL THAT'S LEFT OF SUMMER."

Now for some of the ontological implications. First, the concretion of the leaves in their empirical zigzag is depicted in the graphic detail of the drawing, if somewhat modestly. Any logical classification of this varied detail may well equalize the manifold zigzag by subsuming it as characteristic of the species leaf under the genus plant. Since my bilingual competence is not affected by that categorization, it must lie outside of language and not in either of the two languages I have acquired. Conversely, the wordplay above between the noun for the plant, "leaf" "leaves," and the verb for an activity, "leave"/"left," can be appreciated only through knowing a specific language, English. While German has terms for the plant and the activity, this language cannot engender the intersecting nuances of the cartoon because these, in a manner of speaking, belong to the signitive "zigzag" of one language.

As for Dennis, he is reacting to a diverse programming that is only partially linguistic as he perceives the leaves in all their presentational immediacy. Still reacting mainly to an ostensive level of use, his perception of words is geared to their related sounds. But for the more sophisticated readers of the cartoon, the visual levels of words are equally conspicuous. Either way, native competence is guided by the sound that is heard or the sign that is visually perceived while reading, but never by viewing the real leaves in their graphic depiction in this cartoon. Alone the word leads speakers to the coercive and yet procreative power of linguistic reference. This power has neither being nor meaning outside of the language its speakers, here this young boy, wield, even as he commits a type of ontological category-mistake by type-trespassing from empirical conditions such as the transitory state of leaves into a semantic association. The critics of metaphor will often evolve as no less naive, mainly because they underestimate those unequalizing powers that pertain not only to such purposive states as Nietzsche had defined for his esthetic "Bild" but also to language.

Etymologists and related professionals certainly may use their expertise in order to substantiate the connecting root between the object designated "leaf" and the activity to "leave." However, even advanced speaker competence does not need to go further than this child to fathom the diachronic past of semantic stages. Wielding the word correctly does not depend on such awareness. The cartoonist certainly knew how the words of his choice were to be plied in order to please all those speakers who, like myself, got the *pointe*.

The graphic and orthographic zigzag have nothing in common in actual appearance, and thus speakers, beyond the perceivers they are, must have their minds locked into the forms of language, which is where each language begins. If these appear unfounded to the point of being "mendacious" in Nietzsche's extramoral sense, so is the concrete counterpart since that, too, depends on some human faculty, if not the capacity of speech. No Kantian "things-in-themselves" pervade this cartoon for human awareness.

Yet there is "truth" in terms of human effectiveness of passing on the message, even if linguistic validation forced speakers into accepting such "odd couples" as the German donkey-fool, the English cuckoo-fool and/or the dog/god palindrome. Furthermore, lop the "g" off "dog" and the verb "do" arises; lop the "d" of "god" and the verb "go" arises. Coincidental from some vantage point, these associations have been ingrained in those fluent in English. The fact that the words are legitimized makes them come "true." Conversely, "*og" and "*od" remain "untrue" insofar as they possess no meaning. Truth here, however, is positive; speakers focus only on what language, the Mother, has made available for speech since from that repertoire alone the "thought" arises that is indigenous to native competence.

Sorting out the Crucial Domains: Realities in Circles

The next task for non-Aristotelian semantics is to *identify* language in concept and domain. Methodologically, that is the only approach: there is simply no way of arriving at a semantic principle like metaphor before defining at least cursorily what meaning is in conceptualization and essence. By the end of this chapter, the ontological placement of language will have been completed in rather concrete fashion as, with the aid of diagrams, language is separated in a circle from the extralinguistic domains. After the ontological isolation, the detailed Picture of Language takes over, probing every facet of meaning, from its most "degenerate" ground "up" to full generation, for which part the semiotics of Peirce is needed. The immediate discussion, however, explores fundamentals mainly with the aid of Cassirer and Ingarden, including to a limited extent their most relevant intellectual precursors.

In the last chapter Nietzsche was seen to posit a rational equalizing "Begriff" and an esthetic "Bild" of unique combinatory proclivity. The concept indigenous to language should go somewhere between these two extremes since it possesses equalizing powers along with unique synthesizing prowess. The amusing concoctions used for prior illustrations are really nothing more than redundant norms native speakers have assimilated in the languages involved, from the "fool" that came with English "cuckoo" to the German equivalent for a word meaning "donkey." The analogies embodied in these animals for designating a human simpleton are nowhere extant in empirical reality but still exist differently in the words of a language. While animal imagery still leaves colorful traces, contents such as the (former) "working" machines are so flattened in English for rendering gadgets which work that only bilingual consciousness arouses any awareness of a figure of speech suggesting a nine-to-five job.

Diverting as those illustrations were, the time has come to probe these phenomena more theoretically. Cassirer's ideas implement this investigation by stressing indigenous concept formation in language, although he is still insufficiently recognized for this important contribution. The historical link is Cassirer's dual approach: as philosopher of *language*, he inherited as much neo-Humboldtian as neo-Kantian roots, while the Humboldtian legacy in turn traded on the insights of the preceding "energetic" tradition, as that evolved from seventeenth-century British neo-Platonism. The value of these historical connections lies primarily in exhibiting concern for language as unique bearer of meaning, long before Bréal had actually coined his "semantics" to delineate a scientific approach to this field of study which, sadly, never materialized.

Cassirer's voluminous *Philosophie der symbolischen Formen* appeared in 1923, according to the foreword in the first volume on language. With so many English cognates in the title, translation becomes unnecessary. The term "symbolism," of course, has been subjected to various construals; for Cassirer it embodies active intervention on the part of human consciousness in the task of effecting semiotic synthesis. This interpretation is not far removed from the one given the etymology of "symbol"--by such philosophers as Heidegger and Peirce (1952, pp. 9-10; 1960, pp 167-168, par. 2.297): something is being thrust together through "convention" or "contract." Such a confluence, indeed, obtains for Cassirer's idea of the symbolic "form" upheld by intersubjective "contract," as all conventional systems are.

The symbolic forms encompass language, mythical thought, and aspects of empirical science. The order itself, by beginning with language and myth, permits Cassirer (1972, p. 11) to claim that Kant's "Critique of Reason" needed extending to a "Critique of Culture." Moreover, what unites all symbolic functions is spontaneity in the mode of synthesis; what separates their products is "modality," a Kantian precept, albeit extended to meet the cultural reorientation cited. Modality emphasizes constitution over sheer content (1972, I, pp. 29 ff.; 1969, II, p. 78, passim). To illustrate with one of my former examples, God as word, concrete object of worship, or abstract supernatural being in a sense becomes diffracted into multiple deities, essentially into different objects of consciousness, by fulfilling a disparate function. Only the word "God" bears that linguistic modality which in one language such as English gives rise to the palindrome discussed before, in conjunction with the canine "dog"--specifically (and humorously) the English creature's other side. As for the knowledge of immortal transcendence in the case of a deity as supernatural concept, this rests paradoxically in the knowledge that such a state of being eludes all investigation as object of knowledge--outside of, those clever ontological arguments once posited by medieval Scholastics.

The linguistic modality, of course, will be of major interest here, leaving Cassirer's first volume on language of primary concern. Indeed, critics like him aid non-Aristotelian semantics in warding off those contemporaries who back up their awareness of language by logic, as befits the error in the ontological category-mistake. There will be sufficient evidence to indicate how neo-Aristotelians posit ontological arguments for the existence of language that resemble in basic intent the medieval endeavor. Yet despite Cassirer's early "cultural" avowal in this volume, even he ends (1972, I, p. 280) by recapitulating steps taken in linguistic development that seem based mainly on "Critical" cognitive hierarchies: he moves from intuition, the Kantian "Anschauung," to conceptual thought, and concludes with logical judgment. With that "logical" epitome at his conclusion, the author's original cultural aspirations become somewhat attenuated, causing my analysis at that point to switch over to Ingarden's theory.

Despite some of these reservations about the ultimate ending of Cassirer's first volume, it does have much to offer in the area of language, particularly its chapter IV (1972, I, pp. 249-279) that deals with language as very expression (Ausdruck) of conceptual thought. Early in this chapter (pp. 250-251), Cassirer presents the amusing analogy of critics who search for glasses that are already on their nose. He is talking about the way in which critics look for concepts in language they possess already outside of language, mainly through the deductive (but not signitive) process applied to logic. "Abstraktion," he says, is the origin of logical subsumption, whereas concepts of language arise from "Selektion" and "Induktion" (pp. 260-261, 269). Again, these Latinized terms need no translation; the last two stress the intrinsic nature of a linguistic concept since it has to be embodied in the choice made during linguistic activity. Products of logic and language therefore go their separate ways.

The failure to realize the distinctions Cassirer makes here has plagued neo-Aristotelian approaches to metaphor through the ages, with the contemporary scene being no exception. This problem, indeed, is endemic in the ontological category-mistake, which mostly turns out to be the only unwanted consistency for an otherwise inconsistent handling of metaphor in language. Ironically, this ontological mistake seeks erroneously nonexistent "mistakes" in lexical incompatibility by really imposing mistaken, preformed, or logical categories on meanings which thus do not belong to language in the first place. The English word "cuckoo" permitted and actually sustained the connotation of the human "fool." This linkage arose inductively from concepts and categories indigenous to, and selectively derived from, wielding words in this language. Real cuckoos or fools, on the other hand, that are perceived and cognized outside of words break into human and avian species through the abstracting process of which Cassirer spoke. Indeed, a real bird precedes the human mammal historically, although from an aspect of evolutionary or religious hierarchies--in the order of the Great Chain of Being--this animal may well be the "lower" species compared to humans. The point is, however, that words stay equal in semantic essence, no matter what their specific lexical denomination.

The two English meanings of my example have been thrust together; they have firmed and solidified into synchronic values, to become invested with a positive-privative relation which all entities of one linguistic corpus share, curiously, in their very difference. Linguistic competence is guided alone by those relations, where simple surface deviance has no place. The resulting network of disjunctive relations is far too huge for such a criterion. To speak of "words" in the above examples, furthermore, seems somewhat inappropriate since the "fool" was treated mostly as an implicit semantic value, as a connotation within another word, the "cuckoo." What exactly constitutes relations of this nature is something which requires more coverage than this introductory chapter can offer. But the topic will not be neglected since so many defaults characterizing traditional semantics are connected to it. In yet another modest introspective endeavor, let me stress for now that my very need here to exteriorize "fool" into a separate denotation rather than keeping it a connotation causes vital changes in essence.

For the present both word meanings, "cuckoo" and "fool," suffice to illustrate that semantic contents remain exclusively functional; their use *is* their being; their existence "directs" speakers toward fluency in future performance. Yet when neo-Aristotelians cry "metaphor," they really type-cross language with logic by merely *sensing* categories in conflict with what other forms of programming have engendered, not language in a language. So this assumed encroachment actually does not disturb competent *signifying*. Since the "-mistake" in the category-mistake implies a negative truth factor, it is not surprising to find this issue surfacing with almost *every* detection of metaphor as lexical deviance, and Cassirer helps me to combat some of those unwarranted notions.

Without delving into such metaphysical problems as Nietzsche's all-encompassing extramoral lie, Cassirer discusses truth early in the volume on language by ridding it of the static old verities known as reality and truth--twinned in the German alliteration of "Wirklichkeit" and "Wahrheit" (1972, I, p. 48). Instead, Cassirer regards truth as sheer evidence of spontaneous activity on the part of the human spirit (Geist). The affirmation of truth as disclosure of function also endorses tacitly the modalities noted, and Cassirer's symbolic forms bear the imprint of that activity.

In language, therefore, a "true" content is a validated functional entity endowed with "sense" for serving linguistic activity; an "untrue" content, such as the starred "*undercat," stays literally "non-sense": except for a limited deployment as neologism, it bears no functional potential and is not even an "it" as a word of English, despite a combination of letters. The "*undercat" thus contrasts with the unstarred English "cuckoo" as respective "untrue" versus "true" meaning, as existing in limbo versus residing in a language. For the "cuckoo" is extant, replete with full semantic-syntactic codes which certainly do not even embody "nonsense" when designating a human "fool." This word possesses a lexical core and a concomitant implicit periphery duly imprinted on signitive consciousness from past usage and then shared among native speakers of the language in potential readiness for the next recall by authorial intent.

Under those conditions, to repeat, truth prevails, yet never as an instance of verisimilitude conforming with states in empirical reality. How could it be otherwise? Even the plain "cuckoo" that conveniently stands in for the bird so named violates slavish representation since it does not name the animal directly but rather its sound. Fortunately, speakers are not encumbered by such discrepancies in diachronic inception; their role is wielding words competently in an acquired reference through a linguistic sound sufficiently ingrained to override awareness of any onomatopoetic vestige, here a creature's sound in reference to the creature itself. At that point, a speaker has gained the capacity for interlocutory partnership, permitting the entity that is the "cuckoo" to exist intersubjectively among speakers, if only in one language at a time. Yet anyone who insists on a "transposition" here, which goes from bird sound to semantic name for a bird, may convert even this ordinary meaning, "cuckoo," into a "metaphor" and claim violated categories by such flimsy standards as neo-Aristotelians apply. Ultimately, where would such a naive realism of conforming to facts and when categories stay that superficial? There would be no determinant for effectively separating the true from the false, the straight from the deviant, and thus any meaning from a supposed metaphor. Gauged by wrong norms, the ontological category-mistake thus spawns much confusion.

In essence, Cassirer's idea of truth as functional disclosure also touches on the original Greek word for truth, the "aleytheia"-literalized as "unhiddenness of being" (Unverborgenheit des Seienden) by Heidegger, in lectures on the origin of art (1952, p. 25). Something new unfolds with spontaneous mental activity in that very symbolic confluence elucidated above. While the "cuckoo"/"fool" example may seem a blatant case of a combination wrought from diverse concepts, a confluence is always in effect when conventional media, adopted through human assent, force their members to "convene" by accepting what is offered. The purposive foundation of language is thus missed when a narrow perspective seizes on the wrong categories in presumed category-mistakes. Then a skepticism inadvertently arises by seeking the aid of logic rather than language if only for the want of a better solution. Certainly, the explicit lexicon becomes an easy target for surface verisimilitude and is pursued for that reason. Since persons who are not necessarily critics of language can cull deviance from a seemingly "odd" content in a given context, no special expertise is needed; anyone may label a human "fool" expressed through "cuckoo" a "metaphor."

If the acknowledged experts of language, however, do not transcend such conspicuous phenomena as a more or less figurative style based on some taxonomy of contents, their expertise has to be sorely affected. Then they do not rise above the level of the ordinary perceivers of warm red who never learned to grasp a physicist's scientitific or "cool" alternative--in reference to Calder's example from my introduction. Then meaning and metaphor become anyone's game of lexical anomaly in the sphere of language. Stylistic phenomena, to be sure, justifiably interest the scholar of literature. But noting *what*, descriptively, language carries does not lead to assessing *how* it is put together, and that problem a theoretician of language has to address. Otherwise "truth" turns into "lie" by locating only a "metaphor" of loose verbalization. As shown, a meaning judged on surface appearance quickly changes into a dubious metaphor. And, as was seen with Nietzsche's peculiar brand of metaphysics, any extralinguistic (empirical) object equals a metaphorical "lie" as a state of being that is barred from an extramental sphere because it has to be observed filtered, through human faculties.

A study of metaphor thus succeeds only after meaning has been apprehended first as its obverse side, leading finally to a distinguishable reverse which bears *bona fide* idiosyncrasies. The linguistic validation of "cuckoo" for rendering a "fool" may well seem false when compared to epistemological concepts which separate avian and human species, but for language in one language the linkage embodies plain semantic "truth." Extending this conception of truth to Heidegger's notion of unhiddenness was not entirely fortuitous either since, as indicated, it appeared in the context of art--whose purposive autotelism resembles that of language. Indeed, the issue of the essence governing art and language is endemic in the tradition Cassirer inherited as well. While purposive indenting by language upon the mind will be probed later in utmost detail, the major ideas that influenced Cassirer and were recognized by him in the volume on language take precedence in this discussion. As already stated, Humboldt (1767-1835) constitutes one important link in Cassirer's focus on linguistic concept formation. Humboldt in turn came out of the energetic tradition which endorsed intuitive rather than rational faculties, an emphasis then continued in the era of nineteenth-century Romanticism. That entailed the programmatic attempt to harmonize two domains closest as human self-expression--*language* and *art* rather than *language* and *logic*!

This radical "estheticization" of language, as it may be termed, was thus based on identities of autotelic spontaneity, without the language necessarily having to be literary. Added to the trend was the "Critical" strain embodied in Kantian and ultimately Idealist philosophy, a connection to be inferred from Cassirer's (1972, I, p. 102) calling Kant the "Critic of Cognition" and Humboldt the parallel "Critic of Language." Cassirer's own "cultural" orientation founded on both Kant and Humboldt is central to this Critical link. Language became in essence the fourth constitutive domain after Kant's nature, art, and moral freedom (with Cassirer's myth readily subsumed under art). A very explicit link between Cassirer and Humboldt when moving chronologically backward is the frequent allusion to "linguistic imagination," German "Sprachphantasie," in Cassirer's crucial chapter on linguistic concept formation (1972, I, pp. 275, 279). Similarly Humboldt's work on the *Variations of Human Speech*, published posthumously in 1836 (1963, pp. 284, 469-470), cites "Phantasie" or "Einbildungskraft" to project the imagination as the catalyst of speech (pp.473-475). Speech in "variations" (Verschiedenheiten) is indeed the result of an inspirational drive that erupts as the *vernacular* among the many speech communities harboring their respective mother tongues.

One is tempted to resort once more to Luther's vulgar "muzzle" which the speakers of each of these languages own and share collectively. No less diverting than Luther's inelegant organ was the beak objectifying similar "variations" through the ways roosters crowed in the languages presented. Diffracted by these languages, the bird cry became a series of cries with their onomatopoetic ring subordinated to the regulative power of the particular language. For the priority is adapting sound to sign, often quite disparately in the languages offered. These cries may never come together again as one rooster cry because each now belongs to a different linguistic inventory, an affiliation that must take priority. Because of this priority, (epistemo)logical categories in genus and species denominations, which neo-Aristotelians foist on incompatible lexical meaning in metaphor, needs to be discarded from the start as linguistically "use-less."

Humboldt's *Variations*, of course, stress human exchange in decidedly *verbal* applications, as is made explicit by the titular reference to "speech," in German actually "Sprachbau," where the suffix "-bau" literalizes into "building" and thus serves as a loose reminder of Heidegger's house wherein native speakers feel at home enough to overcome all the apparent oddities that neo-Aristotelian categoricians detect in metaphor. With Humboldt's marked emphasis on speech, gone is also the universal monolith Latin had represented in written form throughout the Middle Ages and beyond as an artificial uniformity (Crystal, 1971, pp. 54-55 ff.). Instead, the *Variations* project what remains crucial to non-Aristotelian semantics: the great need to affirm meaning on its own ground, within one language, instead of exploring contents as though they rested in universal concepts and categories equal to all languages, which would bar all genuine diversity. Equally important is the way in which Humboldt anticipates Cassirer on linguistic concept formation as he reiterates (1963, pp. 191, 223, 426) that language constitutes the very "Organ" of thought, a tenet this study will have much cause to reinvoke. Small wonder, then, that Cassirer, who regarded Humboldt as the "Critic" incarnate of "Language," consciously identifies with this forebear when taking up linguistic cognition.

Cassirer (1972, I, pp. 85-98) additionally pinpoints ideas that are historically relevant to the wider "energetic" tradition. They hark back to the emanation theories of Shaftesbury and Harris, thus to seventeenth-century British neo-Platonism, and the effect these had upon the language theory of Herder (1774-1803), the German Enlightenment thinker who nevertheless opposed undue Enlightenment emphasis on reason. Instead, Herder emphasized the compelling force of genius as an inspirational faculty at work in human endeavors such as language. This shift in focus made possible the transition from an "energetic" theory of art to one of language, notes Cassirer (1972, I, p. 88; also 1965, pp. 312-317 ff.). Certainly, Herder's indigenous "Volksgeist" seems only one remove from Humboldt's "Sprachgeist" which spawned the linguistic "variations" (see Schaff, 1974, pp. 20-25).

Although in its focusing on intuitional capacities the energetic trend is non-Aristotelian in my understanding of this term, the etymology of "energetic" manifests Aristotelian roots, specifically the *Nicomachean Ethics* (1975, 1098a, pp. 32-33). In this work, Aristotle differentiated "ergon" from "energeia," hence "function" from "active exercise," the latter marking free activity of the "soul." But a context of ethics could hardly befit language directly, and Greek "energeia" has a wide enough application to possess connotations that subsequent discussions of Aristotle's *Rhetoric* will disclose as traits of (Homeric) animation.

What left Humboldt the heir of the energetic tradition as derived from Herder *et al.* is no doubt his famous statement in the *Variations* (1963, p. 418) that language never constituted static "ergon" but dynamic "energeia"--ceaseless regenerative activity. Throughout the rest of the *Variations* Humboldt under-scores emanation in the regenerative force that a linguistic spirit embodies through its unique powers of synthesis (1963, pp. 386, 389, 391 393, 473-475). Because of my limited space, only two other famous Humboldtian statements will be offered in brief reference to their impact on the energetic tradition, which encompasses Cassirer's philosophy, as he himself seemed to have realized. The citations will be identified as the Humboldtian "image" and "interposition" statements.

In the image statement, Humboldt claims that a word is never a mere duplicate of an object as such (an sich) but constitutes an object formed from the "image" or "Bild" of the linguistic "soul" or "Seele" (1963, pp. 223, 433). Here the inchoate nature of linguistic *content* is affirmed, while Humboldt's premise of language as organ of thought, which follows closely upon this statement, seizes on the indigenous essence of the linguistic *concept*. Humboldt is saying that linguistic *reference* is never sheer *representation* of other preformed objects "as such," thus anticipating Cassirer's "form," molded as that is by symbolic synthesis. On the surface, too, Nietzsche's esthetic "Bild" seems to return: as product of the "soul," the word remains a purposive whole and not a surrogate for "objects as such," sartorially covering these in linguistic form.

Returning to my earlier example, Humboldt's object as such would be a real cuckoo as also its cognition as avian species. The English word "cuckoo," however, gives rise to Humboldt's image, has been impressed upon the mind through a particular language in use. Even if once culled from the bird's sound in order to name the bird, the word is a distinctive entity having its place in this language. From a purely rational perspective it may seem irrational to make a direct connection between an animal and its sound to identify one by the other, but as semantic vehicle the word remains efficient. The "soul" as the faculty engendering the image has also been secularized despite its religious overtones and thus merely conveys the intuitive base which the energetic tradition always stressed. Herder for one envisaged in "soul" the seat of intrinsic forces or "energies," say experts such as Schnebli-Schwegler (1965, p. 91), who deal with his *Treatment* (Abhandlung) *of the Origin of Language*. Since Herder wrote this work to refute the divine origin of language, a view still rampant in his day, he was obviously not sanctifying the term. In fact, to stress the decidedly anthropomorphic origin of language, Herder relied on organological descriptions: at one point (1959, p. 77) he discusses the "drive," German "Dringnis" or "Drang," which is as much entailed in the force of linguistic exteriorization as it is in the birth of an infant (see Adler, 1968, pp. 122-130; Clark, 1969, pp. 130-132; Berlin, 1976, pp. 167-168).

All these terms--imagination, genius, energy, and now soul--were to describe intuitive faculties in the liberation of language from logic. Not surprisingly, therefore, Humboldt's statement on the linguistic image turns up in Cassirer (1972, I, p. 256) and is cited to affirm that no synonymy exists among languages. What the energetic tradition as a whole grasped only too well was the "natural artifice" that constitutes the very nature of a so-called natural language in all its metaphysical self-determination. Indeed, artifice is a form of "art," as Humboldt's reference to "image" or "Bild" suggests, and by the time of nineteenth-century Romanticism, the issue was no longer to compare language *with* art but actually to treat it *as* art in essence. Unlike most of the eigtheenth-century Romantics, these successors displayed a keen interest in the literary rather than visual art genres. They called literature "Poesie," but never ceased to concentrate on language as the powerful medium that generated it.

Of the two Schlegel brothers, for instance, both of whom analyzed the role of language as literary substratum, A. W. Schlegel sounds almost like Humboldt and/or Cassirer when observing in his 1801 "Lectures" (Vorlesungen) that language was never a mere product of nature but remained the imprint of an active human spirit (1963, p. 226). My recent study on experimental Concrete Poetry (Gumpel, 1976, pp. 141-144 ff.) credits this period of Romanticism with anticipating what modern experimentalism later practiced in conscious linguistic manipulation, simply because the disposition of language in all its natural artifice became so well understood during this time.

Next in popularity to the image statement is Humboldt's concept of *interposition*. This statement focuses on linguistic *independence* or active *intervention* at the point of inception. Just as the single sound interposes itself between object and person, notes Humboldt in the *Variations* (p. 434), so does the entire language interpose itself between persons and their nature, influencing them inwardly and outwardly. Indeed, Humboldt's style here is so complex in abounding with prenoun inserts and embedded clauses English does not tolerate that those who translate his statement should become immediately aware of that originally willful intervention, especially if untoward sexism is to be avoided by adhering to plural designations for humans. Basically, Humboldt is separating all the "natures" that do not belong directly to language: "inner" sentiments and "outer" sensation, or "inner" feeling and "outer" perceiving are all faculties which, in themselves, do not necessarily coincide in the linguistic sound. Rooster cries can be heard, the birds in question seen, reactions to either experienced, but, ultimately, that sound which expresses "cock-a-doodle-doo" comes between these experiences, intervening on behalf of the unique and yet diverse (or varied) stratum language represents.

In the interposition context, Humboldt mentions a "world-view" and has been misunderstood on that score too; he does not mean the type of "Weltanschauung" linguistic anthropologists often associate with language (see Helbig, pp. 122-127, 130-132, 140-142). That is to say, language does not reflect a view of the cuckoo as human fool or even as a bird sound taken over by the name. The only "views" are the values language has ordained in (unstarred) words. That is not to preclude sporadic vestiges of *Weltanschauung.* The fact that Greek words, for example, predominate in philosophy obviously can be traced to a well developed ancient culture, as made evident by the very term "philosophy," the "love of wisdom"--or even the *energeia* which bore the etymological root of the term "energetic." But again, all such information is ancillary and not primary to the synchronic state of linguistic competence owned by speakers. For example, the "dog"/"god" palindrome cannot be interpreted as testimony of special Anglo-Saxon irreverence. But form the words did, and whatever the diachronic cause, the overt link now exists as potential for inimitable punning.

What Humboldt's "world-view" reinforces is essentially the "word-view" (my neologism) of his "image" precept. In that respect these Humboldtian concepts parallel the disclosure tenets of self-evident truth which came up in discussions of Heidegger and Cassirer. Again, whatever sense it makes outside the sense contained in "cuckoo" to name the bird after its sound, a linguistic perspective has solidified into a signitive value and become ordained as such. Nothing enters language by osmosis. But everything that has entered continues under its own momentum of self-determination. Through renewed articulation language quite literally reasserts itself as determinant of its freely forged determinables, forcing a speech community into perpetuating inimitable sounds that have been adapted further to written signs.

Since Humboldt's interposition precept obviously embodies unique synthesis, it also appeared early in Cassirer's volume on language (1972, pp. 25-26), where the latter discusses how human consciousness steps between ego (Ich) and world in order to forge its combinations. A work, moreover, which by virtue of its very title fills the gap historically between the theories of Humboldt and Cassirer in following one thinker and foreshadowing the other is *Language as Art--Sprache als Kunst*--published in two volumes in 1871 and 1873 and recently duplicated as facsimile (1961). Its author, Gustav Gerber (1820-1901), has not been sufficiently recognized either for his important contribution. In the last quarter of the nineteenth century Gerber's title, too, still makes explicit the Romantic identification of language with the essence of art. And the "Critical" connection is also there, since Gerber (1871, I, p. 279) suggests inadequacies in Kantian philosophy by advocating that the *Critique of Reason* should have incorporated a "Critique of Language" because all mental activity ultimately has its empirical existence in language. Indeed, through language, speakers first interpret reality as a human universe. Here I should reiterate that Kantian "reason," German "Vernunft," is not confined to the rational sphere. When not "theoretical," reason may extend to either the "practical" domain of morals or the esthetic "judgment" of art, where concepts of logical judgment, called "categories" after Aristotle, have no validity (Kant, 1914, Cassirer ed., V, i-9, pp. 270-285).

Gerber (1871, I, pp. 160, 193) also goes on to stress the alogical, intuitive foundation of language which affiliates him with the entire energetic tradition. Nearly all the important Humboldtian statements return in Gerber, as well as the vital terms here discussed--the "Phantasie" for the imagination, the soul, and the image as "Bild," all of them operating in their unimpeded "freedom" (1871, I, pp. 30, 170-175 ff., 200). "Linguistic art" (Sprachkunst) is invoked repeatedly by Gerber to stress how "life-acts" form and transform their products in language (1871, I, pp. 30, 72, 74, 103, 111-114, passim). The first linguistic root, notes Gerber (p. 125), already attested to "creative art" (schöpferische Kunst) because it embodied the first mature "soul-act." Such acts endowing language with life may remind those familiar with Wittgenstein's *Philosophical Investigations* (1963, p. 11) of the "form of life" or more literally the "life-form" (from "Lebensform") introduced with the "language-game" as "Sprachspiel."

However, Wittgenstein's pragmatism precludes any direct association between him and Gerber. Instead, Gerber makes frequent reference to the "esthetic" synthesizing powers of combining and severing which go on continuously in the formation of linguistic products, activities that reappear *verbatim* throughout Cassirer's exposition of language. And Gerber (1871, I, p. 175) anticipates this successor further when describing how a linguistic sound evolves as "Symbol" for the speakers who "enter" a sphere of "art" when they form sound to express themselves through it linguistically. Also, in quoting Humboldt's energetic premise Gerber alludes to "enthusiasm" (Begeisterung), a term both thinkers took from Shaftesburian neo-Platonism (Humboldt, 1963, p. 475, Gerber, 1871, I, p. 180).

A typically Teutonic emanation precept is "Hervorbringen" or "Hervorbringung," which literalizes into a "bringing to the fore"; one of those words can be found in almost any thesis of the proponents marking the energetic tradition. (Humboldt, p. 226, passim; Gerber, pp. 114, 130, 175, 190-193, passim.) The Romantic connection is not far behind, either, this time made evident in the transcendental or "aesthetic idealism" of Schelling (1775-1854). (See Windelband, II, 1958, pp. 600, 607; Schelling, 1858, III, pp. 607, 622). While Humboldt visualized language as the "Organ" from which all thought emanated, Schelling (ibid., pp. 619, 627 ff.) let art itself become the "Organon" or "documentation" of philosophy, since it presented a realm liberated from natural causality and thus a "freedom" whose provenance was solely human creativity. Such a premise certainly complements the various disclosure theories discussed.

Outside of exceptions such as Gerber, however, Humboldtian influence gradually became modified to suit the new Comparatist trends. Indeed, in the *Variations* (1963, p. 485) Humboldt himself seems to endorse this development since he praises the "insight" of the Comparatist proponent, Franz Bopp (1791-1867). Also, Romantics such as Friedrich Schlegel and Jakob Grimm revealed their Comparatist interests when they turned out their respective treatises on Indic languages (1808) and comparative grammar (1818). Comparatism certainly seized on "variations" among languages, if primarily for the benefit of their identifiable roots, tracing back "recorded" to "reconstructed" parent languages (Waterman, 1976, pp. 13-24 ff.). Yet by emphasizing evolution, most Comparatists retained a strong diachronic rather than synchronic perspective, planes Humboldtian theory had not confused. Even Saussure (1857-1913), the modern spokesman for separating these planes, had himself started along that path in his Comparatist study of Indo-European vowels of 1878. Indeed, for that achievement he was called from Geneva to Paris by Bréal, the critic who also gave the modern world the discipline of semantics as elucidated. Bréal in fact translated Bopp's Comparatist endeavors from German into French (Leroy, 1967, pp. 34 ff.). Yet Bréal's Comparatist affiliation should explain also what caused him to fail in his goal of establishing a theory of scientific semantics. On the other hand, Saussure (1966, pp. 65-70, 79-100) went on to distinguish effectively the diachronic and synchronic planes, as well as the arbitrary yet vital nature of the latter, although his *Course*, like Humboldt's *Variations*, was published posthumously (by his students) in 1916.

The late nineteenth century then witnessed the appearance of neo-Grammarian positivism, with its rigorous description of sound laws. The German "Junggrammatiker" looked to their leader Leskien; his treatise, *Soundlaws Know No Exception* of 1876, indicates the focus well enough. One favorable neo-Grammarian "exception" to the rule was Hermann Paul's *Principles of Linguistic Theory*, which first appeared in 1880 and was reprinted four times by 1920. Even in wording there is that slight reminder of the energetic past: like Herder, Paul describes language as possessing an inner "drive" (1975, p. 94) when exteriorized. More importantly, Paul also distinguished "usual" from "occasional" meaning (pp. 74-88), a dichotomy which in some respects anticipated Saussure's *langue* and *parole*, say critics (Ivić, 1971, p. 53). In other words, Paul glimpsed how reference traded on redundance, the "usual" component, since no new speech may result from individual speakers without sharing a sediment antecedently. Any conventionally based medium of expression guarantees its members acquired staples which make possible their potential expansion.

While neo-Grammarian positivism on the whole went in quest of definitive soundlaws, Comparatism turned psycholinguistic at about the same time: the Comparative Psychology of Wundt's *Völkerpsychologie* around 1900 stayed popular long enough to still influence Chomsky's precursor, Bloomfield. The latter's *Language* of 1933 (pp. 18, 386) does credit Humboldt with having initiated "general linguistics" but on the whole makes more of Wundt. In any case, Chomsky, who chronologically followed Bloomfieldian descriptive linguistics, took his predecessors to task for their "structuralist" mode of segmentation. While proclaiming his own Humboldtian roots, Chomsky displayed a strong reaction against everything psycholinguistic and/or "empiricist" in orientation.

At best, however, Chomsky remains a pseudo-Humboldtian who deserves credit mainly for opposing undue description in his own time and for recognizing the value of this German precursor. Indeed, Chomsky's *Cartesian Linguistics* of 1966 (pp. 19, 20-21, 70) did not neglect to cite the three Humboldtian statements-- in German even!--which were included here, the passages on ergon and energeia, on the image and soul, and on intervention. Yet his very allusion to "Rationalist Thought" in the work's subtitle indicates a stance inimical to the energetic tradition out of which Humboldtian language theory came. Ultimately, the fact that Chomsky opposed superficial trends of his era does not *ipso facto* convert him into the successor to Humboldt he deemed himself to be.

Consequently, no one besides Chomsky (ibid., p. 27) should be surprised that Humboldt did *not* "construct particular generative grammars" with an inbuilt "universal schema to which the particular grammar conforms," as he notes with regret. How could Humboldt's intuitive energetic approach to language adopt such set conformity, particularly when a few pages hence Chomsky (p. 35) posits a "universal deep structure . . . common to all languages?" That kind of universalism would annihilate the "variations" on which Humboldt had concentrated. Chomsky's monolith robs language of its true "mind," to trade on the title of his later work, *Language and Mind* (1972), which manifests the two side by side, held apart by a conjunction. His works generally reflect the same stance: a mind rooted in transformations which do not belong to language proper. Rather, Chomsky keeps language the vassal of logic. While trying to restore depth to the investigation of language, he invokes his own "ontological argument for the existence of language" through a universal logic.

Chomsky's rationalism constitutes instead an anachronistic "Cartesius Redivivus" (Esper, 1968, pp. 219 ff.). He certainly does not hide the fact in the works cited that he returns to the Cartesian age, chiefly to endorse seventeenth-century Port-Royal grammar, the *Grammaire générale et raisonnée* of 1660 by Lancelot and Arnauld because of its focus on universal logic (1966, p.31 ff.; 1972, pp. 16-17, passim; also 1965, pp. 6-7). Subsequent discussions should reveal further what problems this orientation causes for any investigation of meaning involving metaphor. From a historical perspective, there exists a definite ironic reversal: instead of fostering a Humboldtian connection as Chomsky intended, he actually sealed its doom by the very impact his Cartesian focus had on the middle of this century.

The same is not entirely true of some trends in the early decades of the twentieth century before Chomsky; they bore signs of combating the then current positivism. A case in point was the work of 1904 by Vossler, proponent of the neo-Idealist school based in Munich; it had pitted against positivism a new Romantic type of esthetic idealism that probed the intuitive depths of language (Helbig, 1970, pp. 22-26, Ivić, 1971, pp. 81-88). Subsequent decades then witnessed other German "neo-Romantic" trends pertaining to "Content-Related (inhaltsbezogene) Grammarians" and "Field-Theory" proponents. These schools tried to keep Humbold's ideas alive, mostly by replacing neo-Grammarian "sound-related" detail with "content-related" semantic spheres (Helbig, 1970, pp. 119 148, 152-154; Schaff, 1974, pp. 26-28). One recent critic (Jost, 1960, pp. 124-127) actually offers tables to show how closely these neo-Humboldtians adhered to their mentor.

Yet none of these developments--including the functional tagmemics of Pike and followers this side of the Atlantic--could resist tranformationalist pressure. Although interest in generative grammar is supposed to have abated of late, nothing substantive has taken its place. In view of the impending year 2000, one gets the impression of heading for the kind of *fin-de-siècle* stalemate that afflicted the turn of the last century in art. Language theory seems to have run the gamut of every field and every professional area from philosophy to psychology and poetics without that discipline forming which Bréal had dimly envisioned in his coinage of "semantics." In the final analysis even Cassirer (1972, I, p. 280), with whom this chapter began, does not take semantics far enough: after treating so painstakingly the spontaneous inductive nature of language, he concludes perversely with "logical relations" as though these were the ultimate realization of linguistic prowess. Cassirer thus came close to undoing the "cultural" expansion he had emphasized at the outset of his volume on language.

With the limits of Cassirer's contribution thus described, as well as the Humboldtian tradition his theory embodied, the analysis turns to the phenomenological semantics of Ingarden. Of course, Ingarden will stay important for many of this work's subsequent chapters, particularly discussions of aspects dealing with the (semiotic) Picture of Language. In the immediate setting, however, he serves my ultimate ontological separation of language by the means of the promised *circles.*

The greater portion of Ingarden's semantic theory appeared in *Das literarische Kunstwerk* of 1931 (though I will refer to the third edition of 1965). Originally written in German, the work was translated into English in 1973 as *The Literary Work of Art.* Ingarden's other important work, *Cognition of the Literary Work of Art,* also appeared in this translation in 1973; it came out first in 1936 under the Polish title, *O poznawaniu dziela literackiego,* with the German translation, *Vom Erkennen des literarischen Kunstwerks,* published in 1968. The dates of the relatively late English translations say something about deferred Anglo-Saxon interest. In one of the posthumous publications containing some of Ingarden's separate writings translated into German from the Polish, the editor, Fieguth (1976, p. XI), points out that Ingarden's style was abstruse in even his mother tongue. Fieguth's volume (pp. 135-140 ff.) also includes polemical passages, essentially arguments between Ingarden and his Marxist compatriots. In a bitter rebuttal against those who opposed the schism he allegedly created between language and the concrete reality (and related issues), Ingarden alludes sarcastically to his own "heresy," a term that should serve as a reminder of the closeness between religious and political dogmatisms.

In the end, at least, Marxist objection should prove wholly unfounded, since Ingarden describes meticulously how language makes repeated contacts with the extralinguistic world. Ultimately, he could only make a case for this contact because he gave language its self-identity. By specifying the bounds of language he could delineate where other domains took over and/or touched on the semantic sphere, which is the very problem neo-Aristotelians never solved while probing metaphor. Since Ingarden approached ontology with full logical consistency for the sole purpose of keeping logic out of language while showing also under what conditions it may enter language, the long awaited science of meaning that Bréal and Ullmann, among others, had sought without success finally reached fruition. So while some critics compare Chomsky's work on syntax to a "Copernican revolution" (Esper, 1968, p. 220), it is really Ingarden who deserves that accolade in the area of semantics. Indeed, so narrow was Chomsky's perception of syntax that, it will turn out, he himself did not know where syntax bordered on semantics, a problem which cannot even arise with Ingarden's dynamic semantic unit(y).

But first, Ingarden actually dared to name the essence of language, calling it "ontic heteronomy," in German "Seins-Heteronomie" (also without a hyphen, or as the adjective "seinsheteronom"; 1965, pp. 104, 120, 127, 131, 141, 172, passim). Leaning on his mentor Husserl, Ingarden describes how in language as ontic heteronomy everything is freely "contributed" (gestiftet), thus has to originate (entstehen, 1965, pp. 106-107) in contents that become spontaneously "created" or "drafted" (entworfen, geschaffen). The very phrasing here evokes the inspirational faculties at work in purposive domains such as art. Thus Ingarden tacitly perpetuated what the Romantics were seen to have espoused.

Moreover, what causes meanings to be heteronomous is their sole dependence on linguistic activity, a point Ingarden never fails to stress (pp. 66, 69, 75, 127, 129, 131, passim). Cassirer's linguistic modality thus also emerges in a new setting. But Ingarden becomes more specific: he traces linguistic activity to binary functions termed "Meinen" and "Vermeinen" (pp. 104, 121-123, passim). "Meinen" corresponds to the *act of meaning* entailed in authorial intent, the will of speakers; "Vermeinen" refers to *signification* or *embodiment* of the act by selected explicit and implicit meanings, whose basic denominations speakers share as interlocutory partners. When thus selected, meanings corporealize and embody a speaker's act of meaning, resulting in a unified sense which harbors what a speaker "meant" to say. In the type of intellectual (Fichtean) introspection my study has advocated from the start, that is also what happens to my writing: authorial intent selected every single word on this page; my meaning becomes conveyed through these chosen meanings. On the surface, the words resemble any discrete vocable in its usual explicit and implicit denominations, but at depth each entity is teleologically bound to, and regulated by, my authorial will, releasing accordingly the connotations relevant only to the whole sentence.

The sentence is thus a holistic constitutive unit(y) that Ingarden designates "pure-intentional sentence (or syntactic) correlate" (1965, pp. 110-121, 133, 138, passim). "Correlation" essentially pinpoints the correlative functions of the two tasks, the "Meinen" and "Vermeinen" that span the length and breadth of such a unit(y). Their resulting interaction brings the *reference* contributed by individual meanings to bear on the *transference* these undergo through the act of meaning as they materialize (explicitly) and engender (implicitly) the act of meaning. Again, my sentences here are no exception to the rule; no new generation of meaning by chosen meanings can occur without a transaction between reference and transference: syntactic entrants shift to release a unified sense relevant to and derived from (my) authorial intent.

In this syntactic-semantic processing, the constituents become what Ingarden (1965, p. 122-124, 127-129) calls "targets" for an act's "intending." Meanings are accordingly "pure-intentional objects," or (loosely speaking) dynamic "mental" entities. Their pure-intentional base keeps meanings sufficiently elastic to retain self-identity while simultaneously undergoing the shift described. In their dependence on signitive acts for every semantic constitution, meanings possess only what their acts intend, be that the "fool" in the "cuckoo" or the German donkey. Referential priority goes to "naming" the acts of speakers and not extralinguistic things or concepts. That is the "natural" task of meanings--rather than hanging labels on antecedent existents for which they serve as mere stand-ins, as the current view of linguistic reference tacitly maintains. In their very dependence on signation, meanings must be confined to the collective acts precipitated (potentially) by one speech community, a numeric qualifier caught in the "hetero-" prefix of "heteronomy." For that reason precisely this study has stressed repeatedly the need to concentrate on language in a language; plurality of use stays confined to one language and ultimately erupts in all the (Humboldtian) variations of different and self-contained languages.

While pure-intentionality is current in phenomenology, ontic heteronomy is Ingarden's addition to assure that these "mental" objects belong solely to signitive acts. Opposed to *ontic heteronomy* he has pitted *ontic autonomy*; it comes either in "real" (corporeal) dimensions or "ideal" abstractions (1965, pp. XIV-XV, 99, 103, 106-107, passim). Illustration may be best at this point: a dog and cuckoo, for example, are perceived as corporeal creatures and thus belong to the autonomous-real state; they are conceived as respective canine and avian species in logical subsumption under the genus animal and in that respect become autonomous-ideal entities. Ingarden devised *just* those *basic* ontological distinctions which help him offset language from other domains. Accordingly, "autonomy" here signifies mainly not being dependent on acts of meaning, thus not on language in a language.

That is always the test, as stated. Logical acts are thus precluded categorically, as is all direct perception of entities which are not (word) meanings. Of course, the semantic entities are "autonomous," more properly *autotelic*, when regarded in their intrinsic, purposive state of being. But without human intervention meanings cannot exist, even if language interposes itself in full self-determination, "coercing" speakers to uphold collectively what has found inception in a language. Conversely, empirical nature may be a part of the human environment but it can also flourish (better?) without being submitted to the perception of humans.

The *collision* between forms of programming mentioned before as the cause for the traditional *metaphor* now can be diagnosed. It occurs when ontic autonomy momentarily obtrudes upon ontic heteronomy, forcing categories of the former into cognizance while dealing with the latter. However, since there is no "dealing" with language except on its own ground, ontic heteronomy cannot be dislodged. The language "works," to resort to my former pun, mainly because autonomy and heteronomy are too disparate in acquisition, thus leaving a mere sense impression behind, but never "non-sense" in language. Even in my bilingual state, I cannot cross over within ontic heteronomy to the other language but must rely on my content acquisition of each, and thus on the contextualization through signitive acts I have assimilated with these contents. This is accomplished by a functional transference occurring within one language at a time--as I express my meaning through the meanings each language holds available. In this very processing, language in a language normalizes constituents within me, forging redundance for some "dead" metaphors that are actually just odd meanings flattened through a frequency of application in related contexts.

Unfortunately, even Ingarden's otherwise clear-cut ontological division into heteronomy and autonomy contains one vulnerable principle. That is his "idealer Begriff" or "ideal concept" (1965, pp. 88-89, 386-390), introduced by him in an attempt to give additional ballast to what he deemed to be the volatile quality of ontic heteronomy. Whatever his reasons, the ideal concept alone by name conflicts with the ontological division he otherwise upheld so consistently, since the ideal throughout his work remains identified with ontic autonomy, and thus should not become any part of ontic heteronomy. To avoid confusion, therefore, Ingarden's ideal concept will be discarded in favor of Cassirer's linguistic concept, whose role of imprinting will be detailed meticulously. Since Ingarden's oversight seems to be mainly one of nomenclature rather than essence, the modification does not erode his theory in general.

It may be necessary also to stress early that Ingarden's autonomous-real and autonomous-ideal states do not reach the Kantian transcendental proportions. The "real" in ontic autonomy does not equal Kant's extramental or transcendentally real noumenon but designates only an extralinguistic state. Since Ingarden's ontological divide governs bounds of language, it stays immanent to Kant's phenomenal domain, where the latter's transcendentally ideal sphere is lodged. Even when thus corrected, however, any direct transition from one thinker to the other remains oversimplified. Thus to thrust in language with Kant's phenomenal sphere is inadequate for reasons that should emerge when levels of time and space regarding literary works are examined later in this study.

But if not in nomenclature, then in precept, Ingarden's phenomenology fits historically into the wider Critical tradition, which, as perpetuated in philosophical Idealism throughout the nineteenth century, stressed the constitutive role of consciousness for human experience. Ingarden aided the development of that perspective by focusing on *signitive* consciousness as the catalyst of language made effective through acts of meaning, a theory that culminates in the disclosure tenets discussed. Simultaneously, Ingarden's ontic autonomy takes care not only of corporeal or "real" entities but of the "ideal" counterparts embodied in Cassirer's deductive "abstraction" or Nietzsche's equalizing "Begriff." The autonomous-ideal thus partakes of the very categories that the ontological category-mistake culls from lexical deviance where ontic heteronomy should prevail, whose entities are pure-intentional "objects" signitively derived, hence not from logical acts of deduction but from dynamic acts of meaning. These elastic entities are indeed inductive, as Cassirer stressed; they are the result of language as the "Organ" of thought, and they constitute the "Organon" of exclusive linguistic productivity.

Indeed, Humboldt almost expressed the gist of Ingarden's tenet when in the *Variations* (1963, p. 226) he observed that to the extent that language remained independent (selbstständig) it embodied an "Object" and to the extent it remained dependent (abhängig) on speech, a "Subjekt." The "subjective" dependence here constitutes the signitive act, and what it "objectifies," the heteronomous, pure-intentional object. Paradoxically, signitive acts are only independent because meanings depend on them for their origination. The great paradoxes Kant formulated in the *Third Critique* (Cassirer, ed.,V, 1914, pp. 290, 312) for the sphere of art may thus be relevant: "free law," "purposiveness without purpose," and "conformity to law without law" are three antithetical phrases that may be used to convey any autotelic, purposive mode of existence. The same applies to the Kantian "Everyman" reiterated throughout the *Critique* (ibid., pp. 280-281, 288, 308, 310). In less anthropomorphic (and sexist?) terms, this concept stands for the intersubjective base through which all persons, and here speakers-- every "man" or "human"--of a speech community uphold values as the only possible means for an "objectivity" in an intrinsic foundation that subsists "without interest" and "without (logical) concept" (Kant, ibid., pp. 271-280, 280-288, 318). Though seemingly odd in wording, Kant's phrasing emphasizes that, beyond their own disclosure, purposive foundations are released from goals, rational or pragmatic, that remain extrinsic to their being.

Below, ontic heteronomy and autonomy become separated in circles to reveal the ultimate "truth" of their disparate natures, fulfilling the promise of this chapter. The corporeal roundness of circular shapes befits continuity and distinctiveness with a touch of global proportion made concrete. Those circular shapes mirror effectively the autonomous-real by "speaking" alike to all individuals, irrespective of linguistic variations. Thus, in their way, the circles project once more the ontological distinction which separates non-verbal contours from those of words, which also come with this diagram. In the way of a warning, the circles foreshadow the adjunct, where they feature in misjudged counterfactuality surrounding discussions on metaphor.

REALITIES (R) IN CIRCLES

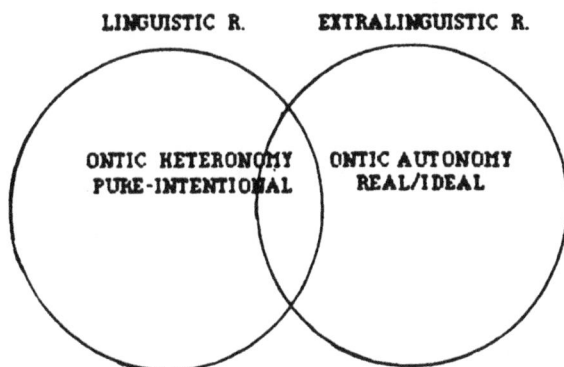

LINGUISTIC R.   EXTRALINGUISTIC R.

ONTIC HETERONOMY   ONTIC AUTONOMY
PURE-INTENTIONAL   REAL/IDEAL

Ontic heteronomy is the left circle, suggesting "first" in the sequence because language as "linguistic reality" stays the primary universe for humans, as Cassirer, Gerber, and others stressed also, before Ingarden. Putting language first also fits better into Ingarden's plan insofar as ontic autonomy, which may be subsumed under the qualifier of "autonomous-objective reality," is posited mainly as counter-reality to ontic heteronomy and thus in traits most basic to that distinction. The extralinguistic reality remains otherwise ramified enough to induce numerous divisions, including also some for the visual arts, since these, despite their purposive state, are not confined to the perception of words. Ingarden's sparse ontological division thus outlines the criteria of fundamentals so sorely needed in any investigation of meaning and metaphor, a problem the pervasive "syncretism" in the adjunct should make abundantly clear.

So with this minimal division language and its counterpart(s) become sufficiently separated to obviate the ontological category-mistake: language of the left circle resides in heterogeneous acts of meaning that surface only with one language. Regarded from the aspect of the right circle, ontic heteronomy appears "arbitrary"; regarded from within its own circle, ontic heteronomy becomes *absolute* if native speaker competence is to govern satisfactory performance. Regarded from the right circle, ontic heteronomy contains violated categories which precipitate "metaphors"; viewed from within their own circle, these metaphors turn out simply to be normalized meanings in a given language, if odd on their (lexical) surface. Ingarden (1965, p. 123) stresses that acts of meaning "transcend" other acts of consciousness; he makes plain that these other acts cannot interfere with signation. As pure-intentional "objects," of course, meanings also transcend their acts; they become their legitimate, and thus validated (unstarred) *products,* even as they attain no being without those acts.

Now, despite their disparity, the circles also *overlap* on the diagram. What the overlap does *not* stand for is that collision between two forms of programming brought on with a sensation of metaphor, since that experience is of no essence. Rather, the overlap marks a particular *use* of language, irrespective of content--cuckoos, donkeys, or whatever. It announces the *contact* language makes with the extralinguistic reality in the separate attachment of a *reality-nexus*, a process called *adequation* by Ingarden in order to designate a juxtaposition of two referents, a heteronomous-pure and autonomous-objective one. Adequation is of enormous importance and will thus be treated in the minutest detail: it is a functional way of making language "literal" as well "logical" by permitting the entry of *truth conditions* that indeed give rise to propositions. Adequation is also the cause of idiom formation through semantic redundancy and, most importantly, becomes the primary functional distinguisher between *literal* and *literary* use without resorting to a "prosaic" or "poetic" (odd) lexical surface. Ultimately, adequation is Ingarden's best defense against unwarranted charges of an elitism, since it necessitates contact between language and the objective reality.

Through the presence or absence of adequation, *three structures* are to be posited, two *non-adequated* ones for fictional and poetic literary genres and one *adequated* alternative which, as already suggested, represents the *everyday* or *literal* application of language. The term "structure" in non-Aristotelian semantics refers mainly to a *nonlexical* orientation. My interpretation certainly includes the basic idea of wholeness and transformation through self-regulation critics generally associate with structure (Piaget, in Hawkes, 1977, p. 16). This structural division, however, should also make evident where Cassirer's logical judgment, which had concluded the latter's work, remained insufficient, since now it can be seen to exemplify only one of three applications in language, specifically the last of the three structures listed here. Beyond the value of the immediate context, furthermore, this structural division will permit the development of a *non-Aristotelian,* structural *metaphor* from one of the non-adequated uses. Since the precise locus of this metaphor involves the complete Picture of Language, the discussion moves next to this semiotic schema, now that the essence of language has been identified and differentiated.

PART II

The Non-Aristotelian Theory, Pure and Applied

Non-Aristolelian Semantics:
Three Trichotomies of Ontic Heteronomy

The "Picture" of Language: General Semiotic Perspective

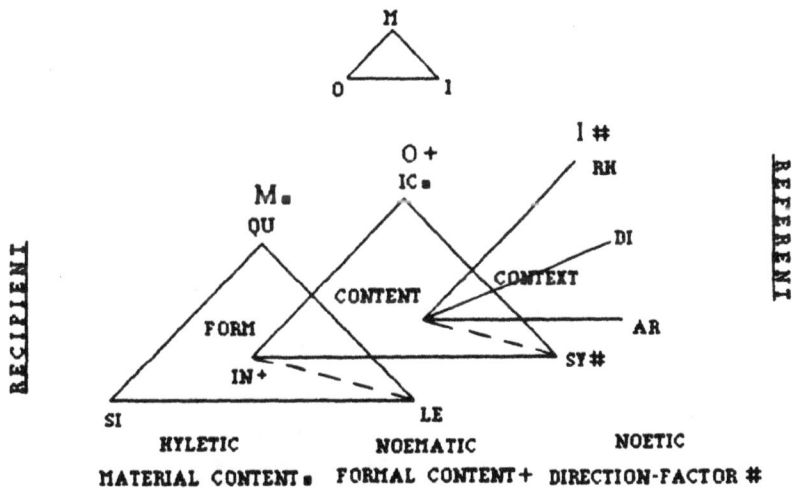

M: MATTER (MEANS, REPRESENTAMEN)
O: OBJECT (RELATION)
I: INTERPRETANT (RELATION); CONSCIOUSNESS

QU: QUALISIGN
SI: SINSIGN   <u>FIRST TRICHOTOMY: PERCEIVING</u>
LE: LEGISIGN

IC: ICON •
IN: INDEX +   <u>SECOND TRICHOTOMY: KNOWING</u>
SY: SYMBOL #

RH: RHEME
DI: DICENT   <u>THIRD TRICHOTOMY: WILLING</u>
AR: ARGUMENT   51

Above is the "Picture of Language" which governs many chapters to come. Language is made concrete or "iconic," and the lower case here indicates that iconization is not derived from a word but a graphic design. The terms beginning with "Qualisign" are, however, capitalized throughout this study to signal my own adaptation of Peirce's "Classes of Signs" (1960, pp. 146-150, par. 2.254-2.265). One basic difference is numeric, since Peirce offers ten classes and the Picture nine, for reasons to be explained. Peirce's "formal . . . doctrine of signs" (1960, p. 134, par. 2.227) is thus not followed slavishly because logic "in its general sense" is to him only another name for "semiotic" (ibid.). By sheer definition, a Picture of *Language* must focus on properties of words if it is to stay "logical" in a systematic approach to this subject. Regarding the qualifier itself, Peirce (1960, p. 134, par. 2.227) traces "semiotic" to Greek "semeiotikey" (in my transliteration). Although his trinary system is followed in Europe by some (M. Bense *et al.*), there exists also the term "semiology," which goes back in part to the binary division of Saussure that side of the Atlantic (Hawkes, 1977, p. 124; Wienold, 1972, pp. 11-12). Those further interested in the development of semiotic concepts might find enlightening Sebeok's "'Semiotics' and its Congeners" (1976, chapter 2, pp. 47-58 ff.).

In any case, the basic nomenclature of Peirce's signs is retained for the Picture of Language though boosted by the following additions. First, there are the insertions within the three trichotomies marked "form," "content," and "context." These nouns designate the material base, conceptual essence, and semantic function of (word) meanings when wielded in the final trichotomy of context. Second, the adjectives "hyletic," "noematic," and "noetic" to some extent paraphrase the nouns; they denote the concrete foundation of meaning(s), the content, and the ultimate act(ivity) that is always involved in context. Next, "material content," "formal content," and "direction-factor" are phenomenological concepts Ingarden coined to designate facets of word meanings. At this preliminary stage, the purpose of the exposition is just to introduce phenomenology in conjunction with semiotics--if the previous effort of ontological placement with the aid of phenomenology is not to be wasted, particularly in view of Peirce's stress on logic cited above. When the detailed specifications take over, the full role of phenomenology for the last trichotomy will also emerge. From an aspect of basic nomenclature, let me stress early that my use of "form" and Ingarden's "formal" are not merely ways of rendering synonyms clad in a noun or adjective. If that were the case, their position would not differ as shown. Rather, Ingarden's formal content will turn out to focalize implicit meaning, whereas the form of the first trichotomy belongs to the *explicit* base of language at its primary level of sonorous and visual concretion.

Now to the trichotomies: they correspond to form, content, and context in a hierarchical order of semiotic generation, reaching their maximal stage of consciousness at the "Interpretant" level, as the readings for M-0-I below the trichotomies indicate. In addition, a *small* triangle can be seen above the trichotomies; its purpose is mainly heuristic for localizing the M-0-I generation. When the trichotomies are taken up separately, the same M-0-I order will be added to each trichotomy. The first two trichotomies in the triangular shape will bear M at their apex, 0 at their left, and I at their right angles. Although the third trichotomy possesses three loose strands, M also commences with the strand at the top, followed by 0 and I at the lower two strands.

For the present, the M-0-I order signals mainly the triadic relation among the trichotomies. Very conspicuous from that aspect is the gradual M-0-I *incline of generation*, made "iconic" or visually concrete enough through the gradual climb to the top. This hierarchy is paralleled by the *broken lines* within the trichotomies that lead "up" to the next trichotomy from the last. Of course, in an organic, hermeneutic relationship, human consciousness alone makes any relationality possible, shaping content through the use of the form. Indeed, this aspect of organic relationality corresponds tacitly to the premise behind Continental phenomenology, which is that all objects are essentially objects of consciousness. Conversely, I-0-M in *decline* marks semiotic *degeneration*. That is the fate of "dead" languages--and not just a "dead" metaphor which has lapsed into ordinary ("literal") meaning. These languages "exist" merely in Qualisign form on stone tablets and equivalent materials. With their semantic content evaporated, the forms disclose only *that* a language once existed in full generation. However, so-called dead Classical languages, such as ancient Greek and Latin, do not belong here, since all they have lost is their viable situational context (at I). Such a degeneration is far less drastic; the same applies to the dead metaphor to be probed further in the appropriate place.

The fact that this semiotic schema projects exclusively a Picture of *Language* is affirmed further by the "Recipient" and "Referent" perpendicular to the trichotomies. Depicted as vertical prongs, these activities constrain the trichotomies like a vise. The terms for these two functions also stay capitalized in order to emphasize their special application to this Picture of Language. "People" as such would be too simplistic in construal. Recipient and Referent denote respectively the linguistic inception and reception entailed in interlocutory partnership. The Referent may be equated with the act of meaning the selected meanings bring forth; the Recipient marks construal of such a Referent through the meanings at hand. Essentially, a Referent and Recipient meet in a given verbal or written message. The Recipient appears at the degenerate end of the trichotomies because it confronts the form of language whereas the Referent belongs to the highest generate point where an Interpretant seeks new contents for contextualization. When following the usual left-to-right sequence in written language, the Recipient seems to come first on the Picture but does not take priority over the Referent. The latter assumption would be misleading, since the Referent is the catalyst for all expression.

To get a better idea of the depth marking the locus of the Referent, the page should be turned *ninety degrees*, leaving the Recipient uppermost. From that perspective, then, the Recipient hovers over the surface of language; it must penetrate form and content in order to arrive at the deep-seated Referent lodged in context for any given contextualization of contents. No less is expected here of my readers; they are not confronting discrete vocables but constituents molded to my authorial intent, be the surface plain or figurative. Indeed, had neo-Aristotelians explored this depth in determining metaphor instead of poring over a lexical surface, this study need never have been written. What Referent and Recipient affirm together is the sphere of *ontic heteronomy* isolated in the previous chapter with the aid of Ingarden. Both stand for exclusive linguistic activity; anything connected with these trichtomies must be filtered through their function. In their way, the Referent and Recipient (in generative order of priority) safeguard against the ontological category-mistake, which causes critics to jump beyond these activities into ontic autonomy as they substantiate metaphor within language in terms of violated categories by violating the very bounds of language.

The same factor of linguistic self-determination governs the three faculties below the diagram of the trichotomies--the "perceiving," "knowing," and "willing" entered for each trichotomy. Though not capitalized here, these faculties must be similarly confined to the use of language and thus embody aspects of *linguistic competence* while anything outside of the word remains (for the present) encyclopedic knowledge. Two of the terms for these faculties were actually extracted from a passage in Peirce (there capitalized; 1960, pp. 198-189, par. 1.375). Peirce associates them with Kant's three "departments" governing a "trisection" of the mind though tracing back their origin further to older "dogmatic philosophers." Moreover, the only "dogmatism" I wish to eradicate concerns the affective ring in "feeling" that Peirce lists for the first of the three faculties. The reference to feeling has thus been replaced by "perceiving." Peirce's allusion to Kant in itself is a constant reminder of those "udders" (quoted in my introduction) that nurtured him. Such is the influence upon him of the man he revered as a "King" of modern thought and as a builder of metaphysical systems second only to Aristotle.

The above faculties thus embody some of that "Critical" heritage elucidated in the last chapter. However, a parallel historical connection does not apply to phenomenology. An exception is Ingarden's mentor, Husserl, who wrote an essay on the logic of signs (1970; see also Sebeok, 1976, p. 49). The essay acknowledges the role of language as an "artifact" whose "artificial" (künstliche) signs remain freely "made up" or "invented" (erfunden, 1970, pp. 365-368). So Husserl certainly recognizes the conventional, spontaneous base of language while dealing with the logic of signs. Still, Husserl did not make full use of that information in the way his successor Ingarden did. Husserl explains, for instance, how "natural thought" (das natürliche Denken) keeps signs under its control (p. 367) when, actually, only that thought which language controls becomes "natural" *in* language. Thought, identified with the second trichotomy of "knowing" in the Picture of Language, must be derived from the word between Referent and Recipient. Authorial "willing" then makes it possible for a context to forge new semantic contiguities in a release of meaning from meanings.

Husserl reappears briefly in this study, primarily in the adjectives taken from phenomenology. For this cursory glance, however, the trichotomies in their basic triadic interaction take precedence: together with the vertical prongs and three faculties they constitute the functional requisites of *reference* and *transference*. Although the very term gives the impression that a "Referent" alone governs "reference," the relation is not that simple. Ultimately, a Referent becomes the catalyst for an authorial will to "form" context (quite literally) by deploying elements of the first trichotomy for purposes of expressing authorial intent at the last. Transference, thus induced, causes selected constituents to *shift* in their reference in order to release authorial intent as new, unified meaning. That is how all content arises at the second trichotomy and becomes recorded in full activity, ready to serve once more the next recall with further expansion of content in contextualization, which is what happens right here. The chosen explicit denominations constitute "reference," while the implicit ones arise with transference in new semantic integration. That is the processing "natural" to a natural language. Linguistic expression is always willed; knowing and perceiving arise teleologically from wielding words through authorial intent.

Despite this affirmation of cognitive independence for each language, the "universal" factor is not ignored either but is at least held in check. Otherwise my reference would hardly be to a Picture of "Language" in the singular. This Picture carries what all languages must possess in essence and faculty. In that respect, ontic heteronomy becomes *one* sphere. The Picture thus treats language as a single substratum just because there is not a language in the world able to flourish without the trichotomies and the activities specified. This universalism notwithstanding, semantic competence resides only in *languages* of specific denominations, just as wielding English remains confined strictly to its community of speakers.

That warning of separate identity has to be sounded regularly, not only to obviate confusion with a Chomskyan type of logical "universalism" but also to resist categoricians at large who fall prey to the ontological category-mistake by detecting metaphor in wrong, wholly universal, categories. Non-Aristotelian semantics instead has as its regulative, cognitive source the act of meaning which comes from *without* by originating with individual speaker intent while it nevertheless reinforces language from *within* by involving only speech activity in one language. The act of meaning would possess no regulative prowess if it did not engender every part of semantic content in all the cognitive bounds a language can muster. This is the reason why ontic heteronomy as one semantic sphere bears entities dependent on "heterogeneous" signitive acts that mold meanings to their meaning, much as the products become "objective" once they are intersubjectively internalized and shared in their given language.

The importance of the above findings should become progressively more evident. At this juncture, the signs are to be contrasted only in their basic tasks. Beginning with the first trichotomy of form, this breaks into Qualisign material, Sinsign composition, and Legisign validation. Though last in the order of generation, the Legisign is first in importance: without its stamp of approval, Qualisign and Sinsign remain quite literally "useless" in any language. In English, "*og" or "*od" may not be deployed because they have not been validated as available vocables; their asterisk thus signals nonexistence for this language. They are unacceptable not from any lack of judgment but simply through being by-passed for validation. Strictly speaking, the above "forms" are then not forms at all, since, despite the recognizable letters, no perception may lead to authorial selection. The opposite applies to the verbs "do"/"go" brought up with the "dog"/"god" palindrome; these unstarred versions equal validated Sinsigns that accordingly bear Legisign endorsement. Since a conventional, volitional system such as language needs validation if it is to *exist* at all for interlocutory partners in individual languages, Legisigns foster *truth* in the manner explained with Cassirer, hence as disclosure of indigenous activity.

Essentially, the Legisign makes an *arbitrary* state *absolute*. That is where the (former) "M" matriarch or "Mother" dominates over native speakers, coercing these into using a "legitimate" repertoire. With conscious assent a requisite, the Legisign must be placed at the right angle that the small triangle reveals as the Interpretant corner. Put paradoxically, Legisign validation invalidates the arbitrary state which, in lingusitic skepticism, too often becomes identified with the being of language. Once a meaning actually exists as Legisign, any Qualisign idiosyncrasy is ready for projecting the material base of a word as sound or visual sign. A conspicuous case of Qualisign dimensions in what might be called orthographic "domes-dots-dashes" surely surfaced with the "cuckoo" of the former cartoon, enlarged in boldface through a generous sickle-shaped "C," a horseshoe "U" and some rings projecting "O."

To be sure, the optic confrontation does not exclude sound either. ɔund is present in transmuted form; no language can be read smoothly if its sound is not in one's ears--a personal experience for which I can vouch when certain target languages start to elude me from lack of practice. However, what matters most at this stage of investigation is the awareness that Qualisigns congeal, forming Sinsign composites that are governed largely by the phonemic makeup of words. In the age of electronic duplication, Qualisigns stay fairly standardized, but Sinsign violation through misspelling, typographical error, and related lapses is harder to circumvent. Let me also stress early that the Qualisigns and Sinsigns validated in tactile-manual forms for the handicapped and similar unique cases will be excluded from my study.

"Up" the incline and/or broken line by the Legisign is to be found the second trichotomy of content. "Second" for this 0-trichotomy between the M-1 trichotomies takes on the real meaning of "middle." The trichotomy's first two signs, Icon and Index, oppose one another as explicit and implicit denominations of content. The Icon thus appropriates the form in explicit denominations at M-locus within this trichotomy, and it is for that reason always protected by copyright laws as the most direct, denotative *reference* in exteriorization of an authorial will. Furthermore, the Icon is crucial for this study because it stands for the *lexicon*, where neo-Aristotelians erroneously place their "metaphor." The Index conversely arises with the *transference* to which the Icon is subjected time and again. Fusing inwardly with the act of meaning, the Index emits connotations relevant to that act(ivity). The Icon and Index are thus the vehicles for any contextualization of contents, irrespective of their denominational appearance. Hence they cannot, by themselves, without an altered function at context (I), give rise to a special "metaphor" of substance. Yet the later discussions reveal how even Peirce could not stay immune to an Iconic metaphor he termed "Hypoicon."

That lexical *neutrality*, in fact, which governs Legisign entry into *any* context forces Icons to discharge their function equally once validated Legisigns are passed on to serve a signitive act, with simultaneous expansion at the level of the Index. Simple "analogies" and/or "anomalies" thus do not account for the formations of Icons and (their) Indexes; these forge instead an oppositional value system derived from the use of one language, hence of synchronic associations so vast that no narrow apples-and-oranges identity in difference could possibly apply. In that network, something like the Index "fool" in the English Icon "cuckoo" constitutes only one infinitesimal positive/privative value that has become sufficiently redundant to have reached full normalization. What is truly abnormal, however, is the way in which neo-Aristotelians turn out to subvert Icons and Indexes through *proxy-tenet* barter, forcing an implicit content into "denoting" for an explicit one in some imagined form of transference.

As noted, the Icon is fixed at (M) apex of its trichotomy, and the Index at (0) left angle in the small triangle. Thus, when both "cuckoo" and "fool" are rendered as explicit Icons, values differ from the seemingly identical denominations carried by an Index. From the semiotic aspect, therefore, the differing denominations "cuckoo" and "fool" have more in common as two Icons than the same denominations "fool" and "fool" when one of them is an Icon and the other an

Index. Otherwise there would be no point in stressing the M-0 locus for each. In my own understanding of linguistic meaning, I am aware that my discussion of the Index "fool" forces me to exteriorize the import in a denotation--at which point the Index has actually become an Icon!

Originally, too, the trichotomies were in color. Considerations of cost then forced me to change to symbols. The color green formerly stood for the first trichotomy of form to suggest the very ground of language; the Icon perpetuated that chromatic identifier, bearing an asterisk of the same color as the immediate beneficiary of validated form. Ingarden's "material content" also bore that color as part of that same foundation, in essence linguistic "matter." Now a dot (.) must present these identifications. Next, the original color for the second trichotomy, which was red, had no significance other than to distinguish from the first. This color linked the Index to its own, second trichotomy as well as to Ingarden's "formal content" with a matching chromatic asterisk, for which a plus sign (+) now appears. The differences in either case, color or marker, certainly sever the meaning of "form" from "formal," as already insinuated. Indeed, anything associated with the Index can be seen clearly as the innermost middle--(0) sign of the (0) trichotomy, the object-relation of object-relation! This is the seat of linguistic *competence* and *concept* formation, giving rise to *categories* indigenous to signitive acts, exactly how will be explicated fully.

Beyond the Index lies the Symbol, at what constitutes the right angle, the Interpretant level of this trichotomy. In that locus, the Symbol parallels the Legisign of the first trichotomy, with a broken line similarly going "up" from its locus to the next trichotomy. The "#" marker now replaces the original identifying color of the last trichotomy, which was blue. The same identifier extends to Ingarden's concept, the direction-factor, which now carries the same marker as the Symbol and last trichotomy. The whole middle trichotomy thus reveals a greater complexity than the first: each sign is linked either degeneratively or generatively with one of the other trichotomies, barring the Index that bears its own identifier. The generate hierarchy has Symbol *anticipate* new *potential* of context in a type of *forward* direction suggesting "future" in temporality, a potential all purposive domains embody in their unpredictable self-determination, as pointed out already. Indeed, the Symbol at the "gate" of context mediates between the dialectics of acquisition and new articulation in *feedback* and *feedforward*. (The latter term was borrowed from a work essentially unrelated to the study of meaning: see Koontz and O'Donnell, 1978, pp. 473-478, 485).

The role given the Symbol here is thus rather specific, certainly more so than the broad application of the term "symbol" which cropped up while discussing Cassirer, Heidegger, and Peirce. Were it not vital to preserve Peircean nomenclature for his sign classes, another term might have been chosen. To indicate that the Symbol from the Picture of Language is meant, my study will not only capitalize the term but add the qualifier "semiotic" whenever possible. How does the semiotic Symbol relate in precept to Ingarden's direction-factor? As cursory answer I might say that the direction-factor, true to its name, "directs" signitive consciousness to assume this or that thought content in accordance with the semantic valence a meaning has formed. In essence, the direction-factor constitutes that intrinsic semantic *pointer* or referential vector invested with the valence meanings acquire from their use, hence in reference through transference. My much reiterated example of "fool" in "cuckoo" is a case in point;

the association between the material content of this Icon and its implicit Index came into being through the dialectics of speech and not as an isomorphic genus to species classification of autonomous-ideal proportions. The direction-factor thus also turns out to be crucial for dispelling the oversimplified notions about a reference divorced from transference which plague traditional approaches to metaphor.

Although the signs of the first two trichotomies have now been introduced, one more criterion of Ingarden's should be added because of its great importance in this study, and that concerns the "schematic" nature of the material content an Icon possesses. Ingarden's interpretation of "Schema" (1965, pp. 64, 264) applies to the *natural ambiguity* of semantic entities, something so often misapprehended today. To illustrate, no creature with feathers can be obtained from the word "cuckoo" even when it names the bird in some context instead of the human fool. All meanings may offer is their Qualisign dimensions. These, of course, should inform a discerning critic of the distinctiveness--that Humboldtian interposition--which sets language apart from the empirical (autonomous-real) domain. But that level was said to be so degenerate that speakers mostly ignore it even if, in their competence, they cannot do without it when they want to avail themselves of their language. Then, too, Qualisigns were seen to be so degenerate that they might continue to exist after a language has actually undergone demise by being no longer "in" the word.

The point is, however, that even when the material stays naturally connected to language in the capacity of the Legisign, a meaning cannot equal the vibrant corporeality of autonomous-real entities. The ultimate point is of course that meanings should not be compared that way; linguistic skeptics who do so obviously invite trouble by not concentrating on the issues. One of these is that the schema invests semantic entities with the requisite suppleness for their task of materializing and embodying an act of meaning without losing their self-identity, something the entities of ontic autonomy, real or ideal, cannot do. The cartoon depicting leaves as natural objects and in words surely made that point: whatever the graphic leaves gained in the vibrant zigzag of their multifarious shapes, only the English words that came in a set print of Qualisign zigzag managed to pun inimitably with the noun and verb as elucidated at the time. That is what words are for, not to imitate empirical things. Only speakers of English glean the orthographic material content which leads--or "directs"--them to "leaves" in all the significance this Icon has amassed through repeated Indexicalization, while the graphic zigzag is anyone's game as autonomous-real counterpart.

Now to the last and open trichotomy of context. Because it is open, a closed alternative has to be added when all the requisite contacts made in the contextualization of contents necessitate a type of "closure." A foregone conclusion of one relevant contact would be the interaction among contents selected to bring forth the signitive act that chose them, and another would pertain to the interlocutory partnership which fosters the reciprocal Referent and Recipient roles. Then language as a whole makes contact with some concrete situational or written setting when articulated anew. The open strands, however, are of special importance for the immediate discussion because they exemplify the three (nonlexical) "structures" based exclusively on units and operations *natural* to language.

The Rheme is the "first" structure when beginning as before with the M-sign, although this is no longer lodged at a triangular apex. My reference to the number appears in quotation marks to insinuate that order in the way of generate hierarchy does not really count here. Yet despite suspending generate hierarchy, the M-locus will invest the Rheme with special significance: as expression of lyric poetry, the Rheme draws quite literally on the pure "material" which marks the disposition the Icons of a language have to offer. My former citation from the Richards poem bore the emphasis of language as "Mother," actually in anticipation of this discussion, since Rhemic Icons in their pristine state become the germinal ground for the intent of the poet, whom Richards relegated to fatherhood.

Dicent, which follows the Rheme spatially in a downward direction, takes its place at 0-level of object-relation insofar as it is the middle strand. Again, a change in generate hierarchy is not so much at issue as is pinpointing the idiosyncrasy of this structure. For Dicent will evolve as the sphere of fictional "objects," hence entities forged from language with an aura of "reality" attached to them, a world consisting of simulated persons in their various preoccupations and places. Finally, below Dicent appears Argument. Though not "low" in a strictly degenerate sense, the structure does not enjoy a higher point of generation because it becomes associated with the remaining I-locus that imparts primarily an Interpretant role.

All three structures are subjugated to the great equalizer of function: it necessitates the instigation by an act of meaning whose selected meanings then Iconize and Indexicalize the act at depth, through the interaction between reference and transference. That equality is further underscored by that point of confluence which takes over from the broken line coming from the (semiotic) Symbol. No matter what the use, language must draw on extant form in order to form a new expression into meaningful content. The Symbol at the gate of the last internalized trichotomy implements that integration through feedforward, feeding back the articulated expansion of meaning for a possible, or future, feedforward. Due to that basic M-0 source at the point of confluence, language indeed always looks the same at the surface, a fact that sadly confused the critics of metaphor, who hoped some colorful surface could make the difference to their principle, perhaps to the point of disclosing a literary use, which cannot happen.

Strictly speaking, to be sure, the differing structures drawing on the M-0 trichotomies convert the signs at M-0 to a "Rhematic Qualisign . . ." and so forth. But that distinction, too, stays functional instead of lexical. Could anyone tell here from my explicit contents (or Icons) that my structure was Argument? As author I can be as figurative in style as I care to be; as critic I must operate within Argument whether my wording is formal or funny. Not reckoning with this rule caused trouble for the Ingendahl Experiment. Structure brands content no matter what the denominations. The third trichotomy is of course complex enough to require the most careful scrutiny. At this preliminary stage, I shall attempt only to elucidate basic connections with Ingarden's findings of the last chapter which were however not entered in the Picture of Language.

First, *Argument* accounts for the one *adequated* "literal" use which operates through the acquisition of a reality-nexus in the juxtaposition between a pure and an objective referent. Conversely, *Dicent* and *Rheme* present two *non-adequated* counterparts that draw only on the pure referent, for which reason alone they attain their *literary* status as respective fictional and lyric genres. Theirs will be a difference in size of constitutional unit(y), with an *extended* transference obtaining for the Rheme. While transference as such logically cannot become an issue when it is always in force as indicated, the Rheme trades on a unique mode of transference. The micro-component of the Rheme subjugated to this modification evolves as a *functional non-Aristotelian metaphor*. Based on a special form of transference, this Rhemic constituent still remains true to the Greek origin of the term "metaphora," denoting a transferral, yet it will have the added advantage that it cannot "destruct," "die," or just disappear from its context.

Although Argument seemed the "last" and "lowest" strand here, it will be taken up first when the third trichotomy is analyzed. One reason for this order of presentation is that Argument in this study accounts for the most basic origin of that mother tongue where every speaker starts, not just the fictional author and/or poet. Going "up" in what would seem a degenerate order, the exposition continues with Dicent, leaving the Rheme to the end. That conclusion returns me to the M-level and amounts to the second reason for the order of presentation since I vowed to finish with the structure harboring the non-Arisotelian metaphor. Such an approach should also benefit the final adjunct by placing the non-Aristotelian and neo-Aristotelian types of metaphors in closest proximity.

To be sure, lexical deviance in any of the structures can be retained for an *ad hoc* type of assessment of metaphor that critics may share with the lay public *at* large, for which reason the neo-Aristotelian precept stays of so little use. I, *too*, avail myself of this descriptive application but am forced to recognize the limitations of such a use. Indeed, the textual analyses will note any possible lexical deviance that may qualify as the traditional metaphor, but never without realizing how little can be gained in semantics by seizing on such a flimsy phenomenon. Nor does my theory have to exclude the more unconventional forms of contemporary literature, such as the experimental vignettes of Concrete Poetry. That assurance can be rendered with full conviction due to my past study of this subject matter. At the time, I posited a "Rheme" also for those types of texts, though generally explored in conjunction with a (looser) "connex" instead of a regular context (Gumpel, 1976, pp. xiii-xiv, 65-66, 90-95 ff.). Still, there is nothing in that distinction which would contradict my findings here, on the contrary, they would complement one another.

With that issue taken care of as well, the theory to be presented here should bring to fruition the search for a science of meaning and fulfill the hopes of Bréal and followers. As one immediate and crucial reminder at this stage, let me show here the conspicuous difference between tradition and my theory: the neo-Aristotelian metaphor is locked into the *second* trichotomy, at the Icon; the non-Aristotelian metaphor appears at the level of the Rheme, hence in the *third* trichotomy. Where the traditional principle is shown, there is no function because activity breaks out only at context. That difficulty in itself should cause instability for the neo-Aristotelian metaphor. Ingarden's contribution of adequation certainly aided me in stabilizing my principle, even if I modified his general binary division by differentiating the non-adequated use further with two literary genres.

The triadic schema of sign classes shown in the Picture of Language has thus been maintained by positing three structures I devised with Ingarden's further help, although this was not depicted but merely elucidated above. The very fact that Peirce kept metaphor confined to an (Hypo-)Icon would prove inadequate for the functional base this study intends to bestow on this principle. Another possible problem with semiotics is that it embraces a so-called synechism. Apparently

Peirce envisaged synechism in an "architectonic conception" based on the "idea of continuity" (M. Thompson, 1963, pp. 118 ff.). Peirce himself alludes to synechism in an instance (1960, p. 470, par. 4.584) that deals with the constitution of knowledge and of nature: he speaks of it as something ready to "burst in upon the mind with cataclysmic multitude and restlessness." Yet too much "multitude" hampers consistency, and continuity must be curbed by incisive boundaries, preferably of the kind Ingarden had so wisely provided through the functional presence or absence of adequation.

One might also take a hint from Hawkes (1977, p. 128), who notes that, in the wide "complexity" of semiotics, anything fit for potential isolation and connection with something else may, in due course of interpretation, end up as a sign. A recent collaborative volume on semiotics, aptly entitled "Perfusion of Signs," displays such an overwhelming profusion of applications that a cataclysmic multitude might not sound exaggerated. One entry there by Sebeok, "Ecumenicalism in Semiotics" (Sebeok, 1977, pp. 180-202), also offers further insight into some of that breadth. The same author in a later work (1979, pp. 61-83) goes on to discuss truly "global properties of sign systems," not forgetting to concede that the "holistic force of semiotics" has also become its "distinctive burden." (See additionally the collaborative bilingual work of Kristeva, et al., eds., 1971.) In Eco's introductory study (1972, pp. 267-292), semiotics is not forgotten in its ramified advertising potential for dispensing soaps and the like--a veritable "logomachy" of "Visual-Verbal Rhetoric," to quote from the essay by Bonsiepe (1972) in a closely related topic.

The Picture of Language thus anchors semiotics in its one exclusive application for semantics. A single example from Peirce might suffice for now to substantiate the need for such delimitation. While discussing "Degenerative Signs," Peirce (1960, p. 151, par. 2.265) seizes on street cries that he reduces from a Symbolic to an "Indexical Legisign." (The terms are capitalized in Peirce's own, often somewhat erratic exploitation of English Qualisign properties.) To non-Aristotelian semantics, street cries parallel content instead of function at context. If part of everyday language, street cries go into adequation, and, if fictional or poetic, they remain conversely non-adequated, in which case their tasks change substantially. Lifted out of context, street cries project only the type of spotsighting criticised with the Ingendahl Experiment. Any lay person can recognize the mundane tenor of such lexical vestiges; only an expert of language is able to explicate where content reinforces contextualization differently, leaving Peirce's "Indexical" qualifier quite literally meaningless for the functioning of language at depth.

The street cries only affirm what I termed Legisign neutrality with respect to lexical denominations. No content as such is barred from any of the three structures even if such prosaic vestiges as street cries hardly call up the imagery of poetry. So nothing of substance is shown with these cries beyond taxonomy of content as specific type of imagery present at the Iconic level, hence without a full Indexicalization. Indeed, the only "ground" for the "streets" of these "cries" Peirce himself had made plain quite inadvertently for this context, namely when he based his "Division of Signs" on "Ground, Object, and Interpretant" (1960, pp. 134 ff., par. 2.227). Well, the context as Interpretant of the third trichotomy alters the very "ground" that has the street cries resound.

To stress the functional aspect, I conclude with a listing of the reciprocal interlocutory roles which amount to equivalents of the Referent and Recipient interaction. Following that listing, the two basic components of language are offered though not without the trichotomies divided between them.

ROLES

REFERENT	RECIPIENT
COMPOSER	CONSTRUER
ENCODER	DECODER
POET	PUBLIC
SPEAKER	HEARER
WRITER	READER

These roles, of course, also reflect a universal factor since no language can exist without them in a literate speech community. The same applies to the two major components of language (p. 63), above which the three trichotomies are placed. Despite the apparent division of the M-0 trichotomies to the left internalized side and the I-trichotomy to the right externalized side, a schism is not really induced. Ultimately only the acquired shared side makes possible new articulation among interlocutory partners.

These set bilateral designations may well be vertical elaborations of one another and, much as they stay vertically divided, they also belong together horizontally due to the dialectic swing which goes from articulation back to acquisition and vice versa. With the reference to "social" and, above the components--where the "roles" are--to a "public," there is the suggestion that language is never without a natural "extrinsic" contact, an issue which crops up with some contemporary dogmatists who insist on keeping language wholly "intrinsic" without proper explanation. That point came up earlier in the defense of Ingarden against his (Marxist) opponents. Every renewed exteriorization in syntagma actually forces language into some renewed contact with the empirical world even when there is no reality-nexus as such, since speakers reside in that world as historically determined beings. This contact becomes indirectly recorded through Symbolic mediation and readied for the next recall "up" any of the three strands, permitting commonplaces to enter the next novel or poem even if made literary in the process, as just illustrated with Peirce's street cries.

In a related issue, the table below (p. 63) indicates that the left, internalized side, rather than the right, stays "free" because it is the locus where discrete vocables, and thus latent values of semantic or "semasiological" differentiation, are lodged. Conversely, the right side is the one which "fixes" constituents by fusing them to the unit(y) that coheres in any transaction between reference and transference. Such vestiges as street cries then remain fused to either a literal or literary setting in full regeneration. The argument over what stays fused or free in linguistic meaning has also been misunderstood. Ullmann, for example, observes in a context describing how language becomes "built up" that it is "language" which is "fixed" while "speech" remains "free" (1972, pp. 21-22). Yet it is the other way around if meaning is to issue from meanings. To be sure, originally the choice for speech is limitless, which is why it resides in that Symbolic "future" possibility elucidated. But the (semiotic) Symbol is still part of the second trichotomy of content. When actualized at context, meanings become set in their (chosen) meaning. That is what Ingarden will be seen to stress also by his frequent reference to "finite" expression.

COMPONENTS

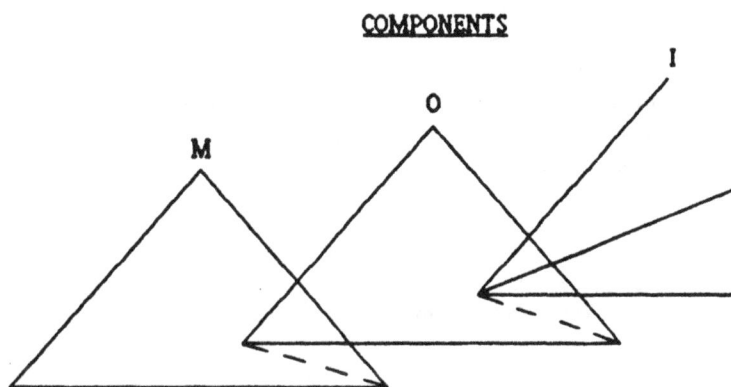

INTERNALIZED ACQUISITION	EXTERNALIZED ARTICULATION
CODE	MESSAGE
COMPETENCE	PERFORMANCE
CONCURRENCE	CONCATENATION
CORPUS (INVENTORY)	EXPRESSION (CONSTITUTION)
DISCRETE VOCABLE	COMPOUND-SYNTAX (SENTENCE)
ENERGEIA	ERGON
FREE	FIXED
HOMOGENEOUS	HETEROGENEOUS
LANGUE	PAROLE
LATENT	ACTUALIZED
PARADIGMA	SYNTAGMA
SHARED	SINGLE
SELECTION	COMBINATION
SEMASIOLOGICAL DIFFERENTIATION	SEMANTIC INTEGRATION
SOCIAL	INDIVIDUAL
SYSTEM	USAGE
VERTICAL ASSOCIATION	LINEAR SEQUENCE

Paradoxically, this type of finitude causes expansion with every use of language, simply because the stricture is purposive. Where critics (Chomsky, 1966, pp. 29, 41, 52) go awry, however, is in the assumption that language offers "infinite" possibilities through "finite" means. In language, finitude and infinitude cannot be pitted that simplistically against one another. Doing just that, Chomsky and one of his cohorts, John Lyons (1970, pp. 21, 36, 51-52, 54, 58-59, 69, 99-100), then look to "recursiveness" for linguistic use. They suggest almost a mode of "recycling" language in the use of language. What they fail to understand is that the latent--leftsided--repertoire is a system held together at such a ramified level of opposition that it remains for all intents and purposes wholly inexhaustible. The more literate the speakers, the more multifarious the positive and privative values. From a certain aspect, these latent components may seem "fixed" in their antecedent positive and privative relations. But for that very reason, full semantic focalization goes on only in the newly integrated expression. And this whole issue touches on metaphor just because the oppositional network is so extensive that any simplistic assessment between analogy and anomaly, of the kind neo-Aristotelians impose on metaphor, does injustice to both meaning and metaphor either when latent or lexical in newly formed expression.

The next point also involving metaphor follows logically from the above discussion: because the leftsided vertical paradigma is discrete and loose by comparison to the linear, newly articulated syntagma, any substitution, such as the proxy-tenet neo-Aristotelians force on metaphor, could occur only within the former. Once the choice has been made, no change or conversion is possible. Again, that is why copyright laws protect the Icon which exteriorizes that choice most overtly, so speakers can probe their signitive consciousness and may even grapple with their thought for the right word, deciding at the last minute to select another. After the selection has been made, however, there is no going back, at least not without affecting the constitutional unit(y) of an act of meaning. Those persons who do that for other speakers, as suggested in the quest for deviant metaphor, inadvertently become pseudoauthors. As will be seen, only the translator is put into that unfortunate position without choice.

One can see how vital it is to understand even the most basic factor in linguistic meaning in order to come to terms with a sound semantic principle that is "metaphor." To be sure, the above table includes many precepts of critics besides those of Ullmann and Chomsky: Humboldt's "ergon" and "energeia," Saussure's "langue" and "parole" (1966, pp. 14-15 ff.), and Jakobson's "concurrence" and "concatenation," among others. Humboldt's criteria were discussed already in conjunction with the "energetic" tradition and the other two recur frequently in this study. Let me add that "concatenation" will also have special meaning for one structure in this study, namely Dicent, or fiction.

The table lists in addition Chomsky's "competence" and "performance." But it is interesting to note in view of the above reservations about Chomsky's idea of finitude that he (1972, pp. 19-20) mistakenly ends up criticizing Saussure's criteria for their undue focus on "parole" rather than "langue." This objection would be consistent with Chomsky's abstract--essentially "finite"--universal, a monolith he regards as something of a catalyst for all "parole" or, to him, "performance." Chomsky certainly has been taken to task for espousing his abstract universal: critics (Esper, 1968, p. 230) say he concocts "manufactured collocations . . . without context," generated recursively from an abstract base that is logical rather than truly volitional and makes evident his belief that finite means serve infinite speech. How problematic such a theory becomes when boosted with contextless collocations in the case of a context-sensitive poetic work, one of my textual analyses should demonstrate clearly--after the trichotomies have been analyzed, a task that is next.

Hyletic Design: Trees in Threes--The Leaps of Language

In calling this chapter the "Leaps of Language," I am playing the devil's advocate; leaps occur only when looking at language from that second circle previously marked "ontic autonomy," where autonomous-ideal classes are derived from autonomous-real objects. Then, indeed, everything that pertains to language remains "deviant," suggesting more of that metaphorical ubiquity which causes this semantic principle to die and disappear by lapsing into ordinary meaning. These leaps are only worth maintaining to prove this very point. In my own chronology, the leaps foreshadow arguments of the neo-Aristotelian adjunct that comes up last, particularly with the metaphor caused by the Ciceronian "transilire" (1960, pp. 124-125), which is the Latin term for leap or jump. Historically, therefore, the time gap predates this leap by close to two thousand years. The fact that my work in that last part almost closes with "conceptual leaps" as a determinant for metaphor among modern contemporaries should indicate the general stagnation of neo-Aristotelian semantics one more time, especially since "concept" remains undefined in the process.

When approached from a non-Aristotelian perspective, however, the leaps of meaning have nothing to do with a special "metaphor"; they affirm merely the indigenous synthesizing powers of language which speakers--such as my readers here--take for granted as norms unless made cognizant of such oddities as this chapter will stress. Then native speakers step momentarily out of the Heideggerian house that allows them to feel at home, thus looking from the outside in, as it were. At that point speakers appear to leave the circle reserved for language, the area marked "ontic heteronomy" in my previous diagram. But since that cannot really happen to sane adults, these sensations do not interfere with linguistic competence.

These leaps can be further explained as the cause of the authorial will, stated earlier to arise from without because it corresponds to speaker impulse. Simultaneously language is made to expand from within by corporealizing and embodying this authorial intent, duly recording the activity in new connotations which serve the next recall. The dialectics of internalizing and externalizing language were said to be regulated by the mediating role of the (semiotic) Symbol as last sign of the second trichotomy before context. Every time a Referent and Recipient go into interlocutory partnership, the act of meaning at context (I) seeks out form (M) to express a unified content (0) which is then bound holistically to the expression, from first to last selected constituent. In acceptance of the Referent, the Recipient probes form until arriving at the authorial intent, the catalyst for the contextualization of content(s). This thetic I-M-0 order, which occurs with every new articulation, thus differs from the linear M-0-I hierarchy in the Picture of Language that characterized the generative incline or, degeneratively, the I-M-0 decline marking the downward triadic relation between the trichotomies.

As each trichotomy now becomes severed from this triadic continuum for purposes of closer scrutiny, an unnatural situation arises. In that endeavor, the broken lines leading to the next trichotomy also become superfluous for the illustration of each separate trichotomy. What has to be there instead is the M-0-I marking of the little triangle in the Picture of Language, with "M" at the apex, "0" at the left and "I" at the right angle of the triangles shaping the first two (M-0) trichotomies. These had both appeared above the internalized component of acquisition on a table that listed as alternative the new articulation on its right side, above which appeared further the trichotomy of context. Therefore, when the first trichotomy as internal component becomes severed from context, one consequence would be that a form may be *sighted* in dictionaries but hardly exteriorized in full *signifying* with embodiment of an authorial will, as speech must be--always. Without that full processing, the forms remain severed from the transference which causes shifts while engendering a speaker's act of meaning. In a curious way, language is then literally rendered "speechless."

Only in such an unnatural situation do forms lapse into something like "replicas" or "tokens," terms that have remained popular among supporters of Pierce (see Fitzgerald, 1966, p. 63). Under normal application of language through an act of meaning, however, replicas do not arise. Peirce's street cries are not separate "symbols" which may shed their sartorial replicas as reptiles shed dead skin. Not the word, but the *wielded* word, in its particular use through an act of meaning confers meaning on this act. Were it otherwise, the authorial will would be reduced to random chance, to an aleatory whim. Then meaning would not become exteriorized teleologically by an act of meaning (I) as the authorial intent which selects explicit constituents (M) and regulates import for its implicit relevance to the whole constitution (0). Only a dictionary item may be uttered or written and erased at will, just because authorial willing still remains outstanding.

For the same reason, any published dictionary listing consists of fragmented context from past usage, causing problems of choice for students of a foreign language. The interiorized oppositional network, on the other hand, is vast though dormant until recall of certain selected forms by a signitive act summons up conscious awareness of the relevant oppositional values for the entities involved. Naturally, a similar level of consciousness is in effect for the Recipient, in the process of penetrating form to reach the Referent, as explicated. In any case, the latent component in the human mind stays inexhaustible enough not to warrant a comparison with finite listings in books, for which reason Chomsky's rather onesided idea of finite means serving infinite possibilities was disputed before.

Again, all exteriorized forms newly fused to an act of meaning are protected for their task by copyright laws. Vocables, however, remain anyone's game as mere (dictionary) tokens. The only other cause for separate replicas or tokens would be the case of a dead language, with degeneration down to the material base itself. Language is then also diffracted at depth, with the unit(y) embedded in the signitive act evaporated from the elements. At a wholly advanced state of degeneration, the form has relinquished all semantic content, with nothing left to share intersubjectively. Such a state reduces forms to the level of skeletons or fossils that now-extinct animals left behind as the only proof of their past being.

Since my task here is to sever the first trichotomy for the heuristic purpose of its exhaustive analysis, I am aware also that, inevitably, language is robbed of "speech" by this procedure. For that reason the Recipient, lodged by this trichotomy in the Picture of Language, can be omitted here, and the same will apply to the Referent for the last trichotomy. Theoretically, of course, nothing may eradicate these two activities; they hold in the trichotomies and thus the sphere of ontic heteronomy. Beyond them there exists only "bedrock," to borrow a Wittgenstein concept (Hester, 1967, pp. 56-57, 108; Hallett, 1977, pp. 492-513).

Turning the Picture of Language once more ninety degrees (clockwise) should provide a useful reminder in concrete dimensions of the way in which the Recipient, placed right over the first trichotomy, actually dominates language at its degenerate end of form.

With these preliminary issues clarified, the first trichotomy of form is next singled out for separate scrutiny. Its base is "universal" in the manner explained previously: language must possess a form in order to exist at all, no matter in what language. The M-trichotomy thus commences at the most rudimentary semantic "matter" and provides the "means" for any possible exteriorization of a signitive act. Though a degenerate base, this very "ground" cannot be ignored, as it is unfortunately by neo-Aristotelians who go straight for the lexicon at the level of the second trichotomy. With the distinctive form, language actually announces itself, disclosing some of that willful intervention discussed before (with Humboldt *et al.*). No sounds or corporeal shapes are intertwined in nature as they are in language. The rooster cries proved that point, despite certain onomatopoetic vestiges which erupted with each of the languages.

The first trichotomy accountable for the sonorous and visual base bore the attributive "hyletic" in the Picture of Language. Greek "hyley" is the etymology embodied in this adjective; it denotes "material" and "matter," as well as "forest" and "timber" (Fobes, 1966, p. 294). But when the adjective was introduced, its more recent use for phenomenology was mentioned. Ingarden's mentor Husserl, whose essay on signs was quoted earlier, spoke about the "hyletic phase," for example, which he connected with the concrete experience of sensuousness (in his *Ideas*, 1958, section 97, pp. 282-283; see also Merleau-Ponty in Kockelmans, 1967 p. 362). Even language has its aura of sensuousness, though this must be traced to perceiving the form.

PERCEIVING

• M-TRICHOTOMY: FIRSTNESS

QUALISIGN

M

FORM:

HYLETIC BASE

O   I

SINSIGN   **LEGISIGN**

The material is perceived in concretion of the authorial will: that is what the heading stresses. Then the form of a language, which has been internalized antecedently in order to be shared collectively, is ready to convert into explicit content the choice of signitive intent. When normally connected, this trichotomy contributes the first sign of the second trichotomy, the Icon, sharing the identifying dot (said previously to have replaced color). While the faculty of perceiving came with the first trichotomy in the Picture of Language, the ordinal number has now been supplanted by a noun: "Firstness" is actually an ontological concept for the degenerate level of being used by Peirce, who correlates it further with a "monad" (1960, pp. 146-149, par. 1.293-1.304). Peirce says in one place (1960, p. 7, par. 1.23) about Firstness that it exemplifies a "mode of being which consists in its subject's being positively such as it is regardless of aught else." This "positive" type of projection beyond "aught else" affirms in essence what has been stressed all along with Legisign validation as the primary cause for a type of "truth." Paradoxically, with its oppositional mode of being the form bears a "-positive" foundation insofar as it exists as a privative state of some other, "oppos(sing)" form. The form can only be an accepted composite insofar as it remains simultaneously a compositional opposite in association.

Motivation is barred from the linguistic form; words need not resemble anything beyond projecting their self-identity in order to provide the ground for linguistic reference. Speakers heed the explicit form because it is extant, sonorously and visually. Indeed, so inescapable are validated forms that Richards let the author become conscious of his "paternal" role as counterpart to an ineluctible "maternal" source which, for his particular poem, came in the English language. In view of the etymology of "hyletic," replete with its several connotations, the word "tree" becomes my next choice for illustration. Those familiar with past studies may realize that this example has enjoyed considerable popularity. Husserl (ibid., 1958, section 97, p. 282-283) for one seized on "tree" while discussing the hyletic source. Saussure (1959, pp. 66-70, 111-117) is another who looked to "tree" for his binary semiology; it comprised a signifying agent as "signifiant" and a content signified, the "signifié." One of Saussure's French successors, Martinet (1970, p. 42), then narrowed down this dichotomy to "form" versus "meaning," moving ever closer to the more recent etic and emic distinctions which separate sheer content from its specific context. Martinet (ibid., pp. 19-24) further listed "tree" in several languages and was followed in that practice by Eco (1972, pp. 86-87), who in the process makes his usual bid for "cultural unities."

Now, to perceive a word may be a "cultural" enterprise in the widest sense, an issue that surfaced also with Cassirer's "cultural" extension of Critical philosophy. Ontic heteronomy is fundamentally a "cultural" phenomenon in that it is based exclusively on acts of meaning. However, this very fact should suggest also that such a qualifier remains too broad: what about those acts of consciousness that cull symbols and emblems directly from spheres outside of language? Briefly, "cultural" is the biblical Tree of Knowledge in Genesis that precipitates the Fall, or the proud Cedar of Lebanon in Kings (1, 4:33). Yet these "cultural unities" are universals in the sense that their significance is not confined to words; they could be recognized in paintings, perhaps, and thus by speakers of any language. To be sure, the provenance of Old Testament symbols is language; these biblical trees did not grow in someone's garden. But the words in which they come "mean" something only to the speakers of the language involved. Without the primary construal of those forms, nothing may evolve either in terms of a Judaic or Christian "culture."

As a Christian alternative, there is the New Testament phrase (Acts 5:30) which has Jesus "hanging on a tree" instead of a cross--supposedly a typically

Petrine expression (Gumpel, 1971, pp. 360-361). Peter's unique phrasing arose from ramified Greek forms for "tree," designating a plant, timber or lumber, and a (wooden) pole paralleling the shape of a cross or a vertical (tree) trunk with horizontal branches. This odd overlapping in Greek then caused the designation "tree" to literally cross with "cross." Such casual naming of the cross--a symbol so "charged" with inherent significance in the intervening years (S. Langer, 1960, p. 284)--could hardly occur today, least of all with the "tree" as form of modern English. In some respects, these odd and yet "cultural" values embody the world-view that came up with Humboldt, in my modification of a genuine "word-view." Language originates as cultural phenomenon yet hardly as a mirror of an extant "Weltanschauung."

Of greater importance for the "word-view" is what Ingarden (1965, pp. 30-38) calls the "wordsound." As suggested by the term, a word draws sound into its semantic threshold as matter turns into meaning, and leads from oral to written (mute) transcription. Again, the former rooster cries showed how sound in each language, even when permeated by onomatopeia, forces the word into a different transcription. The problems with such conversions are experienced by all students of a foreign language. Indeed, staying in touch with a language assures sufficient exposure to the myriads of concretions arising with the mechanical manipulation of forms: the mind penetrates these differences like a laser beam, picking out wordsounds through a type-to-trait relation that eludes all scientific isolation. At the same time, since the mechanics of speech are not germane to my analysis, an "ideal" condition (Chomsky, 1965, p. 3) will be observed for the most part, leaving all lisps, stutters, and other such problems to the specialists of these particular areas.

With this reminder, I introduce the first sign: the *Qualisign* appears at M-apex of the M-trichotomy. The "Quali-" prefix here affirms that M+M locus by denoting "quality" as material disposition. Whatever the quality appears to have borrowed in sound or contour from nature, its disposition goes exclusively into shaping the wordsound "natural" to language at its most degenerate level. Ironically, because of its degenerate locus, Qualisign material may subsist as "dead" matter, while the semantic threshold it embodies at greater generate depth stays fully dependent on it, unless meaning is to remain pure spirit. When Qualisigns stay and their meaning goes, graphic patterns betray orthographic vestiges. Nowadays, the same can be claimed for recorded sounds of a language that has died.

The Qualisign, in an orthographic rendering of English "t-r-e-e," accounts for the bar that is crossed in the "t," for the little hook attached to the "r" and the dome that becomes sufficiently curved in the "e." My readers here are either native or sufficiently fluent in English to have amassed the mutual interdependence between sonorous and visual material. With appropriate (Cartesian) distance, they also notice that "tree" looks nothing like the plant in nature which the lexicon nevertheless reflects. Granted, some Qualisign isomorphism may be found in "t," perhaps, and ordinarily one associates this with hieroglyphics or ideograms. Thus the character for the Chinese ideogram "mu" designating "tree" comes across pictorially as "木" (Babcock, 1963, p. 115), to resemble loosely a trunk with branches. Any such material transparencies, however, are counteracted by the synchronic oppositional states endorsing application of, and not simulation by, a language.

The form, therefore, constitutes the first didactic step toward realizing that language never fosters representation of nature but only presentation of its own reference. This difference was not properly realized by Wescott (1971, p. 420), for instance, who discusses what he deems to be "iconic" vestiges in language, one of them the letter "A" that apparently originated inverted from the head of an ox, though offered in something that looks more like a crossed "V." While such information remains valid when recognized for what it is, namely diachronic contact, it literally means nothing in Wescott's case because he does not synthesize the facts other than to affirm meekly that such representational vestiges suffuse language. No expert is needed for that conclusion. A genuine expert of language recognizes Qualisign *opacity*, not transparency, since the priority is affirming *boundaries* between language and nonlanguage.

Regarded from that perspective, Qualisigns reinforce their positive being beyond "aught else," as Peirce had it above. To borrow a concept from Saussure (1966, pp. 117-123), the forms in their complex but positive foundation stay "in praesentia"; they become "in absentia" only relationally, in their privative association with other forms. An interesting experience involving handwritten European airmail letters may well demonstrate the Qualisign power of sheer presence. When not slit open carefully in their proper place, these letters may cause Qualisigns to become ripped apart. In confronting the damaged signs, I can see nothing remarkable other than a few comminuted curlicues. Perplexed at being left with these almost illegible vestiges, I turn to the tear itself as the only guide--lo and behold!--upon restoration of the edge and its zizag tear, the "t" is crossed once more, the "r" has its hook back as the form assumes shape, perhaps in the Qualisign dimensions of written "tree." "No-sense" or "non-sense" has been restored to a wordsound containing a semantic threshold of "sense," although not as mere replica or token but consonant with the authorial will of the letter writer.

My next experience appears to prove an opposite problem. While the above example demonstrates the power of Qualisigns, this one shows off also the neglect of the form. To my surprise, I discovered that I by-passed the conspicuous differences in German Qualisign concretion between the older "Fraktur" print and the modern Latin version--until some nonnative individual, barred from the "Fraktur," drew my attention to this difference. In my case, the type-to-trait conditioning was so complete that even such conspicuous changes could be overlooked whereas to that other person the language "died" with the older forms. A Referent was present but the Recipient failed the Qualisign dimension and thus could not respond. Yet in my case, semantic redundancy had wrought a kind of "deadening" effect very detrimental to the M-base in literary use. Regarded from one aspect, Qualisign efficacy was complete, regarded from another, it was damaged, had been stunted from overexposure. Whatever swift perception accomplishes for speed reading, it has ultimately also a dulling effect upon the finer sensibilities needed for the enjoyment of lyric poetry and the like. Indeed, that is one "pedagogical" role literature can play--reviving Qualisign interest for its own sake, something that the postwar movement of Concrete Poetry accomplished by stressing the sheer, intermedial disposition of language from every imaginable facet (as discussed throughout my work on this trend, Gumpel, 1976).

Now, semiotic (synechistic) continuity is such that in discussing the Qualisign, the *Sinsign* was tacitly ever present; Qualisign contours become welded into Sinsign composites at 0-level, at the left corner of *object-relation* for this trichotomy. There, words start to cohere in their phonological and lettristic idiosyncrasies, through positive and privative oppositional values, by the very *singularity* each composite projects. That is exactly why for students of a foreign language words run together in dictation, for instance; the mind misses the bounds enclosing each composite.

On the Sinsign, Peirce (1960, p. 142, par. 2.245) has to say the term denotes "'being only once'. . . single . . . simple," associating this further with Latin "semel. The old Greek prefix "syn-," of course, has associations with English "con-," even if this goes back more directly to Latin. The Sinsign thus affirms distinctiveness through a validated composite. In this task, the Sinsign actually opposes any such loose serialization as that of the *alphabet*, whose "a. . .b. . .c" sequence does not compose words. In a particular use of English, "abc" can be applied to signal "alphabet," for instance, as when persons are said to "know their abc's." In this rare instance alphabetic sequence becomes a Sinsign invested with special sense.

An alphabet prevails in "t-r-e-e" insofar as the Sinsign has drawn on it if not in any alphabetic order: the "t" would constitute the twentieth, "r" the eighteenth, and "e" the fifth letter in the alphabetical *serialization* which obviously does not match the word's *sequence*. Moreover, the intricacies involving just one language are such that the names of Sinsign vestiges permit separate punning: there is the "tee" for a golf course setting or, in pure sound, that British brew called "tea," and so on. How inimitably a competent speaker of English can play with these Sinsign ramifications in relation to their possible names, the following "ABC" cartoon from *Peanuts* (*Minneapolis Tribune*, August 12, 1979) should illustrate.

In this flawed communication among the *Peanuts* interlocutors, an alphabetic repertoire is tossed around and made to coincide with the particular names of letters that belong also to other words of English. Mute sound reverberates through orthographic parallelisms. Rarely does English seem more endowed with strange concoctions than in the alignment of these forms! Their connecting points as wordsounds make evident the various regulative adaptations to the written signs. Encased in the second panel (after the title) is the "Y," which in serialization of alphabetic repertoire comes second from last but whose corresponding name coincides with the interrogative spelled out as "Why?" The "O" is used similarly though preceded by its name, which is the exclamation "Oh"; and then one "I" and "C" yield respectively the pronoun and verb "I see" in brief syntagma. On to the "G" for yet another exclamation, "Gee!" Then to the final "U"-- actually more than one--precipitating by implication the "you" that erupts in the response containing "me."

Very clever, as well as wholly irretrievable beyond the oppositional framework of English! Paraphrasing would merely ruin the *pointe* and thus the very semantic sting weaving in and out of these concocted associations. I capitalized the letters, although that orthographic factor does not emerge too clearly from the cartoon. English capitalizes the first-person pronoun "I," of course, thus demonstrating something like that disputed "world-view" brought up before (with Humboldt) but hardly a genuine "Weltanschauung" projecting deliberate egocentricity. In fact that might apply more to the euphemism "Gee!" which circumvents taking the Lord's name in vain --yet cannot become the other side of "dog" in Sinsign dimension.

To be sure, the seemingly flawed conversation is in itself a screen for the *real* communicants, the interlocutory partners which comprise the cartoonist Schulz and his readers: they get the gist of the humor in their decoding simply because they share latently the Qualisign and Sinsign idiosyncrasies of English with this encoder. So the cartoonist's authorial intent comes through perfectly even if his cartoon mouthpieces appear thwarted in their efforts and forced to engage in a travesty of speaker competence. For, certainly, even less than ideal conditions that make interlocutors go awry through some speech impediment or interruption from the situational setting could not misfire this badly. If anything, this setting in ostensive usage should obviate and not increase misunderstanding, with the concrete objects (such as the letters) immanently present between the interlocutory partners.

These "children" have mastered and simultaneously confused the oppositional *leaps* of *language* which are natural to the positive and privative values English harbors. Few examples could show better how language jumps from one thing to another and remains "normal" for speakers of that language. In evidence are the vast strides that lead English from nouns and verbs to pronouns, from interrogatives to exclamations, and so on. A zany zigzag by any other standard, one might say, it certainly differs from that graphic zigzag the leaves of the earlier cartoon displayed; theirs was a concrete dimension and thus hardly confined to the perception of English forms. Here, language in a language celebrates another victory of new completion; no mere tokens compose these language-bound puns since they have become fused to the intent of this cartoonist.

In a way, the interlocutory partners exist at two levels. One partnership stays concrete within the panels, with the female character who writes paralleling a Referent and the confused male character who does not follow her functioning as her (erring) Recipient. The other, major partnership involves the unseen but genuine constitutive consciousness belonging to the cartoonist Schulz and his anonymous readership in their Referent and Recipient relation. The former partners are sheer content, derived from and thus dependent on, this cartoonist's intent. As with the other cartoons, there is ontic autonomy in graphic form and ontic heteronomy in orthographic form, the former aiding presentation of the ostensive usage, the latter projecting only itself--to its own speakers.

The structure is also in evidence as nonliterary use. But since the first trichotomy is the main object of investigation here, the concentration is on the disjointed Sinsigns that collide variously with the full composites identified above. What the example should also prove categorically is that there can be no synonymy among languages, indeed even among forms in one language, inimitable as each entity is in Sinsign composition and possible contextualization. Synonym, antonym, and homonym are terms to be plied as descriptively as the traditional metaphor, but structurally, in mode of function, they cannot be upheld. Homonymy, indeed, will loom on the horizon of neo-Aristotelian metaphors, where the lexicon is believed to harbor dual meaning under one form or explicit content. Synonymy, on the other hand, may be ruled out right here. For instance, German possesses the interrogative "Warum?" to match English "Why?" but hardly lends itself to playing with a loosened "Y" Sinsign bearing the name of this letter, proving positively that "meaning" exudes from the very pores of every facet governing the linguistic form. Accordingly, the apparent nonsense of the *Peanuts* cartoon emerges as very precise "sense" by exploiting English oppositional values residing in wordsounds to the hilt. Though arbitrary by any other measure, the ramifications involved rely on careful, conscious planning.

Ultimately, however, the conscious part remains outstanding in this analysis until the *Legisign*, located at the right Interpretant corner as the most generate locus of the first trichotomy, has been introduced. In the Picture of Language a broken line emphasizes that generate input by connecting with the next trichotomy, specifically the Icon. Now, a Sinsign in itself has no power to ward off the "*" asterisk assigned to nonvalidated compositions as unacceptable wordsounds. Only a Legisign legitimizes the Sinsign Object-relation within this hyletic trichotomy, affecting starkly the oppositional relation of semantic thresholds. To illustrate, English "tree" forsakes just one Sinsign at the sonorous and visual level--and there appear such validated wordsounds as "three" or "free," to name just two. In phonetic transcription the result might look thus: "/tri/," "/Θri/" and "/free/," with Greek theta transcribing "th" in the second example to serve the wordsound of English here. Each Sinsign composite is what the other is not in oppositional wordsound. When the Legisign (I) thus stamps each meaning with self-identity, Qualisigns (M) start to shape Sinsign (0) composites, creating linguistic designs.

In the above example of the added words spun hyletically from "tree," English Qualisigns and Sinsigns have thrust together these forms. As much as they are kept apart, their hyletic base nevertheless preserves a mnemonic tie through the closeness in sound and visual contour. With their Legisign backing, the names comprised in each form become propitiously standardized, no matter how odd by standards of logic or of that empirical existence that classifies the tree as plant, the number three as a quantitative factor, and the freedom contained in the adjective as abstract idea, leaving every association "deviant" or "metaphorical" by any nonlinguistic determinant. Again, language in a language manifests its power of leaping from one entity to another, committing a Ciceronian "transilire" in combination of further "odd couples" to be added to those my illustrations had contained before--if the wrong, extralinguistic vantage point becomes adopted. When it is not, the Legisign partakes of that curious "neutrality" already mentioned in that, no matter how plain or prosaic, no entity is barred from authorial selection on the grounds of its lexical oddities, once it has been validated.

Legisigns thus reinforce the Sinsign connective in unbiased fashion when not wrested from deviance cults, just as my choice here could fall on the most figurative preference. All autotelic, purposive domains rely on Legisigns, forcing speakers to consent through an intersubjective consensus of sharing. "A Legisign," says Peirce (1960, pp. 142-143, par. 2.246), "is a law that is a Sign. This law is usually established by men. Every conventional sign is a legisign (but not conversely)." To rationalize Peirce's capitalization in this passage might be a validating task all by itself. But the "law" he cites is made explicit enough in the "Legi-" prefix of the Legisign. Sebeok (1976, p. 7), in a brief chronological survey of Peircean thought, discusses how "laws" gradually became correlated with the "imputed character" Peirce had reserved for the symbol. The (semiotic) Symbol of the second trichotomy is not at issue as yet, but a basic connection between Legisign and Symbol has to be the Interpretant locus within their respective trichotomies, as the Picture of Language showed. Certainly, the Legisign, too, upholds imputed contiguities, validating a composite such as "tree" without special motivation.

At least the three alternatives above are valid for English while the same cannot be said for the vestige "*ree" that seems to unite them all in sound and spelling; no Sinsign composite, no connective yielding a word, may arise from its Qualisign foundation. Such a vestige thus eludes the "law" embodied in the Legisign and remains an "alien" element within English. Tradition, of course, has recognized oppositional Sinsigns sufficiently well in so-called distinctive features. In that case, "ree" may present a phoneme or morpheme without the asterisk. Then two of the above three composites align as "minimal pairs," designating literally that minimal switch of sound or letter that is capable of inducing a total change in meaning.

Most theorists of language know what Jakobson and Halle (1956, pp. 20 ff.)--later joined by Fant (1965, p. 40)--contributed to the study of phonemic features, with some of those critics the heirs of the Prague Circle founded in 1926 (particularly Trubetzkoy). Interest in the phonological base of language was focal to these groups as their members came to realize that phonemes were not in meanings but rather the cause of their difference. Their "Conclusion" (ibid.) ended with twelve binary oppositions, beginning with the vocalic versus nonvocalic, consonantal versus nonconsonantal, and so on. Saussurean opposition also played a part in positing the phoneme, as Jakobson (1956, pp. 4 ff.) concedes. Perhaps it is true, furthermore, that the binary focus of these critics foreshadowed the "bit" principle in computer communications theory (Ivić, 1971, pp. 210-212). Whatever the case, the binary theories will turn out to be insufficient, for reasons that evolve shortly.

With the Legisign, the linguistic "design" has reached completion at the level of form--ready for the full-fledged designation of the next trichotomy. In the above examples, the "*/ri/" or "*ree" connective among those three validated designs may well present something like an "analogy," if hardly the kind supported by logic. This heteronomous difference can be proven by the fact that German and French, for instance, would not even match the phonetic transcription for the double (or even single) "e" as "/i/," let alone the "*ree" or "*/ri/" association between their Legisign equivalents. Actually, any of the illustrations, including those from the cartoon, are so infinitesimal within the vast oppositional network of a linguistic corpus that my above reference to an analogy becomes almost a joke.

Now, Legisigns validate designs that are in every respect *words*, as suggested already with Ingarden's concept of the wordsound. But issues of minimal units will require further consideration. Crystal (1971, pp. 187-191) has rightly pointed out, while dealing with controversies surrounding the "smallest unit for grammatical analysis," that morphemes do not possess the substance of such function words as definite articles, even, as made evident with the "*ree" above. Also, a noninflected, so-called analytic language like English permits "tree" and "three" to function respectively as noun or verb as well as noun or adjective.

Clearly, Legisigns in their synchronic state remain impervious to the kind of diachronic motivation that was illustrated by Searle in a discussion of "regulative" versus "constitutive" rules (1970, pp. 41-42). There the author contends the reason why the "/ɡ/" phoneme in "finger" is absent in "singer" often becomes discovered by chance, when it is realized that "singer" has this phoneme because it is a derivative of the verb "sing." This information, which I did not possess either, is totally irrelevant to a native competence at the synchronic plane. Were it otherwise, speakers would *have* to be cognizant of it. No rule intrinsic to linguistic competence can be missed and is thus neither truly constitutive nor regulative for speakers--outside of philologists, etymologists and the like.

Legisign validation is therefore purely synchronic, affirming language states and not developmental stages. Only with those indigenous states may a speaker of English trade on a poster or commercial jingle aimed at the sale of Christmas trees through "Three Trees" . . . "Trees in Threes," and related versions, one of which no doubt could add a fourth tree "For Free." What do these words have in common? Why combine the number with this plant? The reason may not be logical but linguistic if advertisers want to trade on their native language with its Qualisign and Sinsign identities. The German "drei Bäume" or the French "trois abres" will not equal the effect and sales may suffer, oddly enough. As with the humor of the cartoons, paraphrasing would not help to coax consumers into a buying spree.

That -is to say, advertising trades on the hyletic base of language, taking accidence right out of Legisigns. The above example reflects the kind of hyletic connection termed *equivalence* since Jakobson's "Closing Statement" for "Linguistics and Poetics" (1960, p. 358). To cite partially from that essay, the "axis of selection" reinforces the "axis of combination," here the internalized sonorous and visual Qualisigns. That such a use can do little for "poetic" language my illustration of a commercial should reveal right here. In fact, this study pointed out early that structure rather than the lexicon is to be emphasized because the literary style may be sober and the commercial alternative ornate. At any rate, since Jakobson first introduced the concept, some critics (Plett, 1975, pp. 346 ff.) now apply equivalence to almost every area of use, in phonological, morphological, semantic, and syntactic manifestation. To be sure, some advertisers may let their greed conquer their delight with the language and by-pass this equivalence by going for five or six trees, not without success either. This result, however, does not detract from the hyletic power of language when in force. After all, the mnemonics of nursery rhymes have traded on equivalence long before its use in commercials--which are now harming young speakers: jingle and jargon hurt linguistic programming in areas where Qualisigns and Sinsigns should impinge on consciousness to let the M-trichotomy take root through active intervention on the part of young speakers.

Take something as fundamental as number: the plural alternatives in my commercial touch on intricacies which even seem to disrupt the oppositional values contained in definite versus indefinite and singular versus plural in a language such as English. Certainly, these bounds seem transgressed in some generic use for definitions, as when speakers realize the closeness of meaning between "The tree is a plant," "A tree is a plant," and "Trees are plants." Indeed, the past decade witnessed a new interest in number to combat sexism through use of the plural. The linguistic "modalities" brought up while discussing Cassirer here demonstrate how something as mechanical as number comes to touch on issues of human bias.

No matter how the hyletic leaps of the M-trichotomy surfaced above, their ultimate purpose is to show how language in a language makes and breaks bounds, sometimes even undoing in certain contexts what generally applies to others. Metaphor would reign supreme in every facet of language, fit to absorb meaning. In yet another "tree" example, the Legisign may validate "family" and "tree" in the compound "family tree" but not isolate the difference which separates the plant in some family's backyard from the genealogical chart so designated, an example cited in an essay by Bruzina (1978, p. 193). However, this critic does no better by the difference than the Legisign itself. In the typical traditional view, he considers the first reference to the plant literal and the second to the chart metaphorical. In essence, what the critic has is validated meaning ready to perform under the "neutral" conditions set forth.

The autonomous-real family tree in one's backyard consists of wood, the one that is a chart, of paper, containing a graphic design. Whatever the similarity shaping those things, the language can pick them up--or by-pass them, as the Richards poem had it. Now, the English Legisign for "wood(s)" is also extant, if not as the substance of a trunk holding up the real plant. Indeed, the Legisign covers an area lined with many trees, although there is also a plural form for the word "tree"--"trees." The jump to that other form seems far afield. So does what might be called the *hyletic doubling* which has English "wood(s)" cover the substance and the area: the composition of the plant and its distribution on the ground coincide illogically when the hyletic ground that is language is not considered. At the same time, to analyze such phenomena as these apparent hyletic doubles necessitates ascending to the higher trichotomies, if something less simplistic than the traditional *homonymy* is to evolve.

Hyletic doubling for now proves mainly what disparities--by any other standard--language forces together. Another reminder should be that, were English to die out, this doubling could not be explained but would merge in one form, just because the Qualisigns and Sinsigns stay the same without revealing differences in wordsound, the semantic thresholds. The limit of Legisign potential has thus been reached, even if there is no going on--or "up" in generation--without Legisign approval since "reference" begins with Qualisign form. That is also the limit for such traditional precepts as phonemes, since their opposition does not explain hyletic doubling. Now, just as hyletic doubling superficially reflects homonymy with the identical Legisign, hyletic differentiation may reinforce synonymy, as in "woods" versus "forest." But the moment overt compounding is attempted the synonymy evaporates: "firewood" counters starred "*fireforest," and "wood fire" does not yield the wordsound or semantic threshold equal to "forest fire." All these vast ramifications of values thrust together and driven apart foil notions of simple similarity or difference, including the "nymy" precepts (homo-, syno-, and anto-) along with simplisitc construals of "metaphor" over meaning.

What the above forms mean is not elucidated further, since no one, if that deficient in English, could read my work here. No reader has to be told either about the adjectival opposition between "wooden" and "wooded" for respective substance and area. When spinning these adjectives further, one may encounter "wooden" in reference to human stiffness or intransigence. Metal may have done better by such a person than wood, but motivation cannot be thus applied, since what a language provides a speaker owns. Now, tradition may easily consider a use of the "wooden" person a "metaphor" since the sense referring to the substance has shifted overtly from matter to mind, one might say. The adjunct later shows how popular such notions were--all the way back to Cicero's and Quintilian's natural or necessary metaphors which, derived from semantic paucity, amplify a linguistic inventory by trading on extant forms. Today, certain such vestiges are called *personality metaphors.* Beardsley (1961/1962, p. 304) cites this type of metaphor while mentioning further the contributions of such contemporaries as Asch, Taguiri, Petrullo and Brown. Although the more common examples list "warm" or "hard," the "wooden" person belongs here too.

Another peculiar use of English "wooden" seems to head in the opposite direction, engendering what Curtius (1963, pp. 136-137) has called a "corporal metaphor," because parts of the body become thrust on the environment or on certain abstractions. There is the "knee" of genuflexion to corporealize humility; there is the "foot," long the traditional favorite, to designate the base of a mountain. (See Brown, 1958, pp. 140-141, more recently, Lakoff and Johnson 1980, p. 472.) Even some of those metaphors recur in later analyses, but for the present, I pick my own corporal vestige: it is not the "wooden leg" of an amputee or a stiff dancer but that curious "prosthesis" which transported the extremity of live beings to such an inanimate quadruped as the "leg" of a table.

To be sure, English preserves the furniture provenance in part by requiring either the compound or genitive link shown respectively in "tableleg" and "leg of a table." German possesses the equivalent compound "Tischbein," but cannot "mean" the same thing when its Legisign belongs to the oppositional values of this language. Whatever the similarity of perception between the (autonomous-)real human extremity and the support for a piece of furniture, such a naive realist stance cannot support semantic identities. Theoretically one would then have to examine all other analogies to justify this usage on the basis of motivation, a task as unpractical as it is impossible. Rather, the linguistic form stands its own ground. Yet attempts at motivation have never died down, least so in the case of the popular "foot" example as (Curtius's type of) corporal metaphor for the base of a mountain. Since this analogy occurs in several languages, it keeps critics preoccupied. Back in the nineteenth century the Psycho-Comparatist Wundt claimed that the mountainous "foot" was *not* truly metaphor because perception outside of language caused its formation within language (Esper, 1968, p. 72; Meier, 1963, pp. 25-26 ff.).

Meaning, however, cannot be involved directly if perception occurred antecedent to the form of words, hence in a purely extralinguistic application. Semantic perception begins with inception and initiation into synchronic planes, with the Qualisigns of English "foot," or whatever. Only the form extant in a language enters an oppositional value system and occupies an unparalleled oppositional locus at the synchronic level. From a diachronic aspect there is one final observation which deserves comment: those personality and corporal metaphors reflect what Cassirer stressed often (1972, I, pp. 159-160, 206-207, 215-216, 227-228): the human body (Körper, Leib) became the first semantic, deictic pivot around which revolved all reference, going out to and drawing from the setting in primeval use.

But that truly corporeal origin pertained to the development of meaning and not some special metaphor, if at times doubling up in the manner illustrated, particularly with the swift use of the vernacular. Martinet (1970, pp. 19-20 ff.) shows with his "tree" example cited before how a modern language such as French also linked "bois," the equivalent form of "wood(s)," to signify substance and area. In addition, similar background is provided with Eco's chart (1972, p. 86-87), for his cultural unities. Interesting as those examples are, they require the type of deeper investigation my next chapter provides, now that the form has been identified. While leaving the hyletic ground to climb via the broken line up that generative hierarchy in order to reach the next trichotomy, I may as well call the M-trichotomy a degenerate "base" or "foot" of a curious "hill" in more or less deviant language. Ultimately, though, my authorial intent has found the forms it sought through the processing of reference and transference, as required of meaning if it is to arise from meanings.

Noematic Designation: Crests and Troughs--The Concepts of Language

The hyletic design has been treated and the full designation follows next. Qualisign disposition yields to intrinsic content once a form has been validated through a Legisign bearing outwardly a Sinsign composite and inwardly the semantic threshold termed wordsound. The purpose of the previous chapter was to show how Qualisigns exude "meaning" in a live language. Yet the discussion reached its limits with the hyletic doubling, since the divergence of such "doubles" at depth could not be explained via the first trichotomy. How do competent speakers deal with "wooden," a seemingly identical Legisign that nevertheless signifies as varied a content as a substance and personality trait? What happened to that curious "wooden" protuberance taken from the extremities of live beings that it should become validated also as "leg" for pieces of furniture? Certainly, the traditional phonemic features of recognizable opposition fail here.

A performance of the Red Riding Hood story, for example, might be described as a "wooden" portrayal of the fairy tale character, who goes into the "woods" or a "wooded" area with a "wooden" basket hanging from a handle that is accordingly composed of "wood." With the identical designations for a human performer and an inanimate object like the handle, language makes evident more of those leaps illustrated before. Yet the sensation of oddity is countermanded by familiarity: redundance has done its work through the prowess of signitive acts. Competent speakers recognize either use of "wooden" as commonplace, perhaps, in the case of the personality trait, as "dead metaphor"--turned into semantic "deadwood," in a manner of speaking.

Ironically, the "live" powers of a language account for that very demise. Moreover, the only "death" non-Aristotelian semantics recognizes is the degenerate kind, either when a language has lost its viable context at the level of the third trichotomy or when it has simply evaporated to the point of mere Qualisigns. Ancient Classical languages exemplify the first and engravings on stone tablets the latter type, at which point all powers of redundance have ceased as well. Beyond an encoding Referent, a decoding Recipient may encounter degeneration or demise. When confronting a foreign language without adequate competence, the construal transcends Legisign perception.

That is to say, consciousness cannot penetrate to the *conception* governing deeper content whose level is the *second trichotomy*. Going "up" the incline of generation formerly depicted in the Picture of Language curiously requires descending into greater depth, as was seen when this Picture was turned ninety degrees, with the first trichotomy uppermost. At this added depth hyletic doubling becomes forced apart, leaving such traditional precepts as "homonymy" also redundant in the suggestion of "one" (homo-) cover for two differing contents. All "nymy" tenets, be their prefixes of the "syno-" or "anto-" variety, this study has repudiated already for a too descriptive approach. What the second trichotomy still shares with the first is its *dormant* state of latent availability for context. The table with the two components of acquisition and articulation kept the M-0 trichotomies over the former, and the I-trichotomy over the latter: form and content are stored for renewed context.

The second trichotomy in the Picture of Language was also seen to occupy the 0-locus of *Object-relation* between the first and last trichotomies. This *middle* position emerges as a curious type of "opposition." Peirce himself hints at this: in contrast to the "self-contained" *positive* state of monadic Firstness, *Secondness* embodies *dyadic polarity*, with "Feeling" replaced by "struggle" (1960, p. 146, par. 1.293; p. 149, par. 1.308; pp. 161-167 par. 1.322-1.33, including "Monads, Dyads, Triads"). Pierce alludes further to "Ego and Non-Ego" (ibid., p. 166, par. 1.332 ff.), a useful connection for the *noematic* factor, the adjectival qualifier taking over from the hyletic one. However, this time the *noetic* alternative of the third trichotomy is discussed simultaneously, just because content and context remain so interdependent.

As with the "hyletic," the root of these two adjectives is Greek: "noema" once meant "what is thought" or, simply, "concept"; "noeo" or "noeso" denoted "to think" or "apprehend" (Fobes, 1966, p. 284). These readings for "noema" affirm cognition, albeit here of signitive provenance, and the issue of the manual or mental grasp connected with such modes of "apprehending" is something that will have special relevance for one of the modern studies on metaphor. Close in significance also is Ingarden's tenet of pure-intentionality: the apprehending noetic factor equals an act of meaning that "intends" its target, German "Treffpunkt" (1965, pp. 122-123), by reaching out to it, converting the target simultaneously into an intentional object. In its "pure" state, this object bears only the content of the act which constitutes it. As a consequence, heteronomous, pure-intentional entities depend on their acts and are *derived* (abgeleitet; ibid.) from these even if, once formed, they transcend the constitution as such by retaining their significance within an expression.

The nomenclature itself goes back to Husserl rather than Ingarden. "Noesis" and "noema," or the adjectives "noetic" and "noematic," appear in his *Ideas*, a work devoted to "Pure Phenomenology" (1958, pp. 255-281, 282-356). The correspondence between a conscious act and its resulting content suggest further Husserl's emphasis on organic "Korrelation" (*Die Idee der Phanomenologie*, 1958, pp. 12, 22, 32, passim). The noesis/noema dichotomy in a subsequent essay by Kwant (1967, p. 379) is further couched in a terminology that approximates Pierce's: ego and nonego surface as respective "'I'-pole" and "counter-pole." Next, an essay by one of Husserl's Gallic successors, Merleau-Ponty, (1967, p. 363), seems almost to paraphrase Peirce by separating "Ego" from "Alter," in the "understanding how *I* become the Other" (his underlining). The wording itself thus helps to bring semiotics and phenomenology (outside of Pierce's phaneron cited in my introduction) closer together. Beyond the formulations, however, their gist stresses only organic interaction between a conscious act and its content, a message which, when heeded, could extirpate the ontological category-mistake once and for all. With this hope in mind, I introduce the second trichotomy.

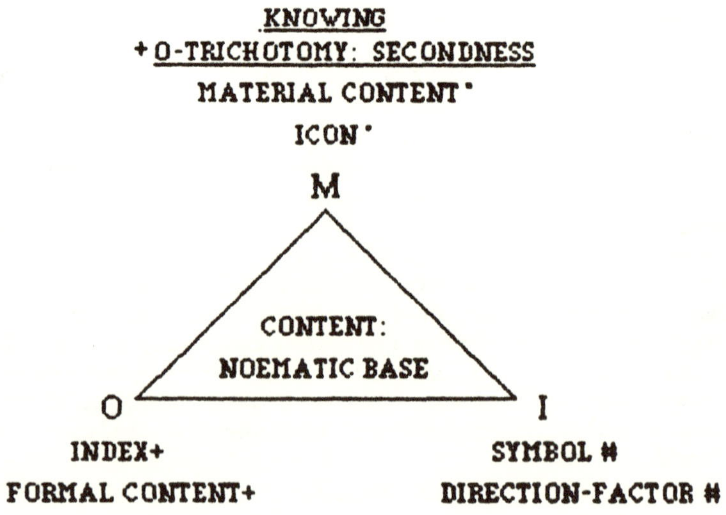

KNOWING
+ 0-TRICHOTOMY: SECONDNESS
MATERIAL CONTENT ·
ICON ·

M

CONTENT:
NOEMATIC BASE

O   I

INDEX+   SYMBOL #
FORMAL CONTENT+   DIRECTION-FACTOR #

As with the presentation of the first trichotomy, the faculty, here of knowing, heads the triangle and is followed by the plus (+) sign that identifies the "0" locus with the ontological state of Secondness. In one of Ingarden's few trinary divisions, his criteria manage to complement the semiotic signs: material content by Icon, formal content by Index, and direction-factor by Symbol. His terms thus share markers with the signs (replacing my previously explained colors). Accordingly, "." goes with the material content and Icon at M, "+" with the formal content and Index at 0, and "#" with direction-factor and Symbol at I. Each marker except the second belongs to a degenerate or generate trichotomy. Such are the dyadic polarities within this triadic setting: M-0 is at the degenerate and 0-I at the generate end. Only the Index amounts to Object-relation of Object-relation, sitting at the very core of the triadic hierarchy.

A parallel dyadic relation is made explicit by Ingarden's material and formal *contents* as italicised, differing in terminology from the (generate) "direction-factor." The semiotic signs reflect a parallel linkage. At M-apex, the *Icon* equals the semantic *name*, thus the *explicit* content or *lexicon* consisting of a *material* base. The Picture of Language showed how the broken line moved from the Legisign "up" to the Icon in the second trichotomy, for which reason this sign shares the "." identifier with the first trichotomy. The Index, conversely--and in that sense as polarity--bears the *implicit* content which yields the crucial *linguistic concept* or *signitive category* grounded only in meaning. The Index harbors the *thought* evolved from language, realizing Humboldt's premise of language as very "Organ" of (its own) thought and, in a particular expression, remains the most context-sensitive component by retaining as import only what is relevant to the constitution, with the rest suppressed.

Despite their polarity, these two signs remain conjoined: the Icon is the *centrifugal denotation*, the Index the *centripetal connotation*. An Index has only a range of implicit meaning and thus depends on the denotative core of an Icon. Every Icon becomes invoked through what might be termed a "natural selection" process of speech. Only then can material contents of Icons corporealize an authorial will. The Index enters with the selection of the Icon as its adhering implicit periphery, releasing connotations pertinent to an authorial will.

How Icons amass Indexes in their wielding is to be explicated shortly under the "crests and troughs" composing the title for this chapter. Let me stress first that the Index has a *subsuming* role, holding its implicit or *formal content* together. So, as stated before, Ingarden's "formal" here does not refer to a concrete "form" but rather to a "formalizing" or inner "focalizing" process. By depending on an explicit core, the formal content becomes signified "along with"--"mitvermeint"--the material content, asserts Ingarden (1965, pp. 69-70). Icons and Indexes obviously present synchronic language states, arising through the agency of the *Symbol*. The Symbol is that motile factor which, placed at the Interpretant corner, parallels the locus of the Legisign at degenerate level of the first trichotomy. That is why the Picture of Language also featured a broken line extending from its Interpretant corner to the next generate trichotomy of context. Since it is the immediate antecedent of context, the Symbol shares the "#" identifier with the last trichotomy. In all respects then, the Symbol constitutes yet *another* polar opposite to the explicit and implicit polarities. No longer content, it is the immediate catalyst for *naming* and *norming* at the degenerate level of Icon and Index. In this active capacity, the Symbol presents an "ego" opposing "an-other" ("non-" or "alter-") ego in the two contents, to trade on some of the terms from Peirce and the phenomenologists.

The implications of these findings are crucial for any study of linguistic *metaphor*. The traditional metaphor is sought essentially at the Icon since that sign approximates the *lexicon*, or rather its explicit deviance. Consequently, the prevalent notion of content expects an Icon to mirror extralinguistic transparencies which, when juggled, spell metaphorical transference instead of standard reference. Yet all linguistic categories have their ontogenetic ground in the Index attached to its Icon from indigenous deployment, while this type of transference lies embedded in a *proxy-tenet* trading on semantic barter which has one meaning stand proxy for another, an Index mostly for an Icon. Obviously, this cannot happen in view of the distinct, polar M-0 locus for respective Icon and

Index. Since the Index is devoid of a denotative core, it may not even become explicit without erupting as an Icon. That happens unfortunately when I discuss import. Even then the Index remains elusive: the description of a "stiff" personality for "wooden" would be only a loose paraphrase of a sense that could be rendered variously. Once articulated, though, the paraphraser equals a *pseudo-author*, an artificial Referent instead of natural Recipient who has made one connotation explicit.

The "wooden" in the Red Riding Hood example does not take its cues from outlying entities and their analogies. Whether implying a substance or personality trait, it is traceable to one cause, the signitive act; in each case, the Icon and its relevant Index come to the fore. Within each meaning is encapsulated that accumulated *valence* composing the *natural pointer*, Ingarden's *direction-factor*, which shares the "#" marker with the Symbol as the product of norming through the activity of linguistic naming.

Peirce's definitions for the Icon, Index, and Symbol can be found in his listing of sign classes (1960, p. 150, par. 2.264). He has the Icon (mainly in the attributive "Iconic") confined to the "Rheme" ("Rhematic"), which would not work for me. An Icon is only material content, not context. While Peirce also says about the "Iconic Sinsign" (p. 147, par. 2.255) that it is "a sign by likeness purely, of whatever it may be like . . .," non-Aristotelian semantics accepts only the *induced* "likeness" wrought by context through the act of meaning. Instead the tradition treats the Icon like an isomorph in material content, confusing lexical *representation* with *reference*. Peirce says also about the "Iconic Legisign" (ibid.) that it embodies "a definite quality which renders it fit to call up in the mind the idea of a like object." To "call up" meaning to bring within consciousness is indeed an apt way of describing the role of the indigenous pointer Ingarden called pure-intentional direction-factor.

Peirce's own problems with the Icon nevertheless surface in his description of the *Hypoicon* which supposedly accounts for *metaphor*. The very idea of placing metaphor at the Icon has Peirce fall in with the tradition. Of Hypoicons Peirce says that those Iconic signs which "represent the representative character of a representamen by representing a parallelism in something else, are *metaphors*" (his underlining, p. 157, par. 2.275). And (p. 285, par. 1.541) he defines a "representamen" as the "operation of a sign or its relation to the object for the interpreter of the representation," adding (just before the definition of Hypoicon) that it refers to "that which represents," while the "act or relation of representing" would be equivalent to the "representation" (p. 155, 2 par. 2.272).

In Peirce's rather circuitous description of a Hypoicon, the representation itself becomes "re-presented," one might say. But no matter which paraphrase one chooses, the above definition bears all the traces of clinging to a traditional view of metaphor. Obviously, his "parallelism" circumscribes standard analogy and his "something else" the anomaly to be bridged by an analogy in metaphorical transference--disclosed here as representing the representation--between contents. Indeed Aristotle's definition of metaphor (in my adjunct) will be so close to Peirce's that the traditional connection can hardly be missed. And that the Hypoicon remains inadequate for language at least is made apparent when next (p. 184, par. 2.320) Peirce illustrates his Hypoicon with such visual artifacts as a portrait, where perception hardly begins with a word.

Max Bense (1971, p. 29), the German semiotician who was influenced by

Peirce, preserves the latter's ideas on metaphor as Hypoicon, replete with a proxy-tenet barter which has his "Iconicity" trade on "another" (ein anderes) Icon. His example (ibid., pp. 53-55) demonstrates an "adjunctive" relation made conspicuous through terms of endearment, all of which go back to the person so described--"Johanna, turtledove . . ." and so on. A series of epithets thus reinforce one another in unique object-relations that are spun off from and refer adjunctively to the same individual in her Hypoiconic description. But that is exactly what the words are, sheer descriptive epithets at the level of content taxonomy. Ultimately this "Johanna" may grace any poster, proverb or poem, leaving "her" literally rendered "use-less"; "she" is kept context-insensitive and veers on collapsing with any meaning when probed in such localized spotsighting --fit for another inconclusive Ingendahl Experiment. The fact that Bense traded on this single example again a couple of years later (1973, pp. 62-63) leaves his illustration more suspect; it stays traditional enough to become invested further with the standard lexical and/or localized transference that Germans generally call "Uebertragung"--literally a "carry-over"--of proxy-tenet barter. (The term came up with Nietzsche and recurs in the neo-Aristotelian adjunct.)

So much for the "Icon" gracing the Hypoiconic metaphor for Peirce and a modern Teutonic follower. Peirce says of the Index that it is "a sign which refers to the Object that it denotes by virtue of being really affected by that Object" (p. 143, par. 2.247). The "real effect" of this "Object" will be demonstrated in my discussion on the indentation linguistic activity causes, with the Index as its ultimate result. Perhaps even Peirce's claim that "Icons and indices assert nothing" (p. 165, par. 2.291) can be accepted, at least insofar as "asserting" belongs to context at the level of the I-trichotomy. Next, the Symbol becomes for Peirce a "sign which refers to the Object that it denotes by virtue of a law," additionally a "general law" (p. 143, par. 2.249). In the exposition, one gets the impression of some of that traditional dogmatism clinging to Peirce's "symbol," a dogmatism which used to consider it the "artificial" or abstract counterpart to a "natural" sign (Sørenson, 1963, pp. 32-40).

Peirce's statement that the Symbol equals a "Representamen whose Representative character consists . . . in its being a rule that will determine its Interpretant" (p. 165, par. 2.292) is opportune. Symbolic determination, indeed, makes Icons and Indexes what they are as material and formal contents, through the mediation discussed. The Symbol maintains a cumulative impact on the Interpretant of the last trichotomy, much as the Interpretant precipitates Symbolic motility. Icon and Index then contain the "reference" which "directs" consciousness accordingly, be it the "person," the substance in the Icon "wooden," or whatever.

An Interpretant sign leading into the last trichotomy, the Symbol does indeed become what Peirce describes as a "law, or regularity of the indefinite future" (p. 166, par. 2.293). *Feedforward* as part of Symbolic mediation in itself makes explicit a progression in terms of the *future* through the last "-forward" segment. But the future must accompany all purposive states in their inexhaustible potential, here at the corner that leads from Symbol to the last trichotomy of context. That is where meaning expands to the possible achievement of ever new integration through an act of meaning. The scope for the new completion of language is provided by speaker impetus (I) marshaling form (M) to release the relevant import (0) in the thetic order described. These parenthetical signs are the *universal* constants, but content denominations vary with one language and its particular application. The act of meaning as such is not internalized but arises with the mature speaker's ability to wield the shared, latent, and differentiated (oppositional) components of the inventory one language harbors. Indirectly the act is recorded, of course: the content of its past use becomes stored through Symbolic feedback and constitutes the potential feedforward for the next externalization.

Peirce's idea of the future additionally touches on the Symbol's *imputed* nature which might be termed adjectivally as "putative." "A reference to a ground," he says (p. 295, par. 1.558), "may be such that it cannot be prescinded from a reference to an interpretant," a condition he then labels "an 'imputed' quality." If followed through logically, this factor disqualifies arbitrariness in language, unless viewed positively as a trait that lends "existence" to signitive entities only through their "ground": putative contiguity is either all or nothing. Let me indicate what happens to the contiguities in supposed hyletic doubling at the level of the second trichotomy when still vertical paradigma and thus in a dormant state.

HYLETIC TRICHOTOMY   NOEMATIC TRICHOTOMY

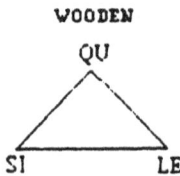

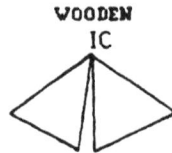

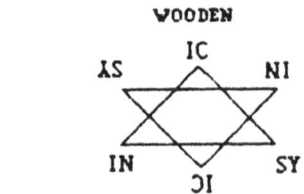

QU = QUALISIGN   IC = ICON
SI = SINSIGN   IN = INDEX
LE = LEGISIGN   SY = SYMBOL

No latent state can be made perfectly concrete, of course, since nobody can enter the mind and its neural impulses. There is nevertheless the foregone conclusion that the hyletic doubling which depicts only one triangle in the first diagram must begin to bifurcate with added generate depth in the other figures belonging to the second trichotomy, as the signs reveal. Icons are thus no longer identical when their Indexes differ through Symbolic mediation of context, whether summoning up the Iconic-Indexical pair "wooden" as "substance" versus "wooden"as "personality" or, in the other example, "leg" as "human" versus "furniture" extremity--in my loose paraphrasing of the left-sided Index. Because dimensions as such do not exist for the latent "vertical" stage antecedent to any exteriorized, linear syntagma, the last diagram may also be valid in its curious antigraviational connections. It shows the Symbols driven apart, like wings, and that distance is apt since Symbolic mediating power separates content in accordance with context. That is also precisely the reason why one cannot confuse Iconic material content with real, classified materiality in the manner of the neo-Aristotelians.

Exact contiguities in their precise locus may be hard to gauge, but not the assurance that they are extant within signitive oppositional values, from the hyletic leap of "tree" to "three" to other unique analogies and privative differences at depth. Certainly, no unilateral relation of some analogy in anomaly equal to extralinguistic autonomous classes can be foisted on these heteronomous semantic vehicles of (one) language. These entities are not stand-ins for . . . things in the world--a "theory" so beautifully expressed in Shakespeare's *Romeo and Juliet* (1952, II, ii, 43-44, p. 484). Juliet appears to project the traditional stance on reference in an implicit analogy which correlates a semantic with a proper name, here of her lover Romeo, a Montagu, whom she, a Capulet, is not permitted to love:

> What's in a name? That which we call a rose
> By any other means would smell as sweet.

Juliet has a perfect right to question the name in her situation; in this analogy she expects the semantic name to personalize the object in the manner of proper names for people. Last names are inherited and first names chosen at random. Icons, of course, are passed on to new, young speakers but never arise from aleatory whim since they are not mere labels standing in for (autonomus-)real objects. Instead, they become themselves the exterior (explicit) portion of pure-intentional objects that exist only for materializing acts of meaning. Unlike the rose in the world, the Icon "rose" of the English word has no smell to make an olfactory appeal to the senses. Rather, its Qualisigns yield the soft sound in the liquid "r," the gently rolling "o," and the "s" sibilant. Any "scent" has to arise as implicit meaning or relevant Index, here obtained in conjunction with the Icons "smell . . . sweet."

This Shakespearean "rose" stays indissolubly linked with the other Icons to the authorial will of Shakespeare. The signitive intent would be impaired, the poetic texture suffer the equivalent of a tear if any Icon were added or removed. That applies equally to the dramatic character and the object of her love: Juliet and Romeo are not "people" who exist by any other name. Indeed, so indissolubly fused to the context are these figures that when wrested from their text, a whole aura of context is removed with them. A critic (Nieraad, 1977, pp. 1, 65) therefore considers the idiomatic adaptation of proper names to a limited contextual relation (knappen Bezugskontext) one of the most fundamental types of metaphors--to wit, any romantic fellow alluded to as "a regular Romeo."

Non-Aristotelian semantics, of course, does not acknowledge a metaphor that switches from esthetic to everyday use on the basis of Icons, because the source stays lexical and the approach too descriptive. Moreover, to consider briefly the Icon "rose" in its latent opposition for modern English, it projects a positive value in mnemonic linkage with the color "rose" as well as the past of the verb "rise" as "rose" and, sonorously, the plural "rows." The obvious differences in meaning and syntax any native speaker recognizes; they amount to privative values, with the Icons trading on one material content while their Indexes harbor various formal contents. Those oppositional values spell potential "reference" for a language, as availability for a future speaker. Although German possesses a similar "Rose" (capitalized as shown), this Icon cannot fit even into the modest presentation of English opposition offered here.

Shakespeare is left the "father" of that matriarch, Elizabethan English, with Juliet not exactly his "daughter" but a "sibling" of that progeny the poem itself constituted for the "family" in the Richards piece. Even if this "rose" were "rose-colored," the shade is not "in" the meaning any more than is the aroma. Autonomous and heteronomous materials are thus two different things. Ingarden stresses that difference with his important principle of the "Schema" (1965, pp. 66 ff.): it designates the *natural ambiguity* of material contents (Gumpel, 1971, pp. 111-113, 377, in reference to Ingarden's "Essentiale Fragen"). A generic code, the schema in a sense equalizes, not unlike the Nietzschean "Begriff," yet not at a rational level. Rather, the schema holds together what Icon amasses at Index through linguistic naming and norming.

Despite its generic quality, the schema remains supple, its ambiguity dynamic. Were it not for their schematic width, meanings could not incorporate an act of meaning--for which reason precisely the apples-and-oranges mentality of proxy-tenet substitution a tradition equates with metaphorical "transference" has no place in language. So the corporeal material of a rose is vibrant in color and scent when compared to its heteronomous, signitive counterpart, the Icon "rose." Such comparisons of states, however, result in ontological category-mistakes--on which the tradition unfortunately thrives. For example, Ullmann, whose work on semantics includes a chapter on "Words with Blurred Edges" (1970, pp. 116-119, 124-125), evaluates "generic abstractness" as a "shortcoming" of language. Ricoeur (1975, trans. 1977, pp. 113-116) concurs with Ullmann while dealing with the general vagueness and "indeterminacy of semantic boundaries." Had greater attention been paid to the forms of language instead of comparing the materiality of one sphere with another, the very distinctive "edges" and "bounds" of language would have been realized.

Qualisigns, indeed, need to be most precise if that semantic threshold, the wordsound to Ingarden, is to be gleaned. Linguistic prowess reigns supreme if viewed less skeptically than the above critics did. A rose-colored rose in words comes across in any colored ink or print and still the Icons remain true to their meaning, because Qualisign curlicues have the priority here, not degenerate print as such. Language transcends any basic color and still conveys color. This chromatic difference prompted the German poet, Stefan George (1868-1933), to speak proudly of his "Dark big black flower" (Dunkle grosse schwarze blume; 1958, I, p. 47) which, unlike the real flower, consists of somber ink or print and thus grows in a garden needing neither warmth nor air, as the text goes on to express. Indeed, how distinctive his flower is George makes known, as one of the first poets who broke with the German syntactic rule of capitalizing nouns. Curiously, while the flower or "blume" stays uncapitalized, the darkness borne by the adjectival Icon "Dunkle" is capitalized because the poet still follows the rule of traditional poetics that requires capitalization at onset of line.

George's linguistic flower, like the Shakespearean "rose," is fused to the text forever, bestowing immortality on its author. Unlike the plant which needs warmth and water, the Icon never wilts. George was a poet who remained keenly aware of his linguistic medium, a cognizance which seems to supersede that of some of the theoreticians in the actual understanding of language. His flower is fused to its text just because heteronomous entities depend on the signitive acts that generated them. Elizabethan English may be "dead" insofar as its context has degenerated through lacking any live situational setting today, but texts such as the Shapkespearean ones keep the language alive in orthographic dimensions.

Not surprisingly, Ingarden (1965, pp. 62-63, 64-68) treats his schema while dealing with the material and formal contents and their direction-factor. He must show how they coincide in reference: the more schematic the material contents, the more indeterminable or "polyvalent" (mehrstrahlig) their direction-factor will be and, conversely, the less schematic this content, the more "actual(ized)" and focalized the meaning. Added to these distinctions are some technical details regarding "variable" or "potential" facets of contents in their impact on the direction-factor. While his exhaustive analysis is justified on the grounds of the intimate correspondence between content and reference as "directed" by the indigenous pointer, it may well defeat its purpose when too excessive in the area of describing content.

A better solution is therefore to aim for *functional determinacy*, since *every* transaction between reference and transference *stabilizes* content by making it point through its denominations at a specific context: meanings become focalized in engendering an act of meaning, with their direction-factors signifying the authorial intent. Although a schema may never be quite exhausted in connotative potential, the teleology of new semantic integration narrows the ambiguity to the immediate relevance of the constitution. Conversely, polyvalent or variable states obtain only for the discrete, latent *vocables* at best sighted in dictionaries when exteriorized. Yet contents fully signified through an authorial will become as much "final" as "finite" by being fused to a specific contextualization, to an act of meaning as its chosen meanings. Actually Ingarden also affirms such a functional difference: he notes that the description of isolated words serves only the heuristic purpose of examining basic characteristics (pp. 62, 94). He then adds in a footnote that single words in their discrete status duly possess a variable and potential direction-factor (p. 73). So he goes here beyond sheer content denomination.

In a way, the very fusion becomes substantiated by Ingarden's language-bound examples: they are the vehicles for speech in German. I thus return to my own illustrations. The Icon "rose" may seem less schematic than "flower," as does the compound "tableleg" in contrast to the "leg" segment alone. But one may well be locked into surface content and identify the Iconic "rose" as a flower species of the plant genus, which is tantamount to stooping to the ontological category-mistake. Context has such an impact on content that the "leg," for instance, may end up being as specific as the whole compound. In some bizarre setting, perhaps, the "tableleg" as the "wooden" prosthesis of some amputee oddly enough could signify a "human" extremity after all! Who knows?

What a critic *should* know is *that* an act of meaning constitutes the determinant of meanings or, the other way around, that meanings function as determinables first and foremost for an act of meaning, resulting in a concomitant schematic contraction. That is also the reason why non-Aristotelian semantics proscribes switching between Icons and Indexes, a thorny issue with proxy-tenet substitution in so-called metaphors. The ramifications of this problem extend to the dichotomy generally termed "in absentia" and "in praesentia" (alluded to briefly in my discussion of Saussure). Presumed deviant meaning in a lexical metaphor is not considered "present" (in less fancy Latinized terminology) due to proxy-replacement (Ricoeur, 1977, pp. 166, 184). Then a "denotation" is torn from a "connotation" through a cleavage that would split meaning from the "meant," reference from its requisite (structural) transference.

In non-Aristotelian semantics, "presence" is not in dispute: first, Icons must be "present" in their centrifugal, explicit material contents, no matter *what* the lexicon displays since this cannot even appear without an Icon; Indexes as centripetal counterparts attain an implicit "presence" in accordance with their relevance to the act of meaning that regulates them; any implication not relevant to the transaction between reference and transference becomes suppressed, is in that sense "absent." So "wooden" as part of the Iconic stretch in the Red Riding Hood example may elicit the subtance of the basket handle at one point in the syntagma and the stiff personality in another. The latter use seems deviant to tradition, suggesting that "wooden" in any shape or form is not really "denoted" and thus not wholly present. Were these theories based on fact, no meaning could issue from meanings (including mine here): every articulated Icon must be "present" or leave a gap in semantic texture. Indexes, though hard to pin down just because they possess no denotative core, must then release the relevant connotations. My various heuristic attempts to disambiguate Indexes exemplified the role of a pseudo-author by forcing Indexes into the strait jacket of Icons, indulging willfully in paraphrasing through artificial "parallel phrases." Only then do Indexes assume an outright, if unnatural, "presence."

The third sign of the second trichotomy, the Symbol, is even more recessive than the Index, and thus less present. As polar alternative to Icon and Index in material and formal contents, the Symbol was said to be their catalyst. The Symbol, standing in generate relation to these contents at the Interpretant corner, guarantees the existence of the explicit Icon and implicit Index. In its latent role of mediation between the trichotomies of context and content, the Symbol leaves Icon and Index language-bound: English "wooden" is tied conspicuously to this language when connoting the personality trait, for example. Symbolic mediation, not the representation of analogous things in the world, forge semantic identities, although die-hard categoricians would have it otherwise. By standards of an empirical isomorphism, the durable quality of metal might seem closer to human intransigence than does wood. Yet feedforward and feedback have ascribed this meaning to "wooden." Because Icons are fused with the relevant Indexes to their particular constitution, they do not record *changing* but register only *changes* resulting from latent Symbolic mediation.

The issue of presence over absence preoccupying neo-Aristotelians in search of metaphor also has Fregean roots. In yet another unfortunate dichotomy, Frege's famous yet overrated essay (1952)--particularly in the Anglo-Saxon community--posits a potential split between "sense" and "reference." To non-Aristotelian semantics that cleavage is as unacceptable as the one between transference and reference. Frege envisaged this schism in literary language, the modern neo-Aristotelians in metaphor, as suggested above by the "nondenoting" of the Icon "wooden" when used as personality trait. Frege (ibid., pp. 62-63) makes matters worse by leaving the sole "sense" relegated to literary use unexplained, other than stooping to a gross affectivism which causes him to lean on the sheer emotional appeal of "feeling." Is that a scientific analysis of anything? Since by coincidence he seizes on the same Homeric works Aristotle cited in his exposition of metaphor, there is indeed a fortuitous "Aristotelian" connection on which to trade.

With half of Frege's dichotomy left unexplained, the other half cannot succeed either, for which reason my study will be forced to include a couple of corrective Fregean "sequels." That decidely "positive" root which has meaning exude from Qualisigns would be contradicted if reference could be severed from sense. Frege, of course, as the logician incarnate managed to do well by the rational concept termed "Begriff," from his "Begriffsschrift." But my study has discarded that type of concept for meaning already. Not surprisingly, Frege's ideas on "truth values" (ibid., p. 63) also fall short of the mark where language is concerned. The primary "truth" in language belongs to the "values" Legisigns validate for Icons and their Indexes through Symbolic mediation. Verification via the lexicon only equals trading on a crude representational verisimilitude.

To illustrate Frege's dichotomy is his own famous example of "Venus" (1952, pp. 58 ff.). Frege realizes that the planet Venus has been verbalized additionally by the terms "evening star" and "morning star"; the alternatives are said to bear the same reference by pointing at the planet so designated while they differ in sense. This is a neat conclusion, but grossly oversimplified! Every extant Icon bears "reference" in material explicit content and so does every Index as implicit counterpart. Any expression containing different Icons changes in both sense and reference, affecting the contextualization of contents; any paraphrasing alters Iconizations of an authorial will, with a concomitant transmutation of import.

Frege's dichotomy, replete with the Venus example, nevertheless spawned a plethora of critical responses: Quine (1964, pp. 9, 21, 62) cites it in a modified nomenclature, using "term" and "meaning"; Ryle (1971, II. p.354) speaks of "two descriptive phrases 'the Morning Star' and 'Evening Star'" and considers them "different ways of referring to Venus"; Eco (1972, pp. 73, also 75, 80, 90) inevitably leans on his cultural unities which set the alternative versions apart; Kripke (1972, pp. 269-270, 306 ff.) adds further names such as "Hesperus" and "Phosphorus" to the Fregean ones as he aims for "rigid designators," although their rigidity is made vulnerable by having to operate in vague "worlds"; finally, Katz (1971, pp. 86-87), of transformationalist affiliation, lets the alternatives "refer to the same object" though they "differ in meaning," while he recognizes dimly that "achievement of empirical astronomy" needs to be distinguished from "achievement of lexicography or semantics."

I say "dimly" because, as happens so often, one point is made and another denied in what should have been an identical case, here concerning achievement in lexicography, as Katz puts it. The fact that the problem goes unrecognized in just another illustration leaves any clear-cut realization of the issue rather questionable. Katz (p. 93) insists, for example, that "synonymous words" such as "bunny" and "rabbit" beyond "certain social conventions . . . have nothing whatever to do with meaning." Yet whatever "social" means here, the signitive "conventions" borne by these two Icons constitute "meaning." As with the astral versions above, separate Icons yield separate Indexes, hence distinctions in reference and sense. A speaker ignorant of their disparities would sound immature, indeed retarded at levels of linguistic competence guiding performance: in the language-game of a biology class "bunny" would sound ridiculous while in a Playboy setting "rabbit" might be erroneous.

Equal to Katz's "social conventions" are the "ways" and "worlds" of Ryle and Kripke, respectively, while Eco's cultural unities have been taken to task already: all fall short of coping with language. There is no separation of ways or worlds from the semantic grooves meanings leave behind and come to own. In this ownership, Icons amount to "rigid designators," not of other "worlds" but of their own words, for which reason they cannot be dislodged from an authorial will once chosen to exteriorize it. Ways and worlds become the very codes guiding signitive consciousness in ontic heteronomy while real animals or planets exist in ontic autonomy. So, in fact, does the goddess Venus after whom the planet may well have been named; she is perceived directly on tapestries or similar artifacts. The Icons of words, however, come with the language; their sole referential purpose resides in that language.

True, without the planet or animal the words may not exist, but, once coined, they reside in their own world. A minuscule portion of such a world which is also thematically close to the above examples I found in a newspaper article (*Minneapolis Tribune*, May 19, 1979, p. 8A) that describes a (British) political scandal involving homosexual lovers. The language is speckled with such idioms as "(poor) bunny . . . frightened rabbit" in reference to one doting and one apprehensive partner. Another political context in dubious metaphors fit for an Ingendahl Experiment, or more hypoiconic terms of endearment added to Bense's adjunctive "turtledove" Johanna? Whatever the case, the Icons in their varied anthropomorphization have parted ways because the "bunny" and "rabbit" no longer can be switched to make sense for these persons as if used in their sheer reference to a hare as one animal. The same would apply if, in a heterosexual relation, that "bunny" had been the turtledove Johanna as "starry-eyed Venus" of perfection.

Just one more popular example is worth adding, especially since two of the above critics also seize on it, and that is the unicorn. Its mythological base resembles the Venus deity and the fact that it is a creature mirrors the rabbit example above. Eco (1972, p. 71) naturally views the unicorn as yet another cultural unity. Ryle himself is "misled" in his essay on "Systematically Misleading Expressions" (Flew, First Series, 1963, p. 16) by asserting, "'Unicorns do not exist' seems to mean what is meant by 'nothing is *both* a quadruped *and* herbivorous *and* the wearer of one horn' (or whatever the marks of being an unicorn are)"--his italics. This unicorn, despite its mythological identity, assumes like Venus a recognizable shape on any painting or tapestry, which is a form of existence, if not of the empirical kind. The English Icon "unicorn," from whose form all linguistic competence proceeds, "exists" only for that goal. True, the "world" outside caused the diachronic contact to be kept transparent in the compounded "one" "horn" as "unicorn" characterizing this creature, as also reflected in the German compound "Einhorn." But each of these Icons stays attached foremost to its oppositional inventory.

None of these conditions for existence can be reduced to Ryle's simplistic empirical data above; as long as they are espoused, no critic can succeed with language. That problem is also made apparent by the Fregean approach to meaning in assessment of metaphor, brought up in conjunction with the traditional view of the "icon." Henle (1966, p. 177), foremost among these critics, invests his "iconic" metaphor with the negative role of "non-denoting" as he singles out *one* word, "enwrap," from a Keats verse in typical spotsighting--like picking a raisin out of a cake! The verb is considered a "non-lexical" type of "icon" because it imparts in its context thoughts of gloom; there is no mention of a garment, some "person with a cloak." How patently absurd! Henle might have probed his native competence and realized that plain English lingo has people "wrapped up" in their thoughts or words "clad" in certain contents. If standard use can produce that much, surely no "lexical" denoting has to get lost.

Yet so traditional is Henle's resort to a sartorial cover, ironically for an image depicting such a cover, that it harks back to a Renaissance "'Garment' of Style" poetics (see Tuve, 1965, pp. 61-78). Underlying this sartorial postulate is the proxy-tenet, of course, with its apples-and-oranges mentality, suggesting that the prosaic reference to emotion has been glossed--"cloaked" or "covered" ("clad"?)--over by the deviant garment image which, because no garment is "meant," stays nonlexical in reference. In a parallel with the visual arts, one might as well posit that the famous blue horses by Franz Marc (of the early nineteenth-century Blue Rider movement) become "nonchromatic" because the color does not represent live horses in empirical reality. In a nonskeptical view, however, the vantage point stays with the *artifact* instead of seizing on conformity to *facts*. Then the color or the linguistic Icon forges its own counter-reality from within the composition or unique context, affirming its function instead of confirming empirical states in the world.

Apparently Henle took his "icon" from Peirce, a connection substantiated by Ricoeur (1975, trans. 1977, pp. 188-189), who himself tries to explain how an "icon" is "not presented but merely described." Yet what all non-Aristotelian Icons are required to do in their "positive" nature is to "present" themselves in their Legisign validation, through which they lay the explicit foundation of an authorial will. So unless "describing" is systematized as specific semantic function, it remains itself a "descriptive" term signifying nothing. If that is what Peirce's "icon" accomplished outside of the hypoiconic metaphor discussed, the need for anchoring content in the non-Aristotelian "Icon" should prove more than justified.

Moreover, it hardly seems fair to bring up the traditional "icon" without at least mentioning the *Verbal Icon* (1967), a work co-authored by Wimsatt and Beardsley. In this work, "icons" are believed to exemplify "counterlogical" rather than "logical" styles--equal to the "texture and polish of the verbal structure" (ibid., p. 217). Since ontic heteronomy is counterlogical anyway, these distinctions would not serve my purpose. In a loose reminder of my own examples, I cite the one offered by these authors (ibid., p. 202). The passage is from Pope and describes in "iconic" circumlocution a door as "wooden guardian of our privacy" (ibid.). The door as inert "wooden" barrier has been anthropomorphized into a watch or guard, in the process exhibiting a style these authors would deem unique in "iconicity" (p. 203). The imagery betrays odd concoctions, to be sure, yet this iconicity is not barred from a commercial selling doors and thus remains a purely descriptive term for a figurative style.

The analysis has now arrived at its own two figures of the *crests* and *troughs*, which convey the functioning of language in its ontogenetic origin. They were taken from a standard translation (1961, I, pp. 285-286) of Cassirer's "Wellenberge" and "Wellentäler" (1972, I, pp. 258) that appeared in the first volume on language of the *Philosophy of Symbolic Forms* cited before, specifically from the crucial chapter on linguistic concept formation. Skimming the Icons yields the literal translation of "waves" for the "Wellen--" segments of both compounds, while the second segments of each go into "mountains" or "peaks" for the "-berge" and "vales" or "valleys" derived from the "-täler." In either translation, these compounds designate mental *undulations* or *convolutions* which evolved from linguistic activity. The troughs are essentially the *indentations* caused by Iconic *wielding*, leaving behind the *imprint* of an *Index* filled with implicit meaning. What prompts Iconic wielding is the act of meaning which, through Symbolic feedforward and feedback, leaves its traces behind.

The "convolutions" are modeled after the perceivable physical convolutions of the grey matter in the brain. Exclusively *signitive*, these convolutions equal only infinitesimal impulses, undetectible to the eye. So these are the very "grooves" speech leaves behind, the "ways," "worlds," or "conventions" within one language the above critics placed somewhere outside of language. Inhering these grooves are *concepts* or *categories* of lingiuistic *competence* in the "knowing" required of a language. This form of cognition is indigenous to linguistic activity, and not logical, deductive processes. No effective performance is possible without these convolutions; speakers share them latently with their speech community. My attempt below to draw a dormant state looks crude but still serves its purpose. First, a *tabula rasa* exists at the tangential plane, showing the smooth line, with the *impact* of the first indentation recorded as mental *imprint*. The other figures depict the indenting in progress with the resulting convolutions, with the final transverse section manifesting mental categories or compartments in the slightly rectangular shapes. (See diagram, p. 93.)

In these concrete dimensions, the arrow in the first figure could as well go up as down to suggest reciprocal hearer and speaker roles. No doubt young speakers hear before they speak. But Recipient and Referent interlocutors take over so swiftly in the dialectic flux of speech that sheer chronology is hard to measure. The Icon is extant for one individual because of the convolutions shared by other speakers. Yet no Icon becomes successfully wielded without a context-sensitive Index which, at 0 in thetic I-M-0 generation, attains relevance only within the specific use and the forged contiguities, as discussed. The second figure thus has arrows going both ways, with the Symbol at right angles to them, suggesting its task of mediation. In the last transverse diagram, the Symbol *is* essentially the adjacent space between the two categories or concepts, in their imputed contiguity. The arrows in conjunction with the Symbol also present the direction-factor as indigenous pointer that has the mind assume the content of the meaning(s).

The *inductive programming* that is in evidence makes concrete the *metalinguistic contiguities* encompassing one system: the deeper the indentation, the wider the implicit radius, shown peripherally in the transverse diagram by surrounding the denotative core. So this is how meanings depend on their act of meaning, here the arrows; this is how noetic activity and noematic content stay intimately linked.

Considering the complexity of the oppositional system, the adjacent category in the last diagram appears far too neat. The many mnemonic layers of positive/privative values can hardly be drawn in without causing havoc. Still, the point is that a purely *linguistic concept* is being illustrated. As stated, it replaces Ingarden's concept, the "idealer Begriff" (1965, pp. 88-89, 386-387, 390); the attributive "ideal" contradicts his otherwise clear-cut ontological division between real or ideal autonomy and pure-intentional heteronomy. Ingarden himself sounds unsure: while defending his ideal concept on the grounds that it averts the "danger of solipsism" (Gefahr der Subjektivierung), he adds weakly that he "believes" (glauben) it will provide the ontological ballast for the seemingly volatile essence of meaning. Yet Ingarden has anchored the "ontic" foundation of meaning effectively enough in the intersubjective base of wordsounds not to require the aid of the ideal concept as well (1965, pp. 385-390, 391-400). Intersubjectivity is the very "objectivity" which keeps language suspended among speakers: it provides the "ontic" ground of conventionally based systems, once interlocutory Referent and Recipient partnerships honor the validated Legisigns.

CRESTS AND TROUGHS -- ICONIC YIELDING, INDEXICAL INDENTATION

I. TANGENTIAL ASPECT

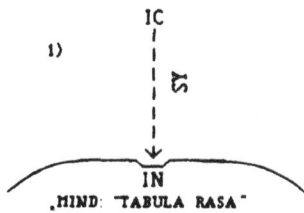

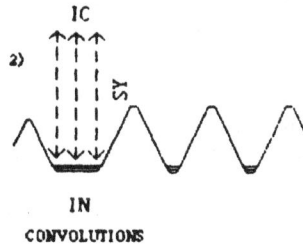

II. TRANSVERSE ASPECT (OF 2)

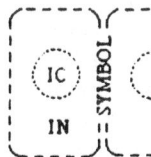

CATEGORIES OR CONCEPTS

IC: ICON
IN: INDEX
SY: SYMBOL

How well Cassirer's linguistic concept fits into ontic heteronomy emerges clearly enough in the following statement appearing near his mention of crests and troughs. Here Cassirer describes how the signitive *mind* becomes imprinted exclusively by *meaning* in the process of what he calls *naming* (Benennung):

die neue gedankliche Prägung, die der Inhalt erfährt, ist die notwendige Bedingung für seine sprachliche Bezeichnung. (the new imprint of thinking upon the content is the necessary condition for its designation in language.) (1972, I, p. 255; 1961, I, p. 284).

A standard translation is offered along with the original because the phrasing is as crucial as it remains complex in rendering. No initial capitalization is in evidence since the passage follows a colon, elaborating on the very possibility or potential (Möglichkeit) for naming, hence involving that futuristic aspect cited before as requisite for purposive domains. Cassirer's "designation" produces a "new" mental imprint, and yet the imprint itself is needed to provide the effective designation for a naming activity. Seemingly circular, the argument is nevertheless that a hermeneutic relation like this forces mind and meaning into mutual determination. The two-directional arrows on my diagram conveyed that same circularity: the arrow downward deepens the indentation and the one pointing upward permits further wielding of the Icon as it burgeons in the area of its periphery, the linguistic category.

Cassirer's "imprinting" and my indenting process thus affirm that no explicit content like an Icon becomes effective without at least a vestige of accumulated import, hence an Index. In the dialectics of acquiring and articulating language through reciprocal hearer and speaker roles, children begin to establish their competence. Their first active attempts remain holophrastic (Gumpel, on "'Reality' as a Construct of Language," 1974, pp. 172-174). An Icon is wielded as a whole phrase in the manner of imperatives and in the process becomes a language-bound, contextual vehicle. With different contexts, moreover, Icons move apart, as might apply to "wooden" in either of the senses shown. Then *two* Icons arise essentially, attached to their polar, implicit Index. To be sure, the explicit (hyletic) identity serves additionally the mnemonics of wordplay, as revealed by the earlier inimitable cartoons.

Just because the Icons separate, speakers may not be immediately conscious of the hyletic doubling: instead of being dual, the Icons seem to differ at depth. Indeed, I amazed a rather literate person by drawing attention to the "leg" for use in the human limb and the furniture support. Instead of explaining, I might have evoked that awareness through a pun, in the manner of the cartoons. That is why traditional *homonymy*, suggesting one (homo-) cover for two meanings falls short of the second trichotomy. Symbolic mediation has done its part. The diagram below should demonstrate that Iconic divergence rules out simple doubling or homonymy. Although the Symbol has been omitted here, its place would parallel that in the earlier depiction.

I. TANGENTIAL ASPECT   II. TRANSVERSE ASPECT
                                                                    (OF 2)

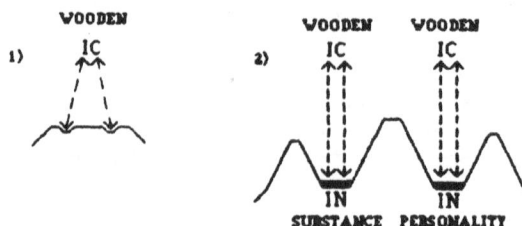

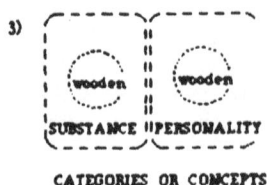

IC: ICON
IN: INDEX

Since this figure is modeled on the prior diagram, it needs little elucidation. According to experts, onset of puberty at around eleven to twelve years is about the right age for gleaning metalinguistic contiguities of this nature (Nieraad, 1977, p. 115). Interestingly enough, children younger than that know how to wield the separate Icons of each "leg" or "wooden," for example, but miss their mnemonic potential for punning (ibid., pp. 115-116, 118-119, 123, 128 on Ash and Nerlove, also Leondar.). Rather significantly, critics in this context cite also the work done by Jakobson and Halle on aphasia: lesions at the speech center result in a type of atavism by loss of metalinguistic--to these critics "metonymic"--connections. No doubt overexposure to commercial jingles that impinge upon the young mind may have the same effect on the forming indentations, even in otherwise healthy young speakers.

With insufficient redundance at the level of normal indentation, moreover, other forms of programming can easily encroach on the linguistic one. Then, in a momentary sensation, that "collision" noted before between two forms of programming occurs: semantic contiguities appear "odd"--lo and behold!--the lexical metaphor has occurred. However, since only linguistic activity and not sensation can govern meaning(s), there is no genuine interference with intrinsic competence; the signitive convolutions are accordingly unaffected--as they are by the movement of the earth around the sun no matter how "real" the path of the sun is to the senses.

Unfortunately, there is confusion about even the presence or absence of a diachronic metaphor, just because critics are not clear on where language begins and ends. One minute this metaphor is considered an early and the next a late phenomenon (ibid., p. 118, on Leondar). A favorite example of early children's metaphor appears to be "moon" as "ball." None other than Ingendahl of the Experiment cites this example in that very essay (1972, p. 268), though he was not the first (Landmann, 1963, p. 136). The case seems transparent enough: children are familiar with such round toys as a ball but less likely to encounter the moon when keeping a regular bedtime. Should they perceive this round stellar object one night, they might form their own analogy and call the moon a "ball." Fascinating as the example is for revealing a child's imagination, the young speaker in question is not in language. To be so, the child must know the accepted Icon and wield it. Otherwise no indentations will form, no intersubjective sharing be possible.

The "shape" of the English Icon "ball" will eventually lead a child to glean the Index "dance." Though this diachronic connection may be opaque, the synchronic state is extant and shared and thus securely anchored in signitive convolutions, irrespective of round shapes or anything else. To be sure, sophisticated speakers can wield "ball" also to mean "moon," or vice versa; within a particular constitution of thetic I-M-0 generation anything is possible. But that is hardly a child's game. Indeed, where the child's perception of the moon itself started, primitive humans once began. By coincidence, Cassirer's chapter on linguistic concepts also includes a moon example (1972, I, pp. 256-257). This stellar object became perceived as either the "measuring one" (Greek "meyn"), still present in the English-German Sinsigns "moon"/"Mond," or as "the shining one" (Latin "luna," from "luc-na": "light"), which French "lune" still manifests. Once the original percipience has become language-bound, the Icon, no matter what denomination, serves speech.

If there is any chance to salvage the neo-Aristotelian metaphor from its solipsistic sensation by straddling bounds of language and the extralinguistic forms of programming, I advocate a *quantitative* rather than *qualitative* approach. That is to say, if the sensation described in the collision could be measured on the basis of *frequency* and *familiarity*, the "life" or "death" of an Iconic, lexical metaphor might be gauged. At what point, in other words, does redundance block the encroachment of other forms of programming, as it seems to do with my former example of the "working" machines? Normalization has been so perfect here that only a bilingual awareness reveals the oddity of this verb in its nine-to-five job connotation.

This quantitative remedy might be applicable to the findings of W. Köller's work, *Semiotik und Metapher* (1975), particularly the chapters dealing with cybernetics and communication processes (pp. 75-83, 187-206). Although Köller's basic idea of metaphor does not transcend lexical "Anomalie" either, he offers some interesting pointers governing a regulative *"disturbance-factor"* (Störgrosse) that balances *Is-Values* with *Ought-Values* (Ist-Wert/Soll-Wert, pp. 78-96). Any discrepancy between these values causes a sensation of metaphor, although the real "disturbance" here remains the encroaching extralinguistic programming that should belong to ontic autonomy in any perception of ... which is outside of words.

These values perhaps could be measured, that is, by numerically determining the discrepancies between Ought-Values and Is-Values. When these values reach confluence at zero point, the Ought-Value essentially disappears, metaphor dies and meaning takes over as all-absorbing Is-Value, with any disturbance-factor removed, as applies to the working machines cited. Perhaps one might look additionally to the studies of Breuer (1974, pp. 121-128) on the self-regulatory processing of language, where set "algorithmic" nodes counter the unique "creative-heuristic" expressions of poets. But Breuer exhibits that common penchant for describing metaphor with metaphor when he goes on to contend that metaphor conquers deviance, German "Abweichung," by forming a "bridge" between the "already-known" and "not-yet-known" (pp. 133-134). He fails to realize that linguistic competence in the use of any meaning is always known to be used but stays relayed in the unpredictable future of potential manipulation insofar as the act of meaning selecting meanings remains an unknown until it becomes articulated through reference with transference.

What this chapter tried to prove can be summed up best by Edie's essay on "Expression and Metaphor," particularly the section on the "Arepresentational Structure of Language" (1963, pp. 540 ff.):

> Thought and meaning are fully incarnate in language; the thematization of meaning does not precede language but rather language makes such thematization possible.

Edie himself is interested in the seventeenth-century Italian thinker Vico and his influence on modern phenomenologists, particularly Merleau-Ponty. Vico realized that "minds" are formed by language, not language by "minds" (Edie, 1969, p. 488). That view is of course also espoused by the Humboldtian tradition to which Cassirer was still seen to belong. The signitive convolutions, formed by Iconic indenting, surely embody that "mind." When this source is known, one no longer needs to raise the questions Ricoeur asked with respect to the presence of metaphor (1977, p. 137): "First deviation from what? ... Next, what does one mean by 'deviation'?" The point is that nothing may "deviate" from the convolutions where Icons have left their Indexical traces, and any metaphor that does is not even a truly semantic phenomenon.

Toward a Non-Aristotelian Metaphor: From Syntatic Noun to Poetic Nominalization

Noetic Constitution, Open and Closed: The Structures of Language

The *I-trichotomy* of *context* is the vital link that provides the two degenerate (M-0) trichotomies with their reason for being. By the time context has been thoroughly explored, the Iconic or lexical metaphor will have been replaced by a structural counterpart which, literally, cannot "destruct." Although I entertained the idea of saving the traditional metaphor by the means of a quantitative approach that measures frequency of use as a corollary of Is and Ought leveling, such results would be of only limited benefit. All that is assessed in this type of pursuit concerns sensation of familiarity with certain contents instead of grappling with genuine functions of signifying.

Full signifying leads to the *noetic* trichotomy which always precipitates contextualization through the agency of acts of meaning whose products, the explicit and implicit contents, have been examined at the degenerate noematic level. In contrast to the last dyadic trichotomy, this one is no longer in the shape of a triangle and yet appears "triadic" through the three strands it comprises. Insofar as all three strands draw on M-0 contents of the first hyletic-noematic trichotomies by departing in confluence from the Symbol, they are identical in source. At the same time, each strand has to brand its signs, beginning with the Qualisign as "Rhemic," for example, since it represents a *structure* and as such a function determining the essence of the selected constituents.

What difference a structure makes the textual analyses should reveal later. For the present, it is more important to note the separation of the strands, which characterizes this trichotomy as "open." The open aspect affirms the distinctiveness of each structure. However, in any immediate constitution there must be always teleological "closure," or no constitutive unit(y) can form and carry the fundamental tasks of meaning and signifying, hence reference and transference in interaction. In fact, *context* always initiates a series of *contacts* during constitution. Briefly, the signitive act and its selected entities coincide as, simultaneously, there is interanimation between the entering constituents. The resulting expression is then projected into a setting which, if situational, forces language into contact with a reality-nexus. Since the expression harbors the encoded Referent, an interlocutory partnership presents yet another association with a decoding Recipient.

These contacts have validity for the closed formats which follow the presentation of the open trichotomy, including two of its modified versions, the long-range impact and formation of texts. I begin with the open trichotomy.

WILLING
#1-TRICHOTOMY: THIRDNESS

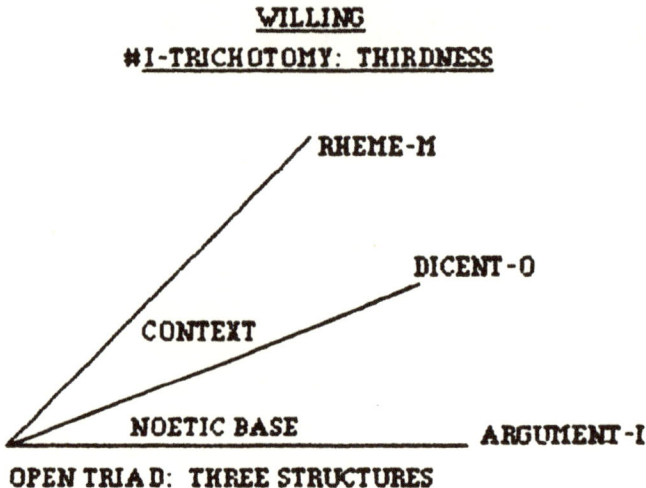

OPEN TRIAD: THREE STRUCTURES

Willing hovers over all three strands as the guiding faculty of this trichotomy, instead of the perceiving and knowing that characterized the first two trichotomies. My occasional reference to an "authorial will" made this connection rather explicit. (See also Hirsch, 1967, pp. 67, 124, 127). Throughout this study, the role of speaker intent has been stressed as the only recourse to initiating thetic I-M-0 generation. The fact that this activity is willed suggests also the inherent spontaneity in language use. Of *Thirdness*, Peirce has this to say:

> Not only will meaning always, more or less, in the long run, mould reactions to itself, but it is only in doing so that its own being exists (Peirce, 1960, pp. 173-174, par. 1.343).

This "molding," in fact, not only applies to the noetic act imprinted on the noematic content but also to the functional or structural *metaphor* my theory develops. Such a metaphor will turn out to be a micro-component of the *Rheme*, which is the literary genre of *lyric poetry*; it has been placed uppermost at M-level. Below the Rheme appears *Dicent* at 0-locus. As second literary genre, Dicent presents the *fictional* alternative to the Rheme. This structure shapes simulated worlds composed solely of words in mimetic augmentation. For "Dicent" as term one might look to Latin "dictio," the etymological root of "speaking"--not far removed from the type of "telling" that occurs in fictional narration. My *genre* determination is thus *binary*, with Dicent comprising such composites as the drama and novel, for example. One *nonliterary* strand is then covered by what appears lowest on the diagram. That is the structure of Argument at I-locus, where the detailed discussion will begin, working "up" to Dicent and Rheme so that my theory concludes with the non-Aristotelian metaphor before the textual analyses illustrate the structures and the adjunct takes over in a final survey of the traditional metaphor.

Argument appears as a rather broad category by representing the one nonliterary use; it must encompass propositions as much as idiomaticity, but, for reasons to be explained, that division suffices. To be sure, critics such as Käte Hamburger (1968, pp. 41-42) have made a valiant attempt to subdivide what she terms a nonliterary "statement-subject" into a "theoretical," "historical," and "pragmatic" kind. But the bounds of these distinctions would not jell and in the end became too content oriented to serve units *natural* to linguistic functioning, as mine have to be. Once basic units are isolated, certainly, there may be a "post-Aristotelian" method for devising further subcategories. To succeed in non-Aristotelian semantics, however, the structures must be identified categorically in their functions, because present studies have not yet come that far.

Since the noetic trichotomy is open, its strands are not in a hierarchic relation of generation, as their M-O-I locus may suggest, and yet each sign characterizes its structure in some way: M may be explicit for the "metaphor" the Rheme harbors, but stands here also for the "materiality" which enhances this structure through the "M-base," down to the degenerate Qualisigns; 0 becomes just as explicit for the fictive "objects" Dicent produces; I is then left as the locus for Argument. In their equality, however, all three structures originate each time through the teleological closure that goes into effect during constitution, as when the act of meanining as authorial will (I) is corporealized (M) and embodied (0) by selected meanings.

The long-range effect, to be demonstrated next, is emblematic for *linguistic historicity*. Because this effect is diachronic in application, it has an *indirect* impact on the disparate structures: today's lingo may become tomorrow's fictional or poetic vestige, and (occasionally) vice versa. The ordinary romantic fellow from my previous illustration who becomes a "regular Romeo" has made that descent from exalted dramatic figure at Dicent to a figure of speech at Argument. A simple yet conspicuous case ready to go the other way and make its literary ascent might be the recent Sinsign shrinkage from "Mrs." and "Miss" to "Ms." The original salutations embodied something like the old-fashioned "feminine mystique" that kept women in their place by making them hide behind their marital status, not unlike a type of "linguistic veil."

At this point in time, the "Ms." has equalized the sexes by corresponding to the male Sinsign "Mr," which reveals no special marital status. Argument, which possesses the capacity of contact with the extralinguistic reality, registers such changes in attitude first, no doubt strongly boosted by mass media attention. Eventually, though, Dicent and Rheme may carry this Sinsign shrinkage, accordingly dating a novel or poem. Through the long-range impact, then, language always possesses an "extrinsic" component, a point I make to counter the simplisitic notions about an exclusive literary "immanence." However, beyond this diachronic development, there has to be the synchronic affirmation: the "Ms." Sinsign must be validated--unstarred--as Legisign, hence as a composite yielding an Icon with an inner, indented core, the Index. Even if such an address or salutation possesses a rather narrow circumference of import, it must still cohere within an oppositional system as one accepted synchronic state. Bearing these conditions in mind, I illustrate what is involved.

LONG-RANGE IMPACT

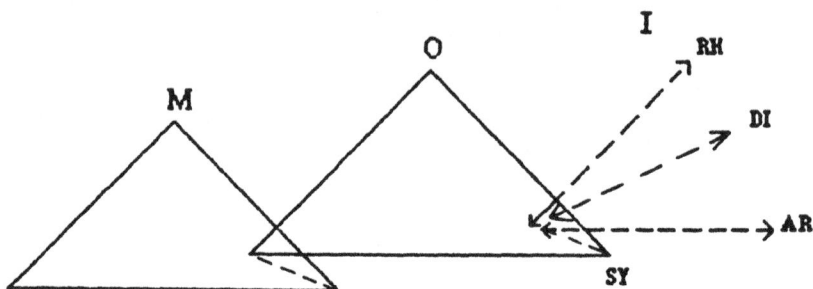

The strands, though appearing "open" in their disparate locus, are rendered in broken lines, with pointers at each end in order to suggest the *flux* of feedforward and feedback, recording contents for latent M-0 levels and recalling them for the next entry into one of the three structures. Since these tasks are primary to the mediation of the (semiotic) Symbol, this sign (SY) is the only one added from the second trichotomy. Of course, contextualization can only go up one strand at a time. But since modern poetics eschews what P. Goodman (1971, p. 152) has called the poetic "guild language" of elevated diction, no content is barred from getttting to any of the structures, with the Legisign itself preserving the "neutral" validation previously discussed. Next, however, I shall depict what happens to such entries during textual formation.

THE TEXTS

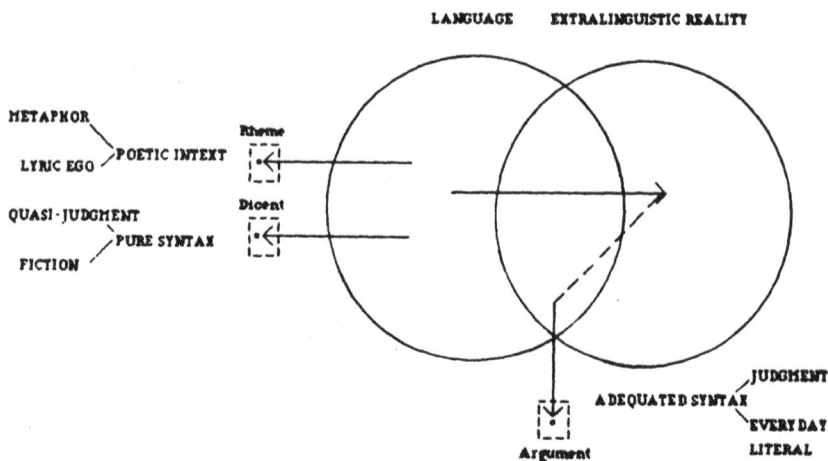

The old circles from my chapter on ontology for "sorting out" the realities are back again, replete with the overlap for adequation. Those little rectangles suggest loosely "texts" in the shape of pages, as, once more, I attempt to draw the impossible with the one priority in mind, which is to help readers understand what is involved. That goes especially for the non-Aristotelian *metaphor* which has now been entered at the Rheme. As micro-component of a "poetic intext," it is governed by a "lyric ego," which is not a person as such, but the constitutive consciousness suffusing this structure and the special transference on which it subsists irrespective of content. Now, both the literary genres, Rheme and Dicent, remain *non-adequated*: their arrows enter texts directly from language. Thus they must originate at *zero-point*. Argument, on the other hand, whose arrow is depicted going the *opposite* way, tends toward the extralinguistic reality once the expression has been formed. The deflected pointer is supposed to illustrate adequation in the acquisition of a reality-nexus, entering the text only from the overlap.

However, it is also important to note the *identical origin* of all *three* arrows: they must arise in *language*, because only ontic heteronomy accounts for a successful manipulation of meaning through reference in transaction with transference, yielding full semantic constitution. The consequences of this finding rectify all the "dilemmas" voiced by (Fregean) critics who do not understand how literary language and/or metaphor "denote." The evidence is thus cursorily presented that language precipitates these functions, causing the sentence to take shape *before* it emerges as adequated "judgment," in contrast to the non-adequated "pure" syntax of Dicent, termed "quasi-judgment," which relies on indignous denoting. The related terminology suggests that Dicent and Argument also share something, namely *the size of the constitutional unit(y)*--syntax as opposed to poetic intext--even if Dicent and Rheme remain tied to their non-adequated state. Dicent at 0, wedged as it is between the other two structures, thus partakes of the idiosyncrasies involving both. Exactly what is entailed in all these identities and differences the detailed discussions of each structure will disclose.

Instead, I next demonstrate context in terms of "closure" by the means of three graphs which reveal the shapes of triangles, in that respect matching the M-0 trichotomies of content.

I: THE CLOSED TRIAD -- A CONSTITUTIONAL UNIT(Y)

CONFIGURATION; ICONIC UNFOLDING

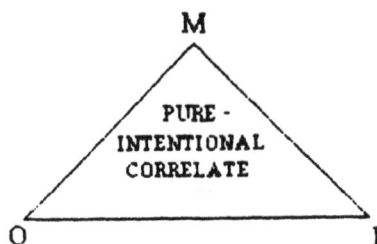

M

PURE -
INTENTIONAL
CORRELATE

O   I

CORRELATION: INDEXICAL   CONSTITUTION: GENERATION
INTERLOCKING   UNIFIED SENSE

Every time (any) meaning is authorially willed in units consisting of meanings this type of closure must be in effect, regardless of the particular structure. Otherwise no teleology exists for the contents that are being contextualized through the agency of a signitive act. The simplest way to exemplify this triad is to draw on what Ingarden calls an "Einwortsatz," literally a one-word-sentence (1965, p. 112), which he illustrated with "Fire!" Why is this single word a sentence? In writing, the capitalization at one end and the exclamation mark at the other indicate the beginning and end of a brief sentence. So the vocable "fire" as mere dictionary item is not involved. Rather, an act of meaning (I) has become fused to one centrifugal Icon which unfolds as explicit content (M) in the simultaneous release of a centripetal Index (0), the relevant import. Accordingly, a meaning has been willed, an act exteriorized through the "reference" of this willed Icon which, in a transaction with transference, caused a shift to elicit the relevant connotation.

This one word has become an integral part of a new expression. Indeed, that is how words first become contextualized: through the holophrastic wielding of young speakers (Gumpel, 1974, pp. 172-174) contents are assimilated and the minds of these individuals indented, giving rise to the signitive convolutions discussed. Moreover, a brief expression such as this is highly context-sensitive, necessitating a situational or written setting to boost constitution. For example, if contextualized in an ostensive situation marking a conflagration, the Icon "Fire!" may release the Index "Help!"; if uttered when an order goes out to a firing squad the Index of this Icon may convey "Shoot!" As stated, Iconizing an Index like this is artificial since an implicit meaning has no denotative core and may thus be variously articulated. But the example suffices to stress that each expression would give rise to a different "sentence." Functionally the expressions are the same, and I use the plural because the exclamation and command would be in essence two disparate sentences, having been willed differently. There is not one "fire" but two such contextualized Icons in their material contents, each of which stays fused to a selectional bias that engenders different implicit meaning. The outcry may be closer to "fire" as noun, the command to "fire" as verb (also in the wider sense of "Open fire!"). No matter; of primary importance is the constitution as meaning arises from each meaning.

To be sure, my example remains somewhat oversimplified--until I discuss contextualization through multiple constituents in subsequent chapters. Structure, too, has been ignored since the heuristic aim here is to demonstrate closure. Normally, "Fire!" must go up one of the three strands after leaving the (semiotic) Symbol, entering either Rheme, Dicent, or Argument--which is something neo-Aristotelians always forget in their exclusive scrutiny of lexical content. The transference they seize on is there anyway, as explained; the structure they ignore will turn out to make all the difference to the contribution each such vestige makes to its context. So, again, the outcry and order in Dicent, for instance, would have more in common as identical structural entities than their difference in content. The same condition has to apply to any non-Aristotelian metaphor.

How easy it is for context to convert a lexical item into a "metaphor" when that flimsily assessed, can be shown too. Thus a speaker utters "Fire!" in the setting of a race and may mean "Go!" or, loosely, "Shoot!" The authorial intent here is to tell the decoding Recipient of the order to start--without expecting firearms to go off. Most people would consider these uses standardized, but those intent on making a case out of deviance in localized spotsighting will never be free of doubt; their metaphor "dies" right under their noses, to put it bluntly, and no "fire" can keep it alive. At this point I have not even mentioned all the Petrarchan figures this Icon has enjoyed as the symbol of romantic passion. Fortunately, non-Aristotelian semantics adheres only to criteria of constitution and structure. Of course it seems easy to say that a recognizable poem, for instance, consists categorically of poetic (here Rhemic) elements. But this study probes in minutest detail what it is that makes a language truly "poetic," even when its surface registers a mundane "Fire!" with a particular context.

Willed meaning, which is the only means of applying language, has to be "symbolic" in contiguity, a relation shown next with the aid of graphs presented by Bense in *Sign and Design* (1971, pp. 37-38).

I - CONTIGUITIES OF "SYMBOLIC" REFERENCE

M - ACTUALIZED DENOTATION:
EXPLICIT MEANINGS

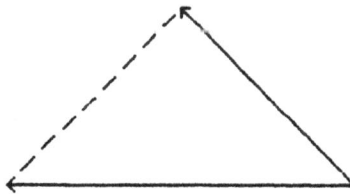

O - RELEVANT CONNOTATION: I - SIGNITIVE REGULATOR:
IMPLICIT MEANINGS   ACT OF MEANING

This graph displays the "symbolic" gap, with the word in quotes not capitalized because it is not equal to the narrow designation of "Symbol" as the sign occupying noematic Interpretant locus before the eruption of noetic context. Instead, this is the principle governing all volitional, anthropomorphic enterprises; purposive domains draw on a confluence that has been "thrust" together, as went some of that etymology discussed while treating Cassirer, Heidegger, and Peirce. I filled in the symbolic gap with a *broken* line, to suggest repeated closure through contact, whenever meaning emanates from meanings, as happens here, too. What the symbolic contiguity does *not* involve is the *anomaly* in *analogy* critics try to extract in localized fashion from the lexicon. Bense, using Peirce's Hypoicon, could not transcend that focus either: be his "Johanna" plain or a "turtledove," she has undergone reference through transference, in order to be in *any* context at all. The content by itself thus cannot project a solid idiosyncrasy as "metaphor" if the assessment is to be more than a sheer reaction to sensation. Otherwise Johanna stays too lexical to be worth her mettle, with those adjunctive object-relations Bense posited for this supposed metaphor also unable to penetrate a structure. What happens in semantic generation I demonstrate last in "thetic" closure, relying once more on Bense's graph (ibid., 1971, p. 37).

I - CONTEXUALIZATION VIA "THETIC" REFERENCE

M: MATERIALIZATION OF ACT

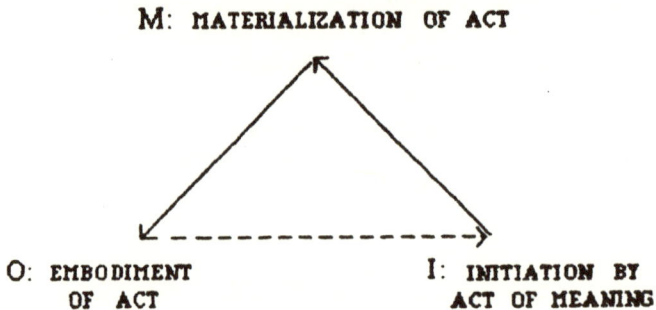

O: EMBODIMENT   I: INITIATION BY
   OF ACT   ACT OF MEANING

This graph describes how an act at I seeks out the vocable "fire" in order to name and "materialize" the act at M through Icons, with the intent of conveying either of the connotations of order or command at 0, the context-sensitive level embodied by the Index. Full meaning then issues through an authorial will at I, marked by my broken line. That is how all contextualization proceeds as speakers engage in the selection process, including myself here as author. That is what the lexicon must contribute at M for I in the generation of 0 instead of some dubious "metaphor"--long before it may be equated with conditions in some extralinguistic world, relevant as such a world may become when Argument is involved. All these graphs affirm *reference* and *transference* as requisites for incorporating a signitive act. As stated, a new I-M-0 contextualization of contents differs from the linear M-0-I incline and I-0-M decline of generation (in the Picture of Language) that keep a language alive or cause it to die, much as thetic generation needs that full viability to go properly into effect. With these general aspects considered, an extended correlate will be analyzed next, followed by entry into the first structure under scrutiny, Argument.

Hierarchy of Syntax. Empirical Contact Through Context: Argument

The structures are to be singly introduced, beginning with Argument, after the basic constitutional unit(y) has been analyzed. The diagram of texts revealed that this unit(y) is *syntax* for two of the structures, Argument and Dicent, in adequated or non-adequated usage. Syntax, however, is given a phenomenological interpretation here, bringing my ideas in line with Ingarden's "pure-intentional sentence (or syntactic) correlate" (1965, pp. 111, 121, 132-133, 138, passim). Correlation is a term used to describe the duality entailed in an *act of meaning* (Meinen) and the *meanings* that *signify* (Vermeinen) the act. With correlation, *pure-intentionality* culminates in *double-intentionality*: not what meanings are as vocables but what they become during new constitution receives ontological priority, asserts Ingarden (pp. 124-12 5). The teleology of "closure" that was examined earlier is directly related to syntactic correlation, hence to the transaction between *reference* and *transference*.

When this transaction prevails, a sentence has gone into effect. So far a "sentence" has come in just one word, "Fire!" The act of meaning had endowed that word with specific meaning, be this in the sense of the order or the outcry. The order and the outcry constitute separate correlates, each of which harbors a distinctive authorial intent. From a functional standpoint, if not from the aspect of content, both correlates are equal. One reference, the vocable "fire," had shifted differently as syntactic "Fire!" through the transference each act of meaning precipitated. Any articulation of meaning, however, requires the correlates to enter one of the strands borne by the open trichotomy. For a syntactic correlate, that entry could be either Argument or Dicent.

The holophrastic "Fire!" is now ready to be replaced by a correlate extended to multiple constituents. With several constituents, a *syntactic hierarchy* arises, according to Ingarden (1965, pp. 79-80). Placing the *noun* first, he ascribes to this constituent the task of "objectification of the meant," from "Vergegenständlichung des Vermeinten" in my rather literal translation. As phenomenological principle, the noun does not necessarily equal a traditional part of speech, although its powerful role as a grammatical *subject* may not be ignored. Rather, the noun is the prime constituent that signifes an act of meaning, if this is not to remain pure spirit. The noun thus initiates the actualization of speaker intent, as the major chosen content. Yet signitive initiation should not be confused with word order. Since the correlate is a holistic unit(y), its first and last elements mutually determine one another; they are integral parts of an organic whole, purposive determinables of their determinant, the act of meaning.

Through the noun, then, an act first engages in the type of "bestowal," "lending," or "endowing" ("Verleihung" and "Verleihen," pp. 69, 103-104, 124-125, passim) which lays the foundation of signifying ("Vermeinen"). The noun bears through its content the authorial will, and in that task reflects also the *noetic-noematic* correlation elucidated in discussing the last two trichotomies. Indeed, so potent is the role of the noun as syntactic agent that my structural metaphors will turn out to have become "nominalized" (Gumpel, 1971), no matter what their surface registers. Even the tradition going back to Aristotle stresses the role of the noun while examining metaphor, although a part of that interest may be traced back to the very inventory of Greek: it had *onoma* comprise "noun," "name," "word," and "meaning" (Fobes, 1966, p. 286).

Ingarden tries halfheartedly to contrast nominal constituents with "Synkategorematika," the function words. That is, he stays rather unsure of what he is classifying, mainly because function words, while limited in Iconic-material range, contribute more to syntax than merely filling in gaps for smooth interaction. The "pro-noun," for example, spelled this way to show that by very definition it covers "for a noun," absorbs the content of a noun into its own Index and yet, like the noun, often assumes the powerful role of a syntactic subject. To be sure, since the indigenous pointer, the direction-factor, "is" what material/formal contents provide, a pronominal pointer stays delimited in signitive width, assuming instead a stronger functional input.

A similar functional preponderance Ingarden (1965, pp. 76-85) ascribes to the verb. It must be remembered that Ingarden wrote his *Literary Work of Art*--cited most so far--in German, although Polish, a Slavic language, was his mother tongue. Both these languages are highly inflectional and thus belong to the synthetic rather than the analytic kind English represents. Not only are nouns variously declined, but finite verbs conform to nouns and pronominal subjects in every grammatical person. That is why "dummy subjects" are inserted when conjugating finite verbs in grammatical paradigms. Not surprisingly, Ingarden (pp. 71-72, 80-81, 83-86) maintains staunchly that all finite verbs possess a more functional direction-factor than nouns--a recursive (rückweisend) kind, in fact, which seeks out the nominal counterpart to interlock with it. This syntactic finitude places verbs below nouns when they reinforce the "meant" at predicate level. Of course, adjectives also adapt their endings to nouns as they shape nominal compounds with articles.

Though fundamentally valid, Ingarden's syntactic hierarchy stays somewhat open to dispute. It may be pedantic to view verbs that way when, after all, their extended predicates control nouns or pronouns as grammatical objects. The unique power of verbs also surfaced in such holophrastic imperatives as "Fire!" that conveyed the order to shoot. If that capacity is any test, pronouns would be low in syntactic hierarchy, despite their ability to function as subjects within an extended sentence. Ultimately, even a preposition such as "Out!" yields an eloquent command, if more so as elliptical verbal complement for something like "Get out!" Yet a definite article may not appear in the imperative form of "The!" and thus lacks such power of constitution. Indeed, it should be starred for making no sense. Moreover, the hierarchy Ingarden proposes here should not spawn the age-old noun-versus-verb controversy, which leads nowhere. In defense of nouns, my earlier doubling of "wood(s)" demonstrated how nouns controlled adjectival and prepositional qualifiers in their almost unmatched comprehensive width: "in"/"of" or "wooded"/"wooden" are just a couple of the numerous syntactic derivatives that native competence culls from the respective Icons signifying area or substance.

Since I keep function closely allied to structure, I shall use the terminology of Köller (1975, pp. 119-120, 191, passim): function words are to be called "operative signs," in contrast to (nominal) "eidetic signs." Köller, in fact, was cited for a possible quantitative stabilization of the traditional metaphor which may be achieved by measuring the level of Is-Values and Ought-Values. That is, semantic redundance, the enemy of the traditional metaphor, could then be determined by degrees of frequency of use and the concomitant sensation of familiarity any repeat perfomance causes. That any solution is better than a qualitative lexical one becomes apparent in even this context of the discussion. Thus metaphorical deviance is still gauged so superficially today that it encroaches on the most basic of operative signs, where it may aid neither meaning nor metaphor. Prepositions are not only verbal complements that may elicit commands by themselves as indicated; they apparently become the mainstay of "metaphor" as well. So it is claimed in Embler's *Metaphor and Meaning*. In his chapter, "Metaphor in Everyday Speech" (1966, pp. 27-44), he expresses surprise that ordinary speech stays so metaphorical--down to the "up and down" that he lists, one might pun. If metaphor resides in such basic syntactic elements, how far can its bounds extend before attenuating those of meaning as well?

To separate momentarily the "ups" from the "downs," English permits birds to "rise," along with successful people, expensive prices, doughs baking in the oven, and even that sun which was cited already to illustrate discrepancies between scientific (heliocentric) fact and (geocentric) sensation. Often a polysemous equivalent of "go up" that manifests two Icons with one indentation can compensate for a verb with a single Icon, as "rise" manifests above. Of course, one word cannot replace another without altering the correlate; that would be proxy-substitution. My point is mainly that these ramified applications with either version--going from voluntary movement in ascension to no genuine movement at all--only affirm the power of *meaning* as ontic heteronomy, a sphere that *breaks* the bounds of ontic autonomy in order to *create* its own bounds, ready to flatten the unique metalinguistic contiguities of its own making.

An essay by Lakoff and Johnson, "Conceptual Metaphor in Everyday Language," which is of still more recent vintage than Embler's work, also covers metaphorical prepositions. For their example of metaphorical everyday speech, the authors (1980, pp. 461-462 ff.) delve into certain English prepositions they term "orientational metaphors." Among these are figurative vestiges that come in various "spatial orientations" of "up-down," "front-back," and "in-out." Grammarians at large have long plied the rubrics "figurative" or "abstract" to describe prepositions of a nonspatial application. But, logically, if every commonplace crosses bounds between meaning and metaphor with such ease, the critics struggling with their classification land in a labyrinth, probably where the Ingendahl Experiment ended.

Embler (ibid., p. 33) himself makes that evident. In the typical neo-Aristotelian penchant for subverting the very terms tradition tried to standardize, he claims to be taken aback by the following discovery: while everyday language is metaphorical, the poetic kind stays "literal" because its "exact," "correct," and "concrete" diction steers clear of the "patois" of "daily talk." Stylistic preciosity is what Embler tries to address here in twisted terminology. Others did so before him; the Imagists (Pratt, 1963, pp. 22-23) specifically espoused such poetic exactitude. Later followers went on to label the phenomenon "ideogrammatic" (Frye, 1967, pp. 275, 333-334), and then linked the ideogrammatic with the concrete "iconic" (Riffaterre, 1978, p. 54). Yet this study will show that structure through a change of function, rather than explicit content, accounts for all these phenomena. This solution is obviously an improvement over loose descriptions that convert everyday meaning into metaphor and esthetic use into literal exactitude. What might be more constructive for differentiating operative from eidetic signs on the basis of Ingarden's hierarchy is the following triadic schema of semiotic generation (p. 108).

The operative signs are at M-apex as the most degenerate syntactic elements. The eidetic counterparts separate simultaneously into the greater functional contribution for verbs at 0 and the heightened constitutive prowess for nouns at I. The schema indicates how these constitutents then implement what Ingarden (1965, pp. 119-120, ff.) calls *nominal-verbal unfolding* and *nominal-verbal interlocking*. In the very phrasing of the italicised words, the noun is explicitly the first component while the verb follows. Yet the verb engages in that recursive function which, as explained, has its pointer seek out the noun-subject. When that happens, the nominal-verbal direction-factors coincide; explicit centrifugal Icons let the correlate unfold in extension and implicit centripetal Indexes *effect* a parallel intension as contents band together and release connotations relevant to authorial intent.

OPERATIVE SIGN =
INTERSYNTACTIC RELATION
NOMINAL-VERBAL UNFOLDING

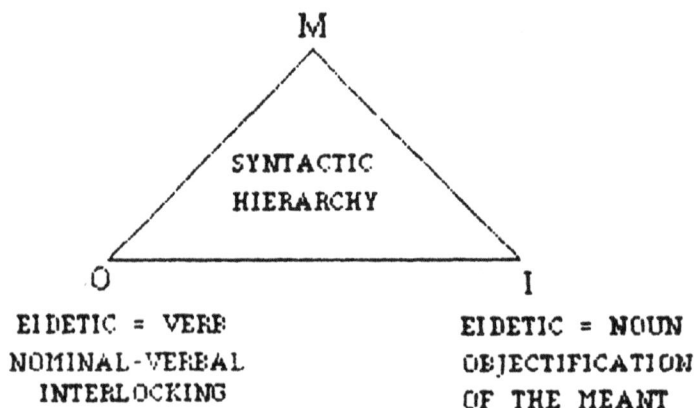

M

SYNTACTIC
HIERARCHY

O   I

EIDETIC = VERB   EIDETIC = NOUN
NOMINAL-VERBAL   OBJECTIFICATION
INTERLOCKING   OF THE MEANT

Sheer sequence and full signation may not coincide, even if most modern languages bear the standardized word order that commences with the grammatical subject. Whatever the order of the syntagma, the correlate is a product of double-intentionality, as this arises through an act of meaning (I) which has selected certain meanings (M-0). The I-M-0 constants have to be present since they affirm the thetic order of generation, even in the case of the holophrastic imperative. Every articulation of meaning necessitates this order, in contrast to the linear generate M-0-I incline which keeps the language alive or the opposing I-0-M decline which leads to its demise. Despite its inherent duality, or just because of it, every sentence possesses just *one* correlate, notes Ingarden (pp. 118-121). The only exception may be an "opalescence" (pp. 149-151, 270), when connotations appear to fluctuate, or oscillate in rich poetic texture. Affirming a single correlate is important, since studies of metaphor based on proxy-tenet theories end up bisecting the organic unity of a correlate.

Ingarden, in fact, lauds the supreme achievement (Leistung) of language for amalgamating an aggregate, the "sentence content" (Satzsinngehalt), into a unified sense, a holistic unit(y) called "Sachverhalt" (pp. 113, 120, 198). The "nominal-verbal" makeup suggests the presence of a grammatical subject and object. Indeed, one may look to the type of "ego" and its "object" the phenomenologists had posited also in their ideas of the noetic-noematic correspondence between an act and (its) content. Syntactic processing thus gives rise to an *interanimation*, which *always* accompanies the generation of speech. According to Landmann (1963, pp. 121-122), such animation in syntax is rudimentary. The very idea of a "subject" embodies an agent taking over an inanimate "object." Yet the tradition, all the way back to Latin rhetoric, has plied animation tenaciously to extract from it some putative metaphorical deviance. The adjunct will go into that fallacy of long standing, but the problem is mentioned here to demonstrate once again how greater methodological consistency of treating *obverse* meaning before jumping into a supposedly *reverse* metaphor would have benefited the tradition.

One may certainly describe syntactic interanimation as a type of "focalization," as did Ricoeur (1977, p. 132, leaning heavily on Black and Ullmann here). Again, this characteristic is not reserved for some "metaphorical" trait but occurs with every generation of meaning by meanings. As long as "statement" is equated with the signitive act, Ricoeur's phrasing applies to (any!) sentence formation: "To the focalization of the statement by the word corresponds the contextualization of the word by the statement." A good example of such a focalized interdependence, which also causes me to reinvoke the "tree" Icon, is offered by Hirsch (1967, pp. 58-60, 91-92, 220). Real trees, observes Hirsch, have roots connected to them permanently, but the meaning "tree" harbors the connotation "root" only when relevant to a particular use of "tree." Expressing the wish to climb ("up") a tree, for instance, would leave "root" suppressed as irrelevant implication for that statement.

Hirsch (pp. 81-87) makes this point to endorse his idea of a holistic "intrinsic genre." But, as happens so often, the principle is not followed through systematically to its ultimate conclusion, at least not when Hirsch lauds Sandmann for having made the "sagest" comment by claiming that just because some languages did not possess a certain meaning does not prove that they lacked a parallel "thing-meant" (pp. 28-29). Hirsch seizes on such designations as "ice" and "mist," among others, while asserting that the words "merely represent different states of the same thing. . . ." Obviously, Hirsch does not trace a "thing-meant" or "state" to their indigenous provenance, in his case the intrinsic genre. Alone the "ice" could spawn enough synchronic contingencies to spin off a series equal to the concoctions of the *Peanuts* cartoon. A few "I's"--instead of the "Y's" in that cartoon--could start forming Sinsigns with "ice" or "eyes," going on from there. Locked into English, these states are inimitable because they evolved from one language to serve correlate selection in that language. No paraphasable "thing-meant" equals their unique foundation.

Hirsch's other meteorological example, the "mist," proves the same point: in my bilingual competence, I know that English "mist"--in Index close to the Icon "fog"--translates into German "Nebel," which still resides partially in the English adjective "nebulous." Yet the German Icon "Mist" carries as its Index a totally different scatological Index, a "thing-meant" of "dung" and "manure." Every intersecting and diverging Icon or Index equals a language-bound "thing-meant," to what extent will become apparent later with this very meteorological example.

At the same time, my emphasis on signitive acts should not be construed either in terms of a linguistic pragmatism or behaviorism. Wittgenstein's *Philosophical Investigations* (1963, p. 20), for instance, is a work that exhibits a strictly pragmatic orientation: it defines the "meaning of a word" as "its use in the language" but still fails to draw use into the dynamic essence of the meanings themselves. The behaviorist stance of Morris misses the mark on the same grounds. In his "Pragmatical Dimensions of Semiosis," Morris (1938, pp. 32-33) defines "linguistic structure" as "a system of behavior" which makes signs come "true" when the behavior anticipated with the use then becomes "released." Such a release, in effect, speech-act theoreticians would meet with a "perlocutionary act." According to their progenitor, Austin (1975, pp. 109 ff.), speakers "first" perform locutionary and then illocutionary acts that impose on locution "informing, ordering, warning . . . ." Perlocutionary acts then take over and "bring about or achieve by saying something, such as convincing, persuading . . ." (his italics).

Diffracting linguistic activity into multiple acts would obstruct the harmony between function and essence. The same is true of the way in which Austin (ibid., pp. 92-93) divides acts into "phonetic acts" confined to "uttering . . . certain noises," "phatic acts" that conform to rules of grammar and intonation, and "rhetic acts." The latter must be capable of bestowing upon the other acts a "more or less definite 'sense' and a more or less definite 'reference.'" What is "more or less" here? The separate quotes in themselves shroud the genuine confidence of the author in doubt. "Noises" may only be gleaned by themselves at their degenerate level, as they were with the bruitistic elements in the cartoons, bereft of meaning. Nor can the parallels of syntax and semantics, the phatic and rhetic acts, be severed from one another with Ingarden's type of correlate, whose two essential acts remain the act of meaning and its signifying meanings.

Unfortunately, subsequent speech-act theoreticians, who added their own *Essays* on Austin (1973)--among them Searle, Forguson and Strawson--eradicated none of these problems but traded on the same basic ideas of speech-acts which may be summarized as follows:

PHONE   PHEME   RHEME
      LOCUTION   ILLOCUTION   PERLOCUTION

Searle, one of the foremost American proponents of speech-act theory, was quoted before on some misconceived notions involving intrinsic "rules" in language that turned out to be diachronic. In addition, he leans on extrinsic "devices" (1970, pp. 39-40), such as behavioral acts of promising. Certainly, these are identical in English or French, just because they are behavioristic criteria and thus not "in" either language--any more than Hirsch's states above. A truly linguistic "device" does not bear separation from its designation. The very fact that English shares its Icon "promise" with both a noun and verb, which is not the case in French, would disrupt the organic identity by causing syntactic-semantic values to diverge.

The same applies to precepts of "communicative competence" a German follower of Searle, Habermas, has set forth to improve on linguistic competence. In the lengthy essay (1971, pp. 101-141), Habermas departs from speech-act precepts of "issuance" (Äusserung, pp. 101-103, ff). He draws up a series of pragmatic categories whose cognates stay close to English: "Kommunikativa, Konstativa, Repräsentativa" and "Regulativa" (pp. 111-14). The first class depends on such performatives as "say, speak, tell," the second on "assert" or "claim," the third on "know" or "mean," while the regulativa seem to cover illocutionary and perlocutionary acts entailed in command, challenge, and so on. Added to these classes are tenuous ontologogical dichotomies of long standing in German thought, such as "Sein" opposed to "Schein" and "Wesen" opposed to "Erscheinung"; they designate "reality" versus "reflection" and "essence" versus "appearance."

These categories, accompanied by their dubious ontological distinctions, are too behavioral and descriptive to aid classifying any vital activity occurring in language and the intrinsic competence on which it relies. The "Konstativa" actually go back to the "constatives" of Austin (1975, pp. 67, 88, 109-110, 141). Their task was to pinpoint true and false conditions; they contrasted with the performatives confined to so-called (happy or unhappy) states of felicity, while these in turn differed from the "verdictives" serving a legal context. My divisions are not complete but stay too descriptive anyway: structure subordinates them, since fictive persons in any novel can utilize apparent constatives or equivalent acts. When they do, "truth" remains confined to Legisign existence of the contents involved and to the proof that a given stucture obtains. Matters are not helped either when Furberg (1971, p. 154), in some polemics over the truth factor of constatives between Austin and Strawson, contends that "Facts are what statements, when true, state." The point is, what are "true" statements to these theoreticians?

To non-Aristotelian semantics, the correlate of a natural language is, in the meaning of Nietzsche, extramorally a "lie" because its very nature remains metaphysical and thus "beyond" nature in the manner described earlier. Ontic heteronomy, in its own circle, never directly "pictures" states of affairs, as claimed in the early Wittgenstein's *Tractatus Logico-Philosophicus* (1961, pp. 36-42). To borrow from Tarski (1944, pp. 343), truth as an "agreement with (correspondence to) reality" in terms of an "existing state of affairs" is possible only when the correlate enters one particular structure, Argument, to acquire truth claims in the function of linguistic verification. Once the correlate has been forged, the Tarskian type of truth may be realized only when the correlate goes "up" the strand bearing this structure in the open trichotomy at I.

With *Argument*, the empirical (autonomous-objective) reality enters language because the *pure referent* embedded in the correlate becomes juxtaposed with an *objective referent* (German "Sachverhalt"). The *contact*–previously made concrete with the *overlap* between language and the extra-linguistic reality–then comes into its own in a *reality-nexus*. With that acquisition, language harbors *truth claims* at the level of the syntactic unit(y) and becomes functionally "literal" or "univocal," no matter what the lexicon registers. The contact involved also serves redundance in idiomaticity, to be exemplified shortly. For Argument, as here understood, is the structure where all speakers begin to acquire their language in ostensive application as they wield their mother tongue in an empirical setting, from the first bisyllabic gurgles, holophrastic exclamations, and mnemonic nursery rhymes to sophisticated, theoretical pronouncements. Though *post-factum* to the formation of the correlate, adequation leaves behind no sensation of a time lapse between encoding a pure referent and juxtaposing this with an objective counterpart. Native speakers are too adept at their craft and the tool, here English, they have wielded since childhood to pause between these functions.

Once the correlate yields the pure referent in the amalgamated direction-factor, it is projected "out into"–Ingarden's "*Hinausversetzung*" (1965, pp. 164-172,)–the extralinguistic reality. With this projection, the correlate becomes an "assertion-sentence" (Behauptungssatz) or "judgment" (Urteil). In that projection, then, the pure-intentional fabric of the correlate is pierced, as it were, in order to meet an objective counterpart in signation as the ultimate content that is "meant." Ingarden uses for adequation "Anpassung" or "Anpassen" (as gerund rather than noun), and occasionally also "Deckung" (pp. 171-175, 177, 179, passim; also Gumpel, 1974, pp. 12-16). Moreover, what the overlap of my diagrams affirmed additionally was the *retention* of both referents, the pure and objective one. Thus Ingarden (p. 175) states firmly in (my translation):

So even with true judgments, the persistence (Bestehen) of the two contents (Sachverhalte)--pure-intentional and objective--is undeniable.

How important that dual existence of contents or referents is, this study should prove conclusively after all the structures have had their due. The point is, the two referents may become aligned but in their distinctive ontological makeup cannot merge. At the same time, the shift in orientation through the adequating process also causes *perforation* of the pure-semantic texture. That effect Ingarden terms a "transparency" (pp. 172, 351; 1976, pp. 60-61) mostly with the adjective "durchsichtig," to imply that the pure referent is left threadbare (see also his essay, "Poetics and Linguistics," 1961, p. 7). But this effect results from the immediate impact at context. Content, on the other hand, gains in amplification in the long run, as the earlier diagram illustrated.

Enough has been divulged about Argument at this point to compare it with Peirce's concept: under his "Ten Classes of Signs" (1960, p. 146-150, par. 2.254-2.264) Argument is the tenth, accompanied by the "Symbolic Legisign." Argument linked to the "Symbolic" affirms that "its object must be a general" (p. 149, par. 2.63); Argument as Legisign means that it must be a "Sign of law . . . an ulterior sign through a law" (pp. 144, 149, par. 2.252, 2.263). In some contexts Peirce aligns Argument in function to the judgment and proposition, alluding in addition to "an actual existent" that "tends to the truth" (pp. 144-145, 149, par. 2.252, 2.263). "Ulterior" indeed is the adequating process when taking over from a finished correlate to make a sentence tend toward truth through an objective referent that signifies an actual existent. The fact that adequation must accompany Argument certainly amounts to a "law" for this structure. What has to be modified, however, is Peirce's idea of Argument as highest (tenth) generate class, since the open state of the noetic trichotomy keeps generation equal if separate. This change is to be expected when one remembers Peirce's (purely) logical orientation. Earlier, I was forced to abandon Cassirer's symbolic-semiotic synthesis because this ended with logical judgment. Ingarden's extended treatment of literary use restored balance to that one-sided focus.

The *example* Ingarden himself supplies (pp. 164-170) for his "assertion-sentence" or "judgment" will help illustrate my comments. That his choice falls on such an ordinary sentence as "My pen lies on the desk"--"Meine Füllfeder liegt auf dem Schreibtisch"--makes evident that his idea of "judgment" is linguistic rather than purely logical here. The sentence could be as much part of a real letter as a novel, which presents the very challenge non-Aristotelian semantics must meet in avoiding a lexical explanation. In an amusing way, one can almost visualize Ingarden sitting at his desk and staring at the pen before him. Beyond such facetious conjectures, however, there remains the scientific fact that, for there to be a linguistic judgment, Ingarden would have to be a real, nonfictive speaker. The correlate then acquires a reality-nexus and bears a truth claim--which does not mean that the statement has to be true. As Ingarden notes (1965, p. 176), the truth claim also can be fulfilled "negatively." Put paradoxically, an apparently "false" statement remains functionally "true" insofar as adequation has occurred, which is a rather different finding from Furberg's simplistic notion of "true" statements. Ingarden's premisee will be of great importance to all the deviance cults in terms of ontological category-mistakes that arise with the traditional view of metaphor.

In detailing Ingarden's model, it is best to adopt a Cartesian stance of taking nothing for granted. The opening "My" is derived from the extant "my" vocable and thus enjoys "true" Legisign status. Through that existence, Iconic indentations may form their Index within the signitive convolutions speakers of English share intersubjectively as partners. The "My" is in capitalized Qualisign form to signal onset of the correlate. Fused to this correlate, the centrifugal Icon denotes possession in the first person. Through the centripetal Index, possession connotes whatever becomes relevant to the constitution. The "My" suggests personal ownership of a pen and is heightened perhaps by the illocutionary force of pride.

This tentative construal necessitates completion of the entire correlate. The fact that this "My" belongs to an adequated correlate takes priority in converting it into a "true" designation by virtue of the structure, Argument. With a reality-nexus attached, the "My" may designate the abstract (autonomous-ideal) idea of ownership and a concrete (autonomous-real) phenomenon of possession, as when the pen in the situational context has the speaker's name engraved on it, perhaps. The primary truth for this heteronomous entity consists of its extant Legisign *existence* and the secondary type necessitates adequating with *existents* of ontic autonomy, be these corporeal or (abstract) ideal. Accordingly, this "My" becomes functionally "literal" and/or univocal, along with all the other constituents, operative and eidetic in contribution.

Of course, the neo-Aristotelian tradition has many confused notions of the "literal" qualifier besides basing it on a nondeviant lexicon. For instance, a "literal" univocality is obtained through *skimming* the Icons, an artificial practice to non-Aristotelian semantics because Icons should not be detached from their Indexes. When done, the German explicit content, the "Füllfeder" above for the "fountain pen," delivers an English "*fill-feather," and the "Schreibtisch" a "writing table." While the latter compound is still permissible instead of my brief "desk," the former has to remain starred for English despite the separate existence of the compound's segments. Thus "*fill-feather" as synchronic state is no Legisign and prevents an Icon from indenting further as one Index where this language is concerned. However, what the Icons yield when skimmed at the *diachronic* level is the viable *contact* language once made with the extralinguistic reality through adequation. The German "filling" and "the feather," as well as the English "fountain," all bear traces of their respective situational contexts, from the quill pen to the cylindrical applicator filled with ink that often caused this liquid to squirt, which speakers of English then viewed as a "fountain."

These transparencies mirror stages of linguistic historicity and as such *date* the expression, as reflected in the Icons. And of late there is also that device with the round nib English Iconizes as "ballpoint pen." Contents, when properly understood, thus bear an "extrinsic" relation to the empirical world no matter how distinctly "intrinsic" their (non-adequated) essence. Therefore, Ingarden's theory of ontic heteronomy should not offend anyone, not even die-hard Marxists, since it guarantees such contacts.

To play the devil's advocate a moment longer, in the traditional purview the same "literal" surface could join ranks with the "metaphorical" prepositions: a fountain gushing ink? Who ever heard of that beyond an odd English designation? Apparently the Germans stayed more sober by adhering to the filling action. So there is a nice "metaphorical" transference from cascading water to squirting ink. To non-Aristotelian semantics this compound simply demonstrates how Ought-Values have flattened into Is-Values; language and not logic has eradicated the sensation of metaphor, leaving the surface no less "strange" if one wants to make a bid for the lexicon. While knowledge at the diachronic level remains encyclopedic--fit for an etymologist, philologist, and equivalent professional--all native speakers trade on synchronic states that let their meaning (I) emerge through Icons (M) with their relevant Indexes (0). The "*fill-feather" stays "dead" to English by not being able to rise to such heights of generation while the "fountain pen" quite literally has the word.

A translator, of course, has a problem grappling with these distinct Icons and Indexes. My translation proves it: I reduced the "fountain pen" to plain "pen" in reasoning that, no matter which kind, only one major tool existed at the time of Ingarden's writing. For this type of heuristic illustration such a strong reliance on the inference may be permissible but not in a literary, non-adequated text where Icons are everything because no reality-nexus exists. Caution must be exercised in the area of inference lest the translator slip into a pseudo-Referent. At the level of synchronic states, though, another unique contiguity arises, since the English "pen" bears a potential Index of "animal enclosure." Also, the "ball" in the modern "ballpoint" pen has been validated as part of its compound--but not that juvenile "ball" for "moon" the critics (Ingendahl, Landmann) mistakenly wanted to foist on a linguistic "metaphor." Whether or not a moon is rounder than a nib is not at issue; language does not ask but ordains in that "coercive" manner my study first discussed. Thus German carries the related Icon "Ball" for the toy and dance, but has opted for a "Kugelschreiber," something compounded into a "disk" that "writes," as the Iconic equivalent to the "ballpoint pen," and speakers may either take it or leave it since private alteration is strictly ruled out.

Even a setting may be adventitious enough to relativize the traditional view of "literal" versus "metaphorical." Such a problem surfaces in what I shall call the *metalinguistic gesture*. Metalinguistic is the mode of describing what is being done while speaking, and gestural the histrionic pointing in the metalinguistic reinforcement. The "literal" gesture motions to Icons, as when a speaker drops a fountain pen into a real fountain and says that, "literally," this is now a "fountain pen." The other gesture has the same speaker draw out the Index when, while filling the pen, the person says that with the squirting ink a "fountain" is meant only "metaphorically" insofar as no water cascades from a genuine fountain. As pure gestures, neither type can affect the structure. But non-Aristotelian semantics at least identifies all possible nuances of what tradition throws around as "literal" and "metaphorical." None of these conditions effect correlate formation at the level of the pure referent or adequation at the objective referent. Still, until all the possibilities are probed and examined, such a conclusion cannot be reached. Neo-Aristotelian semantics has never reached them by not taking the pains to sort out the nature of meaning. Basically, all the above instances of "literal" or "metaphorical" dissolve into meaning, unless the attempt is to describe a style and/or a metalinguistic surface. Exactly what makes language functionally literal, the following diagram should demonstrate conclusively.

ADEQUATION IN PROGRESS

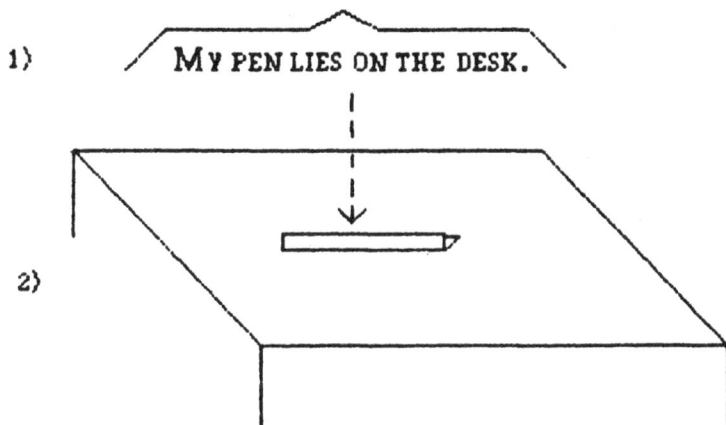

1) ⌢ MY PEN LIES ON THE DESK. ⌢

2)

1) CORRELATE = PURE-SEMANTIC REFERENT
2) REALITY-NEXUS = OBJECTIVE REFERENT

Again, I try to draw for the sake of clarity what eludes all concrete manifestation. Though crude, my diagram nevertheless depicts the *two levels* of contents that arise with the adequating process and have been presented so far in the overlap between two circles. The numbers are supposed to stress the order of priority: formation of the correlate, (1), precedes juxtaposition with an objective referent, (2). The sentence must *form* before it can *conform* to any *fact*; only linguistic competence shapes the former, while encyclopedic knowledge enters language with the latter. When in progress, adequation is not sensed as a dual task. Only the keen introspection of a theoretician of language would lead to such cognizance.

The correlate displays capitalization at one end and punctuation at the other to demarkate its bounds. The nominal portion "My pen" comprises a possessive and a noun-subject, while the predicate with its intransitive verb "lies" encompasses the prepositional unit "on the desk." Now, the verb bears the recursive direction-factor that counters the overt sequence by seeking out the noun and interlocking with it, in the manner explained, whereupon nominal-verbal unfolding goes into effect at M and interlocking at 0. At that point a signitive act has induced closure (I), with signitive contiguities forged in the process. The constituents interact by "correlating" with one another and double-intentionality prevails in thetic I-M-0 generation as an act of meaning (I) becomes corporealized and embodies explicit and implicit meanings (M-0).

Through adequation, the correlate is then projected "out" into the extralinguistic reality: on the diagram, the amalgamated direction-factor is shown going *downard* to meet this objective referent. At that point, the graphic objects become aligned with the contents. With no other graphic means available, the white interspaces between the words may depict the *perforation* caused by adequation, even if language always looks that way when printed. So, when the (autonomous-)real entities become signified in the juxtaposition, the shift in focus moves away from the meanings themselves to the things "below" that are now "meant." If the adequated use is ostensive, the presentational immediacy is such that the "My"-speaker assumes a face and perhaps confronts a hearer directly. These interlocutory partners then actually hold the reality-nexus between them. Ingarden terms such an ostensive setting a "concrete instance" (konkreter Fall; 1965, p. 65). Not only the speakers but their environment becomes rounded off in corporeal dimensions, lending constitutive support to the schematic material contents, as would apply here to the color and contour of "pen" and "desk." In the process, a type of disambiguation (Gumpel, 1974, pp. 180-185) occurs that reduces Icons to sheer labels for . . ., causing maximal semantic depletion in the narrowed-down schema through the obtrusion of an objective referent. This is how primeval language must have begun. Today, Icons no longer depend on such ostensive support but flourish in their dynamic significance.

When *written*, an adequated work--like mine--undergoes *depletion* with every unfolding correlate, ironically, as context progresses and seemingly becomes augmented. Thus all my sentences here go into adequation, one by one, since I am a real author in aim of truth claims. As my study progresses, it receives ever-greater backing from the objective referent of the conditions about language I intend to reveal. But I could not get to that point without the linguistic competence which first shapes the pure referent, the correlate. However, no matter how figurative the style, my language stays functionally literal. The language I use becomes instrumentalized to verify language use.

Another example might be a manual for the use of pens: no one is going to concentrate on alliteration and other such stylistic niceties; reading a manual on pens is strictly informational, not esthetic. The instruction matters more than carefully structured sentences. Indeed, so crucial is the information itself that the correlate may be violated through *paraphrasing*. A sentence differently exteriorized becomes a "parallel phrase" and thus another pure referent or correlate before adequation. The correlates must differ in their nominal-verbal unfolding and interlocking. But both correlates may converge on the objective referent at the second level, much as their pure referents differ. The semantic telos then becomes replaced by a pragmatic goal.

A related issue arises with the verb "lie," which has some rather interesting "Aristotelian" repercussions. In the first place, my choice of words was guided somewhat by the translation because the German verb for designating the position of objects usually has them "lie" when flat and "stand" when vertical. However, in the context of the correlate and its subsequent contact with the reality-nexus depicted, the choice of "is" may have said as much about the tool's presence. To be sure, this modification affects the correlate at nominal-verbal unfolding and interlocking. Nothing can alter that fact. But from the standpoint of the objective referent, perhaps, either word may have done as well by this "pen" and its position.

The "Aristotelian" aspect is that this ancient propounder of metaphor trades on a similar example involving a predicate. In anticipation of his exposition, then, the argument would be as follows: the fact that the pen actually "is" on the desk converts "lies" into an usurping, deviant content which, as proxy stand-in, has taken over. Since "lies" denotes a more specific action than mere being, the transference would be to Aristotle of a species-to-genus order. Non-Aristotelian semantics, of course, cannot accept such a localized function. The principle is not indigenous to shaping the correlate but comes closer to rupturing it, since that other predicate is not there as Icon and could at best be engendered through the given Icon as relevant Index. So the pen that "lies" on the table also implies that it "is" on the table. But to impose the concrete position on the wording in essence would force the arrow to go from (2) back "up" to (1), a most unnatural situation.

For this English version, the inventory governing the content and the context may certainly work together. If the "My-" owner were a less than scrupulous person, for instance, the double entendre might arise that the pen which "lies" on the desk also "lies" in words. This phrasing makes the pen sound animated, but no more so than when one says in English that a given pen "writes well," as though this thing possessed voluntary movement. Adequation may well provide the missing link, quite concretely the hand of the person trying out the pen. Whatever the case, irrespective of all these embellishments, the language remains "literal" as long as the reality-nexus obtains.

The diagram for adequation brings me also to the promised Fregean sequel. The juxtaposed objective referent is loosely what Frege meant by "reference"-down to the "rigid" designators Fregean followers such as Kripke were seen to relegate to vague "worlds." Well, the "world" is herewith identified; it belongs to the reality-nexus at the second level. The first level corresponds roughly to Frege's idea of "sense" which, unfortunately, he couched in nothing but affective designations of sensuous appeal. So Frege's planet Venus would be located at the second level where the graphic pen is. But the meanings "Venus" or the other linguistic versions, the "evening" and "morning star," reside at the level of the pure referent, as parts of some correlate. As explained, these meanings may converge on the reality-nexus, but as teleologically bound syntactic constituents they remain distinct. Unless included in the same sentence, they have no contact, outside of that vast internalized oppositional network speakers share.

Frege may have been right when he suggested that literary use traded on "sense" only, hence the correlate at (1). But Frege was guilty of failing to explicate sense and suggesting tacitly that reference had stopped when, actually, that is where reference begins. Were it otherwise, adequation would not have to depend on those curious "linguistic doppelganger," to borrow a figure from Furberg (1971, p. 136). Ingarden (1965, p. 174) makes a point of stressing that the pure-intentional one stays inimitable; ontic heteronomy and ontic autonomy never coincide. The "My" possessive proves his point as well as the demonstratives he uses for the illustration. Where is this "My" at the lower level of the diagram? There is nothing to see, although, as suggested, the pen could be engraved with the speaker's name to weight the possessive. Whatever the case, meanings are not semantic marbles; neither their concrete nor abstract states identify with those of ontic autonomy, as reiterated throughout this study.

Not that adequation does not make enormous contributions to the amplification of a linguistic inventory at that long-range level explained. The best illustration of that input is idiom formation. Idioms project their own type of an extended, or syntagmatic, dead metaphor, at least for the tradition and not my own theory. That is, overtly idioms are frozen Icons, mostly at the predicate end of the correlate while nominal heads are kept floating. A whole predicate, therefore, goes into one indentation as though it were a single word. Thus several Icons share one Indexical groove as one internalized word. Obviously, idioms are the products of semantic redundancy through adequation, in a long processing of literalization. But appearances delude: literalization is long-range whereas an immediate contextualization could force these seemingly redundant vestiges into one of the literary strands, where they turn up in novels or poems and become revivified by that change in structure no matter how transparent their lingo.

Idioms would certainly qualify as some of those "everyday metaphors" the earlier-cited critics envisaged with prepositions. In the loose traditional nomenclature, most idioms come off as literal-metaphorical hybrids. From an aspect of sheer semantic redundancy, the literalized idioms are "old" (Gumpel, 1974, pp. 36 ff.). But their abrupt introduction into a context and possible literary resuscitation lets them appear "new" as well. Their curious potential for sudden inclusion as well as their outer color and rigidity make for a unique combination of characteristics. The colorful nuances are obvious in "seeing the light" and "falling off the wagon," for instance. So is the need to cling to the definite article. What the definite points to here is a stabilized projection of the direction-factor in its set Index rather than to some nominal antecedent. That is why "the" light or wagon may be introduced without any prior reference to those nouns; that is why their article embodies a transformational defect. When changed to indefinite "a" light or wagon, the individual correlating Icons return and no longer cohere to convey together a sudden realization or a state of sobriety.

As for vibrant color, there could hardly be a more ironic example than the colorless fish English reserves for a "phony issue," the "red herring" (Gumpel, ibid., pp. 24-25). That is to say, the Icon in the color "red" and the entire "fishy" expression are colorful enough for an Index of a seemingly abstract connotation. Still, that fish is also colorless because there is no such objective referent by that color in empirical reality. Some interesting conjectures on that diachronic inception by U. Weinreich (1969, p. 42) have been entertained. But far more fascinating is the power of language to force through its "lying" contents nevertheless and keep them extant. Strictly speaking, of course, this "red herring" possesses truth as Legisign and attains additional truth claims if it lands in the structure of Argument. Once the adequation through some situational context forged this idiom. Now it may enter any of the structures.

Related to the idiom is the *proverb*, where an entire sentence and not just a frozen predicate coheres in one basic import. For that reason, proverbs are colorful like idioms, but also terse enough to facilitate fast oral transmission and retention. A good case in point is "Misery loves company," and this is offered by Chomsky (1965, pp. 149 ff.) to illustrate violation of "selectional" rather than "subcategorization" rules. The latter kind break syntactic norms, such as the transitive rule in "John compelled," whereas selection supposedly counters semantic norms. The other difference is that selectional violation keeps sentences construable, indeed, it accounts for the presence of metaphor and personification, contends Chomsky (ibid.). Both rules are questionable, since they will turn out not to affect the other two structures.

But to dwell briefly on this proverb: as with the idioms, the proverb draws on semantic redundancy and thus could have registered practically anything in semantic selection on the surface. The objective referent, consonant with a situation which pertains to the comfort of sharing grief, has come to obtrude on these Icons through repeated adequation, almost as though that arrow on the diagram could indeed reverse and go from the second level back to the first, where the pure referent resides. Next, the selection itself, which has stayed a big issue in linguistic explorations of metaphor, is a tenuous principle nevertheless. Actually, Chomsky is the one who, in questioning selection, violates the natural selection of language. His own native competence should have told him that the English oppositional system has aligned the social and human aspects in the additional "business" Index of "company." Language selects as it sees fit. The same applies to the verb Icon "love"; it does not always render emotional involvement but also serves as an intensifier of "like."

Plainly, in the dynamics of semantic material contents, where collective nouns thwart number by conveying plurality in the singular, the initiating "Misery"--obviously standing for humans--is no special case either. So, if anything, all selections here cling to the English lingo if not to Chomsky's logic. The nouns, "misery" and "company," each reflect instead the "metonymic" type of singular which renders the many through the one and preserves the priority of terseness. No wonder Chomsky (1965, p. 163) misses the "boundaries of syntax and semantics," as the chapter bearing these rules is called, conceding that he is forced to "conclude a highly inconclusive discussion."

Idioms and proverbs may be submitted to yet another and more constructive dichotomy than Chomsky's, one that became known as "foregrounding" and "backgrounding" (Plett, 1975, pp. 127 ff.). The terms as such may be traced to the Czech Structuralists, specifically to a collaborative volume entitled A Prague Reader on Esthetics (1964, pp. viii-ix, 9), where the editor, Garvin, offered these translations for Czech "actualisace" and "automatization." Idioms or proverbs are automatized expressions, backgrounded in a rigidified import, if often foregrounded in the ("metaphorical") color noted. So "background" equals the stabilized direction-factor in the objective referent whose power is such that the arrow on my diagram seems to go the opposite way, from the second--back up--to the first level. Correlation for the constituents is kept at a minimum. Originally perforated in the frequent adequation, such contents have become annealed. The individual choice cannot be broken down further since multiple Icons possess one indented groove as though they were one word that the authorial will (I) selects in content (M) to obtain the Index (0).

Under those circumstances, the backgrounded import may have to determine the foregrounded Icons. Any of the above examples display that: the "phony issue" guides the "red herring" which otherwise possesses no reference to anything. However, the Czech Structuralists --Havranek and Mukarovsky (ibid.)--make their point with greetings and the social etiquette accompanying them. To use my own example, German "Guten Tag!" yields a foregrounded "Good day!" Yet in English backgrounding the greeting connotes, not a polite salutation as it does in German, but rather a tart equivalent of "Scram!" on the order of the "Out!" cited before to show that prepositions could generate commands. In a more homespun German equivalent of a salutation, "Grüss Gott!" when foregrounded yields, not a provincial greeter but someone resembling a religious fanatic who insists on the need to "Greet God!" everywhere. The backgrounding, however, resembles a colloquial English "Hi!" Even "God" has featured in my study, beginning with its English Sinsign reversal from "dog." "God" in this case, is part of what Austin (1975, pp. 81, 83, 88, 150-162) has called a "behabitive" by triggering a certain behavior. In that capacity, a greeting lapses fast into a stereotyped utterance: to Jakobson (1956, pp. 59-60) it is a shrunken "phrase-word," of which the monotonous "How do you do?" may be one of the best examples. (See also Gumpel, 1974, pp. 20-25).

The primary purpose of these behabitive idioms is to signal social etiquette through their automatized backgrounding which then determines the foregrounding in another language. However, even when that is done, the foregrounding cannot be adapted slavishly. A case in point is the dubbed Western for German television: to hear a sturdy American cowboy utter his colloquial equivalent to English "Hi!" as "Grüss Gott!" may not be disconcerting to the German audience but amuses the bilingual speaker. Despite the seemingly correct choice of Icons, these are too ethnic in flavoring to cross the Atlantic as natural vernacular and eradicate the German muzzle.

These examples all seem to stress behaviorism, but that muzzle serves as an important reminder that idioms are Legisigns with the literary potential elucidated and thus a capacity equal in signation to any constituent. Also, what these greetings reveal, the single Iconic Legisigns affirm within latent opposition. Only translators who tread on foreign (Qualisign) ground may have to sever Indexical background from Iconic foreground. That problem is shown below with examples from Ingarden's "pen" sentence for adequation. The English "pen" is backgrounded as animal enclosure and writing tool, while the German "Feder" becomes backgrounded into a bird feather and writing tool. How the Icons in the last two versions draw a blank with the wrong Index is clearly shown, though unfortunately not demonstrable without mixing the languages.

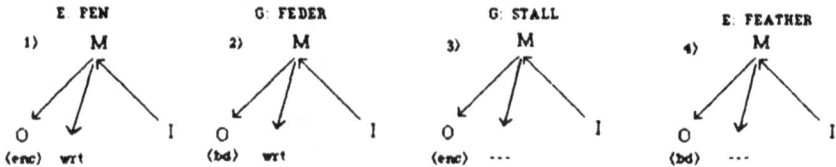

E = ENGLISH, G = GERMAN
enc = enclosure,   wrt = writing tool,   bd = bird feather
() = parenthesis added import (Index)
--- = blank

Ontologically part of the second trichotomy, the "M" equates with the foregrounded Icon and the "O" with the backgrounded Index. Figure (1) manifests how two backgrounded Indexes, the enclosure and the writing tool, foreground into "pen." Figure (2) similarly has the backgrounded bird ruffles and tool foreground into the German "feather" (Feder). Yet in Figures (3) and (4), the foregrounded enclosure into German "Stall" and the foregrounded bird ruffles into "feather" no longer yield the German "pen" as "Feder" nor the English "pen" as "feather." With the context-sensitive Index obliterated in the blank areas of the last two figures, no meaning can result from an act of meaning at I, picking up the wrong Icons. In my analysis of indentations and hyletic doubling, the Icons were separated with their respective Indexes, as would apply to "pen" in (1), for instance, when given twice for each Index. But with the one Index in parenthesis anyway, a single Icon suffices for this heuristic illustration. The two Indexes, incidentally, were listed partially in diachronic consideration. In the second figure, for instance, the bird feather had to precede the quill pen as artifact.

Speakers cannot elude these differences in oppositional values. However, that there is such a thing as occasional speaker rebellion, a mass media controversy demonstrates as diverting proof. Certain letters addressed to Ann Landers followed one another closely in the *Minneapolis Tribune* (April 5, July 31, August 13, November 9, all in 1979, pp. 4B, 3B, 2C, respectively) to show by that frequency how much the subject preoccupies speakers, specifically writers. These blamed Landers for her past willingness to accept the senseless question in the greeting "How are you?" where any attempt at an answer unleashes a superfluous "rundown" of ingrown toenails and the like. Landers readers thus offer a "warmer" alternative with "Howdy!" while Landers herself reneges on hopes of future "Howdying" due to the foregrounded provincialism, fit for a "bowlegged cowboy." After explaining that "Howdy!" came from the equally senseless greeting "How do you do?" and thus the meaningless question "How do I do what?", Landers pointedly thanks one communicating "Pardner."

Other entries challenge the sexist salutation of "Dear Sir" for letters as also that "gesundheiting" behabitive triggered with every sneeze as a more or less polite reaction (actually transported into English from the German). These disturbed "pardners" do not realize they are up against a coercive power so strong that, curiously, although they helped to make it they cannot break it without severing that intersubjective bond of interlocutory partnership. In some respects, "God" Himself could not be more omniscient--had indeed not eluded the English whim of trading on the other side of "dog," or finding His name taken in vain by provincial Teutonic greeters.

Dicent and Rheme as Constructs: Quasi-Judgment versus Metaphor

The other two structures, the literary genres *Dicent* and *Rheme*, will be discussed together, but they require two chapters. One chapter deals with the *constructs* as encoded by a Referent and the other with their decoding in *concretization* by a Recipient. In concretization the constructs become "reconstructed" by passing through the consciousness of a Recipient. So the literary genres are first treated as holistic composites and then tested in their construal. The reciprocity between Referent and Recipient roles may complicate separating the topics on occasion, but the subsequent textual analyses combine the topics anyway by proving how the constructs reveal their structure when concretized in selected texts.

In non-Aristotelian semantics, content must be probed functionally in its specific contextualization. Critics should be alerted to Legisign neutrality: surely they see that modern literary texts may exhibit any of the idioms, behabitive greetings, or proverbs that came up in illustration under Argument, from a "red herring" to a "How do you do?" or a proverb on the order of Chomsky's "Misery" example. Any "Howdying" among fictive communicating "pardners" will differ in essence from the Landers correspondents. Even the metalinguistic gestures discussed before are not to be excluded, be they "literal" or "metaphorical." A fictive dinner guest, too, may motion to Icons and say, "Literally, this is a red herring," in reference to some such fish dipped in a red sauce (or a red light?) while the conversation revolves around a phony issue; another may motion to the Indexes and affirm that the phrase was meant "metaphorically" since neither the stated color nor species of fish is really being signified.

If not confined to a structure, these seeming everyday vestiges are to non-Aristotelian semantics neither truly literal nor metaphorical: Argument brands them literal and the Rheme, it will turn out, metaphorical. Once contents have entered the strands of Dicent and Rheme, they must remain non-adequated. Adequation is thus the pivot for literary use, negatively or positively. The negative prefix "non-" in itself underscores that no juxtaposition with an objective referent occurs. The lack of adequation leaves the pure referent, which is always primary anyway to this juxtaposition, to its own devices. A non-adequated correlate thus consists of natural units wholly indigenous to the pristine essence of linguistic meaning.

The diagram of texts showed nevertheless that Argument and Dicent shared the size of the correlate, a syntactic unit(y) designated respectively "judgment" and "quasi-judgment," so that the "quasi-" prefix implies lack of adequation. The same diagram demonstrated also how Dicent and Rheme had parallel arrows which went straight from the circle of language as ontic heteronomy into their respective texts--a graphic means, therefore, of depicting their non-adequated status. Where these two structures differ instead is in the size of their constitutional unit(y), since the Rhemic correlate has been extended from syntax to context, specifically poetic intext. And the "metaphor" identified with this intext supersedes lexical neutrality by belonging only to the Rheme. Still grounded in the meaning of Greek "metaphora," this non-Aristotelian metaphor continues to underscore transference, if not as something pitted against, but coordinated with, reference and yet modified exclusively for an extended correlate.

Obviously, non-Aristotelian semantics does not give priority to "genres" that consist of the multiple formats dictated by sheer fashions of taste, hence the literary etiquette popular in different phases of history. Where necessary, the structure of such formats will be identified. In literary scholarship, with no ambitions of isolating semantic essence, a descriptive approach is also valid. Critics embarking on such ventures study the taxonomy of contents and the stylistic impact of the imagery borne by a work. But those data elude any functional contextualization of contents, a difference of approach that must be recognized if in no way disparaged.

However, any such awareness among critics at large remains doubtful. As late as 1966, Fowler, the editor of Essays on Style and Language (p. 10), complained in the introduction to his collaborative volume that, so far, no "formal feature, or set of features" had been found which could identify "literature" unequivocally and that he accordingly doubted their existence. Fowler's significant problem is not realizing that his "features" are reduced to the lexicon. His perspective is equivalent to assuming that a cigarette stub in a collage will alter visibly just because it has become an esthetic component. Of course, changes occur in the esthetic setting of a composition, but the piece of refuse as such remains. At least, the materiality is conveniently visible on a collage, whereas linguistic Qualisigns may be perceived concretely and yet stay on a page with their language gone in total I·0·M degeneration, something that could not happen to visual art forms. At the higher degenerate levels, however, the identity of function and essence is even closer than in compositions of the visual arts. So despite lexical appearances, the substance of meanings changes considerably with the structure.

To date that message has not sunk in. Barely three years after Fowler, Baumgärtner's (German) essay on the "methodological status of a linguistic poetics" offered an international survey of twentieth-century theories, up to the date of his essay. Baumgärtner (1969, p. 27) concludes by referring to Fowler's pessimism. Nor does he himself (pp. 38-40) offer a solution, since he trades on the figurative lexical surface considered "formal" in Fowler's sense. In typical spotsighting, Baumgärtner probes isolated contents by the means of that old standby my study has disclosed as so fundamental in syntactic-semantic interaction that it proves nothing at all--animation. Not without irony, Baumgärtner (p. 15) actually begins his survey by citing Jakobson on the "flagrant anachronism" committed by linguists who stay "deaf to the poetic function of language" or by literary scholars who remain "indifferent to linguistic problems and unconversant with linguistic methods. . . . "

Such a confident opening is shattered when Baumgärtner (p. 26) throws Jakobson's equivalence on the discard pile with the other modern theories for failing to differentiate a "poetic" from a "standard" language. Even the timing of Jakobson's pronouncement on which Baumgärtner trades has an ironic twist: it appeared as the "closing" part to Jakobson's own (1960, p. 377) "Closing Statement," which covered linguistics and poetics along with his equivalence. Yet by the time of Baumgärtner's essay, no "closing" argument had appeared in the way of a solid conclusion. Jakobson, the linguist who was certainly not "deaf" to or unconversant with issues governing linguistic poetics, had thus failed too. His equivalence has been cited before in this study, where I covered the leaps of language and the intrinsic categories they forge to prove that, indeed, the principle is not a unique "poetic" phenomenon. Of late, Culler observed in his *Stucturalist Poetics* (1977, p. 75): "Semantics has not yet reached the stage where it can characterize the meaning of a text." Culler claims that even the more modest attempts in that area of semantics fall short of expectations. His prognosis (p. 162), too, is pessimistic since any theory aiming to base poetry on "special (linguistic) properties" seems to him doomed to failure.

My analysis of Dicent and Rheme, in that order, does trade on a "structuralist poetics" which may remove some of these gloomy predictions. While it may sound like a tautology to state *that* a component of fiction is fictional irrespective of content, non-Aristotelian semantics will indicate *how* that difference is to be assessed. Etymologically rooted in (Latin) "telling," *Dicent*, the first structure to be examined, is here the genre of fiction, which on a functional basis includes not only epic prose but the dramatic kind as well. And drama may be versified as shown with the Shakespearean excerpt from *Romeo and Juliet*. In my structural alignment, I followed the genre determination of Käte Hamburger (1968, pp. 15-52; trans. 1973, pp. 8-54). What a novel and a play share functionally is *mimetic augmentation*. No matter how such works differ, they commence at *zero-point* and lay their foundation cumulatively by the means of concatenating non-adequated correlates, the quasi-judgments. Since these correlates are not singly perforated as in Argument, there is *progressive amplification* rather than *regressive depletion*; no obtruding reality-nexus grows at the expense of the pure referent. Instead, a simulated world emerges, invested with only those characteristics the unfolding correlates yield piecemeal at their Iconic-Indexical levels and cumulatively in their concatenation.

Before detailing non-Aristotelian Dicent further, I turn to Peirce's ten classes of signs (1960, p. 150, par. 2.264). There, "Dicent" is given in attributive form with an Indexical Sinsign as well as Legisign and a "Symbol Legisign." No matter what the obvious generative discrepancies among the three, they would not serve my purpose without modification, if for no other reason than that all become subordinated to the tenth class, Argument, as elucidated. The open format of the last trichotomy broke through such a hierarchy for the three structures. Nor is Dicent in attributive form helpful to non-Aristotelian semantics, where it is a structural determinant in full control. An exception, to be sure, is the categorical qualifier invoked while discussing the Picture of Language: all signs, beginning with the Qualisigns at the first trichotomy, become branded by the structure they enter as "Dicentic" or "Rhemic" components.

For an illustration of Peircean ideas, I go back to his former standby, the street cry. Peirce (p. 151, par. 2.265) first refers to a "Replica of a Dicent Indexical Sinsign" and then offers this example. The street cry presents an "Indexical Legisign" insofar as its tone and theme identify an individual and, as "Replica," arise in a "Dicent Sinsign" for the "individual instance." A street cry in non-Aristotelian Dicent lays the foundation of a fictional world through its Iconic Legisigns; "Indexical" is its deeper meaning, perhaps part of the theme and tone Peirce mentions. But so interwoven is this vestige with a purposive literary foundation that it cannot be a mere replica of anything but itself. In teleological constitution, this cry has become fused to its context. What may be salvaged from Peirce's Dicent instead for the intrinsic foundation of language can be found in his assertion that its

> intended Interpretant represents the Dicent Symbol as being, in respect to what it signifies, really affected by its Object, so that the existence or law which it calls to mind must be actually connected with the indicated Object (p. 149, par. 2.262).

Dicent, as postulated in my analysis, certainly becomes "affected by" and remains "connected to" its "Object" through a particular mode of "existence" that is the very "law" of operation. Indeed, through the task of Dicentic presenting that is shortly to be explained the object really is being "indicated." In addition, an "Object" is also relevant to my placement of Dicent on the open trichotomy, where it occupied the "middle" or *0-locus* between M-Rheme and I-Argument. Although this open format had eradicated any hierarchy of generation among the structures, the locus helps to characterize Dicent: it is neither mere expression nor container of an objective referent attached to a reality-nexus. Dicentic "objects" of people and places thus arise from language, ontic heteronomy; they may be termed *emergents* rather than *existents* insofar as they evolve solely from concatenating correlates.

My idea of Dicent would thus also oppose Bense's (1971, p. 27), who said under "Interpretant-relations" that "dikentisch" identifies with the "assertoric" (behauptungsfähig) sentences which are either true or false, whereas "argumentisch" governs axiomatic-deductive conditions of apodictic truth. Dicent as non-adequated structure cannot aspire to any kind of truth beyond Legisign validation and structural self-identity. To posit otherwise would get no further than espousing the "constatives" and equivalents Habermas classified for his communicative competence: any novel or drama may harbor these activities as Icons if the plot revolves around a fictive theorist. But in that fictional setting persons and their apparent propositions stay caught in the web of non-adequated correlates.

The Dicentic micro-component, the quasi-judgment correlate, also affirms the middle 0-locus for its structure: like Argument it still partakes of syntax as "-judgment"; like the Rheme its "quasi-" prefix keeps it non-adequated. Accordingly, Dicentic idiosyncrasies still reflect those of the other two structures in a type of transition though belonging to neither one. Insofar as the Dicentic unit(y) is still syntactic, furthermore, it retains the basic correlate hierarchy elucidated with Argument, as this begins with the noun initiating "objectification of the meant." The "-judgment" part has thus been covered in the preceding chapter; the "quasi-" prefix reassigns the literary contribution to this correlate as Dicentic particle. Of course, the essence differs quite drastically in accordance with this change and thus "quasi-" by no means suggests any half-hearted measure. Rather, Ingarden (1965, pp. 175-176) affirms that the quasi-judgment must be derived exclusively from a "pure expression-sentence" or "reiner Aussagesatz."

The Dicentic correlate as quasi-judgment has its tasks cut out for it, central as it is to the four strata Ingarden posits for the literary work of art. The first two strata, covered by the fourth and fifth chapters in the Literary Work of Art (pp. 25, 30-61, 61-196), take care of semantic constitution in forming the sentence, much as was analyzed in this study under the hierarchy of syntax; the last two strata, treated in Ingarden's succeeding sixth to ninth chapters (pp. 196-270, 270-307), engage in a function designated "Darstellung," which may be translated as "representation" as well as "presentation," and I choose the latter term. Language presents itself instead of being representational of other worlds while "indicating" its sphere, to draw on Peirce above. The Dicentic quasi-mirror seems to imitate an extralinguistic reality of persons in their various pursuits but actually reinforces indigenous presenting through the selected Icons and their relevant Indexes. What Icons "present" in an amalgamation attains "presence," one might say, in a world that is shaped and yet held in check by the selectional bias of authorial intent.

Icons as pure-intentional objects lay the very groundwork for the presentational objects that arise with the higher strata, where the amalgamated contents of the concatenating correlates are further knit together into unified wholes. The correlate is thus pivotal for this stratification: the first two strata shape the correlate and in the last two strata a series of correlates fashion the fictional world of presented objects called "dargestellten Gegenständlichkeiten" by Ingarden (ibid.). These objects are thus the higher generate products that result cumulatively from several concatenating correlates, down to their precise (Iconic) aspects in which they must appear. That, indeed, is the contribution of the fourth stratum, much as the presentational aspects are preordained by the Icons and their Indexes that enter at the lower strata in accordance with authorial choice. A character is only what "his" or "her" Icons bear in material contents and relevant Indexes. Such are the peculiar properties of linguistic meaning when a pure referent obtains, without any ostensive backing from a concrete situational context. So organic is the relationship between object and aspect that the last two strata might be reduced to one. But from a heuristic standpoint the strata are better separated because they help demonstrate individually idiosyncrasies of meaning.

Ingarden's *Cognition* of the literary work of art (1968, p. 264)--which was introduced with my ontological placement of language and will play a greater part in the ensuing chapter--additionally refers to wordsound formations and semantic unities as the "linguistic strata" (also Ingarden in Fieguth, 1976, p. 144). The last two strata then may be subsumed under a "presentational" qualifier. So the "-judgment" part of the correlate belongs to the linguistic strata and the "quasi-" prefix to the presentational or literary alternatives. Such a binary division also reinforces the break between Dicent and Argument through the "-judgment" both share in syntactic size. That is to say, in Argument only the linguistic strata take effect. The presentational strata are blocked from forming due to the perforation of the pure referent that adequation causes. Ingarden supports this bifurcation tacitly in the *Literary Work of Art*, since adequation is discussed toward the close of the chapter (section 24, pp. 164 ff.) covering the second stratum.

It is to Ingarden's credit that he avoids the defaults of past critics, such as the Fregean neglect of a literary "sense." Although Ingarden's primary interest is non-adequated literary language, he deals with the adequated literal kind as well. So he adopts a method equal to the obverse and reverse order I proposed for maintaining logical consistency instead of developing alleged idiosyncrasies for poetry and/or metaphor that are basic to meaning. One logical outcome is that the pure referent as primary constituent carries out its presenting without the conflict in "(non-)denoting" that afflicts Fregeans and followers. Everything the Dicentic quasi-mirror bears a language owns naturally. This "nature" as ontic heteronomy is already arepresentational, grounded as it is in signitive acts instead of empirical facts.

To illustrate quasi-judgment, I return to the prosaic looking sentence from Argument, "My pen lies on the desk," since non-Aristotelian semantics must meet the challenge of surface identity. Certainly, the Icons as lexical elements look the same. But their essence differs from the moment this sentence opens a novel, for example. True, basic nominal-verbal unfolding and interlocking proceed as before (under Argument) at the level of the linguistic strata, where reference in transaction with transference forms the correlate. Indeed, any constitution of a correlate, be it Dicentic or Rhemic in size, follows the rules of "closure" shown by the graphs that were presented where I introduced the last trichotomy. Beyond those tasks, the correlate as quasi-judgment stays in sole control. Beginning in a vacuum at zero-point without any backing from a reality-nexus, the correlate has recourse to nothing but its own contents.

Negative as this change of conditions sounds, it remains entirely positive. Instead of being perforated through adequation, the pure referent begins to lay the fictional foundation. All it offers in the way of persons rests with the bare and schematic opening, "My." This first-person possessive comes together with an object, the "pen," and that in turn is located lying in the space provided by the prepositional phrase "on the desk." "Who" is this "My" person, a man or woman, hero(ine) or villain, (dramatic) protagonist or antagonist? What significance does the "pen" play, and how will the fictive "space" widen from that one piece of furniture, the "desk," to a possible room, house, or whatever? Recipients do not conjecture this way. Led by the Referent, they remain locked into the Icons, glued to what is *there* and not missing. That goes also for the relevant Indexes weighting the Icons in their material contents with special significance. Everything is to be *derived* piecemeal from the correlates in their progressive unfolding and concatenation.

Language, in a nonskepical view, serves a Recipient through its Referent as its natural, schematic ambiguity drives the concatenation forward in an inbuilt type of suspense--thus not necessarily of the contrived kind found in a thriller. Everything is meted out in the selected contents. The dynamic elasticity, so typical of heteronomous, pure-intentional objects, permits meanings to incorporate the meaning of the fictional author through their own explicit and implicit denomination, in denotations and connotations. Beyond these contents, no one can check up on that "My" person, for instance; no vital statistics may compensate for what is not there. Only ensuing correlates offer more, a little at a time. But everything the correlates *do* provide is kneaded together into people and human preoccupations. Although these presentations go back no further than to their respective correlates, their ultimate composition transcends each single correlate.

With this kind of Iconic *steering* power, any *paraphrase* becomes truly a "heresy" (Brooks, 1947, pp. 192-213) for disrupting the quasi-mirror. Since a translation induces paraphrasing, I could take the "fountain pen" as closer in meaning to the original "Füllfeder" than "pen," but not the foregrounded "*fill-feather." Translators, like Referents, must adhere to accepted Sinsign composites that culminate in the Legisigns validated by one inventory, and this has to be shared in indented signitive convolutions by a speech community. The "*fill-feather" does not fit into that inventory as oppositional value and thus would distort the translated quasi-mirror. Having a "*fill-feather" lie on the desk and/or belong to a "My"--would be meaningless, at least without the kind of text-critical apparatus often added to Elizabethan plays for readers of modern English.

When Icons become thus contextualized and expand Indexically in the elastic ambiguity that is theirs, the literary work they compose radiates its own unique "aura," to borrow a term from Benjamin (1974, pp. 440, 489). A new, meaningful world comes to the fore with the unfolding and concatenating correlates, similar to the (symbolic) precept of disclosure cited with Heidegger's etymological construal of Greek truth as "unhiddenness." There is literally no predictable "telling" what the work will reveal and where it will end before it comes to a close, lending new significance to all its meanings, from the beginning on. The sequence of nominal-verbal unfolding and subsequent concatenation is thus *countered* at depth by the organic constitution. In the hermeneutic relationship typical of purposive wholes, last and first elements determine one another.

Temporal issues of this nature are largely reserved for my next chapter. What should be clear from the start, however, is that even a seemingly superficial phenomenon such as *length* plays a crucial part in the formation of literary genres. Dicent requires a certain length for correlate concatenation to proceed so that the presentational strata may go into effect. Argument on the other hand, may be projected singly, as was shown in various instances, just because the reality-nexus provides such strong backing, particularly in ostensive usage. Therefore, the one sentence given here actually would stop dead at the linguistic strata without the "My," for example, transcending its correlate to erupt eventually into a hero(ine) beyond this (proud) possessor of a pen. Accordingly, each correlate is something like a *mosaic*; Ingarden (1965, p. 217) speaks of "little stones" (Steinchen). Readers may interrupt their decoding which locks them into the Icons by leaning back to peruse the correlates bearing these contents at a distance. This "analytic" approach has the pure correlate manifest a type of blotchy *tachism* Ingarden renders with the adjective "fleckenartig," meaning "mottled" or "speckled."

All such phenomena reside in the essence of ontic heteronomy. The correlate of a pure referent is sprinkled with a series of Icons, such as the ones in the above sentence. Though cohering at depth through syntactic subject-and-object interaction, the correlate at its most explicit level seems to have varied material contents juggled together. These contents also rest in the schematic ambiguity that enables them to absorb the cumulative significance of the work. Argument could disambiguate the "My" through its objective referent, and I suggested such possibilities as having a person's name engraved on the pen. But a fictional context has to render any such connection through unfolding correlates. In the case of the "pen" and "desk," neither their colors nor contours are as yet disclosed, the way some were in Argument with the graphic counterparts. But this suppleness precisely succeeds where rigid ontic autonomy would fail.

To be sure, the correlate also manifests a type of *rigidity* that Ingarden (ibid., pp. 286 ff.) labels "Erstarrung." Ironically, however, this curious finitude rests in the spontaneity of all autotelic domains, specifically the selectional bias once the choice has been made, in the past tense. When the regulative act of meaning (I) determines the reference (M) in transference (0) for the constituents of its choice, there is *purposive fusion* of the one to the whole once the correlate unfolds and interlocks. Beyond the correlate constituents, the concatenation also consists of a set number of correlates. Without this finitude, nothing could be "derived" (abgeleitet, ibid., pp. 122-123) from pure-intentional objects. While autonomous-objective entities are perceived in bounds that stay fluid, "fliessend" to Ingarden (pp. 167-168), heteronomous ones in their purposive yet piecemeal foundation are "finite" or "endlich" (p. 209) insofar as they are bound to their selection.

Take the "desk": this is all the meaning yields from its Qualisign foundation on, whereas the real piece of furniture may be perceived from the front, the sides and back by walking around it, with the visual aspects changing accordingly. Although there is a type of "movement" with the correlate sequence and its concatenation, a decoder of texts gets only what the meanings yield. So the authorial will as act of meaning has ordained "My pen" and not anyone's long or short, red or blue pen, much as "later" correlates may carry these other qualifiers, explicitly or implicitly. In that natural heuristic foundation of language, encoder becomes known to decoder through the text—down to the very generate depth of the full Index, where meanings expand in their connotations. So literary works are *finished* products insofar as a choice has gone into effect. This type of finitude is, however, counteracted at depth by Indexical expansion in the meaningful relevance these schematic contents attain.

There is no manufacturer of pens, only a manipulator of native English competence who wields "pen." The person so far caught in the "My" possessive also has an identity as first presentational aspect of some fictional figure. That is an equivalent "birth"*qua* language, ontic heteronomy in new completion. When, however, the author works very consciously at manipulating the heuristic steering power of language, the aspects of *potential reinforcement* arise, Ingarden's "paratgehaltene Ansichten" (pp. 282-288, 293-295, 301-302). These aspects accentuate the presenting prowess of language. A case in point is the stylistic device, known as "leitmotif," which manifests reiteration of precise words for purposes of characterization and related emphasis. Ingarden uses the past participle "aufgezwungen" (pp. 282, 287, 293, 295, 301, passim) to underscore how these aspects are "forced" upon the Recipient by the Referent. Ironically, the extensive pagination shown for these aspects demonstrates Ingarden's own critical reinforcement of them where his readers are concerned.

Certainly, leitmotifs are inescapable enough in their Iconic intensity to invest any character or object with an identity through a reiterated identifiable trait. For instance, if the syntagma "My pen" appears often, the fictional speaker behind the possessive starts coming across as being "possessive," also self-assertive, perhaps, to the point of sounding defensive or aggressive in accordance with the development of the plot. Simultaneously the "pen" also assumes this Icon "My" as repeated presentational aspect. Fictional leitmotifs have long been popular and were utilized by such great novelists as Dickens, Flaubert, and T. Mann, among many others.

Ingarden's reinforcing aspects, however, raise some concern: they are difficult to separate from ordinary (schematic) aspects, aside from conspicuous leitmotifs. The end result, again, would be left to the devices of the lexicon. To forestall that problem, let me suggest the following modification for which Ingarden actually provides the clue. After concluding the analysis of the four strata governing the literary work of art, he turns briefly to a nonliterary "scientific" (wissenschaftliche) alternative, "the mere report" (der blosse Bericht, pp. 350-353). This is where he rightly brings up again the transparency caused by the perforation of the adequating process. The explicit contents are drained of their rich semantic potential and thus bear aspects that are skeletal, he says, because of their function rather than appearance. Consequently, I took the hint and thus suggest that all adequated works carry schematic aspects since no genuine presentation takes place here anyway, as explained, while literary counterparts possess ipso facto reinforcing aspects irrespective of appearances. Since such works start at zero-point, everything their Iconic-Indexical potential offers becomes intensified as the only source for a fictive sphere, even if conspicuous leitmotifs further accentuate reinforcement.

So much for a structural solution of aspects. Ingarden's opposite criterion to aspect reinforcement appears to be a phenomenon he (ibid., pp. 261-268 ff.) terms indeterminate spots or pockets, in German, "Unbestimmtheitsstellen." These hollow pockets seem to have the opposite effect, but they affirm in their subtle way the pure essence of linguistic meaning. Tacitly, they occur wherever the schematic material contents are invoked. In mimetic augmentation, the pockets weight Icons with relevant Indexes bearing the significance of the whole, just because the meanings stay non-adequated and thus "fill" out in their indigenous elasticity. Accordingly, these pockets parallel the conspicuous, explicit aspects as an implicit mode of reinforcement. Their indeterminateness then constitutes yet another seemingly negative factor that turns out to be positive. Certainly, few criteria of Ingarden's theory have enjoyed more attention than these indeterminate pockets (Iser, 1975, pp. 234-235).

For an immediate illustration, "My pen" may be more determinate than if the noun were preceded by an article or appeared by itself. With this compounded stretch the indigenous pointer, the direction-factor, is somewhat less polyvalent within each material content. But no matter how many attributives surround the "pen," these do not match the "determinate" vibrance of corporeal (autonomous-real) materiality; there will be pockets in "pen" omitting its color, contours, or whatever. Positively viewed, that fact makes the selection of the contents all the more important. In any case, the degree of determinacy is not really at issue since these pockets become suffused with significance from their contextualization, at which I hinted when discussing the possible construal of the pride released with the "My" possessor. The concretization plays an important part in this unique permeation.

This element of pride could exemplify an aspect of speech-act theory that Ingarden does not neglect either, which is an illocutionary force, and to that can be added a perlocutionary resolve in the developing plot, such as affirming or denying ownership of the pen. Ingarden uses the term "Kundgabe" (ibid., pp. 40-41, 193-195) for this phenomenon of speech. That it resembles illocution becomes obvious from his examples: he offers questions, wishes, and commands. At the same time he stresses that these functions become subjugated to the fictional quasi-judgment sphere: there are no real questioners, respondents, or well-wishers. All these persons remain as fictive as their actions; all are caught within the network of the unfolding and concatenating correlates. Indeed, he (pp. 135-136) uses questions and commands as examples for proving the independence of ontic heteronomy, since they cannot refer directly to anything in the world in the manner of most declarative sentences.

A corollary of Ingarden's "Kundgabe" in extended form at the level of the presentational rather than linguistic strata seems to be the "metaphysical qualities" (he took from Heidegger, pp. 310-319). Although the attributive is a bit difficult to justify in this context, the presence of these qualities is not: they emerge in the exultation or anguish of joy or fear, but do not in themselves compose a stratum. In a way, these qualities might be considered the perlocutionary impact in a fictional domain. They depend upon the intonation of words when enacted in dramatic performances, possibly making their entry behind the scenes through the stage directions, which are always read when a play is concretized that way rather than performed.

Yet another point of identity between Ingarden and the speech-act theoreticians concerns the issue of fictional "nonserious pretense" as well as a "parasitism," concepts that are implicit in the "quasi-" prefix. Indeed, the quasi-mirror of linguistic presentation by its very nature resembles a type of game, of language at play, purporting to offer the "real" thing when this is not so. Basically, however, such a game is endemic in all purposive states by trading on the materials of existents for their own whim, something taken up effectively by Kant in his (Third) Critique of Judgment (Cassirer ed., V, 1914, pp. 266, 292, 295, 298).

Where aspects of the game surface in Ingarden, he also seems most likely to be misunderstood. Ingarden (1965, pp. 176, 178) suggests the game when he says that quasi-judgments do not have their amalgamated direction-factor projected in the manner (Modus) of full "seriousness" (eines vollen Ernstes). Such ambiguous wording led critics not unjustly to disapprove of his "pseudo-statements" (Stankiewicz, 1977, p. 56). Yet Ingarden does state clearly a few pages hence (p. 182) that quasi-judgments forge only an "Illusion der Realitat." The capacity to create such an illusion of reality is indeed a power to be attributed to language in the area of the presenting strata. But even that point becomes partially misunderstood because in the context of discussing his idea of illusion Ingarden claims that quasi-judgments are not really "pure sentences" (keine reinen Aussagesätze). Also Gabriel (1975, p. 55), though generally discerning, was confused by such observations: is it not paradoxical to base quasi-judgments on pure, non-adequated correlates while denying their identity? The answer is, theoretically, that a pure sentence stands for a non-adequated correlate whereas, positively, a quasi-judgment performs the presenting tasks demanded by the last two strata of a literary work of art.

Admittedly, the distinction may be too finely cut, since a pure sentence by itself is nothing. But in defense of Ingarden (ibid., pp. 164 ff.), his ontological dichotomy involving judgment versus quasi-judgment is there from the outset. And if he does seem to play at words here in raising the issue of seriousness, he is stating something in circumlocution that non-Aristotelian semantics has stressed all along, namely that the lexicon deludes. The non-adequated sentence looks "for real," to put it simply, and gives the impression of being projected into the extralinguistic reality although this is not, and cannot be, the case. Some of these aspects concerning Ingarden's poetics have been covered satisfactorily in a recent (1981) treatise by Falk. An earlier work on phenomenology by Magliola (1977, pp. 107-141) is also helpful in part but still grapples with Ingarden's ontology between real and ideal autonomy as well as the "intentional object" belonging to ontic heteronomy. In view of some of Ingarden's less than lucid definitions one may not wonder why Magliola (p. 111) finds certain areas of the second linguistic stratum "very entangled" in explanation.

Experts on speech-act theory no doubt may point out also that notion's of literary nonseriousness were familiar to them. True, Austin (1975, p. 22) touched on something that resembled a lack of adequation when he said of an actor's performative utterance that it stayed "in a peculiar way hollow or void." Austin then goes on to maintain that the language of poems or soliloquies is "used not seriously, but in ways parasitic upon its normal use . . ."(ibid., his italics). To be sure, the pure referent feeds upon itself, in a manner of speaking. But the parasitism Austin posits suggests that literature exploits so-called normal use. Underlying such a literary parasitism is the notion among Fregean followers that the language of poetry and/or metaphor cannot denote or refer to anything without being propped up by standard language--a theory not far removed from the proxy-tenet.

Indeed, the East German critic, Bierwisch (1965, pp. 53, 59 ff.), espoused such a poetic parasitism in defense of lexical deviance (Abweichung). Not surprisingly, the Baumgärtner survey covering a linguistic poetics cited before (1969, pp. 26-27) rejected that theory as inconclusive, along with the rest of the recent attempts. Plett (1975, pp. 134-135) then dealt with Baumgärtner's reaction to Bierwisch in terms of the imposition of "secondary structures" upon "normal" ones such a theory involves. The great advantage of Ingarden's position is that the pure referent stays primary just because it never goes into adequation.

The idea of a literary parasitism coupled with the "pretense tenet" in nonserious performances were nevertheless passed on from Austin to followers. Two particular essays by Ohmann (1971) and Searle (1974-75) make that legacy evident. Even their phrasing is similar: Ohmann has "stretches of speech," Searle "stretches of discourse"; Ohmann seizes on an illocutionary force which stays "mimetic," Searle on an illocutionary act that is "pretended." Searle (ibid., p. 327) further makes his indebtedness to Austin explicit by quoting him on how an author of fiction "pretends to perform illocutionary acts by way of actually performing phonetic and phatic acts." In addition, Searle's work on speech acts (1970, pp. 78-79) echoes Austin when he labels literary use a "parasitic discourse and meaning" aimed at a "let's-pretend mode of discourge."

A nice colloquial description, if one goes in for that kind of thing! Of greater benefit may be Searle's two planes which distinguish "horizontal conventions of fiction" from "vertical connections of serious speech" (ibid., pp. 327, 331). As my next chapter will reveal, succession in non-adequated ("nonserious"?) spheres like those of quasi-judgments is indeed confined to textual chronologies rather than to the vertical historicity of genuine temporal succession, no matter how faithfully time becomes simulated through the quasi-mirror. If Searle got that far with fictional time, he unfortunately did not extend that wisdom to fictional space, since he is inconsistent enough to claim (ibid., p. 330) that "London" and "Baker Street" in a Conan Doyle novel, for instance, remain "non-fictional" vestiges. What Searle should have said was just the opposite: these lexical place names, too, become incorporated into what he terms the horizontal conventions of fiction. So here is a typical case of being deluded by the nonserious pretense of a lexical quasi-mirror.

Fortunately my textual analyses will contain so many place names that, by the end of this study, no one will be able to doubt their use in non-adequated, horizontal, structures. At least, Searle touches on the very problem this study has taken up. He (1974-75, p. 320) realizes that the traditional "metaphor" may occur either in "fiction" or "nonfiction." Then he adds that "some jargon" is needed to keep "metaphorical" synonymous with "nonliteral" while opposing "fictional utterances" which are instead "nonserious." Searle is trying to say that "metaphor," as he understands it, should not be "serious" just because it is "nonfictional" or "literal," and yet it cannot be "nonserious" if it is definitely not "fictional" or "literary."

Well, non-Aristotelian semantics will provide what Searle irreverently calls the "jargon" which places metaphor categorically within its structure, just because a localized, lexical surface fails to sever the literal from the literary alternative as he just proved. That is to say, the non-Aristotelian metaphor will be "nonserious" in Searle's terminology insofar as it stays non-adequated no matter what its surface registers, and yet it will be "nonfictional" by not sharing the constitutional unit(y) of Dicent. When separated by proper functional differences, "metaphor" evolves as a structural idiosyncrasy that cannot die or disappear as it did in the Ingendahl Experiment. The structure to which it belongs as micro-component is the Rheme, and the works that harbor it partake of lyric poetry. Though based fundamentally on Ingarden's phenomenological semantics, this structure required modification because his theory did not take it up in detail. Indeed, Ingarden (1965, p. 188) had to defend himself against Käte Hamburger by saying that as a foreign speaker he deemed it inappropriate to tackle such a language-bound phenomenon as lyric poetry.

Actually, Ingarden's Cognition of the literary work of art, which (my study has indicated) first came out in Polish, does cover lyric poetry. This work becomes more relevant for my next chapter on concretization, and that it does may prove in itself that Ingarden did not explore the lyric construct with the same consistency he applied to fiction. Of immediate relevance to my analysis may be merely a comment from a Polish essay that was translated into German (Fieguth, 1976, pp. 102 ff.) and finds him probing the experimentalist style of a native poet, Tuwim. Ingarden notes that such a poem yields no genuine presentation of fictional objects since it lacks the progressive continuity of plot formation.

What became apparent to Ingarden in this extreme case applies categorically to the Rheme. A plot is obviously something lyric poetry does not possess: the Rheme tells no story, is not preoccupied with "doings"--in my translation of the Aristotelian "prattontes" (Käte Hamburger, 1968, p. 17). To be sure, Icons always "present" through the very material contents they carry. That is the natural function of explicit contents, for which reason they are made so easily the target of erroneous categories, as in the case of the traditional metaphor. However, the Icons that go "up" the strand into the Rheme have become *expressants--objects of expression* for a *totality of expression* within which lies embodied the authorial will. The correlate, called "poetic intext," is no longer *syntactic* but *contextual*. That is to say, correlation as embodied in the double-intentionality between act of meaning and meanings proceeds through teleological "closure" as before, but the transaction between reference and transference now *extends* to the circumference of the entire context.

The impact of those changed conditions will be given after adding some relevant pointers from Peirce (1960, p. 150, par. 2.264), taken again from his ten sign classes. My selected presentation here of the Peircean Rheme might be expressed figuratively as the degenerate "left corner" of his schema.

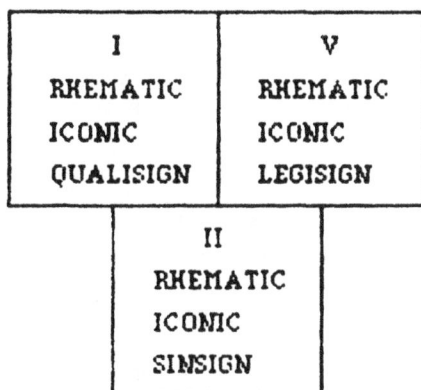

I RHEMATIC ICONIC QUALISIGN	V RHEMATIC ICONIC LEGISIGN

II RHEMATIC ICONIC SINSIGN

As with Dicent, the term "Rhematic" appears in the attributive, which is not suitable for designating a vital structure in non-Aristotelian semantics. The part of the Peircean schema included above, moreover, was not chosen for the "Rhematic" qualifier alone but also for its linkage with the "Iconic"--made "iconic" in this conspicuous association, I might add. Out of a total of six Rhematic classes, Peirce's other "Rhematic" signs accompany the "Indexical Singsign" (III), "Indexical Legisign" (VI), and "Symbol Legisign" (VIII). So in semiotic hierarchy of generation, the Rhematic ascends to eight of Peirce's ten sign classes, with "Dicent" interspersed (in IV and VII). When one confronts his whole schema, the

Rhematic factor sustains that diagonal "left-corner" appearance even after adding all these sign classes.

The *Iconic* "corner" is relevant to my own placement of the Rheme at "M." While this M-locus applies to the third trichotomy, it reflects the Icons in that M-position within their second trichotomy. Now that the open format of the last trichotomy is complete, one may well contrast the Rheme with the other two structures. In what is for the strands a "degenerate" direction although a hierarchy between them does not count, the Rhemic M-level might exemplify a "Hypoicon"; it neither shapes the fictional "objects" governing Dicent at 0-locus nor accounts for an "objective" referent, as did Argument at I.

My allusion to the Hypoicon for the structure that bears the functional metaphor may seem apt. The Hypoicon came up in discussing Peirce, who used the term for his semiotic metaphor. However, at the time, I stated that as single entity Peirce's concept was not far removed from the traditional metaphor with its localized analogy-in-anomaly precept and the proxy barter this induced. Peirce (1960, p. 157, par. 2.277) focused on the representation of a representamen that represents "a parallelism in something else." The phrasing I reiterate here verbatim has analogy and anomaly clad in the respective "parallelism" and "(something) else"--to the extent that the fidelity to tradition harks back to Aristotle's concept for semantic alienation, the "allotrios," which surfaces in the adjunct of this study. But even those who followed Peirce could not improve on that inherently lexical orientation of the Hypoicon, as was shown with Bense's turtledove Johanna, whose terms of endearment certainly clung to Legisign neutrality and thus could not be contained by structure.

Nor were Peirce's other Rhematic signs included in the above schema, simply because they do not have sufficient bearing on any facet of non-Aristotelian semantics. "Sinsign" and "Index" have their locus at Object-relation, while "Legisign" and "Symbol" occupy the Interpretant corners of the respective M-0 trichotomies. To be sure, the signs that enter a structure are branded by that structure, so that from the first Qualisign on, the signs have to be "Rhemic" ("Rhematic") when they forge lyric poetry. That condition applies so unilaterally that I omitted it from the presentations although not without a comment.

As for my suggestion of using "Hypoicon" to characterize the entire Rheme as structure, this works in the way of a reminder that the M-base becomes a type of logo for "Metaphor" as well and, indeed, for a distinctively "metonymic" *parts-to-whole relation* that remains nonlexical. Neither Johanna nor a string of endearments affect this relation but only the extension of one correlate for a context which no longer is shaped by a series of smaller, concatenting correlates. Since non-Aristotelian semantics has proceeded methodically in an obverse and reverse order, "transference" as such is not at issue but only a modified--specifically an expanded--form of transference. Accordingly the Rheme becomes differentiated systematically from Dicent and Argument in the switch from a syntactic to a contextual type of correlate that stays also non-adequated in usage. The "literal" language of Argument is thus cut off categorically from the literary "metaphor" of the Rheme. And structurally, Dicent bears neither literal language nor metaphor. The colorful, deviant lexicon can still be described as "metaphor" in any of these structures but certainly stays loose "jargon," to echo Searle, just because of that ubiquity.

Even non-Aristotelian semantics may draw on the convenience of concrete manifestations, although never with the idea of reifying these by making them into "semantic" criteria of function. One case in point is *size*, which may be distinguished as *Dicentic length* versus *Rhemic width*. Ironically, it is the *extended* correlate of the Rheme that necessitates the greater *brevity*, although when followed through logically, this makes sense. Dicentic concatenation needs a degree of progression, if without specifying the length in actual number of words; Rhemic breadth cannot absorb the same voluminous continuum. Beyond appearances, the reason for curbing size concerns the manner in which poetic intext acquires its circumference. The act of meaning (I) that Icons (M) corporealize and Indexes (0) embody becomes engendered *directly* through the contextual whole. In mimetic augmentation, this whole forms *indirectly*, since constitution begins within the smaller units of the correlates and then progresses with their concatenation. Argument is not confined to size, since the reality-nexus supports the single statement, as was brought out with the idioms, while extended written works undergo depletion anyway through the perforation of each concatenating correlate.

With the breadth of the Rheme, the activities of *reference* and *transference*—Ingarden's "Meinen" and "Vermeinen"—span the whole through each part. Each micro-component as structural metaphor consists of a centrifugal Icon whose *reference* causes the poetic expression to unfold and whose centripetal Index *shifts* with the extended transference to release the connotations relevant to the whole in maximal compounding. In this manner, the Rhemic constituent effects constitution between the one and the whole as direct part of an entire context. Micro-component and macro-structure then become immediately intertwined as cohering *lyric ego* or *subject* at depth. Yet "ego" is a constitutive principle here, implicit in a poetic Referent; it does not apply to a psychological disposition or an author as "person" who is rendered in an "I," or in the "My" above, for that matter.

This Rhemic extension from syntax to poetic context is thus the only other possible alternative for positing a structure based on *units natural* to language in the constitution of a correlate. To be sure, when the text exhibits concrete evidence, the structure is easiest to prove. A surface registering disrupted syntax down to asyndetic elements projects the Rheme conspicuously. In view of my analysis, I can add that such a surface substantiates the Rheme at depth. At the same time, non-Aristotelian semantics claims that even when sentences are present they are no longer the fundamental constitutive unities where this structure is concerned.

If a last alternative, the Rheme has to encompass the experimental endeavors of Concrete Poetry as well. This postwar trend really tries to "concrete" the M-base, down to its most degenerate material in Qualisign dispositions. Words cluster together while shaping patterned "Constellations" (Gumpel, 1976, pp. 90 ff.). Instead of tightly interwoven lyric contexts, the Concretist vignettes give rise to loose "connexes." Their selected Icons and Indexes appear so disparate in choice that they resemble discrete vocables, keeping the transaction between reference and transference at a minimum. Whatever the variation in Concrete Poetry, none is so drastic as to require a separate structure. Although the loose connexes seem "open," a selection of contents has occurred as always, demarcating authorial choice in teleological fusion through the closure discussed. Perhaps it seems less fitting to call components of these connexes outright "metaphor," just because transference has been attenuated as noted. But then again, the minimal regulation of Indexes by an act of meaning permits these to burgeon in their implicit range, with few implications suppressed, since none becomes irrelevant. In that respect, then, connotative compounding is met. And Concrete Poetry certainly fits into the non-Aristotelian division: since it possesses neither a syntactic circumference nor an adequated objective referent, Dicent and Argument are ruled out, leaving the Rheme.

The changed priorities of the Rheme logically influence two vital areas. One of them concerns syntactic hierarchy and the other stratification. With syntax no longer in constitutive control, the noun is no longer highest in that constitution. Expressed positively, every Rhemic particle as structural metaphor is a *noun* in essence. Of course, I am applying Ingarden's dynamic phenomenological interpretation of the noun here, which was "objectification of the meant." This task now extends directly from the single constitutent to poetic intext, causing the direction-factor to intensify as though it possessed the range of the pointer nouns carry, even when operative signs rather than eidetic ones are involved. Semantic functioning at the level of the Rheme is thus a process of *nominalization* (Gumpel, 1971), embedded in the extended transference of these non-Aristotelian metaphors. With nominalized expansion rather than mimetic augmentation in the presenting Ingarden had claimed for fiction, the strata, too, have to be modified as shown.

RHEMIC STRATA

1) LINGUISTIC WORDSOUND: HYLETIC BASE
2) SEMANTIC UNITIES: EXTENDED TO INTEXT
3) BACKGROUNDED LYRIC EGO: INDEXICALIZATION
4) FOREGROUNDED LYRIC EGO: ICONIZATION

The original binary division of two linguistic and two literary types of strata is kept intact. First, there must be wordsound formations yielding semantic thresholds that Legisigns have validated. Except for Concretist extremes, semantic unities must also form. Due to the contextual immediacy of the Rheme, however, the second stratum is harder to separate from the following two, for which reason I almost reduced Rhemic strata to three in all. Semantic unities, after all, cohere differently when backgrounding is next in line. Still, there is cursory interlocking especially when whole sentences are present, no matter how amplified these become from the full nominalization. This coherence spreads to a fully backgrounded and foregrounded lyric ego at the third and fourth strata. With the final stratum, the original wordsound becomes nominalized: the compounded connotations seep into the M-base. reaching all the way "back" to the degenerate sonorous and visual Qualisigns.

It should be a foregone conclusion for Rhemic immediacy that the foregrounded M-base cannot be severed from its compounded background in the manner of the automatized expressions that were discussed with the Czech Structuralists. On the contrary, so interwoven are these strata that *bilingual* versions should always accompany a translated text of the Rheme. Then decoders may see at least the original foregrounding of the M-base even if it cannot be transported closely enough into the other language. From a pragmatic standpoint, the greater brevity of the Rheme facilitates such bilingual presentations. My treatment of the textual analyses will underscore the crucial need for such considerations given the literary strata of the Rheme.

Indeed, so intimate is that coherence in the Rheme that a *recursiveness* obtains, and not just for the verbal direction-factor that meets and interlocks with a preceding nominal counterpart in a syntactic correlate. Rather, that recursiveness was insinuated when I described the nominalized wordsound as flowing "back" into the M-base after full generation of the strata. That is also why I kept all four strata. The linguistic strata go *forward* with the sequence to effect the semantic unities cursorily; the literary-Rhemic strata permeate the whole in a *backward* direction, giving the backgrounded, nominalized parts their full chance to intensify in every corner of poetic intext, in a *vertical* as well as *horizontal* dimension. So semantic unities are forged but not reinforced in full compounding until pulled through--to put it simply--the last two strata of backgrounding and foregrounding. Because of that recursiveness, in fact, Rhemic foregrounding displays utmost *fusion* on the surface; "meaning" here penetrates to not only the selection of explicit and implicit denominations but their very positioning. Accordingly, the constituents do not fall as they may at the edge of a page but have been carefully spaced in their textual sectors. In view of these changed conditions, let me offer a listing of priorities.

RHEMIC HIERARCHIES

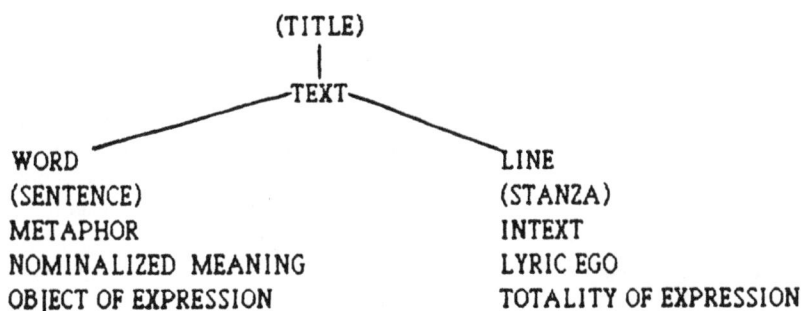

```
                      (TITLE)
                         |
               _____TEXT_____
              /                    \
      WORD                          LINE
      (SENTENCE)                    (STANZA)
      METAPHOR                      INTEXT
      NOMINALIZED MEANING           LYRIC EGO
      OBJECT OF EXPRESSION          TOTALITY OF EXPRESSION
```

The elements in parentheses are optional, the others obligatory. A title may be omitted in lyric poetry although it plays a vital part when added by the poet. In the recursive nature of this structure, the title-to-text relation has the text rush forward while simultaneously the title gains in significance "back" at the top, where it appears in this table. This significance may be reinforced explicitly at the *Iconic* level or implicitly at the *Indexical* level. Either the title is concretely *expressive* by matching the material contents of a text or it is mainly *interpretive* of the import that evolves. Käte Hamburger (1968, pp. 213, 214), though using the dichotomy of "object-relation" versus "subject-relation," made me cognizant of this distinction between title and text.

The "Text," following a title when present, then introduces a couple of other optional elements. Whether optional or oligatory, the textual listings to the left divide vertically into micro-components and to the right into corresponding macro-components. Thus "word" is met horizontally with "line" in obligatory pairing while the "sentence" and "stanza" become the optional counterparts. "Metaphor" is complemented by "intext" as constitutional unit(y) and the fully "nominalized" (backgrounded and foregrounded) meaning coheres as "lyric ego." The task of each element is to serve as "object of expression" for the "totality of expression" that goes with authorial intent. All Rhemic constituents thus equal "expressants" instead of the (progressive) fictional "emergents." Of course, the left-sided specifications are just facets of the structural metaphor.

There is a reason for the extended listing and the various facets. First, the "word" is not to be taken too literally. The textual analyses will reveal that "metaphor" as nominalized meaning and/or object of expression--may sink to the level of a punctuation mark! So "word" affirms mainly a unit smaller than the sentence or phrase. Second, the poetic line, though one convenient mark for identifying the presence of the Rheme, needs the kind of underpinning it is given in the table above just because both Dicent and Argument may contain it. Shakespearean drama is one case in point, while any versified commercial jingle proves as much for Argument. There are thus "lyric" accouterments outside of the Rheme which do not account for structure. To be sure, the line of Dicent also breaks up syntax and depends on a degree of recursiveness. But the Dicentic line is nevertheless subordinated to mimetic augmentation in concatenating correlates. And the perforation caused by the adequating process blocks thorough foregrounding and backgrounding in some commercial use of the line. Although the line is mandatory for the Rheme, its outer ubiquity thus necessitates the type of backing the Rhemic hierarchies above include.

All three structures have now been analyzed, the two literary ones so far only as constructs. Let me repeat that these structures are based on *units natural* to the *disposition* of *linguistic meaning*, to the point of permitting no further alternatives, unless there is an interest in *historical genres*, in which case I recommend the detailed exploration of genre theories by Hempfer (1973, pp. 18-19, 23, 143, passim), although his is the typical diachronic approach that offers little genuine synthesis beyond describing the varied theories of critics past and present.

Now, what of the "pen" sentence? It was carried forward from Argument to Dicent, and nothing is to stop lexical neutrality from letting it open a line of a poem. However, because of the immediate, recursive nature of poetic intext, this structure is toughest to fragment for the heuristic purpose of illustration. Also, aspects of concretization assume greater importance in the Rheme than in the case of the other two structures, for which reason more detailing will be postponed. The subsequent textual analyses, however, are exhaustive, let the reader be assured. They will not proceed either without pointing out advantages of a non-Aristotelian over a neo-Aristotelian metaphor left to localized spotsighting. The only identity between the two principles may well be the etymology of the original "metaphora" to suggest that "transference" matters to both if hardly as a function opposing reference.

Briefly, the possessive "My" initiating this correlate is not the holistic lyric ego despite the first-person Icon. As Rhemic particle, this "My" becomes *ipso facto* a metaphor, a nominalized meaning though outwardly still an operative sign. The "My" thus interlocks at the horizontal level with elements of its line and at recursive-vertical levels with titular elements, if present, as well as textual components; anaphoric, prosodic, assonantal, rhyming, and alliterative relations form and eventually heighten this Sinsign composite in foregrounded Qualisign resonance. An otherwise modest entry, "My" is here an object of expression, fixed in exact location just because it coheres precisely with the whole as one speck occupying space in a totality of expression.

While a basic presenting of the "My" as "person" may not be eradicated from the Iconic material content, it hangs suspended instead of being cumulatively augmented as in Dicent; no presentation converts the "My" into one aspect of a fictional character. Rather, the priority goes to what the "My" contributes to the whole through its Iconic value and Indexical interlocking, even if full construal is even less predictable here without a whole context. The point is, nevertheless, that the overt possessive as operative sign has become a nominalized meaning, a functional metaphor geared to constitution of the whole through its own denominations. The textual analyses will hold a few surprises in store for the reader by demonstrating how far such a constituent may strain in this task. A unique coherence results from that "metonymic" relation of carefully spaced parts to the whole. That is about as much as can be disclosed before dealing with the concretization of these two literary constructs--next.

Dicent and Rheme in Concretization: Time and Stance Through Genre

Concretization is the term Ingarden uses for assimilating a literary work of art, when a construct assumes what he (1965, pp. 353 ff.) calls "life" (Leben) as it passes through the consciousness of a reader. This topic will be discussed in conjunction with *time* and *stance*. Concretization is time incarnate. As a process, indeed a processing of the construct, concretization proceeds in phases that synchronize the continuity of decoding with the encoded sequence of a work. Stance promotes such synchronization; it is a constitutive rather than psychologistic principle and will be accompanied by the concept of a "superreader." Although the term resembles the "archilecteur" Riffaterre (1975, pp. 177-181) introduced as a means of responding to textual control, my superreader is adapted to the structural divisions of non-Aristotelian semantics.

The issues surrounding time and stance in the area of concretization are certainly complex, occasionally to the point of seeming paradoxical. Since the textual analyses follow, all the idiosyncrasies involving the constructs and their concretization recur and are thus clarified further in the full application of my theory. The applied part also includes Argument with its reality-nexus, since all three structures are then to be tested empirically. On occasion Argument also enters into this discussion, particularly when needed to indicate differences that affect the presence of a reality-nexus, because the juxtaposition with an objective referent induces the presence of (autonomous-)real time and space in language.

Even my exposition up to this point has provided a variety of clues that should seem vital to concretization. Despite the fact that literary genres do not partake of "real" time because they lack a reality-nexus, they give rise to temporal features at the level of the linguistic and the literary strata. The strata themselves embody an element of succession through their hierarchy. That the linguistic strata go by sequence was indicated above when I mentioned the synchronization effected during concretization. But even that relatively conspicuous evidence is eradicated by the fact that word order is not consonant with hierarchies of semantic constitution. There is succession on the surface and teleological fusion at depth; the organic whole knows no "first" or "last" based on sheer sequence. In Dicent the word order of the syntactic correlate is partially countered by the recursive direction-factor of the verb, and in the Rheme the entire poetic intext is characterized by a recursive trait that prevents doing justice to the title until the text has been read. While all extensive nominal-verbal unfolding in modern Western languagues occurs in a left-to-right sequence, this order is countermanded by the intensive nominal-verbal interlocking, or the connotative compounding of the Rheme. Without such organic interaction, no "closure" occurs and no semantic contiguities arise.

Icons, too, may reflect time through their material contents. Yet it is that degenerate "material" of Qualisign sound or print which ironically survives Icons by existing permanently in (autonomous-)real time and space. When written, Qualisigns cling to their pages even after their language has died. What they lack then is the semantic threshold which resides in the first linguistic stratum of (sonorous and visual) wordsound formations. However, as long as Qualisigns stay suffused with full generation, they support the four strata the constructs own; they are never material replicas of words but the very "ground" of the entire purposive work they compose.

If that ground never becomes activated, however, even when there is every chance of doing so, the construct also loses touch with the times: the only means of bringing literary works back into time is, indirectly, through the interlocutory partnership consisting of historically determined beings. If less than a handful of literary scholars peruse a work just long enough to paraphrase its fable or the gist of its lyric expression for others, an artificial mediation exists between a Referent and Recipient. A construct needs active "renewal" of communication between an encoding Referent and a decoding Recipient, as well as the multiple Recipients among one another. One might quip and say that the further generation of a work depends on the future generations of readers; the work survives as they revive it in different periods. As long as these concretizing agents share the signitive convolutions and linguistic indentations of the inventory a Referent used in selection, they may become effective Recipients of the work.

Drawing all that information together from the standpoint of temporal perspectives, a work bears a *past* as inception, and breaks into the *present* through its immediate concretization. Since concretization is never cut off, the work enjoys a "posterity" in the *future* as well. A unique contemporaneousness thus clings to the work, yet its past cannot be buried. The linguistic strata keep the meanings anchored in the lingo of their period and the literary strata bring the construct forward in ever expanding meaningfulness. Accordingly, the linguistic strata *fix* the time of diachronic stages, while the literary stata, trading on atemporal *synchronic* states, keep time *fluid*. The linguistic strata thus force a Recipient to "return" to the stages of oppositional values reached at the time of Referent inception. Once the stages have been recognized as synchronic states of an earlier inventory, the reception can bring the Referent *forward* in the growth the work experiences as it "speaks" to succeeding generations of Recipients.

The linguistic strata register the idiolect of their author in commonplaces current at the time of inception, even if a work is anonymous. When not misread--as mistaken lexical deviance!--these commonplaces become part of the poetic diction that identifies a Referent in many works. The incipient perpetuation of a work then immortalizes its author. That is to say, through the "life" a work attains from concretization its creator, though long dead, continues to live. A human corpse cannot be activated in the manner of degenerate linguistic Qualisigns. To be sure, sometimes the popularity of a work over time is *cyclical* rather than linear.

An illustration for the ramified temporal aspects covered so far is yet another Shakespearean work, *Hamlet*. Its language, Elizabethan English, is essentially "dead" since no one today shares this inventory except at a written and mostly literary level. All modern Recipients, therefore, must "return" to the Elizabethan oppositional system where this differs from their own English or misconstrue Icons that still appear extant but not in the same indented Indexes. A text-critical apparatus may be needed although it will function as an artificial mediating "Recipient" between the interlocutory partners. Fortunately, the majority of Elizabethan Legisigns are still sufficiently intact to permit the work to become concretized often, in readings or performances, so that it may stay "alive" instead of sitting on dusty shelves as Qualisigns. Because such reactivation has been possible, the work has grown in value throughout the years, with the advent of Freudian psychology, or whatever. At the level of the literary presenting strata there has been growth, but the linguistic strata continue to reflect unchanged the Elizabethan era.

Accordingly, the diachronic linguistic strata of *Hamlet* bear *ipso facto* the historical background of Shakespeare's own English, from whose inventory he selected Icons and Indexes. Conversely, the choice of historical background for the plot of his drama at the literary level was entirely up to Shakespeare once he dealt with Legisigns validated in his era. The same rule applies to the space: even the geographical verisimilitude of setting Hamlet's Elsinore in Denmark is only a signitive game for that simulating quasi-mirror, a theatrical illusion that should not delude an astute Recipient as reader or spectator of the drama. Denmark, the country in that Northern Baltic region, does not come to the text as an adequated reference; this Iconic "country" has as its "ground" only degenerate Qualisign material, going back no further. Yet from that material arises a fictional country whose "rotten" state has become famous for all time. This work is cited also because it opens auspiciously with something like the street cry that came up variously while discussing Peirce: a "Who's there?"uttered by castle guards rings out on streets and over moats paved with words. "There" or "here," "now" or "then" are adverbs in Icons that have relinquished their space and time, beyond their validation for a language which in this case sees modern English match its Elizabethan forebear.

Any concretization thus resuscitates a construct, curiously by bringing it back into a new time period with its old time intact. This "old" diachronic time, above the Elizabethan English, proves indirectly that the author began as speaker, deploying Argument in full contact with the empirical reality and through interlocutory partnership with other speakers of that era, none of whom may have possessed the skills of a Shakespeare. Behind the validated Icons and Indexes deployed by these speakers resides the (semiotic) Symbol which in its motility mediated the feedback and feedforward that recorded the modes of externalizing Elizabethan English as it internalized them for future recall. Through this activity, Elizabethan English became indented and preserved in the signitive convolutions its speakers shared intersubjectively and of which the linguistic strata continue to provide the proof.

Although many ordinary speakers may never deploy literary language themselves, they possess the full power of recognition they need in order to communicate with such a dramatist or poet. They may have acquired their "Mother" tongue by projecting language into the extralinguistic reality first. But soon they confront the "fictional" base of fairy tales as well as the "lyric" mnemonics of nursery rhymes, since all my structures are based on units natural to language. A superreader thus monitors appropriate Recipient compliance with comparative ease. Recipient *stance* is the means of culling the Referent as authorial will (I) from explicit and implicit components (M-0), and everything divulged above applies to that rule. Through stance, Recipient "meets" Referent by way of the text. Obviously, nothing like the "intentional Fallacy" of Wimsatt and Beardsley (1967, pp. 3-18) is involved in such a meeting ground: "people" or "persons" with their private thoughts, motives, sensations, and purely biographical backgrounds are not at issue. The point is that the "mind" of an author as creator of a work resides as constitutive consciousness within that work, specifically through the words it comes to carry.

The reciprocal roles first presented in discussing the Picture of Language showed that a single author or poet often becomes numerically countermanded by the multiple recipience of a "public." The superreader thus resembles in function a type of collective noun by appearing mostly in the *singular* and yet covering an effective readership at large. This use of the singular is an exception and may thus occasion the use of sexist pronouns, something this study has tried studiously to avoid. But the singular has certain benefits. It underscores the fact that concretization is always individual, as all conscious acts have to be, even in the more passive role of Recipient rather than Referent. Despite the one concretizing subject, all "-subjective" inclinations nevertheless stay suppressed, affirming the "inter-" link for the intersubjective state. This state is the only recourse to any "objectivity" for purposive media such as language, including the meanings that compose Hamlet's state of Denmark.

As for the "super-" prefix of the "-reader," its positive connotations are supposed to stress the fundamentally *ideal* condition on which this study has relied from the start. Thus little or no emphasis will be put on distractions, pathological aberrations, outside interruptions, and related obstacles that cause flawed concretizations through various mechanics of construal. Naturally, borderline cases that threaten the "super-" prefix in vital areas of semantics will come up in their proper place.

When concretization in conjunction with time and stance has been analyzed exhaustively, I shall add just a brief survey to indicate where these issues surfaced before and what became of them. Since I mentioned Riffaterre in conjunction with the superreader, let me begin there. I draw on the essay that aimed to rectify an approach to (Baudelaire's) poetry others had attempted. Under one of the sections entitled "The Poem as a Response" (1966, pp. 202-205) the superreader is cited as a convenient "tool of analysis" by mediating between the poet's "message and the addressee--the reader." The superreader, says Riffaterre, manages to "reconstitute" a "context" and keeps the "contact" decidedly "assured by the control the message has over the reader's attention . . ." The idea of reconstitution and contact through textual control is apt. But, unfortunately, Riffaterre's approach does not by-pass lexical deviance by implication when he declares in the same context that where the text "holds up" the superreader one may reckon with "poetic structure."

Plainly, Riffaterre goes nowhere near far enough. A hold up of this nature relies on surface oddity, which can happen in any of the three structures when the language is not that conspicuously "literal" or "literary." Therefore I turn once again to Ingarden, although Riffaterre will be cited sporadically. This time, it is Ingarden's *Cognition* which plays a major part in the ensuing analysis. Dicent and Rheme are semiotic concepts but, ontologically, they need to be boosted by phenomenological semantics. Similar to Riffaterre's above reconstitution is Ingarden's "Rekonstruktion" in the *Cognition* (1968, p. 294; see also excerpt in Warning, ed., 1975, pp. 57-58).

Concretization thus reconstitutes and/or reconstructs a literary work of art. In its most rudimentary aspect, *time* is to be detailed first as succession in terms of the *sequence* which surfaces as *horizontal chronology*. Concretization adjusts the encoded syntagma to the decoding process. This synchronization affects modern literary works of art in visual or orthogrpahic dimensions since the oral tradition is ancient. But mute sound accompanies the visual base as well, for which reason I kept Ingarden's "wordsound." My study on the whole has concentrated more heavily on the written language, even while treating Argument, since my own role as author facilitates an illustration in written form. Here I display the left-to-right sequence, for instance, as it spills over onto the line below when the edge of the page has been reached. Accordingly, the syntactic correlates break apart on the surface, if not as units of semantic constitution, as they are pushed onto the next line. Conversely, the line of verse curbs sequence by predetermining all breaks.

Ingarden uses for sequence the term "Aufeinanderfolge" (1965, pp. 326 ff.; 1968, pp. 95 ff.). In a literal translation the term refers to the manner in which elements "follow (upon) one another." What the sequence of encoding and decoding reflects is the inner consciousness of time, which philosophers have recognized at least since Kant. At its level, linguistic sequence thus reinforces the "mental" origin of ontic heteronomy as pure-intentionality. Since even Argument forms first at the pure referent, this basic condition applies to all structures. After all, despite the reality-nexus Argument acquires through the objective referent, it shares the linguistic strata with the other two structures.

Moreover, the *overt sequence* becomes counteracted by *covert simultaneity*. The act of reading counters the act of meaning that extends holistically along the length and breadth of any correlate, small or extended as in the Rheme. That is to say, thetic generation and/or double intentionality, as this involves the transaction between reference and transference, must stay *atemporal*. Otherwise there would be no teleological unit(y) where first and last elements mutually determine one another irrespective of the precise word order. Consequently, only the actual act of reading takes place in real, vertical time, with minutes and hours ticking away, days or months passing. The sheer temporal occurrence of concretization is thus *Newtonian* enough to permit the more mechanical types of measures just cited.

Larger Dicentic works have their concretization interrupted and meted out in other, later periods. A novel also may be serialized in some journal over months or years. Such a duration, built on interruptions, could heighten suspense in so-called cliffhangers as well as weaken concentration sufficiently to impair the "super-" prefix of the reader by operating under these less than ideal temporal conditions.

Just as degenerate Qualisign material stays with a work, so does real vertical time in historical occurrence cling to the act of reading. However, minutes or hours do not satisfy that "inner" aspect of satisfactory superreader assimilation. Accordingly, Ingarden's *Cognition* (1968, pp. 106-107, ff.) introduces *qualitative* in addition to *quantitative* time phases. Contradictory as qualitative time sounds, it remains valid as an appropriate *mnemonic* device which monitors the requisite assimilation. Though stated by Ingarden to be ruled by a "time differential" (Verschiedenzeitigkeit) among readers or readings, the qualitative phases resist mechanical time. Their "clock-time" (Uhr-Zeit) is still temporal insofar as qualitative phases have one phase yield to the next. But the priority here is on grasping the deeper semantic integration and not on a time span doled out in set amounts. Obviously, Riffaterre's notion of textual control is relevant to these qualitative phases as more complex works lengthen their duration. (Since mnemonic phases embody "inner time," it is not surprising that Ingarden in this context mentions the early exponent on this subject, the French philosopher Henri Bergson, 1859-1941).

Next is what I shall designate *epochal* time, which governs discrepancies between the *inception* and *reception* of a literary work of art. The epochal dichotomy was implicit in my introductory comments on the diachronic and synchronic distinctions. Where there exists an epochal gap between inception and reception, alert superreaders must "return" to the inception because this mirrors the linguistic inventory of the era in which the work was written. The epochal time factor is tremendously important for the traditional view of *metaphor*, just because neo-Aristotelians neglect it by not making that return. Instead they foist their own sensation of deviance upon an earlier language which, obviously, would bear some "strange" elements. What these critics do is to superimpose wrong reception on inception, resulting in an exegetic practice as fallacious as that used by early analysts of the Bible--as the adjunct will demonstrate.

Today, of course, the mass media exert such control that Ought-Values normalize swiftly into Is-Values: the odd wording of today becomes the semantic staple of tomorrow. Conditions can change rapidly either way as commercial jingles automatize today what remains unused tomorrow, reverting to an Ought-Value. All of these conditions would exacerbate determining a semantic item on the basis of familiarization even if some aspect of frequency could be measured, thus dooming the neo-Aristotelian metaphor more than ever. Regarded positively, epochal inception, too, endows a work with life through the constitutive consciousness of a Referent, just because the encoding act occurs at a certain period of historical time. That is how language even in literature preserves some attachment to the extralinguistic reality without being anchored in it. Reception, as already indicated, then perpetuates the "life" of a work and indirectly that of the author as Referent by respecting epochal distance instead of closing it artificially in ignorance. Inception thus dates the work, while reception conversely has it transcend any date when the epochal perspective is observed.

To illustrate epochal time with the Icon "weed" in two other Shakespearean plays, there is *Henry VIII* (if somewhat doubtful in authorship) and *Twelfth Night*. In the former work (V, i, 52-53, Harrison, ed., 1952, p. 1537) the Icon is Indexicalized to convey a human rogue, rendered as a "rank weed" one must "root . . . out." As basic reference to a plant, the word is familiar to modern speakers of English. Yet *Twelfth Night* (V, i, 262, 280, ibid., pp. 877-78) uses the Icon "weed" with an Index of female apparel that was common in the oppositional system of Elizabethan English. Thus the first reference to the "rank weed" does not create an epochal gap. Rather, the image may become enhanced in significance at the level of the presenting strata, considering how many wastrels, such as the "weed" image elicits here, still populate the world today. However, the sense of apparel cannot be extracted from this Icon today. A modern Recipient returns to that earlier Index, since the "plant" Index does not befit the Icon either in this context. The wide epochal gap is then properly observed instead of being artificially narrowed, releasing accordingly what Shakespeare "meant" to say through the Icon. Otherwise the double-intentionality comprising reference and transference for the correlate becomes subverted at nominal-verbal interlocking: Referent selection (I) of explicit (M) content is then distorted at the implicit level (O).

That is to say, the indigenous pointer, the direction-factor of the material and formal contents marking "weed" and "attire" differed for Elizabethan English. The Index "attire" cannot be foregrounded into "weed" without drawing the blanks of my previous "pen" and "feather" examples. If not realized, the difference conflicts with the authorial intent and inadvertently changes a Recipient into a *pseudo-Referent;* the "super-" prefix has then been relinquished and/or replaced with a "pseudo-" qualifier for this "-reader." Either Dicentic plot formation or Rhemic compounding will then suffer at the higher literary strata. Briefly, in *Twelfth Night* a character named Viola has donned male apparel; at this cited point in the plot, she decides to reappear in her female "weeds," her womanly garb, whereupon the comedy reaches its happy, romantic denouement of reunited couples. Skimpy as my construal is, it makes the point of superreader obligation rather than option. An added solution may be supplied by the scholar of literature (as Harrison in my edition) who mediates somewhat artificially between Referent and Recipient through text-critical amendments.

This vital distinction between epochal option and obligation also surfaces somewhat confusedly in *Validity of Interpretation* by Hirsch (1967, pp. 215-216), where one may wonder at the "validity" of the critic's solution. Hirsch discusses the image "vegetable love" used by the Metaphysical poet Marvell (1621-1678), certainly a closer contemporary to Shakespeare than to Hirsch, which may be part of the problem. Hirsch (who supports the findings of Wellek in this context) may be right in suggesting that the same attributive today would have been "vegetative," with the connotations my own modern readers here would recognize. However, the linguistic change of import in itself cannot provide "enrichment" for the poem, as Hirsch claims, since this Icon must be read with the Index given by this poet. Yet Hirsch proposes that the only way out of what he views as a dilemma "is to perceive that the meaning of a text does not change and that the modern, different connotation of a word like 'vegetable' belongs, if it is to be entertained at all, to the constantly changing significance of the text" (ibid.).

Obviously, clear-cut distinctions, of the kind I have separated as set "diachronic" levels for the linguistic strata and dynamic "synchronic" alternatives for the literary strata, are lacking. The former, just because they are in flux, should not be touched once they have become teleologically fused to a work at inception, hence at one point in time. Otherwise, a pseudo-authorship is again forced upon a work, marring the selectional bias of a correlate. Only once that linguistic foundation has been kept may the higher literary strata benefit from semantic enrichment in some changing significance--if romantic vegetation, perhaps, were of special concern today. Otherwise the "literary interpretations" would be robbed of their intrinsic "objectivity" (Juhl, 1975, pp. 385 ff).

One example worth adding also involves a female, if neither in reference to an "Ms." address nor a "weed" attire. The German Icon "Frauenzimmer" used to denote "woman" but nowadays bears an invective closer to "bitch." To read those negative connotations into one of Goethe's novels, for instance, would grossly distort the Indexical relevance since, obviously, it was not "meant" and did not even exist for this Icon extant at the time of inception. No enrichment can result from such a linguistic distortion at the presenting strata either. The work would be encumbered by an *unindented* Index and the female it portrays by an *unintended* aspect, causing the quasi-mirror to go awry by subverting the authorial will. An epochal span thus narrowed falsifies the work just because no attempt has been made to "narrow" construal with the composition at the time of inception and the inventory on which the encoding then relied.

A superreader who relinquishes the "super-" prefix through this negligence of lexical historicity commits an *anachronism*--perhaps more severe than the one Baumgärtner cited from Jakobson. No perceptive Recipient should be that unconversant with a linguistic medium and succeed at literary interpretation. Through epochal time, Referent and Recipient are brought "back" together in curious ways. Careful balancing is then needed between the true linguistic *retrospect* and enhanced literary *prospect* if the work is to benefit from a valid contemporaneousness in its "presence" as well as future *postponement* of concretization. The German philosopher Hartmann (1953, p. 166) describes how the continued existence (Fortbestehen) of a work produces a "going-forward" while recipience necessitates also a "refinding" along with a "reawakening" (German "Wiederfindbar- und Wiedererweckbarsein").

Epochal time thus embodies a type of periodization despite the zero-point origin of non-adequated structures. The higher strata may undergo their own periodization through the cyclical popularity noted, hence of decline and comeback: the work reenters eras when the cultural climate is favorable to the author or theme, and disappears again when the opposite applies. Even Shakespeare, however mildly, was subjected to such cyclical unevenness. Brief pockets of decline appear to have occurred mainly during the eras of French and British neo-Classicism in the seventeenth and earlier eighteenth centuries, partly expressed in objections to Shakespeare's less than streamlined style, although today his contemporaneousness seems assured enough to proceed on a linear course. By sheer definition, the epochal time factor not only plays an important part in coming to terms with metaphorical deviance in language which the tradition plies, but may also disband those embattled "extrinsic" and "intrinsic" factions of literary criticism (Lohner, 1968). One-sided extrinsic or intrinsic "methods" (Hirsch, 1976, pp. 115 ff.) in their simplistic dogmatism may then be shelved for good.

The next temporal criterion is what I term *Iconic time*. As indicated, time here becomes mirrored in Icons, perhaps by deictic adverbs or the morphemic additions of verbs for tense changes. Iconic time thus covers lexical taxonomy of content which, when part of a pure referent, remains heteronomous, pure-intentional in essence, radiating imagery as quasi-mirror or lyric foregrounding. Any "succession" here stays locked into the centrifugal Icons in their semiotic stretch and horizontal sequence. Logically, therefore, Iconic time consists solely of synchronic oppositional states constituting one linguistic inventory. Iconic time is selected for inclusion in the linguistic strata and localizes "time" within a non-adequated setting, Dicentic or Rhemic, as was indicated with the *Hamlet* example.

A German critic, Gabriel, illustrates my last point in a work devoted to "fiction and truth" (1975, pp. 14 ff.). Citing the sentence, "Yesterday was New Year," Gabriel rightly observes that this statement, when true, could be made only on January 2. In non-Aristotelian terms, it could be true only when adequated with a reality-nexus under the structure of Argument, where such vertical temporality as the real New Year of experience enters through an objective referent. For all these reasons, then, the following and seemingly ungrammatical concoction may surface in a non-adequated use: "Tomorrow was Christmas." Käte Hamburger (1968, pp. 65-66; 1973, pp. 72-73) actually extracted this sentence from a novel. Her reason for doing so was to prove quite convincingly that the "epic preterite" ("was") had turned "epic" indeed, less by signifying the past than by providing a literary substratum for fiction. Because the tense has been superseded, the adverb denoting future may combine with this past tense, no matter how weird that sounds out of context. Another critic who examined the preterite was Barthes. Though obsolete in spoken French, the preterite is to him the "cornerstone of Narration," capable of affirming the "presence of Art" through a "ritual of letters" which becomes an "ideal instrument of every construction of a world . . ." (thus capitalized, in Hawkes, 1977, p. 109).

A "ritual of words," one might say, has begun at zero-point when the language is literary; a Kantian type "game" or "play" I called it before that wreaks havoc with time or space in a purposive sphere. Critics such as Gabriel (ibid., p. 29) nevertheless suggest that, ontologically, fictional bounds of time may be "liberalized" on occasion by letting a sliver of genuine history into the literary domain. To be sure, sometimes it seems that way, in the type of documentary drama, for example, which Gabriel cites as proof: Hochhuth's play, *The Deputy* (1974, trans. 1978), covers the role of Pope Pius XII during World War II. To do that convincingly, historical facts are not only included in something resembling stage directions but follow in an added section called "Sidelights on History." I cite this example primarily to stress that only the Sidelights outside of the drama, but not the supposed "facts" inside of it, bear real time.

Even experimental antiart tries to combat Iconic time. A case in point are the "speak-ins" (Sprechstücke) by the Austrian Handke (1974, p. 15). As their name suggests, they are types of spoken "happenings": speakers instead of dramatic characters challenge the audience to synchronize their watches with stage time--a nice modern try at the traditional (Aristotelian) unity of time! Granted, no dramatic quasi-mirror arises from sheer speaking. The time thus appears monolithic. But straining for historical time that way remains histrionic after all. Time cannot straddle the audience arena and the artifice of set performances. Since these speakers are only mouthpieces of their author, they have not shed their "roles" entirely. Ontologically, there is no way to circumvent such distinctions between art and life, illusionary and real time.

Finally, there is *structural time*, which in essence has been a part of this analysis ever since the two constructs were individually identified. Thus, Dicentic *continuity* induced by the concatenating correlates opposes Rhemic *simultaneity* of what amounts to one correlate which burgeons into poetic intext. Dicent in fictional progression achieves constitution by *indirect* means, since a correlate is amalgamated first and then concatenated; Rheme partakes of a *direct* mode of constitution that befits its unique concrescence, to the point of countering progressive word order sequence with a regressive vertical coherence that was designated *recursiveness* before. The *horizontal* sequence goes forward while recursiveness forges *vertical* associations in a backward direction--"up" to a title if included.

This is where Ingarden's *Cognition* (1968, p. 274) also has a valuable contribution to make in quite a lengthy description of the "lyric subject": it constitutes a pure-intentional object that suffuses the full content of a poem (Gedicht), dominating even overt sentences, through an "expressive function" (Ausdrucksfunktion). In the same work, Ingarden speaks of a "condensation" (pp. 101-102, 283-284, 287) and "total immersion" (Versunkenheit, das völlige Sich-Versenken, pp. 137-139) as unique lyric qualities. He also offers an equivalent to my Rhemic recursiveness called by him a "Wiederkehren" (p. 105). In more figurative phrasing, lyric simultaneity is said to resemble the "present" (Gegenwart) in "a now" (Jetzt) phase, a contemporaneous moment (Gegenwarts-Moment) with close to "supra-temporal" (überzeitlich) dimensions (pp. 137, 139, 283-284).

Ingarden is thus aware of lyric "density" or "intensification"--meanings still caught in the German word for poetry, "Dichtung." A superreader honors that difference through a mnemonic faculty of qualitative time Ingarden calls *live memory* (lebendiges Gedächtnis, pp. 101-103, 143-146). Its function is to foster what he terms "Retention und Potention," words which hardly need translating (p. 143). My textual analyses demonstrate best how live memory works. At this point, let me affirm that it becomes the assimilating tool for the reconstruction or reconstitution (à la Riffaterre) of the connotative compounding that forms a poetic intext. Live memory is a capacity that serves the very "potency" of Rhemic width--long enough to retain the backgrounded content for lyric condensation. This faculty aids the concretization of the extended Rhemic transference; it allows functional metaphors as objects of expression to become construed holistically in forging the lyric ego, as the totality of expression takes root within the consciousness of a Recipient.

Fictional augmentation, on the other hand, undergoes a curious binary divergence during concretization that Ingarden calls *double horizon* (ibid., pp. 105, 140). In lyric poetry such a horizon stays "empty" (leer), he adds, meaning it has no chance to form. As indicated with the structural idiosyncrasies of the genres, the very *length* of Dicent necessitates stoppage in concretization, often spread out over several days. Dicentic assimilation is more localized and the concretization accordingly more gradual; it may be disrupted at various stages of the augmentation. Indeed no superreader possesses an attention span capable of covering a long novel in a single reading. What happens is that parts of the text are knit together and disclose features of the characters in their activities, while the ongoing concretization has not yet reached the same stage of amalgamation.

Moreover, Dicent basically creates a double horizon because each concatenating correlate needs separate construal before some portrayal can be combined in further augmentation from the parts decoded.

Horizons, of course, have long been of interest in literary criticism. Gadamer, whose studies on hermeneutics (1960, specifically pp. 373-375) are widely known in one of his essays (1975, p. 117) describes the movement of a horizon: a Recipient "wanders into" a text which in turn "wanders along with" the recipience. This Gadamer essay is contained in a collaborative volume with the self-explanatory title of *Rezeptionsästhetik* (1975); an excerpt from Ingarden's *Cognition* sets the tone; other critics (such as Jauss, pp. 131, 133-140) are shown to work also with horizons in their impact on recipience. (Also see Hirsch on Gadamer's horizons, 1967, pp. 245, 252-253). Basically, to be sure, horizons cannot be eradicated from any concretizing process through the very continuum of the word order sequence, even in construal of the simultaneity characterizing the Rheme. But Ingarden introduced live memory as the faculty for the lyric genre precisely because immanent retention matters, rather than a gradual knitting together of parts through separate acts of consciousness, and thus the double horizon is blocked from forming.

Full superreader compliance with these structural intricacies of time, however, is best met with the three modes of reading Riffaterre advocated in his recent work on the semiotics of poetry (1978, p. 5): a "heuristic" reading aids a preliminary familiarity with the theme through textual synchronization; a "retroactive" reading then develops perspectives that affect the beginning in relation to the end, particularly when lyric recursiveness is involved in all its vertical alignments; a "hermeneutic" reading aims at the organic whole residing in both structures, even if arrived at differently in Dicent and Rheme. These triadic modes of concretization may be aligned to semiotic generation, from the first M-synchronization of decoding textual material to the full O-processing of mnemonic time phases until an I-synthesis is obtained as an atemporal whole, be this a simulated fictional world of quasi-judgments or a totality of poetic expression. Lighter works such as thrillers may then trade more on the first type of reading and complex ones on the last.

Ingarden's *Cognition* cites also the reinforcing aspects and indeterminate pockets that reside within the schematic material contents (pp. 49-59 ff.). Both came up in discussing the constructs. Obviously, the reinforcing aspect leave their impact on the Recipient from the first heuristic reading on, while the schematic pockets get a chance to fill out, especially the structural metaphors which burgeon in all their connotative circumference, during the hermeneutic reading. A by-product of the hermeneutic reading is the harmonious interaction among the four strata that Ingarden calls consistently "polyphony" (1965, pp. 61, 397; 1968, pp. 93, 234, 284; Fieguth, pp. XLI, 24, 94).

So far stance has remained uniform, because it was largely discussed in conjunction with basic contextual controls of time. However, stance as superreader posture may be divided into roles that separate the *critic* from the *connoisseur*. The nomenclature is my own, but Ingarden (1968, pp. 233-234, 246-249, 264, 425) suggests this dichotomy in his *Cognition*, where he differentiates the "artistic" (künstlerisch) from the "esthetic" (ästhetisch) "values" that inhere in a literary work of art. The artistic values govern the construct in what might be called the "inlaid" compositional areas; the esthetic values take effect in the appeal of the work during concretization and thus affect the sensibilities of the decoding consciousness. In the etymology of "esthetic" from Greek "aistheysis" (my transliteration), the term signified sensuous appeal (Fobes, 1966, p. 266).

Basically, therefore, these values split into Referent and Recipient priorities. The esthetic values induce that very vibrance of experience during concretization that caused Ingarden to speak of "life." Fundamentally, to be sure, the Referent predicts these effects in the selection of contents, but their *appreciation* emerges with the concretizing process when proper superreader response actualizes the esthetic values. For dealing with the artistic values, Ingarden reserves the *analytic* or "pre-esthetic" stance of cool observation (Betrachtung, pp. 248, 272, 284, 286-289). Instead of yielding to the sheer continuum of concretization in its full esthetic actualization, the analyst coolly appraises the compositional merits of a work. Unavoidably, this analytic stance causes a type of "vivisection," whose negative effects Ingarden makes explicit with such terms as "zerschlagen," "Zersetzung," and even "Verletzung" (ibid.) The German prefixes "zer-"/"ver-" bear pejorative connotations of disintegration, fragmentation, or diffraction, and these effects are a necessary evil of strenuous concentration on isolated detail. To mitigate that problem, the esthetic stance of the connoisseur takes over from the pre-esthetic stance of the critic and becomes immersed in a last hermeneutic and polyphonous concretization that once more cements the work in its ultimate if stratified coherence.

The superreader stance discussed so far reacts to the controls of a construct. However, what happens if the controls appear to conflict? To make sure they are not taken for granted, I introduce *second* stance, whose role is proper *authentication*. The number does not imply "secondary," since this stance is as crucial as what will now be differentiated as "primary" stance in designating all the aforesaid aspects. Rather, "second" signifies only that this stance is not always consciously invoked when no problem of authentication exists. Second stance prevents what might be termed figuratively an "identity crisis" of the two constructs, at times even involving Argument. Context, with all the contacts previously specified, possesses many safeguards against structural subversion, not to mention that the structures were all grounded in units natural to language. Even a less literate but mature speaker has become innately aware of differences between ostensive-everyday use and "fictional" storytelling or "lyric" mnemonics in rhymed formations.

Outside of such Recipient awareness, the inbuilt Referent as authorial will induces barriers between structures. Limitations of length certainly exist for Dicent and Rheme if in diametrically opposed ways: no genuine mimetic augmentation can be confined to a couple of correlates, and no Rhemic immediacy in conjunction with live memory could grapple with the length of the majority of novels, even dramas. Also, prose cannot obtain for the Rheme even if verse is not confined to the Rheme as stated. So there is some recursiveness in versified dramas, too, as lines make vertical contact for the benefit of rhyme or whatever. Still, superreader stance follows the guidelines of Dicent since the formation of a plot drives the text forward in Dicentic augmentation. The same applies to a Homeric type of versified epic; it still "tells" a story and is thus Dicent. This point should be noted early, since Aristotle will be shown in the adjunct to rely heavily on these works for his dubious "metaphor." The versified ballad, like the Homeric epic, partakes of mimetic augmentation in non-Aristotelian semantics; a "story" is being told, involving figures and their activities that must be knit together in smaller, syntactic correlates, even if these are broken up by lines through such poetic accouterments as rhythm and rhyme.

Käte Hamburger (1968, pp. 233 ff., 240) considers the ballad a borderline case. Non-Aristotelian semantics, while not positing many structures, eschews hybrids: either a work is intended for mimetic augmentation or for lyric expression. Ultimately, there is Argument, too, in the possible form of a versified commercial. Thus the billboard poster may bear verse. But the very contact Argument makes with the extralinguistic reality necessitates everyday authentication as the units become perforated in the manner explained. Actually, my interest is not so much in providing an exhaustive list of examples where formats seem at odds with their essence but rather to deal with the problem of authentication itself.

Ingarden's *Cognition* pp. 232-233 ff.) hints at second stance, where he refers to an "attitude" or "Einstellung" that is mandatory when the title of a text "informs" recipients as to the presence of a poem, drama, or whatever. Part of that information, of course, becomes relayed to that innate awareness of linguistic competence, which may be called "literary competence," a term used by Sacks (1968, p. 110). The latter suggests that there must be "certain formal ends . . . known in advance by any reader capable of reading a comedy as comedy, or, indeed, by any writer capable of writing one." Sacks unfortunately does not define those ends. Each work harbors "intrinsic imperatives" (Hirsch, 1976, p. 115), and concretization meets these.

The human capacities and textual imperatives embody respectively the modals "can" and "should." Nothing prevents readers from making a versified commercial out of a poem or vice versa. But Recipients then violate the imperatives of the work albeit possessing the power to do otherwise. To obviate such perversion of an authorial will, I introduce the *esthetic ought* in cognizance of Kant. His *Third Critique* cites it in conjunction with the "Fourth Moment," that of "modality," which governs the esthetic judgment (Urteilskraft) of taste after the moments of quality, quantity, and relation (Cassirer ed., V, 1914, section 18, pp. 307-308). Kant used for the esthetic ought the same modal--"sollen"--that formulated his famous ethical maxim, the categorical imperative in the *Second Critique* (ibid., p. 35). The indication is that where the human will is in control it *should* aspire to doing what it *can* (können) achieve. Whatever the differences between ethics and esthetics, there is that related volitional base, although entirely spontaneous in goal for purposive wholes that rest in their own autotelism.

That language is basically "coercive" my study proved from the very start. With the esthetic ought, that coerciveness preserves the distinction between literal and literary alternatives, and for that matter also between fictional and lyric dispositions. Let me provide a few examples. Since the early "lyric" mnemonics of nursery rhymes were mentioned, I cite from the famous T. S. Eliot poem, *The Waste Land*, because this is what one of its lines (1971, p. 146) contains: "London Bridge is falling down falling down falling down." Out of context, the words are part of the nursery rhyme. In context, this atavistic vestige, with its monotonous repetition (bereft of all punctuation), has become poeticised. As an integral component of the "Waste Land," it supports the theme rendering a desiccated society that is close to "falling down."

Again, my interpretation may suffice only to make the point that this nursery rhyme is no longer the game of children but a part of the esthetic "game" which has

Icons render a serious theme through juvenile imagery. The line was chosen also for the geographical reference that so confused Searle. Whether plain "London" or "London Bridge," the British landmark and its city are not meant directly but belong instead to the nursery rhyme which in turn fosters the significance already explored. This geographical vestige, then, is in reference as remote from the stone or pavement of the real thing as it would be if it were composed of canvas on a painting; its Index of decay supersedes pointing to that actual place in Britain's capital city, whether or not the real bridge is in good shape. A superreader knows all that when heeding the esthetic ought through authentication of the Rheme. Then Icons are probed for their foregrounding until their relevant Indexes interlock in satisfactory backgrounding to convey the desolate societal landscape that goes right back "up" to the title. Involved are structural metaphors that contribute through their explicit and implicit denominations to the whole, whether deviant or standardized in appearance. A poetic intext has thus enveloped this nursery rhyme, inclusive of its "London Bridge."

Curiously, an entire poem may be additionally enveloped by fiction. The nineteenth-century penchant of (German) Romantic novelists, for instance, was to include whole poems in novels. Since non-Aristotelian semantics has ruled out hybrids, what obtains here? The answer is--Dicent. Surprisingly, *length* dominates in structure: the poems are surrounded by mimetic augmentation since those who recite them will be fictional characters. Put the other way, these poems characterize some figure. Should the poems be severed from their Dicentic environment and be read by themselves, particularly with an author's endorsement, the esthetic ought ordains concretization of the Rheme with the agency of live memory.

Another example for seemingly crossing structural bounds between Rheme and Argument is offered by Käte Hamburger (1968, 191-197; trans. 1973, pp. 237-246). It involves a devotional cycle by the Romantic poet Novalis which was at times read either as *poem* or as *prayer* in church. Hamburger notes rightly that the two are intrinsically no longer the same thing. Without an author's consent, the prayer remains a subversion of the authorial will, the poet's act of meaning. But even with his consent the poem now serves real speakers in reference to ulterior pragmatic goals, no matter how deserving these are, and the very term "ulterior" came up with (Peirce's) Argument. That, indeed, is where the prayer belongs; the focus is no longer on a pure but an objective referent and justice cannot be done to lyric foregrounding and backgrounding. For functional entities like meanings, the essence, now perforated as described with adequation, changes accordingly. Structurally then, this poem has become "literal" instead of literary, leaving the term "poem" essentially a misnomer. Put another way, these words have relinquished the esthetic ought.

Even this example was chosen for more than one reason. It forestalls Aristotle's problem with the prayer which, in its effusive eloquence, he has pitted against the theoretical proposition. Non-Aristotelian semantics keeps both these uses under one structural qualifier insofar as they necessitate adequation, whether the objective referent is utilitarian or logical-theoretical, for reasons explained earlier. Unfortunately there is no room here to enter into the controversies surrounding biblical language which my comments on the prayer may have unleashed. Let me say only that a document of this nature cannot be a blanket case of non-adequated language, even if "poetic" vestiges such as the Song of Solomon seem to merit outwardly such a classification.

A convenient signal in accommodation of the esthetic ought would seem to be a title or subtitle specifying the genre. But often titles render little more than what Wimsatt (1967, p. 51) has termed "superficially inspectable shapes." Indeed such information may entail a histrionic type of "proffering" on the part of authors who are less intent on verifying a genre than on finding fancy terms for describing their works. Sometimes the intent may be deliberate enough to delude or tease Recipients. Not that this is a judgmental observation of such practices; the author's right is not challenged, only a superreader's acuity to reach the genuine Referent during concretization, especially when functioning in that analytic stance of the critic rather than the average connoisseur.

Goethe's *Faust*, for example, was proffered as "A Tragedy" without actually being a drama. The subtitle mainly underscores the theme of human striving against the metaphysical odds and thus does not touch any functional depth of contextualization. This work also has been classed loosely as a "dramatic poem" or "poetic drama," where the critics following Goethe leaned on sheer descriptive epithets, which is less acceptable. Indeed, the identification of tragedy would not affect non-Aristotelian structures, since Dicent covers it anyway as mimetic augmentation, despite the rich poetic texture. Whatever the case, a superreader authenticates this structure as Dicent. And, certainly, while the work is too long to be held in live memory, the fate of Faust spells "plot." In addition, the Handke speak-ins, although "true" to the role of speakers, become a type of histrionic proffering by suggesting through the title that Recipients get real speakers--under Argument.

Whatever Recipients get, the esthetic ought does not extend to the lexical phenomena the Russian Formalists term "deautomatized" and/or "defamiliarized" constituents (from Russian "ostranenie"; Lohner, 1968, pp. 152-159; Hawkes, 1977, pp. 62-63, 66, 69; Stankiewicz, 1974, pp. 629 ff.; Bruns, 1975, pp. 71-81). Such an overt alienation may be loosely histrionic as well. Rather, in authenticating the structure and, with it, the underlying function, the content involved becomes *ipso facto* deautomatized to meet the tasks set for the pure referents of Dicent or Rheme. The Eliot poem with the nursery-rhyme line, in fact, abounds with British slang, or Cockney. The Rheme nevertheless deautomatizes that lingo as significant import of the dreary mindlessness this elitist poet attributes to the lower classes and uses here to render the atavistic desiccation from yet another Iconic perspective. Moreover, an epochal discrepancy may arise here, if future Recipients have lost that Cockney inventory and impose other connotations on that type of English.

The esthetic ought is thus not to be misled by the lexicon or titular descriptions and the like; it cannot be "misread" because through all that diversity the structure stays identical. That traditional genre determinations did not overlook time and stance either will be indicated next with a highly selective *historical survey* of trends that may clarify further issues related to my own theory. Recent experts on developments in genre determination (Ruttkowski, 1968, pp. 34-37; Hempfer, 1973, pp. 169-170) cite the various concerns with time in a truly impressive listing of international exponents: among others, they name Humboldt, Paul, Schelling, and for today, Jakobson, Hirt, Kleiner, Erskin, Dallas, Frye, Staiger, and Kayser.

Wading through these theories may be rewarding but not to the point of discovering analyses that deal with bounds on a level of semantic function. All too often the methods resemble those of the neo-Aristotelian approaches to metaphor by seizing on conspicuous surface phenomena. Most critics class lyric poetry in present time, rendered by a first-person lyric "I" that conveys self-expression through a "subject," epic prose in the past as preterite third-person narration geared to an "object," and drama in the future as potential enactment of a dialogical make-up, hence the second person. My synopsis may well by-pass facets of individual theories but none were pertinent enough for my structural focus. With the limited space here, I select the last three names, Frye, Staiger, and Kayser to briefly detail theories that touch on issues I have treated

In the case of Frye, more remarkable than his analysis is his acclaim, if for no other reason than that his much cited *Anatomy of Criticism* (1967) lacks any coherence among the four autonomous essays that were simply reprinted under one title (Daiches, in Hempfer, 1973, pp. 76-77). Frye's fourth essay treats rhythmic temporality through an alleged "Theory of Genres" (ibid., pp. 243-337). While it may be nice to describe "epos," "prose," and "lyric" as rhythmic "recurrence," "continuity," and "association" respectively, matters are not helped if "prose" or "poetry" as opposed to the "lyric," for instance, is never properly defined. Frye's flair lies in what might be labeled the "critical epithet." Original and irreverent, his epithets tag free verse as "emancipated lyrical rhythm," modern poetry as "centripetal wordmagic," and Greek *melos* and *opsis* of sonorous and visual Qualisign dimensions as "babble" and "doodle"--synonyms also with "splutters" and "sparks" (ibid., pp. 273, 275-278). This diverting profusion, however, lapses into uncritical confusion for the lack of a systematic presentation in nomenclature.

The other two critics, Staiger and Kayser, are selected for their relevance to the issues of number and stance. However, with the limited space at my disposal, I arrive at their theory by indirect means, putting the issues before the people. Number is relevant insofar as my binary genre determination breaks with the traditional *triad.* (Hempfer, 1973, pp. 148 ff.; Ruttkowski, 1968, pp. 26 ff.). By the nineteenth century that triad even became linked to (Hegelian) dialectics: Vischer, for instance, reserved "thesis" for the lyric, "antithesis" for the epic, and "synthesis" for the dramatic genre (Ruttkowski, p. 35). Early in this century, Peterson (1926; Ruttkowski, pp. 35, 133) used the criteria of monologue and dialogue for his own triad by linking a monological report with "Epos," a dialogical presentation with drama, and a vague "monological presentation of a condition" with the lyric kind that lacked a plot.

Of these distinctions, it is the monological factor that led to some curious ramifications and will take me back to number and stance. At issue is the German concept "Artistik." The German poet-critic Benn (1965, pp. 500-502) took the term from Nietzsche and had it signify pure "monological" artifice in poetry, which is to say that this type of language is aimed exclusively at the muse instead of a dialogical addressee (Gumpel, 1976, pp. 125-127, 141, ff.). Thus interpreted, "Artistik" connotes something that resembles a lack of adequation for literary use. Moreover, number got involved with this concept when Ruttkowski (ibid., pp. 86-104) confusedly plied the term "Artistik" as a label for a *fourth* genre that was to "modify" the triad of "fundamental poetics." His term, however, looked to performance embodied in the circus "artiste." The concept was thus hardly the same: "Artistik" as fourth genre shed its monological roots to become a dialogical or "audience-related" (pubiikumsbezogen) phenomenon.

Although one may have hoped for another term, any nomenclature is valid when properly defined. And "audience-relation" certainly abounds today. The Handke speak-ins were one instance of addressing the audience on the time factor quoted. One speak-in actually "offends" the audience by hurling invectives at it in an "audience-related" attempt. An earlier didactic rather than experimental goal caused authors like Brecht to posit an audience-related, anti-illusionary theater aimed at breaking through the theatrical illusion in order to keep spectators sufficiently "alienated" from the plot that they would learn from it rather than emotionally identify with it. Stylistically, his plot-alienation is a curious way of "defamiliarizing" drama (in the Russian Formalist "Priem Ostranennija," as suggested by Willett 1964, pp. 179-180).

However, no matter how "pure" or "engaged" the motives of the authors, their method ultimately remains what I called "histrionic" before. Stage and arena belong to two separate realities; the inbuilt "audience" of the former is no ontological clone of the latter. Ruttkowski's fourth audience-related category thus distinguishes nothing the traditional triad could not include. But his ill-founded numeric extension is worth mentioning because he (1968, pp. 47 ff.) posited it as the self-professed heir of the poetics that had revolved around "fundamental stances," in German "Grundhaltungen." This Teutonic interest essentially harks back to Goethe, specifically his "natural forms" (Naturformen) discussed with prefatory comments to his poetic cycle of 1819, the Westöstlicher Divan (1965, II, pp. 187-189). Goethe contrasts the natural forms with the "poetic formats" (Dichtarten) comprising such historical genres as elegy, fable, ode, and so on. The natural forms oppose these diverse formats as three basic linguistic modes, couched in the nouns "Epos, Lyrik, Drama." Yet his description of these nouns seems rather ambiguous, even affective: "lucid narration" goes with the "Epos," while "enthusiastic excitement" and "acting persons" apply respectively to the other two.

So innate is the "natural" state of these forms that they appear in any format--just like the lexicon. This ubiquity is in itself an indication that their root is more anthropomorphic than constitutive, not resting in units whose bounds are truly "natural" to language. Yet this vulnerable omnipresence was passed on to contemporary Teutonic criticism, of which Staiger and Kayser are to be the representatives here (for Viëtor and Cysarz, see Hempfer, 1973, pp. 18-19, 63, 67-79). True, the terms were changed: "fundamental" or even "elemental" replaced the attributive "natural" with the prefix "Grund-"--obviously a cognate of "ground"--which then preceded "concept" or "stance" (Begriff, Haltung, or Einstellung).

Staiger, a Swiss German and no doubt the most prominent among this contingent (1959, pp. 236-237 ff.), also correlated fundamental stance with simple or "primary qualities." To these he assigned the adjectives "lyrical, epical, dramatic" (offered occasionally in the substantive "das Lyrische," and so on). Three nouns, "Lyrik, Epik, Drama," then became the classificatory precepts (Sammelbegriffe) that resembled "slots" (Fächer) and as such could encapsulate the simple qualities. These slots impress one as shells or molds into which the qualities are poured, thus with none of that integral "molding" between content and context my study cited from Peirce while discussing the Interpretant. Here, stance would lose control over the essence of the constituents, since the "ground" is not indigenous to the whole.

Kayser (1963, pp. 330-387), generally a discerning critic, demonstrates that schism between content and functional context well enough when he (p. 335) insists, for example, that an exclamation such as "Ach!", the German equivalent for "Oh!", bears fundamentally a lyric stance. It just so happens that an early nineteenth-century play, *Amphitryon*, by H. v. Kleist (1964, pp. 245, 320), concludes with an enigmatic "Ach!" But no matter how eloquent its illocutionary force, the exclamation belongs to Dicent. Uttered by a fictional speaker, it becomes the last presented aspect to characterize that figure. There is no getting around that function. The same applies to another example Kayser cites in this context which, by coincidence, appeared in my study to illustrate double-intentionality. That is "Fire!" as exclamation (rather than command). Kayser (p. 335) states that it possesses illocutionary force--German "Kundgabe"--as well as a possible perlocutionary "release" (Auslösung) when resulting in the action of extinguishing the fire.

As explained with the aid of Ingarden, illocution and perlocution, too, are content, and thus subordinated to a structure that molds the vestige into everyday or esthetic (Dicentic or Rhemic) use. To be sure, any novel or poem may sound "lyrical" or "dramatic," for instance, when eloquence predominates in one and dialogue in the other. Style may be thus described in literary scholarship. "Stance," however, when thus interpreted merely yields to loose description instead of isolating a "natural" or "fundamental" trait in literary works of art. As for Ruttkowski, the self-acclaimed heir of fundamental poetics, he would have done better by this tradition had he deanthropomorphized stance rather than modified it by what is *qua* language literally a "use-less" fourth division. Who is to arbitrate on the "audience-relation" or the "lyrical" bent of a drama or novel? The question becomes rhetorical.

The issue of number causes me to cite one more theory which tends in the opposite direction to Ruttkowski's by reducing genre to *two* classes from the traditional three. Such a binary division would seem to parallel my own. In fact that same theory made me posit just two literary genres. But here is the difference: in all, I offer still *three* structures, one of them nonliterary. That addition, precisely, is omitted from Käte Hamburger's *Logic of Literature*, as the English title (1973) reads for the last word, "Dichtung." Hamburger goes by the Aristotelian concepts, "poein" and "legein," signifying to "fashion" or "make," and to "say" (1968, pp. 15-19, 187, passim). From these, she draws up two logical forms. The merit of her thesis is that, despite this Aristotelian influence, it stays "non-Aristotelian" in my understanding of the term by going for (logical) function instead of lexical appearances. The "logic," however, suffers because her category of "saying" as "statement" comprises everyday and lyric use. The bounds between literal and lyric statements are accordingly left "open" in a fluid point of transition (ibid., pp. 11, 12, 187, 228, 269, 279-280, often citing Hegel in support).

Literal and lyric statements, claims Hamburger (1968, pp. 28-51, 187-205), require a "correlation" between a subject-pole and an object-pole; the more subjective end tends to the lyric and the objective to the literal. The arbitrary nature on which such a decision would have to be based ultimately forces Hamburger (1968, p. 215; 1973, p. 269) into contradictions. That is where she separates the lyric from the literal statement for possessing a "sense-nexus" instead of a "reality-nexus." With the sense-nexus, the lyric statement has gone into total "recoil" toward the "subject-pole," while the literal statement remains suspended between object-pole and subject-pole (correlation), depending on how abstract or concrete its wording is (1968, pp. 41 ff.; 1973, pp. 40 ff.).

So a cutoff point exists after all, countering her premise of the "open" state. While this solution seems better, it cannot eliminate the inconsistency. Also, by implication Hamburger is then left with *three* alternatives. More effective are her ideas on the mimetic "I-Origines"--essentially fictional "originations" which confirm that works of fiction own no real speaking subjects, whether or not authors and narrators appear in the works (1968, pp. 62-68, 275, 279, passim). The same type of "closure," however, must govern every use, and not least lyric expression. To cite from an essay by E. Stankiewicz (1974, p. 642),

> Poetry delimits the beginning and the end of a work, creating poetic "closure," or a frame which contains the work and sets it off from the "ordinary" language as an artifact which has itself as its purpose and context.

Hamburger's conflict therefore substantiates that three in number is the bare minimum, if one use must be reserved for nonliterary purposes. The issue of "closure" that has now closed my analysis of Hamburger's theory has other curious repercussions in Anglo-Saxon criticism. My study forestalled this problem by indicating that certain "extrinsic" factors do not disrupt the "intrinsic" essence of literary works once their provenance is understood. But this very dichotomy erupted into polemics within this century and began largely with reactions to positivism. It is said (Hempfer, 1973, pp. 9-10) that positivism late in the nineteenth century eluded the Germans due to the influence of Dilthey's humanistic studies, the "Geisteswissenschaften," while simultaneously some Anglo-Saxons put much effort into resisting this rising trend, particularly as espoused by Symonds and Brunetière. The so-called *New Criticism* of the early 1920s to 1930s was supposed to stem the tide of positivism, though not without some confused notions of affiliation. Apparently Ransom had advocated a "New Criticism" (while unaware of Spingarn's forerunner) in the hope of moving away from the focus on detail adopted by Richards, Empson, and Winters. (Brooks, 1965, pp. 567-568; with Wimsatt, 1967, pp. 610-634, 635-656).

Yet ironically the persons cited themselves became known as the "New Critics," with Frye, among others, thrown in for good measure. By the 1950s the New Critics came under attack by the Chicago School--known as the "neo-Aristotelian" group (Brian Lee, 1966, p. 39, and his reference to Burke). "Aristotelian" was supposed to be their attempt to emulate the father of genre, Aristotle, by seeking the holistic perspectives that the New Critics were accused of having neglected. In the compendious *Critics and Criticism* (1952, pp. 13, 556), one Chicagoan, Crane, endorses vague "wholes of various kinds," and another, Olson, looks to some "composite continuum" based on a "perceptable magnitude." The pagination for these quotes demonstrates that I jumped from the begining to the end, mainly because wading through the middle of this treatise offered no "perceptable" synthesis in any critical coherence. (See Wimsatt, 1967, pp. 41-65; Vivas, 1963, pp. 243-259; Scholes, 1974, pp. 80-81). In fact, the more interesting studies seemed to concentrate on the type of detail for which their adversaries, the New Critics, had been castigated.

Equally thwarted in their attempts at defining an intrinsic literary whole were "neo-Aristotelians" in reference to my application of this term. Tacitly, at least, this contingent, surfacing in the last few decades, got caught in a *Fregean* crisis that kept adherents embroiled in a *Contextualist Dilemma*. Those involved--Krieger, Sutton, and Vivas--actually used the italicised terms while entering into the polemics of deciding as to who was a Contextualist and what, essentially, the label meant (Vivas, 1963, pp. 171-202; Sutton, 1958-1959; Krieger, 1962-1963).

In *The New Apologists for Poetry* (1956, pp. 20, 22), Krieger makes explicit the dilemma as he wonders how a poem can "function referentially" as it must in order to make sense while the language dare not "break the context" even as it is forced to "point outside itself." How does poetic language stay "non-referential" as a "special form of discourse," asks Krieger, when simultaneously it must be "referential to be any form of discourse at all." He (pp. 88-89) offers a series of dichotomies supposedly separating the literal from the literay, which his precursors rendered as "tension" versus "intension" (Tate), "logic" versus "texture" (Ransom) and "motive" versus "emotion" (Winters). Then he observes:

> And as we must ask of Winters' "motive" or Ransom's "logic," we must ask of Tate's "extension," whether it desists from its prosaic function of denoting objects under the pressure from "tension" to create a unique and self-contained mode of discourse.

Well, Ingarden could have made these critics realize that their "motive," "logic," or "extension" is actually the reference which "desists" from natural denoting because it must break with that self-contained discourse the pure referent bears--*first!* In that all-pervading skepticism, language cannot be entrusted with "denoting" on its own ground. Exactly how well it does so, the ensuing textual analyses should prove conclusively for the three structures and the two holistic constructs in their concretization.

The Structures Proven:
Argument, Dicent, Rheme in Action

Analysis: Baumgärtner and the Brecht Hypothesis

The time has come to test out the theory empirically: I myself in the role of a *superreader* present to my reader(s) how human consciousness, or the Interpretant in semiotic terms, has Recipient meet Referent in interlocutory reinforcement of a particular structure. Although there is only one lexical surface in a series of words that look the same, non-Aristotelian semantics identifies the structure to which they belong. Three structures have been identified, two of them literary constructs. Since I function predominantly in the role of the critic, beyond a connoisseur appreciating the immediate construal of a text, my primary stance for the two literary constructs will be analytic as, in concretization, I probe their compositional "artistic" values. Second stance, which authenticates a structure, is put to the test especially in this chapter, because one text will be submitted to all structural alternatives. The analysis of this chapter thus differs by being tripartite in application. When adding the two analyses of the following chapters, *five* in all are to be offered in this applied part of the theory. Each text was selected because a critic quoted it in conjunction with a problem pertinent to non-Aristotelian semantics.

Some other basic differences in procedure governing the three chapters may be mentioned right away. Since the first and last chapters contain German texts, their presentation will be *bilingual*. Vital aspects of *translation* are to be treated in the process. Each translation is my own, one of them "official" in the sense that it was published. That difference is mentioned in order to stress that it does not eliminate the problems of translation, which become so acute because selections from two different inventories are forced unnaturally together. Positively viewed, this problem affirms ontic heteronomy, the sphere of language grounded in acts of meaning. The only "universalism" that transcends all languages concerns the *content-insensitive* structures, just because they are not identified by semantic idiosyncrasies residing in the lexicon. Structures thus take over unilaterally under the same conditions in any translation, but never the concretion of language in a language. In the final chapter, optional units such as title and stanza that were listed for one of the structures, the Rheme, are also given their due.

159

The *first* analysis on which I am now embarking violates the esthetic ought by not authenticating the construct right away. Though to be avoided in general, this violation has the didactic advantage of demonstrating to the reader that the same surface no longer bears the same essence when the structure differs. That was the main challenge of non-Aristotelian semantics all along, and it has to be the concern of every modern critic of language who realizes, surely, that lexical deviance is as omnipresent as any standard language literary works in turn may bear on their surface. In essence, then, the first analysis is a type of *experiment*. But in its very attempt and ultimate proof it counters the Ingendahl Experiment, for example, whose results proved inconclusive because instead of considering holistic functions, mere localized spotsighting of metaphorical deviance became the focus.

My experiment first substantiates the presence of *Argument* as everyday or *literal* meaning, then Dicent as fictional alternative, and lastly the *Rheme*, the *lyric* construct bearing a functional *metaphor*. That my experiment is attempted at all may be justified on the following grounds. First, the critic involved seized on an *excerpt* only. He thereby created an artificial situation from the start which could be adapted more readily to the *hypothesis* that the vestige belonged to one structure at a time. Since Dicent, with a certain length mandatory for mimetic augmentation, cannot be presented in its entirety anyway, it may as well be tested with an excerpt. The plan is thus to entertain two hypotheses with Argument and Dicent and then to conclude with the authenticated structure, the Rheme. The English translation will do for the hypotheses after I have offered the whole bilingual version of the excerpt. With the authenticated structure, however, the bilingual version returns, crucial as the original remains for the non-adequated M-base of the Rheme.

That the translator becomes a type of "pseudo-Referent" or locutionary "interloper" has been indicated before. Especially a reader of literary texts should be allowed to glean the "natural" Referent of the original next to the translation wherever possible. Of course, the issue of translatability in itself is important for any investigation into metaphor, because critics at large make it a kind of test for the presence of metaphor and/or literary language. That type of substantiation goes too far and, again, is tacitly a deviance cult. Taken literally, a translation always resembles a "transference" based on a shift that goes from one oppositional system to another. Not only in the role of translator, however, but also as critic do I have to intervene between Referent and Recipient as I, the concretizing Recipient, pass on in turn my construal to readers who concretize my own (adequated, critical) work here. Instead of merely decoding connotations, for example, I have to render them artificially in explicit denominations in order to talk about them.

The critic who brought up the excerpt for the first analysis is none other than Baumgärtner, whose pessimistic essay on what was essentially a nonexistent methodological status of a linguistic poetics was cited before. Baumgärtner, it will be remembered, also echoed Fowler on those "formal features" that simply would not appear to accomodate a linguist grappling with poetic language. Part of Baumgärtner's proof, therefore, is an excerpted prosaic looking poem by Brecht (1969, p. 29) which he goes on to label a *hybrid*, in German "Zwitterding." Since Baumgärtner wants to prove that, if one did not know Brecht had ordained the text as poem, no one could tell that it was not a newspaper item, he seems partially justified in severing the full context this way: without any of the surrounding evidence, the language might be a feuilletonistic fragment.

The very setting reminds of the Ingendahl Experiment since that critic, too, drew on a newspaper article in determining its metaphorical content. So here is a poem which could in fact be part of everyday language because no special metaphorical deviance is evident in the style. That Baumgärtner equates such evidence with metaphor becomes only too apparent when, after citing the hybrid (ibid., pp. 38 ff.), he culls "transfer" from localized (spotsighted) lexical items, where "woods" are "sleeping" or "sleepy." Again, then, a modern critic is preoccupied with such rudimentary phenomena of meaning as animation that ancient rhetoric has plied to little avail for centuries. I cite the contents because "wood(s)" featured in my illustrations of the variegated natural leaps of language. These leaps, however, were identified as being intrinsic to *all* semantic entities because they arise from a functional instead of lexical transference any time an act of meaning is expressed through selected meanings.

With Baumgärtner's interest in lexical phenomena, then, it should come as no surprise that the ordinary looking Brecht excerpt baffled this critic. As shown in the (first) bilingual version to be cited, a deviant surface is hardly in evidence.

Auf der Flucht vor meinen Landsleuten
Bin ich nun nach Finnland gelangt. Freunde
Die ich gestern nicht kannte, stellten mir ein paar Betten
In saubere Zimmer. . . .

In flight from my countrymen
I finally got to Finland. Friends
That I didn't know yesterday put a few beds for me
Into clean rooms. . . .

The ellipsis points indicate where the poem was cut. Brecht's original work came in a volume entitled "Poems" *(Gedichte,* 1961, IV, pp. 220-222), with the dates "1934-1941." The poem had a title, "1940," and consisted of eight prosaic looking stanzas of varied length, identified by Roman numerals. Baumgärtner's excerpt opens the last stanza, "VIII," which consists of eight lines altogether. In fact, the fourth line above is incomplete: where the ellipsis points appear, the text continues with "Im Lautsprecher"-"In the loudspeaker." The enjambement would have left this vestige dangling in the excerpt and was no doubt omitted for that reason. In the way of additional background information, the poem is part of a cycle labeled "'Steffinische' Collection," in tribute to Brecht's collaborator Margarethe Steffin (who died in exile, in 1941; ibid., pp. 229-231).

That much information--none of which Baumgärtner offers--seems fair to include, some of it in anticipation of the authenticated structure that is to be analyzed last. Although Baumgärtner may have seemed justified to quote an excerpt in order to underscore its prosaic appearance, he nevertheless stoops to the "anachronism" he cited from Jakobson by seeming so "unconversant" with literary scholarship that he could not even provide some documentation.

At this point, the *first hypothesis* is ready to be presented. While non-Aristotelian semantics does not go in for hybrids, the prosaic appearance is to be substantiated first by treating the text as though it were functionally "literal" or univocal and thus belonged exclusively to *Argument*. On the surface the words look the same, but they are now borne by a *syntactic correlate* which, through adequation with an objective referent, gives rise to linguistic *judgment*, hence to a unit(y) backed by a *reality-nexus* supporting *truth claims*. The author willing this use cannot be a novelist or poet, but instead the writer of a letter, perhaps, that contains information about himself--and I use the masculine in cognizance of Brecht despite the present hypothesis. Although Argument may be ostensive, my own written communication causes me to continue stressing the orthographic foundation rather than the purely sonorous one. With that perspective in mind, I include a graphic line to suggest a type of "frame" for the edges of a page. Although Argument is versified in some commercial use as stated, the idea is to preserve the "prosaic" nature of these words without making any changes. The words seem to spill over naturally onto the next line, yet they do not fit perfectly: the "I" of the second line could have been included with the first and, of course, the "Friends" are left dangling in the enjambement, since only *one translated* correlate is to be offered for this first experiment.

....

In flight from my countrymen
I finally got to Finland. Friends

By coincidence, the first line includes the possessive about which much was said while going into Ingarden's adequated "pen" sentence. Were the use here ostensive, this "my" could be rounded out by the face of a speaker, perhaps Brecht's before he died in 1956. A person like Brecht as real speaker would be talking *about* himself, and since I vowed to concentrate mostly on written language, such a person could jot down these experiences. Indeed, someone of Brecht's stature could have such a letter (or inverview) published also as newspaper item. None of these conditions detract from Argument and its truth claims, even if they were met *negatively* by being a lie, perhaps in fear of censorship, to protect the "friends" cited. In Käte Hamburger's possible division for statements (1968, pp. 41-44, trans., 1973, pp. 40-44), such a letter actually written by Brecht is the work of a "historical subject."

I gave my reason for shying away from such added categories in Argument since they only end up describing content. The important point is that the function of Argument, adequation, supervenes the content as a particular mode of contextualization. Argument rules that this correlate, after nominal-verbal unfolding and interlocking, becomes juxtaposed with the kind of objective content the pure referent conveys. That is to say, Argument as pure referent starts in (the former circle marked) language, because only linguistic competence can amalgamate meanings into a unified meaning. This particular correlate is (hypotactically) twisted: its subject, the "I" --to be termed the "pronominal hero"--is preceded by a syntactic modifier consisting of two prepositional phrases, of which the second contains a possessive in the grammatical first person that matches the subject.

Significantly, this syntactic deferral complements Iconic timing, since flight and escape from the "countrymen" would precede arrival in Finland, the country of exile. The deictic adverb "finally" becomes the explicit element of Iconic time to reinforce that temporal order. Within the whole syntagma of this correlate, the pronominal hero seems sourrounded by prepositional phrases. In some respects one can glean, too, what Ingarden had in mind when his syntactic hierarchy placed nouns in first constitutive place for their "objectification of the meant." Even though these are noun-objects, with "flight . . . countrymen . . . Finland" tied to their prepositions "In . . . from . . . to," they seem to carry the brunt of the constitution by rendering in full the escape from foes and the safe arrival. By comparison, the subject-pronoun "I," as befits its name "pro-noun," remains a function word, an operative sign, whose schematic material content bears an intrinsic pointer or direction-factor that has been delimited considerably in seman-tic range.

What I just offered is a very careful description of the correlate as pure referent. In an emergency situational context, the urgency would cause adequation with an objective referent to be enormously fast. Thus the readers of these contents in a letter, who may be friends or relatives anxious to get the good news, would force the "I" swiftly into adequation with the known sender of the letter, rounding off this pronoun with his very person and appearance. The fact that he not only got away but has safely reached his destination and was accorded a welcome takes prece-dence over the forming of words. All attention is thus on the reality-nexus, the news value of the message, and on the "truth" in view of this vital information. Put scientifically in terms of non-Aristotelian semantics, the depletion or perforation of the pure referent has occurred; any fancy rhyme would be penetrated just as swiftly, adding perhaps a lighter touch by suggesting that the person had deve-loped sufficent distance from the harrowing experience to gloss it over like that. Even if this author is not backed up the way the "pen" was on my diagram by a graphic "doppelganger," the "I" pointer becomes stabilized through the familiarity with the real individual who hovers behind these contents as writer of the note.

In short, for Argument, the pragmatic message supersedes pure meaning, to the point of permitting the paraphrase. Should others want to know the gist of this letter, they could be given a shorter version of this correlate, as long as it conveyed at the level of the objective referent the safe escape. At the same time, the superreader Recipient who is a critic of language and not emotionally involved in this particular situation also understands that in paraphrasing there has been tampering with the pure referent; the new "phrasing" changes nominal-verbal unfolding and interlocking. That goes for any of the constituents: a different Referent (I) is being corporealized in reference (M) and embodied in transference (O). The actual wording, then, never tolerates any interference in the (thetic) closure of I-M-O generation. The point is simply that since the objective referent has priority here, it wins.

The objective referent wins to the point of dating the message through the adverb "finally"; it also localizes "Finland" on a map: readers may check their watches (although in those days they did not register dates) and look up the country. A superreader as critic, however, realizes that "Finland" at the level of the pure referent stays on a "ground" regulated by Qualisign dimensions. When thus alerted, a Recipient notices the different spelling for German "Finnland." No matter how minuscule the distinction, behind it lies the regulative power of language in a language, as first pointed out with the onomatopoetic rooster and cuckoo cries. What makes the constituents of this text structurally "literal" and not "metaphorical" like those of the Rheme is a univocality that comes from their projection "out into" a reality-nexus.

This univocality applies also to the "countrymen." At the level of the pure referent, they have no human identity, no face or body. Curiously, English *sounds* as though sex is there, but competent native speakers recognize that "-men" is a sexist remnant of English, whose plural usually does not necessarily divulge gender but in any generic context lets the male dominate, even if more women speakers may share the language. All one learns through the possessive "my" accompanying these compatriots is that they are of the same nationality as the pronominal hero. However, if the title of the whole poem, "1940," is to be taken as the real situational context applicable to the fleeing Brecht, the objective referent warrants the import "Nazis," as it would to the Recipients of Brecht's letter. Not until I get to the non-adequated structures, where the pure referent is all, will my reason for choosing "countrymen" rather than "compatriots" emerge.

Well, my *second* hypothesis is at hand to change all the priorities just elucidated. When these words belong to *Dicent*, they form a *non-adequated* syntactic correlate which abides by the pure referent only. As *quasi-judgment*, this correlate becomes the *literary* alternative to "literal" Argument, or plain "judgment." For the mimetic augmentation that is the fictional base of Dicent, at least *both* the *translated* correlates covering the excerpt have to be included. The very condition of augmentation, however, necessitates a hypothesis for this illustration, since even two correlates would not suffice for Dicent. The assumption is now that the two correlates open a novel, or drama. Since "performance" has to be confined to acts of decoding, the written novel works best, yet not without the reminder that the Dicentic construct comprises any short story, versified epic or ballad, for example.

All formats bearing *plots* become subsumed under the "fiction" of Dicent for sharing in a mimetic augmentation which is meted out piecemeal through unfolding and concatenating correlates. The primary issue is not how many formats can be drummed up, but what is entailed in the semantic functioning that causes plots to shape when the lexicon here stays unaltered aside from extending to encompass two correlates. Because Dicent may be in verse, the graphic "frame" is omitted this time. Still, to maintain closest surface fidelity with the former structure, the insinuation tends in the direction of prose and thus toward spatial confines of a page rather than a poetic line.

In flight from my countrymen
I finally got to Finland. Friends
That I didn't know yesterday put a few beds for me
Into clean rooms. . . .

The two sentences may compose a letter which now opens a novel as part of the exposition. The superreader authenticates Dicent in *second* stance, meeting the *esthetic ought* of this construct and its imperative of plot formation. Perhaps the authorial will is made explicit by a title and/or subtitle. But whether or not a "novel" becomes announced in so many words, there are indicators that fiction obtains for the construct. The Recipient is hardly a pal of the author concerned with the latter's personal well-being. That is not the reason for concretizing these correlates. If it is, Argument will obtain, to the detriment of Dicent, naturally. No matter how autobiographical the novel containing these two sentences, the Recipient does not involve the real Brecht in content alignment with a reality-nexus but only as constitutive consciousness of a plot; the Referent to be sought resides in a "story" the correlates bring forth in the "telling" that I identified with the very term "Dicent." There is no "ulterior" motive of juxtaposing the pure with an objective referent. While *syntax* prevails in seemingly forming the "-judgment" part of each correlate with nominal-verbal unfolding and interlocking, the "quasi-" prefix underscores a pure referent that *presents* a simulated world from what Icons mirror and hold Indexically, beginning in a vacuum at *zero-point*.

Instead of the perforation characteristic of Argument, closure obtains not only for each constitutive unit(y) but the entire work that arises piecemeal and cumulatively from the correlates in their unfolding and progressive concatenation. "Closure" becomes a mimetic enclave or "enclosure"--if not on the order of the "pen" that came up with Ingarden's example. Leaning back for a moment in a wholly analytic (or pre-esthetic) stance, the superreader as critic of language may note the mottled surface of the non-adequated correlate, disclosing that curious *tachistic* and *finite* disposition Ingarden had noted. It attests to the selectional bias of a *pure* correlate that stays non-adequated, hence without the backing of a reality-nexus. Simultaneously, there are the indeterminate and yet elastic "pockets." As a part of the dynamic and natural ambiguity of linguistic meanings, these pockets fill out during concretization. The schematic, laconic pronominal hero as an "I" would be a rather conspicuous case in point, even if all material contents of Icons in their heteronomous makeup remain schematic, as explained.

My analysis so far has covered a description of the *linguistic strata* that carry semantic thresholds and unities, although observed with an eye on the two *literary strata* that yield presented objects in the precise aspects the Icons and Indexes submitted. After all, Argument was said to carry the first two strata as well, much as they become depleted through the reorientation to a reality-nexus. In Dicent, however, what the correlates own at the moment of unfolding reinforces thematically what their concatenation will knit together. Thus the pronominal hero may count as the protagonist while "his" possible antagonists erupt as the felonious "countrymen" chasing him. Their faceless, sexless, and curiously sexist nature has been revealed already and needs no reiteration. Through the "my" possessive, these antagonists gain a certain aspect that links them dissociatively to the protagonist, since he has to flee from them when he should belong to them. Illocutionary force may go into the "my" as the hurt experienced at the hands of these infamous pursuers. Ingarden's "metaphysical qualities" may be pertinent here, necessitating a special intonation of bitterness, perhaps, in a dramatic performance of a character reading this letter on stage.

These "analytic" observations bring me back to the superreader who now operates as "connoisseur" by being locked into the Icons that unravel with each unfolding correlate in turn at the horizontal sequence. The *first correlate* plunges the Recipient into *medias res* with respect to the "flight" and escape of the pronominal hero from his "countrymen." So here meaning comes before the urgent message carrying factual "news." Instead, the Icons "urge" a Recipient on to discover why the pronominal hero had to flee--perhaps with subsequent correlates going into flashbacks--and who the pursuers really are. Nothing can be taken for granted that does not come with the explicit and implicit denomination of words.

The second correlate, however, does not delve into the hero's past but continues with the (fictional) present. The "Friends," presumably of "Finland," emerge as "new" characters and oppose the compatriot foes in that very Icon of benevolence. Unlike the pursuers to whom the hero should belong, as the "my" suggested, the "Friends" were not even known "yesterday," before the arrival in Finland, and yet they demonstrate a sense of responsibility toward the hero. That is to say, the "Friends" that initiate the second correlate as noun-subject show their initiative to full advantage as they take over the action which erupts into the kind deed of providing shelter with the furniture described. Indirectly, the "Friends" are reaffirmed by the relative pronoun "That" and this whole clause in content. Unlike the supposedly familiar compatriots from whom the pronominal hero becomes alienated, these foreigners at point of arrival are fast becoming familiar.

In the second correlate, therefore, the recursive direction-factor of the verb "put" bypasses the relative-pronoun clause to interlock with "Friends." The full predicate then produces the objects in nominal-verbal interlocking, directly for "a few beds" and indirectly for the "clean rooms" as objects of the preposition "Into." This preposition underscores the feverish activity of the welcoming "Friends." Curiously, even the adjective "clean" bears part of that action by suggesting the preparation that went into readying these "rooms." Adjectives, indeed, serve rather conspicuously as *reinforcing aspects* in the order of "leitmotifs," just because they can be omitted in nominal-verbal constitution; "beds" and "rooms" would have made the point, but the number in "a few" and the care in "clean" respectively drive home a point. Both individually reinforce the concern of the new friends. The number, tying in with the plural morphemes of "beds" and "rooms," increases the magnanimity; not only to the singular "I"-person in which the hero appears do the friends extend their generosity but also to possible family members and (native) friends.

So one learns through the second correlate that the hero is not alone--for long at any rate. And although the vast geographical space of "Finland" has been narrowed down to the four walls implied by "rooms," the very fact that this Icon comes in the plural suggests largesse, perhaps on the order of a suite. Space has become explicitly rounded out and simultaneously narrowed down from a geographical location to a man-made locus for rest and repose spelling "shelter." To Iconize that Index, the pronominal hero has found a "roof over his head," one lovingly readied.

Under Argument, the readers of Brecht's letter would have known who accompanied Brecht, what family members and/or friends he took with him or would meet there--native German persons, no doubt, instead of the Finnish ones. With the non-adequated zero-point origin, however, the schematic plural morphemes, beyond reflecting the relatively vague number in the Icons "a few," keep the reader guessing. The language via the referent drives the concatenation forward. How may these numbers be filled out? Who are these persons still reduced here to plural morphemes? Are they true friends or more treacherous foes, men or women, adults or children? Only other correlates will "tell." The same applies to the hero, "who" is merely reiterated as "I"-subject in the relative pronoun clause and, outside of it, as an added "me" "for" whom the Finnish friends put themselves out as the Good Samaritans they are. So, certainly, a fascination with this elusive protagonist continues until more emerges from succeeding correlates. In this manner, the unfolding and concatenating correlates combine and, in a curious way, "conspire" by letting out precise Iconic details in some instances while offering only ambiguous Indexical suggestions in others.

All this the very essence of language achieves in the process of *natural denoting* and *connoting*, as acts of meaning become expressed through meanings in their own dynamic, heteronomous contents of explicit and implicit denominations. Let the skeptics, Fregean or otherwise, disappear once and for all! Thanks to Ingarden, language as bearer of meaning has found its substance and its function. A simulated world grows from the Qualisign ground and is presented in set Iconic and yet dynamic Indexes at depth, at the level of import. This presented world is replete with instances of time and space involving people and their pleasant or not-so-pleasant preoccupations. Hostile and hospitable characters have begun to appear in nouns and pronouns, in adjectives and ("s") morphemes rendering their plurality. They are there because the material contents of Icons laid their foundation while their relevant Indexes "filled" them out.

A last note on the "countrymen." This compounded Icon proves many things, first among these a possible *epochal* time gap. Supposing this Icon changed in years to come and referred literally to "men from the country" as rural individuals. Of course, that such an Index hardly befits the context should alert a superreader. Hypothetically, though, a Recipient who artificially closes the gap between inception and reception by decoding the "countrymen" wrongly becomes an unwarranted pseudo-Referent by altering authorial intent at 0 in I·M·0 generation. To avoid the problem, a Recipient must return to the inventory from which the selection was made in order to accord the author the proper signitive act that was "meant" by the choice of Icon.

Now, when stating that, "literally," the Icon refers to "men" from the--and not "a"--"country," a critic draws on that *metalinguistic gesture* for punning I had introduced before. The meaning is then "univocal" by skimming only the material, explicit contents of Icons (M). Conversely, one could say that genuine "men" from the "country" were not meant--or meant only "metaphorically" by designating compatriots at depth. Then, in a metalinguistic gesture, a speaker motions to the Index (0). Whatever the case, these gestures can be deployed under Argument or Dicent. In the latter case the speaker is fictive, perhaps the pronominal hero "who" puns in "his" situation. As histrionic "gesture," anyway, no genuine univocality is involved since Icons are never contextualized without Indexes, and vice versa. Beyond a sheer description of thus skimming Icons, no constitutional unit(y) can tolerate such a split without tearing meaning from the meant, leaving nothing to be "derived" from the selected Icons. Moreover, if the Icon were changed deliberately and/or officially to mitigate the sexism in the compound by switching to "country-persons," it would *date* every such appearance. As patent reminder of inception, the Icon would bring the newly accepted choice forward through future reception, much as the Recipient tacitly goes "back" to that "date" in satisfactory construal of the relevant Index.

Just as important for this study of *metaphor* is the fact that epochal discrepancies affect *deviance* ratios in future receptions; anything no longer commonplace seems "strange(r)." If, for instance, "countrymen" had been replaced by "countrypersons," future Recipients encounter the former as an odd expression for compatriots that are only of the masculine gender. All these problems arise with the lexical, content-sensitive type of "metaphor" tradition has plied. "Metaphor" in structural dimensions comes up shortly. Presently, let me list the facets of *time* that have surfaced thus far: sequential, Iconic, and epochal. *Structural time* is not to be excluded either. Although it is harder to prove with such short length, enough is there to stress that the two quasi-judgment correlates of Dicent become *cumulatively* augmented as the quasi-mirror *emerges* without the direct backing of equivalent *existents*.

In synchronizing the gradual accumulation between encoded text and decoding concretization, the *double horizon* forms: "Finland" has emerged as a friendly place of exile, for instance, a hospitable country providing shelter. As more evolves and becomes knit together, this "country" shifts in whatever direction the plot changes, and that could be drastic if the kind persons, for example, turned into traitors after all. In any case, this double horizon will be mitigated after the first heuristic concretization by the full impact of the qualitative time phases that assimilate the construal as it moves along. Retroactive and hermeneutic concretizations should then weight the work with all its significance, permitting its "artistic" compositional merits to evolve as an organic whole. The first-person pronominal hero may then come off indeed as an egocentric person from the start, or whatever. If Dicentic *verse* applies, as it may here, the final hermeneutic effort of what I qualified as the (primary) stance of the "connoisseur" may then work toward full appreciation of the "esthetic values" that result in (Ingarden's) "polyphony" among the interacting strata.

Polyphony is given its due especially by the *third* analysis of this chapter, in the structure authenticated by Brecht, the author, and that is the *Rheme*, whose *micro-component* is the functional, *non-Aristotelian metaphor*--of substance and not of deviance! The hypotheses are thus concluded and yet also continued insofar as the authenticated form, the poem, stays reduced to the excerpt Baumgärtner cited. Still non-adequated like Dicent, the Rheme additionally breaks with the syntactic correlate and extends instead to the contextual alternative this study has designated "poetic intext." Meanings then become intensified in their "nominalization" of backgrounding and foregrounding a lyric ego, an outward "totality of expression" toward which each such meaning has contributed as "object of expression."

For full authentication, the earlier presented background plays a part. Brecht's poem, I said, was identified as such in the title for the cycle that contained it, inclusive of dates. Its own title, in fact, bore the date "1940." Despite the poem's length, greater than the excerpt that covers only the first half of the eighth and last stanza, there is no mimetic augmentation, no genuine "tale" being told about heroes and heroines. As for the excerpt, it now displays its "expressive" rather than fictional nature. One may then get a glimpse of the direct "saying" that Käte Hamburger classed erroneously with any statement in order to contrast lyric poetry with mimetic fashioning. Regardless of the eloquent appearance that lets the "I"-person "speak out," the Rheme through its centripetal lyric ego demands the same separate and self-contained "closure" of constitution that Dicent owned and which cuts it off from any adequated statement. This "speaker" is not for real, whether or not the surface looks more "literal" than "lyric." In one descriptive concession (only), it may be wiser to call the pronominal hero a "lyric I." But the designation is not synonymous with the Rhemic structural unit(y), the lyric ego. It merely labels surface content. Since this structure was placed at the M-base, the bilingual version returns, with extra space devoted to vital issues of translation.

Auf der Flucht vor meinen Landsleuten
Bin ich nun nach Finnland gelangt. Freunde
Die ich gestern nicht kannte, stellten mir ein paar Betten
In saubere Zimmer. . . .

In flight from my countrymen
I finally got to Finland. Friends
That I didn't know yesterday put a few beds for me
Into clean rooms. . . .

So here is the text once more--the same words but no longer the same constituents of a construct. Keeping in mind that all the entries are now *non-Aristotelian metaphors*, the procedure of concretization differs again. The text has to be pieced together *directly*, with the *lines* respected rather than the syntactic correlates which were given as optional on the schema of Rhemic hierarchies. Accordingly, the poem is to be analyzed in a *tetradic* division matching the four lines instead of going by the two correlates.

"Direct" constitution, moreover, applies to the constituents themselves that support each line, just because lines as such surface in the other structures. So what a line bears here must accompany all non-adequated and nonmimetic elements that are objects of expression for a totality of expression. Ironically, in that very capacity the function of these constitutents turns so-called function words or operative signs around, into *structural nouns, nominalized* meanings. As a consequence, these components still are described by their syntactic taxonomy while at depth they remain metaphors and/or functional nouns through the width their intrinsic pointer, the direction-factor, assumes from the task of connotative compounding. Thus I still speak of "prepositions," for example, to identify the surface but stay conscious of Rhemic synthesis. All elements, in fact, belong to the "metonymic" parts-to-whole coherence which does not go by the lexicon but by the function unique to a constitutional unit(y) that transcends both correlates in this particular text.

Inner connotative compounding must supersede the overt syntagma displaying sentences, and that Rhemic task is carried out at *horizontal* as well as *recursive-vertical* levels--"up-and-down," so to speak, if not in reference to the everyday prepositional metaphors that so intrigued Embler and others in a spatial-to-social reuse. No, what distinguishes these "esthetic" counterparts is that after forming the linguistic strata, they *background* and *foreground* poetic intext at the two *literary strata*, where the lyric ego is pieced together by Icons and interlocking Indexes as coherent import. The processing occurs immanently and not cumulatively.

An analytic approach to basic linguistic dispositions of the Rheme calls for comparing those bilingual aspects that affect construal at the M-base. After that approach, each line will be scrutinized, as the two Dicentic correlates were before. A conspicuous similarity in the bilingual version is the matching relational circumference of lines: they extend in length from one to three and fall off in the fourth line, which the excerpt has curtailed unnaturally. Yet the difference that causes most of the German to appear more elongated than English affirms also the synthetic, inflected nature of the former as compared to the analytic language English represents. Then again the many cognates underscore the Indo-European, "Proto-Germanic" root (Waterman, 1976, pp. 38-51) of both languages, which aids M-base fidelity in retained alliteration for "Flucht" and "Flight," "Freunde" and "Friends," "Betten" and "beds." Yet even these cognates make evident the regulative "coercion" of language in each language with which my study began, and not only with the already mentioned "Fin(n)land," where the added nasal distinguishes even a place name as belonging to one oppositional inventory. Such a geographical landmark at least keeps the capitalization bilingually, as does the syntactic onset from which the friends are seen to benefit above. In other instances, however, German differs from English by its mandatory capitalization for nouns at one end and often a softer feminine cadence at the other.

Only from the *universal* perspective of structure does the Rheme dominate both versions equally, just because the function is context-sensitive but not content-sensitive. That is exactly why such designators as "literal" or "metaphorical" can be applied categorically in non-Aristotelian semantics. The loss in content, however, stays a problem particularly for translations of a non-adequated language located at M-base. It forces a translator into the role of an "after-poet," or "Nachdichter" as the Germans say, not necessarily with a pejorative intent but because the keen sensitivity to content often requires a poet to translate poems.

In my own attempt at the closest "after-poetry," I now explain why the Icon "countrymen" was chosen instead of the less sexist "compatriots," for instance. When simply literalized, one gets the starred "*landspeople" English has not indented as compound--any more than the "*fill-feather" of Ingarden's "pen" example. That is to say, only the segments "land-" and "-people" are Legisigns. And, although the first segment appears to yield the cognates "Land" and "land," the German Icon is not only Indexicalized for that elevated patriotic nuance which English can match, but also for "country" in the dual sense of national home and rural area, of which the former applies to the "countrymen." Thus my choice despite the sexist overtones.

Many other discrepancies cannot be perfectly controlled either. Right away the first prepositional phrase makes known its "national" origin in what linguists (like Chomsky) would call a syntactic subcategorization rule by requiring the (dative-feminine) definite article "der" between preposition and object. That addition right there extends this line further than the English one even before considering the lengthened cadence mentioned, which elongates possessive and noun in (dative plural) to "meinen Landsleuten," as italicised. The second line bearing the first verb tense as Iconic time becomes elongated because of the German need to use the present perfect in "Bin . . . gelangt" while English keeps the (simple or single) imperfect past with "got." True, in the next line additions seem reversed insofar as English demands an auxiliary for the emphatic to accompany negation in "didn't know," even when thus contracted to preserve the "prosaic" tone that confused Baumgärtner. Also, since English bears no distinctive Sinsign for the dative case, this line had to Iconize an extra preposition with "*for me*" instead of "*mir*."

However, even so, inflected German components lengthen their line further than the English, as shown by the extended plural morphemes of verb and noun in "stellten . . . Betten" compared to the blunt, (masculine) equivalent of "put . . . beds." The verb, incidentally, literalizes into "stood," because the German inventory possesses the quirk of having flat objects "lie"--as indicated with Ingarden's "pen" example--and more vertical ones with (wooden?) legs "stand." Again, English had to forego that peculiarity at the M-base lest I become indeed a phony "after-poet." As for the last line, this again forces English into an added prepositional Icon as shown by the pair "In"/"Into," because otherwise the accusative Index of motion gets left out. In that line, too, the German adjective "saubere" assumes the onus of plurality, Iconized as italicised, because the equivalent noun for "rooms" as "Zimmer" bears a null morpheme for number.

From my general observations above, the irony arises that, surprisingly, it is the prosaic type of language which for the M-base presents the greatest number of strictures if one does not want to over-poeticize by emulating the authorial will. A more outlandish style, particularly of disrupted syntax, permits also more departures of norms for the translation. However, to eliminate the sensation of standard language in the Brecht text not only violates authorial intent but would eradicate the Baumgärtner "hybrid" on whose refutation my tripartite analysis is based. Certainly, these mandatory syntactic changes cause horizontal and vertical proximities to go awry. At the horizontal level, the switch of perfect to imperfect tense has the new hospitable persons closer to their country, as in "Finland. Friends" when compared to the original that separates them with the past participle "gelangt" in typical dependent clause word order. At the vertical level, the same tense change pushes the lyric "ich" or "I" over to commence the second line instead of having the reiterated pronouns hover exactly over one another in recursive reinforcement. I myself no doubt added to that distortion by using "finally" instead of the possible "now" which in Iconic stretch and Sinsign composition might have been closer to the "nun." But somehow this adverb did not seem to Indexicalize as well in the illocutionary sense of relief that comes out in my choice. So I believe.

A special case of bilingual entanglement is the *relative pronoun* clause of the third line. Typically, the plural definite article "Die" that German adopts also as relative pronoun initiates the clause. Although punctuation is obligatory for German relative pronoun clauses, the comma after "Freunde" has been omitted in what may be just a modest indication of that "poetic license" the conspicuous prosaic nature of this poem has generally avoided, although it does appear at the end, after the verb "kannte." Had a comma not gone there, the two finite verbs "kannte" and "stellten" would have been thrust unnaturally together, which is indeed the reason for this punctuation. The strange proximity is caused by the mandatory order of verb-end and verb-second-place for the respective dependent and main clauses, thus forcing two finite verbs of different subjects together as shown, even if "kannte" signals "ich" as subject and "stellten" the plural friends "who" then resume their action within the main clause, much as they determine the plural of the relative pronoun.

English, which is not subject to such word order changes, may thus forego the punctuation stricture for the relative pronoun clause. However, truly amazing is the signitive ramification of its relative pronoun. Four possible choices reside in the oppositional inventory of latent alternatives: (1) null entry; (2) "who"; (3) "whom"; and (4) "that." What determined my fourth choice in the translation was, again, its casual nuance. The second and third choices do reinforce the "human(e)" aspect of these friends and are generally standardized for persons. But they seemed stilted for the tenor of this poem, in part because they force the translator into deciding between the proper subcategorization "whom" and the looser but more natural sounding "who." The omission of the first choice might have obviated all those problems. But here is the unexpected result of that choice for the actualized meaning: a vertical anaphora would be created by eliminating the relative pronoun as opening element of the third line, yielding "In"/"I"/"I"/"Into." Very clever! But again, the translator appears inadvertently to outwit the original creator of the poem--ironically in the very intent to save the style from excess. To be sure, this anaphora would have brought the lyric "I" back into vertical alignment, if in first place, but through a drastic measure.

A modest vestige and so ramified the problems! Whether I have solved them to everyone's satisfaction is not so much the point as to indicate, positively, the power of ontic heteronomy, the willful sphere of language in a language, despite the universal nature of the structures as such. The differences came about through the ontogenetic origin of Icons and their Indexes, hence in the indentations that resulted from the transaction of *reference* with *transference*, from an act of meaning corporealized and embodied by selected explicit and implicit meanings. In the renewed transaction through the extended transference this Rhemic construct acquires, signitive values and their deployment become so uniquely intertwined as structural metaphors that the slightest nuance has serious repercussions. Outwardly, to be sure, the words look like the ones that served Argument and Dicent, but inwardly they now point centripetally toward a holistic lyric ego instead of being driven forward by unfolding correlates. The totality of expression still arises piecemeal from these nominalized meanings, but not progressively. To do justice to this holistic immanence and/or structural present, Ingarden's assimilative faculty of *live memory* has to go into effect while following the sequence of the lines, as is to be demonstrated next, beginning with line *one*:

Auf der Flucht vor meinen Landsleuten
(In flight from my countrymen)

The line obviously splits the sentence into the first two prepositional phrases that usher in flight and escape. While the Iconic feminine cadence in "meinen Landsleuten" seems to reinforce a "togetherness" between the possessive and its compatriots, the flight shatters that connection in sense, releasing "enemy," or "hostility" in my attempt here to Iconize this Index. The two nominalized prepositions "Auf" and "vor" add respectively the nuance of a flight in progress and a need to get away "from" the compatriots in pursuit. When observing a further analytic distance, the critic notices a curious Iconic reversal: on the surface the flight is cited first and the pursuers last, whereas in meaning the pursuers are the very cause for flight. With the *second* line,

Bin ich nun nach Finnland gelangt. Freunde
(I finally got to Finland. Friends)

the hostile pursuers are cut off sharply as the auxiliary verb "Bin," in agreement with "ich," also ushers in the lyric "I," the subject, in completion of this correlate. With the "nun nach," time and space appear in Icons and alliterate as Sinsign composites. English could not match that, even if I had settled for "now" instead of "finally." And the perfect-to-imperfect tense change (discussed) severs that proximity anyway, should "now" have matched the nasal Qualisign of the spatial "to." German "nach" as vocable, incidentally, also bears the temporal signifier "after," which becomes suppressed in the Indexicalization when preceding place names such as "Finnland." And there is of course the inimitable assonance between the geographical "-land" and past-participial segment "-langt" to let safe asylum and arrival interlock through place and action. At the recursive vertical level, "Finnland" and "Flucht" alliterate to reinforce a similar import for the anticipated and attained destination. Live memory holds the construed elements together, permitting them to widen in further compounding. Through that capacity of retention, the chiastic reversal can take place between the compounds "*Lands*leuten"/"Finn*land*" as underlined (in italics): the persons from one's ("meinen") own "land" become--quite literally--the ground for anxiety while that new land turns into a blessed haven. The positive import is extended to the "Freunde," who were recently "Finnish foreigners" but became fast friends. The new intimacy surfaces through the further alliterative bond intertwining "Flucht"/"Finnland"/"Freunde." These friends also belong to their line for all the reasons cited, no matter how much they open the next sentence in enjambement, as geographical space takes on a "human" qualifier through them. In their vertical alignment with the "Landsleuten," who broke off the first line, the "Freunde" interlock as "people" and even share the "eu" Qualisign with them. Yet as "members" of their line, the benevolent friends also counter the nasty pursuers, not being merely "human" but truly "humane."

Such recursive interaction could not be given this much attention in the other two structures, even when versified. For the horizontal level of the M-base, the second line radiates a gentleness in the soft nasal twang which weaves in and out of the Incons in their Sinsign composition, from the initiating "Bin" to the "*nun nach Finnland gelangt. Freunde*." These Qualisigns exist in the first line, too, but not to that degree. So far, then, live memory has amalgamated "hostility" versus "hospitality," with "old foe" pitted against "new friend" for the backgrounded lyric ego through all the Iconized foregrounding elucidated. Meaning evolves from meanings because every single element as "metaphor" contributes through its own denominational core what it has to offer in Qualisign material and deeper relevance for the poetic intext, the contextual correlate. Nominalization causes these micro-components to *shift* at *every level*; in their intensified "pointing at . . ." these components assume a direction-factor equal in strength to that of the noun, even if they are not *overtly* nouns.

In the *third* line,

Die ich gestern nicht kannte, stellten mir ein paar Betten
(That I didn't know yesterday put a few beds for me)

the initiating relative pronoun "Die" still carries out the operative task of taking over from a noun antecedent, the "Freunde," bearing "their" plurality. But as nominalized meaning, this pronoun underscores the numerous new friends "relayed" back to the "Freunde" by the reiterated plural. This number English cannot Iconize in any of the four relative-pronoun choices discussed, even if I had given the priority to the "human(e)" import rather than the casual tone by selecting instead either "who" or "whom."

In both versions this line nevertheless begins with the relative pronoun clause, offset in German also at the other end by a comma. Within this clause, the lyric "I" as "ich" continues to be the subject and the friends as relative pronoun--which at the horizontal level precede it as they remain close to it--the grammatical object. The vertical reaffirmation of the lyric "I" deepens into a tone of renewed confidence and self-assertiveness, but also seems to underscore the singular status of the pronoun that contrasts with all the plural nouns of "persons" surrounding it, foe or friend. Yet this lyric "I" is brought closer to the friends in the clause which in horizontal sequence further "seals" this new friendship.

Next in the sequence is Iconic time, displayed by a deictic adverb and verb tense. The original has the adverbs "nun" and "gestern" directly under one another, an alignment the tense change unfortunately disrupts in English, as pointed out. Time in content, reduced to a tiny intextual circumference, becomes boosted by the structural time of Rhemic recursiveness as the vertically aligned adverbs come closer together while their signifance distinguishes *present* from *past*, from a "prior" moment of flight. The sheer sequence driving concretization forward becomes halted as the construal goes "back" or "up" to the preceding lines through the assimilative capacity of live memory. The past belongs to the native foes and the present to the new Finnish friends who, in the recent past of "yesterday," were as yet unknown "foreigners," if never outright foes matching the pursuers. That is how time Indexicalizes within the relative pronoun clause, replete with its verb, "kannte."

The formerly "not-known" friends then erupt positively as subjects of the main clause, where they are found doing things "for" the lyric "I," as is implicit in the dative "mir." At this point the plurality tends away from people to things, first through the adjectival number "ein paar" which modifies the plural "Betten." Ostensibly, the adjective resembles the English cognate, "a pair," but together the Icons Indexicalize into "a few" as shown, hence a number which offers no set quantity and thus rests in that natural schematic ambiguity of material contents; their polyvalent direction-factor does not point at "two" or "four" to suggest either a (married) couple and family or a set number of acquaintances (as the native rather than new Finnish friends). What the number, however, does denote distinctly is the magnanimity of the friends. Their generosity is multiplied by attending not only to the one lyric "I" but "his" company. Through this import, the number and plural noun also endow the explicitly single lyric "I" with number; "he" did not come alone, or will not be lonely in exile. At that point, then, the number and Icons for things interact with the concerns of people.

The number in itself thus conveys positively the charitable nature of the friends and the implied companionship of the exile. There is visual and assonantal reverberation to heighten the significance of the welcome and repose the friends and beds exude, as shown by "*gestern . . . kannte . . . stellten . . . Betten.*" Vocalic "e" iteration is accompanied by the soft nasal twang of the "n" and the liquids "l" and "r" at the level of the nominalized wordsound at the M-base, once the meaning has been foregrounded in all its relevance. The geographical place of "Finnland" paved the way, in a manner of speaking, for the narrowed and yet more humanized, man-made interior, which is evoked in the *fourth* line,

> In saubere Zimmer. . . .
> (Into clean rooms. . . .)

Were this line not cut artificially by the excerpt, one might say that its brevity mirrored effectively the narrowing of space from a country to the four walls of the "rooms," the German "Zimmer." As pointed out before, the original Brecht text had "Im Lautsprecher" where the ellipsis points are. In yet another enjambement, this content spills over into the next line which resounds with the bragging radio messages of the enemy, called "scum" (Abschaum). So the nasty pursuers, the "Landsleute," absorb the invective through live memory and share the alliteration with the "Lautsprecher" that carries their negative message. There are further geographical allusions to "Lappland" and a to hopeful "little door" that is still left open in the extreme North.

But to concentrate on this excerpt, its last line creates a type of implicit epiphora in vertical aligment with the preceding lines, two of which rendered "people" in the pursuers and friends, and the other two "things" in the beds and rooms. At the other horizontal end, the spontaneous activity of the friends is relayed through the accusative which English Iconizes as "Into." The friends gain further in positive connotation since the plural rooms suggest something more lavish than many beds in one area, closer to a suite as noted. The cleanliness of these several rooms, which was stated to bear the onus of number in the plural ending of the adjective "saubere," also becomes compounded, or magnified in size: every place is spotless. Although Iconic reinforcement is still part of the "clean" adjective, a fictional type of *leitmotif* in recurrence must be ruled out, letting Rhemic recursiveness instead underscore what is there. The same goes, of course, for this lyric "I" which remains suspended in its pronominal rendering; a genuine hero will not emerge--ever. Nor is this lyric "I" the poet Brecht. As poet instead of real speaker, Brecht is the inhering Referent of that constitutive consciousness which merges with the holistic lyric ego as authorial intent.

As for the Recipient, retention of live memory enabled the foregrounded M-base to meld into the poetic intext for the decoding consciousness. The whole context then hangs together through the meaning culled from these few meanings in their unique "metonymic" parts-to-whole relation. The full nominalization of structural metaphors has made that possible: whatever compatriots or Finland or beds, and so forth, designate elsewhere, here they came to interlock through an extended transference in order to lend their explicit and implicit meanings to a poet's meaning in maximal connotative compounding. Every vestige contributed to that goal, even such seemingly "grammatical" particles as dative or accusative cases. For that reason I cautioned early in presenting Rhemic hierarchies that "words" as such are not to be taken too literally. Nominalization suffuses everything, and its Qualisigns are no longer the degenerate material that is left on a page. These signs bear a fully generate materialization that causes Icons to back in their idiosyncratic denomination what expanded Indexes gain in inner relevance. That was also the reason why my construal adhered mainly to the original here, always citing words in full inflection to stress that chosen constituents and not loose, latent vocables were involved. Although English matched few of these, the translated version was kept in tow for specific issues.

My analytic approach stayed diametrically opposed to that of the tradition: neo-Aristotelians use "metaphor" descriptively and I applied terms such as "noun," "verb," "adverb," "preposition," or "pronoun" descriptively. Metaphor, on the other hand, is for real, since ultimately all the components disclosed effectively their "formal features," shedding Baumgärter's "hybridic" state, once the esthetic ought was met by proper (second) stance of construal. Indeed, when the critic yields entirely to the connoissuer and moves from heuristic and retroactive readings to a hermeneutic concretization, Ingarden's *polyphony* can go into affect among the interacting strata of the Rhemic construct, disclosing a transmuted rhythm which might be labeled "free verse" for its lack of set meter and/or neat rhyme schemes. Simultaneously, all the foregrounded sonorous and visual aspects of the M-base (I treated) come into their own.

To be sure, the content in the area of connotations may differ slightly, but not the basic procedure outlined for a superreader as Recipient. Construal needs full concentration on the given Icons, focusing only on what is actually there, put there by the authorial will which may then be culled successfully from the constituents--without any proxy-tenet substitution of guessing what analogy prompts a superficial anomaly in replacement. What Brecht *meant*, his *meanings* disclosed in their circumference and deeper content; his intent was *derived* from their contextualization at depth, going "up" to the (mute) sonorous and visual idiosyncrasies that hover at the surface. *That* is the procedure: there were no existents to "prove" the veracity of any occurrence in time and space; there were no fictional "emergents" that solidify into persons with set traits; there were only "expressants" that kept an Iconic lyric "I" afloat and yet forged coherence at every level, horizontally in foregrounded sequence and vertically in backgrounded recursiveness. Since the esthetic ought is intrinsically spontaneous by challenging a Recipient, a reader who relinquishes the "super-" prefix could approach the text as elucidated, under the other two structures. With Dicent the Recipient quite literally would not get far, but with Argument the semantic depletion of adequation would cause all rich nuances to evaporate.

Brecht as person is thus not at issue, despite biographical overtones. Had this not been an excerpt, the title, which was said to read "1940," certainly would have played a part in the recursive significance that belongs to the structural time of Rhemic immanence. In the process, the date would have been combined at the implicit interpretive level with the Iconic time the text displayed. But a real date it is not. To be sure, the background and/or biographical circumstances should not be ignored in full literary scholarship, yet they cannot compensate for the actualized I-M-O generation which has Recipient communicate with Referent. That goes even for a type of Whitmanesque Song of Myself Brecht had forged (1963, pp. 148-151; Esslin, 1962, pp. 177-178). The poem's very title, "Of Poor B.B.," cites its poet's initials while its text commences with "I, Bertolt Brecht, . . ." More for didactic purposes of spreading his socialism than in sheer affirmation of a Rhemic M-base did Brecht insist on a "faithful word-for-word reproduction of the

German," as one of his translators, Bentley, put it in an "Introduction" to one of the plays (1978, p. 10). Yet even Bentley saw fit to disobey the author by offering a more "nonliteral" translation in the end (ibid., p. 11).

My bilingual analysis has tried to uphold such fidelity in reproducing a text, as Bentley has it, without literalizing the Icons for the sole purpose of foregrounding the M-base when that practice threatened to distort the backgrounded Indexicalization and thus the significance of the lyric ego. Making the decision was not always easy. Still, the analysis proved that, with proper authentication of poetic intent, Baumgärtner's "hybrid" is unmasked as bogus: all "formal features" of the poem appeared. The next analysis should have been a straightforward case since the text includes those features unmistakably. But even such overt backing from the language apparently does not prevent a critic from forcing a literary construct into the strait jacket of compliance with logic, making the text seem "prosaic" by forsaking the decidedly "poetic" Icons the author offered.

Analysis: Levin on Nonrecoverable Compression in Dickinson

The second analysis is based on a text with decidedly "poetic" traits. Unfortunately even that kind of textual control does not prevent a critic essentially from turning the construct into yet another hybrid by neglecting the esthetic ought and taking recourse in logic rather than language. The critic is S. R. Levin and the example a poem by Emily Dickinson. Levin cited it in his essay entitled "The Analysis of Compression in Poetry" (1971). Compression should be a fitting qualifier for the type of condensation characterizing Rhemic coherence. Unfortunately, Levin bases compression on the traditional notion that *linguistic reference* actually *represents* the empirical world in matching classes of epistemological or so-called encyclopedic knowledge. Levin fails to realize, therefore, that language presents only itself through concepts derived from signitive acts which guide linguistic competence in further use of such acts. This failure leads him tacitly into espousing the *ontological category-mistake* as he seeks to explain *linguistic meaning* through *logical mediation*.

Levin's idea of compression is thus not a matter of centripetal denseness but one of *deletion* in a "reduction" of logical connectives he sees fit to fill in through a process of semantic *recovery*, even as he claims that poetic language should be "nonrecoverable." It appears, therefore, that Levin can find no other method of dealing with construal of literary language. His general procedure becomes equivalent to taking a photographic transparency of some subject matter a painting contains and placing this over the canvas in order to fill in what the artist has left out. Whether or not the omissions actually are painted in, they are to be pointed out by him. His vantage point of naive realism is not unlike trying to extract chlorophyll from a painted leaf. Such skepticism assumes that the purposive medium under scrutiny cannot be evaluated on its own ground.

In language, which as purposive domain resembles art even before it is literary, that ground is the linguistic Qualisign, the base of all perception from which arise the validated contents, the Legisigns that erupt into the explicit Icons. Any attempt to by-pass that ground induces the *paraphrase*, which Levin readily endorses. When attacked by Kintgen for this parasitic approach to meaning, Levin staunchly defends the paraphrase: in his "Reply to Kintgen" (1972, pp. 109-110), Levin insists it helps avert "random generation" in language. His rebuttal demonstrates that typical neo-Aristotelian perspective which non-Aristotelian semantics has tried to eradicate from language theory. Since all "generation" of language is willed, there is no such thing as random chance. What Levin confuses is the *volitional autotelism* of a purposive state with a *volatile* contingency whose *aleatory* outcome resembles the tossing of dice. From the intrinsic vantage point, Legisign validation creates *norms*. Ordained to serve speaker competence, these norms become *absolute*, much as they seem "arbitrary" from any other standpoint.

By coincidence, I made that very point in the same journal a couple of years after Levin's "Analysis" appeared. My article (Gumpel, 1974) treated the "essence" of a "reality" that evolves as a "construct of language." Such a sphere can be traced back no further than to the signitive convolutions speakers share intersubjectively as interlocutory partners within their speech community. Only acts of meaning through authorial intent have indented signitive consciousness, and every content serving these acts acquired its explicit and implicit denominations through composing a constitutional unit(y) that engenders the new completion of language. No single speaking "subject" can alter a language without conflicting with the intersubjective consent Legisgns embody, nor interfere with a choice based on those signs that a given speaker has already made.

The paraphrase, then, is one attempt to meddle with an authorial will in a particular constitution. My previous bilingual presentation forced me partially into such a role as translator, and so did the need to express my construal of implicit meaning which, as analytic critic, I had to pass on to my own readers. In that capacity, I intervened artificially by Iconizing Indexes in a type of explicit "recovery" process to specify what the meanings "meant" for the reader of my study. Yet I remained ever conscious of the "mediating" role that interposed me between the original Referent and its Recipient. At the same time, my fundamental method proceded unhindered by "recovering" only from the Icons offered by a text. This focus is the sole recourse to *reconstructing* and *reconstituting* the Referent in conjunction with the textual control the structure exerts and an alert superreader recognizes (or "re-cognizes") under the conditions specified. Whatever my inevitable encroachment on the original encoding of the authorial will as translator and/or critic, I decoded the text methodically from its Iconic base and simultaneously encoded its significance in my analysis of it. Since my readers got the text, (bilingually) reiterated for every structure, they certainly could engage in their own construal as well as following my theory.

Nothing was lost, therefore, concerning the intimacy between Referent and Recipient in an interlocutory partnership. By comparison, Levin's recovery becomes literally "unauthorized" by not focusing on the Icons of a text but on norms that anticipate a compliance with logic. Consequently, instead of "receiving" what the nonrecoverable poem actually owns in contents, Levin is constantly "reasoning" with it. Endemic in his approach is the deviance cult which compensates for selectional violation by the means of proxy-tenet substitution, here the recovery. That issue is hardly irrelevant to Levin since he subsequently devoted a work to the *Semantics of Metaphor* (1977). I cite the title because, much as the work offers some insight into current linguistic theories on metaphor, its allusion to "semantics" remains a misnomer for the reasons noted.

The underlying problems, therefore, are rooted in the outlook, not of literary language but language itself as bearer of meaning. That becomes clear with Levin's brief excursus into daily discourse before embarking on his analysis of poetic compression. He may be right in saying that in everyday use "reductions" of content are often not sensed as compression (1971, pp. 41-42). But he does not offer a satisfactory explanation for the reasons. One reason pertains to semantic rendundance in that normalizing power language possesses, which is exactly why it becomes foolish to reify lexical deviance by logical means. As my study has shown, constant usage in set situational contexts with the aid of adequation flattens the most outlandish behabitive or idiom, from an asyntactic "How do you do?" to a seemingly meaningless "red herring" speakers wield confidently. Also, in a particular ostensive setting, the objective referent as reality-nexus provides sufficient backing for the expression, as was shown previously with my orthographic and graphic 'doppelganger' for Ingarden's "pen" sentence, including some of the more detrimental side effects of the processing involved in adequation.

Since Levin offers examples (leaning heavily on the linguistics of Katz and Postal), my points may be illustrated once more: *imperative* and *intransitive* uses are "reduced" by missing a grammatical subject and object, respectively. Imperatives call to action and thus the verb as predicate for once takes priority over the subject, which is confined anyway to a second-person address, a set "you," and for that reason warrants suppression more readily, or so semantic redundance has ordained. A strong exhortation may then "recover" the subject, as in, "*You* do (this or that)!" However, the moment that happens, another correlate has been created, a different constitutional unit(y). So "recovery" of one and the same "reference" in a transaction with transference is not involved and remains impossible. Strictly speaking, therefore, there is no "compression," and no "reduction" or "addition" either. Instead, two commands arise; one bears an implicit subject at 0 and the other an explicit subject at M in thetic I-M-0 generation. In one command "you" must be released as relevant Index of a verb Icon and in the other "You" is the initiating Icon, posessing its own denotative core with an illocutionary type of urgency.

There is no getting around those conditions; every copyright law protects the explicit base, as stated before. The same rule applies to the presence or absence of a grammatical object in an intransitive or transitive use. Levin's example, "John is reading," is a complete sentence, a constitutive unit(y) bearing the teleology of its contextualization through an authorial will. Should some grammatical object such as "a book" be added, a new syntactic unit(y) will have to be generated, with a signitive act differently corporealized and embodied in shifts of natural (structural) transference. The two sentences are no more related than paintings within their own frames, irrespective of their matching themes. Either one artifact is willed or the other, unless one wants to "repaint" the canvas by emulating the original artist. In language, too, only the author makes the choice and accordingly becomes embedded as the Referent that a Recipient may cull from the explicit and implicit contents.

At the level of syntagma in some extended (concatenating) context, the two sentences may follow one another, but they cannot be superimposed upon one another. Again, only adequation effects a type of juxtaposition where a reality-nexus may help out: John still reads but the *sentence* is backed by a *situational context* where said person holds a book. Then the objective referent backs the amalgamated pure referent after it has been projected "out into" the extralinguistic reality. But at the level of the pure referent, implicit relevance and logical or factual recovery are inimical: one must be *derived* from the given explicit contents while the other obtrudes on meaning from the outside. All these conditions need to be examined and kept in their proper perspective; they have no bearing on non-adequated, literary use, anyway, but explain only under what circumstances the type of paraphrasing Levin advocates becomes at all plausible. No pure "phrasing," however, can ever be replaced by a "parallel phrasing" without lapsing into a "pseudo-phrase" that destroys the authorial will as inchoate Referent.

It is doubtful that a critic who has not come to terms with these issues is likely to succeed with an analysis of poetic compresssion as genuine semantic idiosyncrasy. Levin's particular recovery method is to be demonstrated with one of the texts by Emily Dickinson (1830-1886) that he offers, "When Etna basks and purrs," as the opening line of this untitled poem reads. What seems startling right away is that Levin, the linguist, pays so little attention to the language that he uses a *bowdlerized* version of the poem. Such a lack of authentication becomes in itself a type of "recovery" right there! Also, as with Baumgärtner, no background is offered for the poem. In Baumgartner's case this limitation seemed more acceptable since he settled openly for an excerpt to prove the language looked ordinary. Yet Levin wants to explain how "poetic" the "compression" is in this text without honoring the poetic Referent as compositional medium. It looks as though he settled for the first version he came across, in total ignorance of the controversies revolving around the unwarranted emendations of Dickinson's poetry.

Clearly, in all this shortsightedness Levin displays the very "anachronism" Jakobson invoked as he castigated linguists who are impervious to vital matters of literature. Such an anachronism assumes double meaning. Not only did Levin, in Jakobson's sense, neglect the most rudimentary aspects of literary scholarship. Levin also became literally out of step with the times by accepting misconceived emendations that were based on dogmatic ideas of literary etiquettes from an earlier era and had long been rectified by the T. H. Johnson editions of the 1950s. The authenticated versions are now readily available, either in the voluminous variorum edition (1955), or in the single volume of "Complete" (1960) poems (republished in paperback in 1975). Just a modicum of research would have produced that much information. The fact that Levin still has not seen the light, unfortunately, can be observed in a recent essay on "Literary Metaphor" (1979, pp. 131-132), which draws on yet another bowdlerized Dickinson poem.

Let me do the honors once again, then, by filling in the most basic background any literary work of art requires. As revealed in the variorum edition (1955, p. 803) and the compact single volume (1960/1975, p. 513), the "Etna" poem, number 1146, was actually written in 1869 but not published until 1914. Such an epochal gap between the original inception and its postponed official recording is rather typical for this diffident woman poet, whose recognition had to await the twentieth century, a situation that in part was to blame for the patronizing emendations of her early (male) editors. To compensate for Levin's neglect of the poet in favor of her dogmatic editors, this study is forced to entertain yet another type of "bilingual" version, not in aid of a translation but an artificially created epochal gap.

The authentic version at the time of inception, so vital to the M-base, appears first, as it was taken from the Johnson edition, while Levin's corrupt version (1971, p. 42) of a later reception follows.

When Etna basks and purrs
Naples is more afraid
Than when she shows her Garnet Tooth —
Security is loud —

When Etna basks and purrs,
Naples is more afraid
Than when she shows her Garnet Tooth;
Security is loud.

According to the Johnson variorum edition (1955, pp. lxvi, 803), the first authentic version came from a manuscript written in pencil around 1869 (presently at the Houghton Library of Harvard). Even the first publication of this poem in the anthology *The Single Hound* (1914), edited by the poet's niece Martha Dickinson Bianchi, honored textual fidelity. Yet these many years later the reception by a linguist goes awry because greater comfort is taken in the standard punctuation the editors have foisted upon the text in obliteration of the *dashes* so eminently characteristic of this poet. In the original, the dashes reinforce a poetic type of *anacoluthon* as will be seen. But some of that characteristic can be gleaned right here since any "syntactic" coherence becomes markedly suspended by the dashes in the original and artificially preserved by the emendations in the bowdlerized version. Fortunately, even the bowdlerized version left intact another Dickinson trait, the *deliberate capitalization*, which becomes carefully planned to create a unique correspondence with constituents that are thus marked automatically through the onset of lines or by denoting place names.

Surprisingly, even her discerning editor, T. H. Johnson (1960/1975, p. xi), sees fit to describe Dickinson's capitalization as "capricious," suggesting that nothing but whimsical poetic license accounted for it. The issue of capitalization, in fact, would produce some curious reversals if offered in yet another bilingual version that included a translation into German this time. As was stated when analyzing the Brecht poem, capitalization of nouns is mandatory in German, and thus any poetic whim of an Anglo-Saxon poet on that score would evaporate with that syntactic rule. Going the opposite way, to uphold poetic self-assertion by keeping the nouns earmarked for lower case would only destroy the foregrounded M-base. Indeed, to stress that kind of independence the German poet George--already cited for rendering the dark black flower composed only of print and meaning--went the opposite way. As pointed out at the time, he did *not* capitalize nouns, a practice quite common nowadays among avant-garde German poets (see Gumpel, 1976, pp. 90-118). Here the problem would be reversed in an English translation by obliterating authorial intent.

These difficulties concerning translations cannot be overlooked even if none is added to this analysis. In the case of Dickinson, it is just possible that an *epochal* time factor may be involved as well. Her capitalization may not be so capricious or unique if one attempts to study the literary etiquettes of the time of inception. Some capitalization was more common in Dickinson's day. At least, that is the impression one gets from citations of Dickinson forebears, all the way back to Colonial days, which appeared in a study on *The Poetry of American Women from 1632 to 1945* by Watts (1977, pp. 23-27).

Levin pays little attention to these Iconic idiosyncrasies anyway, for which reason I keep stressing them. His approach to this text may be divided as follows: (1) the comparison, (2) the collocations, (3) the additions, and (4) the tree diagrams. Because the poem bears a comparison with the "more"/"Than" of lines two and three, Levin tries to *restore* the lacking "symmetry" of poetic compression by introducing an unrelated logical comparison of four fixed terms (1971, pp. 42-43). This very idea stays so true to traditional semantics that it falls right in with the *proportional metaphor*, where Aristotle (1960, Loeb ed., pp. 80-81), in a typical ontological category-mistake, claims that proportion within a logical correspondence of four terms comprising an analogy permits their juggling to keep any lexical anomaly comprehensible.

Levin's contextless collocations may seem more "modern" in the development of linguistics, but by that contemporaneousness insinuate how "far" theories treating language as bearer of meaning have come. Instead of staying with the text, Levin strays from it by offering a series of concocted strings generative grammarians like to present. Rendered in everyday lingo and not even remotely connected with the content of the text to be analyzed--something about a "Jon" and his "wife" (pp. 42-43)--the collocations are simply too ridiculous to detail further. The space nevertheless devoted to them seems out of all proportion to the the amount provided for direct analysis of the poem itself.

More interesting are the additions because at least they involve the text, which is their main saving grace, unfortunately. What makes this practice questionable from the start is that to nonrecoverable poetry one is not supposed to "add" recovered parts. So Levin gets busy dabbling in his own type of editorial amendment of the text, as italicised in the following citations, ". . . shows her Garnet Tooth *and roars*," "Security is loud, *not soft (or 'quiet')*" (p. 44). In support of his curious reasoning for an esthetic deployment that hardly permits such a measure, Levin introduces the criteria of "approbation" and "opprobium." That is, he speaks of having to "justify" his addition of "roars" because "loud" (otherwise) "implicitly confers disapproval on 'purrs'" (ibid., p. 44). The suggestion is that a loud purring is a roar, and thus he restores this missing connection--in more than one sense, I might add. He is not only concerned about the disrupted meaning but the five senses of perception which, among others, involve sound and sight, as is made evident in his second addition, the parenthetical "quiet." It is almost as if Levin has never heard of synaesthesia, although I shall demonstrate shortly that he must have done so to be competent enough in English to wield "loud" at all.

Expansively, Levin adds that no one should be concerned with the reason why this poet "thought there was security in loudness" (ibid.). It is nice of him to rule out Wimsatt and Beardsley's intentional fallacy. But the comment is also wholly gratuitous: an author's "thought" is not at issue unless made explicit in imagery (M) and implicit in relevant connotations (0), at which point the Referent (I) obtains as the Interpretant or authorial will that selected what the contents carry. Anything else in the way of private motives, personal feelings and the like stays literally "immaterial" and thus "use-less" to the poem, hence also to its Recipient.

The irony is that Levin's normative stance, aimed at justifying his logical "judgment," entangles him further in illogical conclusions, because a literary work of art cannot tolerate such an approach. His next addition tells him apparently that the volcano, or Etna in this poem, stands metaphorically for "a lion" (p. 47). Cats purr and lions roar, would be the logic, although he himself and not the poet contributed this roar through the reasoning elucidated. The "random generations" against which his logical recovery was to guard thus abound through such arbitrary additions, and they certainly seem "aleatory" in relation to the poetic context.

Where the rationality of Etna's lionization then falls apart is in Levin's dissection of Etna in supposedly semantic markers which are really logical, or epistemological classes termed "+Animate," "—Masculine," and "+Feline" (ibid.). These categories, even in their explicit form, are typical of markers and distinguishers linguists (Katz and Fodor) employed in attempts at a rational semantic "disambiguation" of meaning, an approach I discuss in the article mentioned at the outset (Gumpel, 1974, pp. 180-185). But the obvious question arising here is why Etna needs to be given an oblique "non-Masculine" (—) marker when the third line has her decidedly (+) "Feminine" in the pronoun and possessive "she" and "her," whether or not Levin likes that gender. Here he almost seems to subtract from the language what rightfully belongs to it while adding what it does not own. Put another way, the text blatantly "approves" the feminine gender while Levin's logic disapproves of it.

In the way of an explanation, there is once again a curious neo-Aristotelian root which will emerge in the adjunct but is pertinent here: Aristotle exemplifies the simile in a comparison with metaphor (*Rhetoric*, 1959, Loeb ed., pp. 366-367) by "lionizing" Achilles, that bravest of masculine heroes. His followers, from Quintilian on, have emulated Aristotle, never letting go of the lionized human male in their analyses of metaphor, particularly the animation which one of Levin's markers bears also. The leonine connection with humans is thus traditionally *masculine* and Levin, well imbued with convention, apparently cannot bring himself to equate "a lion" outright with a female. Then why go to all the trouble of foisting the lion on poor, feminine Etna? It is the ontological category-mistake that causes Levin to confuse logical with linguistic categories. In the process he converts feminine Etna into a leonine creature of his own making through a (lexical) "transference" which goes from the inanimate topological phenomenon to the feline that, in his stubborn insistence, also assumes a "non-Male" qualifier! Anomaly is bridged by the analogy of a roaring noise that exists only in the ear of this beholder. Levin's straining for logic has somehow caught him in a logical hiatus. Why, if at all, not make Etna leonine by describing her as "lioness" to match her authenticated, poetic sex?

Levin's last critical offerings to be discussed, the tree diagrams (pp. 45-46), certainly keep him in the transformationalist fold of the twentieth century. These diagrams are consistent only in making conspicuous his own anachronism of not being conversant with the purpose of literary language, since they typically shift the word order around to suit standard language. Thus little can be done with these unwarranted blueprints for a language the poem does not own.

To rectify some of Levin's suppositions, let me briefly examine the Icon "loud" that led to the "roar" and the non-Masculine "lion." Had Levin probed his native competence as this poet did instead of plying logic, he would soon have realized that English has already provided natural *synaesthesia* for "loud." Surely he is aware that the word may designate garish color schemes. So the explicit reference may be to sound but the implicit periphery has been indented to cover for sight as well--which fits right in with the showy dentine image of the preceding line. Indeed, "loud" is a good example for demonstrating what Ingarden meant by the dynamics of heteronomous, pure-intentional "reference," whose indigenous semantic pointer, the direction-factor, owns everything the material and formal contents offer. All Dickinson had to do was to follow up on that very "directive" and endow it with new relevance for the transference intrinsic to this poem.

Next, Levin's non-Masculine "lion": why not adhere to the "cat" the poem "approves" through the purring? The poem also justifies that construal by depicting a stealthy surreptitious "Etna"; a roar would give it away. Again, English native competence has provided the potential "feline" and "female" associations that meet in the Icon "cat." In one of those animated types of "personality metaphors" discussed before, an envious, underhand female is referred to as a "cat" or being "catty," something the indigenous pointer, the direction-factor of the English word, encompasses naturally. The diachronic transparencies for this feline-female linkage may be there or absent, fair or unfair. What matters is that these synchronic states have solidified. Dickinson certainly plays on those intrinsic connotations as she displays supreme awareness of that "Mother" tongue; one wishes her theoretician here would demonstrate a similar cognizance. As a translator, I certainly would have experienced difficulties of integrating these contents with the intextual whole, just because they reside in a specific language and not in universal logic. Although German "laut" seems almost a perfect Sinsign match for English, its indentations do not permit the synaesthesia elucidated. Neither does the feline "Katze," despite its feminine gender.

In addition, Dickinson's femininization of "Etna" gets some help from its Qualisign closeness to the proper name for a female, "Edna." Whatever the case, Dickinson knew what she was doing as Referent of this poem by palpating, in a manner of speaking, every oppositional value of (hyletic) form and (noematic) content of the meanings at her disposal, which cannot be said of Levin as a Recipient. In his preoccupation with logical recovery and dissection, Levin never really made it his business to "receive" the poem in its Iconic base. By converting meaning into semantic marbles for logic, all his collocations and additions only proved literally "use-less"--like the overgrown "weeds" that were the topic of some of my earlier "epochal" investigations.

Let me now indicate what causes poetic "compression" in this poem, in a *line-by-line* analysis of the authenticated version, although not without reinvoking some of Levin's *points where* relevant. At the end, the entire text is recapitulated in order to get a better glimpse of the hermeneutic and polyphonous interaction among the lines and the inherent Rhemic strata. The procedure thus follows basically my former approach to the Rheme. Not some dubious lexical "lion" but every Rhemic particle is "metaphor" and/or nominalized meaning. With that reminder, I introduce the *first* line:

When Etna basks and purrs

Iconic time leads this line, capable of creating only a "temporal" association within this context, specifically poetic intext. The "When" bears the Index "whenever" and thus the qualifier of potentiality that when Etna engages in certain actions something happens, and not necessarily that they occur there and now. As subordinating conjunction, "When" also initiates the dependent clause which has "Etna" as its noun-subject. Any educated superreader recognizes the narrow Indexicalization typical of geographical place names. But an informed superreader knows also that the Icon as image encapsulated in this text is just that, as remote from any real place as Brecht's "Fin(n)land" turned out to be when composing the Rheme and not Argument.

In further syntagmatic extension "Etna" soon erupts in the activities that endow her with her feminine-feline nature. The recursive direction-factors of the finite verbs "basks"/"purrs," linked by the conjunction "and," interlock with "Etna" in nominal-verbal unfolding of this clause, completing the first line. Also, I exteriorized "feminine" before "feline" as relevant Index for the verb "basks" since this may signify humans more readily than "purrs," thus in anticipation of the later Icons registering Etna's sex that a retroactive reading would substantiate. In any case, the action borne by the first verb conveys languor. The second verb, with its foregrounded *onomatopoeia* through the doubled Qualisign liquids in "rr," adds contentment as it imitates that real feline sound, droning on. "Etna" has become Indexicalized as a seemingly innocuous domestic pet, the "cat."

If one wants to be pedantic, the verb "basks" approximates a violation equivalent to Chomsky's type of subcategorization rule. For this intransitive verb usually precedes a prepositional phrase, such as "in the sun," perhaps. Although this import may be contained in "basks," it cannot be recovered to make the language more logical. What "basks" nevertheless releases effectively is the Index of inertia. It imparts the prone posture; Etna appears flat, almost crouching in a submissive gesture. However, that comparative calm is shaken by the *second* line:

Naples is more afraid

The new geographical place name takes over as subject in the main clause. Live memory intertwines the two geographical Icons into an inimitable as well as intimate "poetic anagram," as it may well be called. In a vertical recursive Sinsign correspondence, "*Etna*" and "*Naples*" enter into their own chiastic reversal, which is in some respects not unlike the "*Lands*leute" and "Finn*land*" of Brecht's text. These two Icons become indissolubly and yet also contrastively linked since the calm of one arouses the fear in the other. That import is boosted by their sonorous and visual Qualisign dispositions, which are the "ground" at the Rhemic M-base to be considered, and not the topology of the real places that might end up being signified in adequation. The state or action of the one causes the emotional reaction in the other, as the predicate "is more afraid" elicits at the level of the horizontal sequence. Thus, the Iconic geographical intertwining when further backgrounded is unmasked as a dissonant relation since gentle "Etna" instills greater fear in "Naples," as underscored by the numeric qualifier of the first segment "more" comprising the comparative.

Not only "Etna" but "Naples" deserves Levin's "+Animate" marker through the predicate that interlocks with this subject in the denotation of fear. However, even this example causes me only to reiterate my point of linguistic competence on which the poet draws so cleverly. It is quite common for geographical place names to become *anthropomorphized* and *pluralized* at depth, operating as type of collective nouns that cover for many inhabitants. Thus one says "Washington," meaning all the politicians residing there, for example. Of course, "Naples" may not be quite as famous (or firmly indented) to evoke that swiftly a similar implication. But in this context with the predicate extension elucidated, Naples is not only animated but anthropomorphized. Indeed, in its sharp Iconic singular number, "Naples" becomes a type of *metonym* or *synecdoche*, conveying "one" though meaning "many" inhabitants. Of course, one can look to a selectional deviance here in terms of *personification*--as Chomsky was shown to do with his "Misery loves company." The function of Naples parallels that usage as a singular noun working through a "collective" group of people.

If, however, language as ontic heteronomy is capable in a language of violating selectionality in the most common expressions, such discoveries help mainly the construal, not the semantic substance based on functioning. From a descriptive standpoint, it is interesting to note that while the imagery of the Brecht poem traded more on plurals, this one reinforces outwardly the singular. In the former poem, "people" in meaning stayed devoid of gender because the plural was prevalent; here geographical place names such as "Etna" that could be rendered in an asexual third person become feminine.

Upon a further discovery, ontic heteronomy and ontic autonomy become curiously pitted against one another, and this issue also involves Levin's study on the semantics of metaphor (1977, pp. 95-99), where he struggled with the "problem" of "encyclopedic knowledge," which he could not address conclusively. That is to be expected for someone unclear on the bounds separating logic from language. Thus, let me attempt that resolution right here. A Recipient well versed in geography is most likely aware of the *fact* that the real volcano called Etna is located on the East coast of Sicily, whereas Naples remains closer to Mount Vesuvius. While the place names in the poem suffice for their geographical landmark as such, they might be considered to approximate misnomers if thus regionally displaced. However--and this is the important point--for this poem, their "placement" in the text gets priority, relevant to that intextual poetic anagram construed recursively, in the precise positioning on each line. The priority of these non-adequated Icons is to foreground a lyric ego instead of signifying a land of actual existence. Any cognition in my Picture of Language was seen to follow from the perception of the linguistic form which yields the Legisign that in turn erupts into the Icon, which in this instance foregrounds the poem through these particular names, "Etna" and "Naples."

So even if Dickinson has made a mistake, she is not the author of a *National Geographic* article, conveying facts about the volcano and the town in "truth" *claims* that, at the level of the objective referent, identify such a statement as *false*. The poem instead remains "true" when it consists of validated Legisigns and carries out its function for the structure in which it comes. Thus any encyclopedic knowledge about the erroneous geography recedes behind the semantic task at hand, since the "cognition" here goes into the constitution of a poem depending mainly on the performances of encoding and decoding. In other words, the poem makes sense and permits construal without relaying accurate information about the empirical world. That is not to say the error could not be noted in a text-critical apparatus, but certainly not in editorial emendations that destroy the poetic anagram of this tiny poetic inscape, to borrow a term from G. M. Hopkins (in Frye, 1967, p. 121).

Surprisingly, encyclopedic knowledge also becomes contingent on philology here. For any literate Recipient knows that Dickinson's place names "Etna" and "Naples" are standardized *Anglicized* versions of Greek "Aetna" and Italian "Napoli." If the language belonged to said magazine in adequated use, the original Greek and Italian terms might be preferred and paraphrased accordingly, in aid of any geographical, etymological and/or mythological information. However, to a poem like this which depends on direct Iconization of meaning by meanings, any paraphrase is anathema. While "Aetna" may sound more "erudite" than "Etna" to those keenly aware of a Classical past, no such choice of alternative exists for the inherent Referent of this text. The poetic anagram and related associations construed so far would disintegrate, a deleterious effect that could only worsen with the important foregrounding revealed in the *third* line,

Than when she shows her Garnet Tooth —

First in order is the second comparative segment and, at the other end of the line, the first punctuation mark of the authenticated version. This dash, incidentally, should explain also why I have refrained from adding any of my own punctuation to integrate the end of each line with the syntax in my continuing sentence. That is something handbooks on manuscript style apparently have not solved as yet, at their level of lacking awareness of where "encyclopedic knowledge" stops, since they always insist on punctuation inside of quotation marks. In a case like this, such a practice would only amount to yet another type of bowdlerization. Also, I have spoken of "syntactic" elements such as "clauses," although this unconventional punctuation shatters that idea. Still, since all these terms apply descriptively to these structural metaphors, as was pointed out with the very first analysis, such a nomenclature presents no problem.

This third line appears longest, as, by coincidence, was Brecht's in the previous analysis. Ostensibly "logical," the comparative segment "Than" in onset capitalization counterbalances its comparative predecessor, the "more" of the preceding line that first led into the comparison. Simultaneously, the reiterated Iconic time "when" which initiated the poem now succeeds the comparison. Horizontal sequence, therefore, has pushed Iconic time over, as it were, by opening with the comparison; at the vertical, recursive level, the link is thus diagonal rather than anaphoral. Still, the pleonasm of Iconic time itself cannot be missed, since the "When"/"when" of the respective lines shows Etna in reverse. Still pivotal to Naples and the comparison, subdued Etna is "more" dangerous "Than" flashy Etna.

"Etna," of course, is not there as Icon, only as "pro-noun" and possessive in the definitive feminine "she" and "her," identifications Levin tried to elude in his indirect non-Masculine marker. Etna's pronominalization in these operative alternatives may be a subtle way of announcing her more harmless state. Certainly, this change permits the alliteration of "*she shows.*" More likely, too, these modest operative signs in lower case allow for projecting the final image caught in the "Garnet Tooth"; it juts out all the more, willfully capitalized as it is. What about this curious dentine object? Grammatically, this fang is easily identified in that it differs as the only direct object of a verb, "shows," amid all the intransitive verbs and predicate adjectives. Why is it there or, put another way, what does it mean in relation to the whole?

For an alert superreader the significance of this object is not hard to isolate. Momentarily, I break with the sequence as analytic critic and begin with the dentine: the "Tooth" itself ties in with the emphasis on the *singular* in this context. As one of the traditional parts of speech, this "Tooth" amounts to a "count noun," a qualifier relevant to number here. For, certainly, from a logical standpoint most mouths commonly possess more than one such fang, at least a bilateral match. What the singular accomplishes better than an amorphous plural is this "metonymic" or "synecdochal" affirmation of the one for the many. In that manner, the singular reinforces at its numeric level the stark verticality of the Qualisign dimensions bearing the capitalized "T": this fang is not to be overlooked. As the object of the Iconic showing its verb contained, this "Tooth" becomes "showy" to the point of ostentation. Indeed, this prominent "Tooth" with its pronounced Qualisign disposition becomes a type of poetic "hieroglyph" or "ideogram": it conveys the outer, histrionic fierceness of Etna baring her one-and-only fang in what seems like a menacing stance that turns out to be relatively harmless.

Etna, of course, is not neglected either in Iconization by the other side of this fang, its modifier, "Garnet." First, the Icon of this attributive embraces both the geographical place names in an extended *poetic anagram* that works recursively with the aid of live memory, as shown italicised in *"Etna"/"Naples"/"Garnet."* *This* is poetic compression, indeed, but intensified through the repertoire the text offers. In this Iconic pleonasm, "Naples" gets caught in the middle, as it does at the deeper backgrounded level, since its fate hinges on fearing "Etna" when there as Icon but not showing off her "Garnet Tooth." The foregrounding, indeed, exudes a symmetrical and yet reversed type of "syllabic palindrome," with the last syllable in "*Etna*" reinforced as first syllable in "*Naples,*" while the first syllable in "*Etna*" ends up as the last syllable in "*Garnet.*" Dickinson's intuitive genius of probing oppositional values in her native language seems complete. "Space" moves together in closer recursive coherence, whether or not the real volcano is elsewhere.

Dickinson almost unwittingly becomes "didactic" here in "teaching" Recipients of language how geographic place names may work as semantic entities when they reside within the oppositional system of one language. This point was first made, of course, with the "beak" emitting those onomatopoetic rooster cries. Even if the onomatopoeia there or the geographical label here had produced the same words, they lie differently within the semasiological system of one language. That goes especially for the relations "Garnet" is capable of forming with these (Anglicized) place names. The noun "Garnet," as opposed to the "Tooth," is not a count noun but may be classed conventionally with "mass" nouns. This Icon in its attributive role thus provides the suggestion of "substance" for this fang. Since "garnet" signifies a stone consisting of a mineral in a reddish hue, this import affirms the "composition" of this "Tooth" in its hardness. There exists for this "Garnet" dentine also a similar metalinguistic contiguity that was discussed with "Etna" and

"Edna." This time it is "Garnet" and "granite," which affirm additionally the hardness of this "Tooth." With the chromatic implication noted, the Index of molten rock becomes released, glowing red lava. The implied buccal cavity through the dentine image may evoke "mouth" for the rim of a crater.

At this point, then, the meaning evolves that when Etna spews fire for all to see "she" is safer than when she is "smoldering" in faint rumbles that keep her relatively motionless. Etna is deviously tame and fierce, to be feared when quiet and not feared when fiery. Nor can a certain gory implication be ignored with this predatory "red" fang, if "blood" outright may go too far. In this manner, then, the carnivorous, dentine image and the active volcano interlock through connotative compounding, made possible through live memory that retains the construed elements. To be sure, the "encyclopedic" knowledge that lava is red, as is the mineral, seems to hover in the background. Also, not every literate and competent native speaker comes armed with the type of lapidary information needed for "Garnet," which, in fact, I gathered from a dictionary. But nothing can detract from the evidence of the contents; they count because they are there in all their idiosyncratic disposition; they expand inwardly as outwardly "Naples" becomes intertwined with both sides of "Etna."

Indeed the coherence of this tiny poetic intext is such that part of my construal actually kept anticipating the *last* line, which is to be entered with the entire text:

When Etna basks and purrs
Naples is more afraid
Than when she shows her Garnet Tooth —
Security is loud —

Outwardly, to be sure, the fourth line enters abruptly, a type of *anacoluthon* in disrupted thought, reinforced outwardly by the two dashes that keep it apart from the rest of the text. That is to say, the *two dashes* as *nominalized* punctuation marks contribute their significance to this poem. They cast the last line as a type of poetic "islet," ringed off and kept suspended by not coming to a close through a period. So these elements, too, are nominalized to exude "meaning" that is relevant only to the extended transference of this poetic intext. Indeed, the dashes lend a rather literal meaning to the term "punctuation" since they appear to "puncture" the text through the horizontal "barriers" they manifest in their Qualisign disposition. These dashes *halt* decoding in sequence and *hold up* live memory momentarily as they "fence off" the last line. They help to project this concluding line as a type of "afterthought." Sadly, the bowdlerized version depletes the poem of all these rich nuances by omitting Dickinson's unique punctuation.

As for the last line, despite being encased by these dashes, there is no genuine disjointedness. In effect, through the dashes, this line becomes rather conspicuously "hooked on" to the rest of the poem. The line obviously jumps the gap by complementing the predicate adjective parataxis of the second line, though somewhat contracted for missing the comparative segment, as shown in "is . . . afraid"/"is loud." Again, the outer Iconic link is inwardly relevant in opposite meaning insofar as the fear follows from Etna's subdued side and the loudness from her ostentatiously fierce demeanor. The parataxis extends to the left in the vertical alignment of the two initiating noun-subjects, "Naples" and "Security." Rather cleverly, the mandatory capitalization of the geographical place name is passed on to the other noun, though only for intitiating its line. What both nouns also share conspicuously is that sharp *singular* circumference in a *metonymic* or *synecdochal* presentation of the "people" they harbor at depth. At the level of the Index, "Security" contrasts also with the predicate adjective, keeping Naples pivotal to living in fear of Etna and sensing security in Etna's outer show of fierceness.

In conventional semantics, "Security" denotes an "abstraction," despite its obvious "human" import as a sensation. In that respect, "Security" resembles Chomsky's "Misery" example more closely than does Naples. Yet, again, Dickinson knows better than that and intuitively grasps the dynamic nature of meaning, here the natural, transmuted personification characterizing all such abstractions for denoting human dispositions. And, although this last line is not a saying as familiar as Chomsky's example, its very generic tenor has a sententious ring to it that is reminiscent of a *proverb* or adage.

Certainly, with all the connotations and alignments elucidated, this line is not in need of Levin's earlier cited amendment, "not soft (or quiet)" (p. 44). What is the flashy fang of the preceding line if not "loud" in its garish visibility? Dickinson, as stated, trades effectively on the sonorous-visual nuances embodied in the *synaesthesia* of this adjective. The sight of this dentine is reassuring because it is so "loud" in its visibility, and the assonantal relation between "loud" and "shows" supports that import. That is not to say the sound image in "purrs" does not become contrastively reinforced as well. The point is that, *qua* linguistic competence, loudness here remains as "normal" in its acquired visual connotation as it does overtly in its sonorous denotation.

Everything set forth here has been derived from the Icons directly in their M-foregrounding and their deeper backgrounded 0-import. If intent on attaching to the meaning of this poem yet another loose proverb, one might Iconize its gist as, "There is safety in the devil one knows or sees." In any case, there was not a single element, down to the operative punctuation marks, that did not contribute to the expression of this poem. All these constituents are structural metaphors that shift in order to lend their individual meaning explicitly and implicitly to the poet's meaning because they were carefully selected for that purpose and none other.

As for the prevalent, indeed omnipresent "+Animation" Levin reserved for Etna, it could apply to almost everything, from Etna to Naples or "Security," and even the "Garnet Tooth" as part of Etna's "mouth." In addition, Naples and Security became anthropomorphized in the manner explained. And Etna, as the female-feline "she" is, does not lack that "human" touch either, for reasons of the indentation marking English "cat." The point is, where does "metaphor" as lexical deviance begin and end by such assessments? If a "metaphor" of greater reliability than that of the Ingendahl Experiment is to be isolated, something more substantial must be sought for a domain such as language that crosses these bounds with ease in the most ordinary lingo. Now, Levin may be right, basically, by saying that the imagery "shows her Garnet Tooth" is equivalent to "a metaphor of a volcanic eruption" (pp. 43-44). He is thus positing an analogy between the display of such an eruption and the showy dentine that bridges the anomaly in their different states as topological and biological phenomena. That association has partially evolved also from my own construal, but only by heeding the meanings in all their essence. This is where Levin should put function before detail and then substantiate the function through the detail to demonstrate inductively how it goes into effect.

As was stated in the last analysis, the connotations may expand and/or shift somewhat in meaningfulness for the individual construer. But there is no getting around that careful, painstakingly positioned foregrounding Dickinson offered and which, when scrutinized, led to a fully backgrounded condensation or "compression" of a lyric ego at depth. All a non-Aristotelian metaphor needs is "approval" of the structure by the conditions outlined. Then even dashes as punctuation marks do their part as objects of expression for a totality of expression in accordance with what the author "meant." This meaning was held together until the last dash had been decoded through the capacity of live memory, intensifying into a holistic intext.

A last analytic consideration before switching to the impact of an esthetic concretization is what might be qualified loosely as the wider "extrinsic" input. Thus Dickinson imagery may be secondarily supported from further evidence of her poetic diction. Literary scholarship has been much aided on that score by the availability of a Dickinson *Concordance* which covers the 1775 poems numbered in the Johnson editions. In brief, the concordance (1967, pp. 232, 516) lists just one other reference to "Etna" and "Naples," from a couple of poems written somewhat earlier than this one, in 1862. Number 422 in the *Complete Poems* (1960/1975, pp. 201-202) refers to "Etna's Scarlets" and the other one, number 601 (p. 295), has a "Volcano" made explicit as Icon along with "Naples." This poem closes also with dashes, for an imagery of "Cities" that " - ooze away - ". To indicate how these dashes also hold the imagery between them in a usage similar to the poem construed here, I have kept my own punctuation, the period, outside of them, as should be done. Besides the inclusion of dashes, the above imagery reveals also unique capitalization, although the singular seems less in evidence than in the poem I analyzed.

From an epochal standpoint governing inception versus reception, it is worth noting that the above two poems were subjected to an even greater time span than the poem of this analysis. Though their inception is dated 1862, their official entry in the way of publication did not materialize until 1935 for the first and 1929 for the second poem. And, of course, had there not been precursors to Levin's logical dissection--apart from the bowdlerizers of his edition --those epochal gaps would not exist either, even for this reclusive woman poet. That issue is a full topic in itself when one looks into the posthumous fate of Dickinson's work (as I have done).

With those added considerations at least adumbrated, I return to the poem of this analysis to give the esthetic values their due after having probed the artistic compositional values. Ironically, in piecing these together, I often had to fragment the poem by dwelling on odd and complex detail. To compensate for the analytic stance, a continuous, sequential concretization follows that is simultaneously "hermeneutic" enough to give live memory its due by heeding the assimilative or mnemonic-qualitative time phases. The fruition of this recipience should be harmonious *polyphony* among the interacting strata of backgrounding and foregrounding. In addition, a fully nominalized foregrounding in conventional scanning reveals what Dickinson experts (Pederson, 1944, pp. 80-82) have called the "short meter." It consists mostly of trimeter, with an exception in the third line of this text, which displays tetrameter. So the conspicuous Garnet Tooth in its capitalized Qualisign dimensions ends up with strong rhythmic reinforcement as well. Careful scanning shows the rhythm supporting the capitalization of the poetic anagram by stressing first syllables in "*Etna,*" "*Naples*" and "*Garnet.*" In the case of the place names, the second,.weak or unstressed syllable of "Et*na*" is then "bestowed" on the city of "*Naples*" in Sinsign reversal, and returns, if modified, in "*Garnet,*" as italicised. The full schema is offered below, first with and then without words.

```
      -  / -  /    -  /
When  Etna  basks  and  purrs

 /  -  - /    -  /
Naples  is  more  afraid

      -    /   -    /    -    / -    /
Than  when  she  shows  her  Garnet  Tooth -

- / - -    /
Security  is  loud -

- / - / - /
/ - - / - /
- / - / - / - /
- / - - - /
```

The above schemas have the Garnet Tooth projected vertically in its Qualisign capitalization and horizontally in prosody through its extended length, invested as it becomes with its own two stresses. In a way, a climax is reached for the first three lines through this strong accentuation and the following dash which momentarily wards off the final line until this brief pause is overcome, whereupon this "afterthought," as I termed it, takes full effect. As suggested, the intonation concluding the last line should not descend entirely either, as though the poem closed in the period of the bowdlerized version. Rather, the line holds its pitch sufficiently to keep the sententious nuance quizzical, as a partially enigmatic end. With added retroactive and hermeneutic readings, the staccato tenor of the dashes may subside somewhat, but not disappear.

By that time, live memory on the part of a superreader's faculty will have gone into effect sufficiently well to assure the full expansion of the connotative compounding to which structural metaphors lend themselves. Aided by what the analytic stance culled from the various facets of the text, these metaphors display their nominalized wordsounds. During the esthetic concretization, these elements should make the poem come truly "alive" by appealing in vibrancy to all the senses and the fullest sensibilities. As the construct passes from encoded composite to a decoding and appropriately concretizing Recipient, the comment of the poet-critic Benn (1965, p. 510) begins to ring true, where he said of the poetic word that it becomes the very "phallus of the mind."

Analysis: Hamburger on the Lyric I: Semantic Content or Connective in Celan?

The last analysis deals with a poem containing *title* and *stanza* as some of the optional components listed in the table of Rhemic hierarchies. An issue more important than these additions, however, is the question of *Rhemic identity* in a poem that manifests an *asyntactic* style. Actually, the more "poetic" the style, the easier it becomes for non-Aristotelian semantics to prove the structure. My theory was challenged most by the type of construct Brecht's poem presented, since the "prosaic" surface seemed to counter its "poetic" depth. Below this illusive surface lay a structural connective which changed the essence also of the Icons with the proper Recipient response. I termed this holistic essence *lyric ego*. Amalgamated by the linguistic strata into semantic unities, the lyric ego becomes condensed into a backgrounded import and is made to cohere as a foregrounded Iconic M-base through the two literary Rhemic strata.

The poem to be treated in my last analysis, however, was chosen by Käte Hamburger on account of a disrupted surface that posed problems of lyric identity for her. Hamburger's *Logic of Literature* has been cited more than once in this study, in part because the work, despite its title, manifested a "logical" breakdown by aligning literal and lyric "statements" as one function. Although Hamburger's logical focus is on the whole to be commended for avoiding a lexical orientation, in this case she unwittingly falls prey to content by supposing that lyric self-expression incorporates a real "self" as speaking subject. She assumes that just because the eloquent "lyric I" of poetry seems to "say" something rather than "tell" stories, this saying equals the essence of any statement. "The much-disputed lyric I," she claims confidently, "is a statement subject" (1968, p. 188; 1973, trans., p. 234).

Terms as such are not at issue: Hamburger may call the lyric ego a "lyric I" and/or a "statement subject." But there has to be a definitive boundary instead of the "open" transition between everyday and esthetic use Hamburger maintains. Leaning on an occasional "sense-nexus" that is to distinguish poetry from the language bearing a "reality-nexus" only exacerbates problems of consistency, unless such criteria are systematically differentiated. They obviously did not aid Hamburger either, since her application of the "lyric I" sometimes designates a functional nonlexical base as in her above assertion and in other instances amounts to little more than content taxonomy.

Hamburger's asyntactic example for illustrating a problematic "lyric I" is a poem by Paul Celan (1920-1970), who, though born in Rumania, has been classed with "German" authors since he wrote mostly in that language. His *text*, which stems from a cycle entitled *Mohn und Gedächtnis* (1970, p. 45), exhibits a disrupted syntax to some extent and is in that sense "modern." Still, I put this periodic qualifier in quotes because it should never be reified; even the most avant-garde antiart attempts (Gumpel, 1976, pp. 49-52) do not break away entirely from conventional art, a fact this poem should prove conclusively. Certainly, the surface does not affect the Rheme as structure but still supports its function, as stated. Hamburger (1968, pp. 203-204; 1973, pp. 253-254), on the other hand, is sufficiently taken aback by the asyntactic surface to insist that it requires a *reverse* procedure in construal. The lack of a thematic unity, which she terms "object·relation," causes her to contend that single words need to be probed first in order to arrive at any sense·nexus (Sinnzusammenhang).

Well, since I have followed such a procedure all along, this particular text should present no problem other than paying special attention to the new additions cited. The bilingual version below, incorporating my own translation, appeared in the Hamburger edition (1968, p. 203; 1973, p. 253). Her comments on the "lyric I" in reference to this poem are to follow. My bilingual presentation, moreover, enables me to illustrate further the "coercive" role of language when involving a non·adequated structure located at the M·base. The startling impact of the minutest change never ceases to surprise me, and I shall express this reaction in what appears to be occasional misgivings about the choices I made. But underlying these reservations is mainly the didactic intent to let the reader glean once more the tremendous power of the non·Aristotelian, structural metaphor that suffuses every facet of a text. Well, here is this metaphor, concreted in Icons and interlocking Indexes.

    Ins Nebelhorn
Mund im verborgenen Spiegel,
Knie vor der Säule des Hochmuts,
Hand mit dem Gitterstab:

reicht euch das Dunkel,
nennt meinen Namen,
führt mich vor ihn.

    Into the foghorn
mouth in the concealed mirror,
knee before the pillar of disdain,
hand with the grid·iron stave:

pass on the darkness to one another,
call my name,
lead me before him.

On the basis of this text, Hamburger (1973, p. 253·254) contends that the "lyric I does not experience itself as a personal whole, but as mouth, knee, and hand, which have no mutual connection . . ." She is interpreting content, similar to my calling Brecht's "pronominal hero" a "lyric I" when analyzing that text as Rheme. The "lyric I" as structural concept, however, is contextual and not a "personal" whole; its "mutual connections" lie in poetic intext irrespective of content. Nor is "experience" involved, but rather a mode of expression whose ground lies in an extended transaction between reference and transference. The "lyric I" Hamburger cites here is just M, the content in thetic I·M·0 generation. Yet the true catalyst should be I, the Interpretant as signitive act, deploying these selected explicit and implicit contents for its foregrounded materialization in Icons and backgrounded embodiment in relevant Indexes.

An analogy that might be pertinent for Hamburger as a neo-Kantian would be the transcendental ego posited by Kant in the *First Critique* (1913, Cassirer, ed., III, p. 114). Kant presented this ego as a metaphysical connective for all possible self-consciousness, thus not as "physical" consciousness of the self in this or that content. Without going into such weighty matters as a transcendental divide that encompasses all being, one nevertheless may draw on the parallel that a lyric "I" here transcends content as the *apriori* connective without which no concretion of the Rheme is even possible. Once the connective is there in compliance with the esthetic ought through appropriate Recipient stance, the Referent will be disclosed accurately--and no differently here than in any other case, thus without any modified or "reversed" procedure.

Let me begin, then, with the analysis to prove my point by following prior methods of construal after submitting content to a first heuristic scanning, which reveals immediately the presence of a title and two stanzas as the new elements cited. Beyond these obvious inclusions, few poems bear Rhemic recursiveness in spatial fusion more conspicuously than this one, making it relatively easy to endorse the structure. That applies even to certain areas of translation. In Brecht's prosaic poem, the translator is challenged to follow parallel rules that closely intertwine syntax with semantics ironically, to affirm what must still surface differently, thus forcing the M-base further apart. A case in point was the relative pronoun: in the transition from German to English it split into four versions, each of which contained a different problem that could not be solved conclusively for the sense in conjunction with changes in sequence, a relation so important for Rhemic intextual fusion.

Indeed, the Celan text projects that fusion rather conspicuously. While my illustration of Argument included a page "frame" to suggest margins within which the text falls loosely, the Rhemic frame itself holds each element to its precise positioning. From the title on there is a marked horizontal or bilateral *symmetry* which in turn reinforces paratactic vertical identity. Bare nouns and verbs lie to the left of the respective stanzas, prepositional phrases and/or direct objects to their right. Accordingly, there is a type of conventional anaphora and epiphora, even if not accompanied by intricate rhyme schemes. The right, prepositional side establishes a direct Iconic linkage between title and text to illustrate the original "steering power" of the title. The more interpretive, Indexical associations in this relationship have to be culled from the detailed construal of individual lines.

Convention is certainly presented by the other new components, the stanzas. Despite lacking rhyme schemes, these stanzas in their triadic patterns reflect tradition by simulating the *tercines* that hark back to Dante (1265-1321) and possibly also the tercets that composed parts of a sonnet, the popular historical genre of long standing. When one distinguishes the stanzas, the first may appear more "modern," since its lines are asyntactic by lacking predicates. While the second stanza instead has no subjects, this omission is supported by the fact that the initiating verbs are *imperatives*. As discussed in connection with Levin, imperatives generally suppress their subjects. Both stanzas, moreover, comply with careful *punctuation* at the end of lines--replete with standard commas, a colon, and a concluding period. In one way the punctuation makes all lines appear "syntactic" and in another it helps to "serialize" them as one takes over separately from the next in continuation of the tercines, demarkated at the other, left side by the initiating elements described. There is thus an overall impression of an "orderly" style. In comparison to this text, Dickinson's poem may have been somewhat more "syntactic" and yet stayed "asyntactic" through its unique punctuation.

However, one stylistic feature Celan's first stanza shares with the former poem is the appearance of the *singular* in the initiating nouns. True, there is just one mouth per face, but knees and hands usually come in pairs--and more numbers for quadrupeds. Their marked "singularity" also is enhanced by their lack of the usual accouterments regarding articles and/or adjectives. Thus stark and bare, the tenor of these nouns reinforces that *metonymic, synecdochal* quality cited with the former poem: the nouns stand as "one" for the "many" and in that capacity also assume the semantic nuance of collective nouns. The "collective" aspect, in fact, receives some special significance when the nouns gain a certain communal relevance recursively through the imperatives that German casts in the plural, as these "usurp" the left-sided slot in the second stanza.

Since the nouns designate parts of the body, they readily depict the traditional "corporal metaphors" which were treated briefly in this study (in reference to Curtius, 1963, pp. 136-138), mainly to be contrasted with "personality metaphors." In the latter case, the human disposition becomes endowed with the qualities of inanimate matter while corporal metaphors impose parts of the body upon matter. In trading on a conventional fund of imagery, then, these nouns may well recall the "places," the Greek "topoi" ("topos" in singular) which anchor content with a certain subject matter. On the other hand, in their left-sided rank-and-file serialization, both the nouns and verbs may reflect additionally a "modern" style by creating types of "rows" or "columns" not far removed from patterns of the experimentalist clusters that compose some "Constellations" of Concrete Poetry (see Gumpel, 1976, pp. 39-41, 50-57, 92-95 ff.). Thus, in this poem new and old stylization coincides in unexpected and yet harmonious ways.

By comparison to the symmetry of the original, my translation may be described as "sprawling," especially since it does not taper off the way the original does in the last two lines. Yet another one of those frustrating changes mentioned in my other analyses stems from the need to preserve the nouns in lower case as befits English syntax, but that decision may not have been my happiest choice either. So this is yet another instance where capitalization becomes a stumbling block when the translator has to second-guess the authorial will in the "coercion" of the language at hand. My decision was based on Celan's standardized usage in German. Celan's adherence to syntactic norms of capitalization rather than the more recent experimentalist tendency toward lower case also forced me to omit this practice unnatural to English syntax in order to convey a parallel standardization. Indeed, Celan put the priority on syntactic norms rather than conventional poetics, since he ignored the onset of lines sufficiently to keep the imperatives of the second stanza uncapitalized. Due to this subtle antiart phenomenon, I dared not capitalize the nouns simply because they initiated their lines. Yet the detailed construal will disclose that the nouns serve as "vocatives" and, thus confronted in a type of address, they might have tolerated capitalization. Since Celan traded on what his language offered, my vacillation may never be resolved.

With these general comments out of the way, the *detailed* analysis begins with the *title*. When the analysis reaches the second stanza, the entire poem will be repeated, mainly to preserve the coherence between what has been construed and held in *live memory* and what is as yet to be decoded. Although a title may be optional, its vital input when added to the intertextual Iconic and Indexical relations should now become self-evident. Because of the strict symmetry of this poem, the lines are "centered" slightly to preserve a bilingual parallelism.

Ins Nebelhorn
(Into the foghorn)

For once English, the analytic language, extends further in syntagma than the German. English has to Iconize motion by the added "-to" of "Into"--as was demanded also of the Brecht poem for the activity of the Finnish "friends"--and the complete definite article "the." Both these elements are caught in the German "s" morpheme of the "Ins," standing for the definite-neuter article "das," which in gender has to agree with the last segment, "-horn," of the grammatical object, the "Nebelhorn." The German preposition "in," furthermore, is called a "two-way" (also "either/or") preposition because it takes both accusative and dative cases, signaling "motion" with the former and the opposite with the latter. Accordingly, this tiny "s" morpheme as nominalized Singsign here conveys "motion" and mediates between the "In-" preposition and its object, the "Nebelhorn."

Something is "moving along" the foghorn; a "passageway" or "thoroughfare" has been created, conveying simultaneously the hollow, cylindrical nature of the "Nebelhorn." In view of the "-horn," this minuscule "s" Icon releases a "voice" going "through" the foghorn as relevant Index. While the (autonomous-)real nautical instrument may well own that type of cylindrical circumference, all "contours" to be perceived here must be gleaned from linguistic Qualisigns; everything has to be derived from the Icons and the Indexes they emit in relevance to the whole.

Although English possesses the adjective "nebulous," which in paraphrasing may loosely describe the first segment of the German foghorn, no part of that Sinsign enters the text in such compounded form, since no such Legisgn exists. While the "-horn" seems to be a cognate of the German, even this identity is misleading since all potential reference lies embedded in the hyletic-noematic (M-0) trichotomies of one language. That point may be shown once more with an earlier example, the "unicorn," thus the mythological, one-horned creature German renders as "Einhorn." Whereas the matching last segment in "Nebel*horn*" registers an Iconic doubling fit for any potential wordplay, English "fog*horn*" and "unic*orn*" remain barred from similar Iconization.

In both languages, however, the foghorn discloses some interesting aspects when submitted to maximal analytic stance. Surveyed at some distance, the nautical instrument sends out one message in attribution and another in linguistic competence. A horn "composed of" fog? That is what the Iconic syntagma renders in Sinsign composites but hardly what the indented Legisign designates, namely an instrument operative in fog which aids sight through sound when ships are stranded by this meterological phenomenon. Native speakers "know" the difference. Such is the power of language as bearer of meaning that it can be so seemingly casual in rendering its meanings. What anchors each Index to its cognition is the *concept* and *category* it bears as indented word, as wielded Icon now residing within the signitive convolutions of one language. No encyclopedic knowledge about worlds, but only a cognizance of word(s) as vehicles for speech determines the semantic roots of language in a language--a truism still ignored today by most critics of language theory (Gumpel, 1974, pp. 180-81).

At the same time, foregrounding is so vital to the Rheme that a Recipient must be a most alert superreader. Thus the "Nebel-" segment of this title becomes a *negative* image of *visual* obfuscation and the "-horn" conversely a *positive* image of *sonorous* affirmation. Each segment stresses different aspects that reappear in the ensuing text. In both languages, the "-horn" provides the type of "thoroughfare" for the voice already noted, and that relevant Index then establishes the textual relation with the nouns as "vocatives." The "voice" erupts as the "addressor" and the following nouns as its "addressees," retaining this relation throughout the first stanza. However, there is little room for a "lyric I" that automatically becomes one with the noun vocatives in the manner Hamburger suggested. So the "connectives" she missed have formed already from the titular-textual interaction as construed so far. If anything, the immediate association between voice and vocatives has to be diverse, imparting an "I-you" confrontation rather than identity even if, logically, one is to assume that the voice talks to itself through (its) parts of the body. The *first* line of the text should lend further support to my interpretation. In the centering mentioned, the German and English vocatives appear immediately below one another.

Mund im verborgenen Spiegel,
(mouth in the concealed mirror,)

While the voice seems concreted as "Mund," it also confronts this organ as though it had a separate being. This noun does not parallel the prepositional unit of the title but instead becomes the "new" textual element which then creates the horizontal left-to-right symmetry typical of the entire first stanza. Although the two-way preposition "in" returns, it is this time contracted as "im," where the "m" morpheme is taken from the definite-dative article "dem" and thus signals "no motion" as explained. As modifier of the preposition's grammatical object, the "Spiegel," the "m" becomes here by coincidence a type of logo for the masculine gender of that noun. With the mouth caught in a static, "concealed" mirror through the attributive past participle "verborgenen," there seems no escape possible from the predicament of visual obfuscation that causes this Index accordingly to interlock with the "Nebel-" of the same import.

What does it mean for the mouth to be in a "concealed mirror"? At first glance, mouth and mirror combine to suggest a type of "vanity," especially since a Petrarchistic past has long traded on the mouth topos of a romantic poetry that rendered the object of one's love in embellished rose petal lips, pearly white teeth, and a sweet breath. Vanity, indeed, may not be absent from the implications here, if more on a metaphysical order of *vanitas*, a mortal state. For it is the curious fate of the holder of a mouth never to behold it with the naked eye. "Real" as this organ feels for its capacity to speak, eat, drink, and thus engage in functions incorporating three of the five senses--sound, taste, and touch--it cannot ever be seen. The face containing this organ never "faces" itself in any direct self-identity, one might say. Only another face, a "you" instead of an "I," may espy the mouth of this voice. Who but a poet like Celan would ever draw attention to such a predicament, common though it is and yet strange as it becomes when one is thus made conscious of it?

In a wider Classical implication of ontological hierarchies that hark back to Plato's Cave Simile, reflection is a lesser state of being; never equaling "reality," it is several removes away from it. In that light, then, the mirror becomes ontologically a "mirage" where a primary state of being is concerned. The mirror "conceals" by "keeping" the real mouth and throwing back only a reflection of it which, consisting essentially of glass, is feeble and ready to shatter at any moment. Beyond this mirage, the mirror as structural metaphor of this poem renders all self-identity as another one of those Nietzschean metaphysical "metaphors," the extramoral "lie." Surely, the esthetic image or "Bild" Nietzsche affirmed simultaneously as no more or less a lie and which at least manages to combine the uncombinable comes through in the Icons of this poem. There are no Icons of ships in the text to substantiate the "object-relation" Hamburger sought. But an eloquent coherence begins to form nevertheless between the titular *meteorological* image and this *metaphysical* predicament or, in view of the latest construal, the *metaphorical* type of existence humans are not able to escape, cannot de-anthropomorphize with their limited faculties, of which the corporal and corporeal mouth is one.

Behind that eloquence, moreover, resides that other linguistic "mouth," the Lutheran "muzzle" my study introduced in the early part that also included Nietzsche, mainly to prove the purposive essence of language itself. This muzzle, too, demonstrates how hard it becomes to combine the uncombinable one language has wrought in another language, to the point of converting me unwittingly into one of those "after-poet" translators. Thus the English Icons combine "mouth" and "mirror" in their own Iconic reflection through an "m" alliteration. Language, the "Mother," has cast this Qualisign material so distinctively that I cannot imitate it without distorting the Referent within the translated poem. Thus English also forces me into an overt "the" pleonasm through an excessive Iconic linkage between title and text, simply because the German contractions cannot be copied. With these issues aired, I move sequentially to the *second* line,

Knie vor der Säule des Hochmuts,
(knee before the pillar of disdain,)

The content opening the vocative noun seems to have moved to the other extreme of the human physiognomy. Indeed, "extremity" is the right word, since the "Knie" (with "/kn/" pronounced) designates part of the limb supporting head and torso, thus including the mouth. This corporal metaphor almost picks up verbatim the conventional topos of humility, which was not the case with the Petrarchan mouth. The knee image thus appears in its traditional role of supplication. I recall Shakespeare's *Measure for Measure*, (Harrison, ed., 1952, V, i, verses 436, 439, 442 and 447, p. 1134), for example, where the knee in the act of kneeling and "lending a knee" in deference plays a rather prominent part. What reinforces the Index of "humility" within this poem, moreover, is first of all the "lack of mobility" conveyed by yet another two-way preposition, "vor," which, through the (uncontracted) definite-dative article "der," releases that implication. The knee stops dead before the grammatical object of the preposition, the "Säule," whose feminine gender is carried also by the article. Through the conventional image, the knee indeed is made to "stoop" in genuflexion before the vertical structure this Icon bears.

Were it not for the traditional topos, that full import of humility could not present itself so readily in the inertia of the limb that the dative supplies. Conversely, the pillar image rises in all its tall, aloof arrogance, especially through the *genitive link* of "des Hochmuts" (see Brooke-Rose, 1958, pp. 146-205). In the translation, the uncapitalized nouns quite literally "fall flat" through their rounded Qualisign dispositions, as shown in "der Säule des Hochmuts" versus "the pillar of disdain." A closer Icon to the German may have been "hauteur" or "haughtiness," but either choice would have produced other semantic and rhythmic complications. For once, too, it is English which blocks reiteration of the definite genitive "des" between pillar and disdain, just as German syntax demands. That hurts the import of the original, since the definite pleonasm--doubly so within the genitive link--solidifies all those objects: accusative, dative, and genitive, from title to text, firm into a "definite opposition," to Iconize that Index. Although Celan's use of the definite is not quite "syntactic," because no clearcut nominal antecedents are established for each of these objects (to thus merit rather an indefinite article), the "poetic" application would go too far if I forced "(of) *the* disdain" into Iconization here. That English muzzle, powerful as concreted ontic heteronomy in an unskeptical view, continues to intervene and prevent me from taking such liberties.

The same point can be proven again when glancing at the German Sinsign composite for disdain, the "Hochmut." Its "Hoch-" segment becomes Iconized as "high" and although the compound has its own indentation as complete Legisign, this inference should not be missed by a superreader alert to the M-base. Indeed, even the "H" Sinsign accentuates that height in its vertical Qualisign disposition and as such becomes yet another poetic "hieroglyph" or "ideogram," resembling in that respect the dentine image of Dickinson's poem. Nor can a "Hoch-mut," hyphenated or literalized from the Icons, be dismissed entirely as "high spirits," which in medieval times embodied satanic arrogance. In this context, though, that sense of superiority does not lie on the "mortal" left side of corporal and corporeal organs or limbs, but rather on the "immortal" right side of impenetrable, indifferent opposition--as viewed from that other side. These evolving "sides" reflect German notions of "Diesseits" and "Jenseits," meaning "this side" on earth versus that transcendent "other side" "beyond" it. Thus, the bilateral symmetry of this poem projects a stark metaphysical division between immanence and transcendence, reinforced by an eloquent spatial fusion characterizing the Rheme: the solid opposition cannot be damned but only cursed by those unable to circumvent or penetrate it.

Through the genitive link, indeed, the distance embodied in disdain begins to suggest a type of "conspiracy," more poignant than mere concealment would indicate. The erect pillar, by implication and Iconization towering over the bent knee, has become injected with animation, has been *personified* through the *volitional* stance of disdain. Localized spotsighting thus allows the image to demonstrate a perfect case of selectional violation; the neo-Aristotelian metaphor appears as lexical deviance based on a "transference" between the cold stony edifice and an equally "hard" or "stony" disposition. Indeed, the anthropomorphized pillar becomes invested with a type of "personality metaphor" through its implied human disposition, "cold" and deliberately unyielding of nature. So here is an "anthropomorphic" fate mortals face; Nietzsche construed it as a "lying," "metaphorical" existence. Ironically, the pillar is humanized only to be dehumanized, since that is the only means for dealing with such an unfathomable beyond, imposing a few sensations of self-identity upon an ineffable enemy, which, couched in negative imagery, becomes converted into a mirror or a pillar.

As for the disdainful pillar as localized metaphor, it may be thus described as long as the limits of selectional violation are realized. Anything pertaining to sheer content taxonomy otherwise leaves a critic as undecided about metaphor's extent and state as were the participants of the Ingendahl Experiment. Thus English has already normalized a personality metaphor that refers to an individual as a "pillar of strength." With such internalized redundance, the image here may appear more "literal" than "metaphorical," depending on the frequency of Symbolic feedforward and feedback deployed by the Recipient--in other words, on how often the Icon "pillar" is wielded as idiom by the concretizing person. Mass media exposure would firm sensations of familiarity, possibly to the point of phasing out "metaphorical" Ought-Values, leaving behind instead merely flattened Is-Values of "meaning."

Fortunately, the Rheme's content-insensitive structural metaphors cannot disappear or "die" unless the entire poetic intext degenerated to the level of Qualisigns--a deceased M-base! As long as the language is alive, so are the constructs it forms, as also their components. When Rhemic, these piece together the backgrounded and foregrounded strata of this strucutre, engendering thereby a lyric ego. Thus no vacillation arises on that score, since "transference" is functionally derived from tasks of contextualization, irrespective of deviant lexical pockets. Every nominalized nuance becomes affected by this processing, including also the accusative and dative cases. Live memory then holds in check the compounded import as the right-sided opposition takes yet another turn with the introduction of the noun vocative in the third line,

Hand mit dem Gitterstab:
(hand with the grid-iron stave:)

Although in one examination of taxonomy (of a nineteenth-century woman poet) I discovered that "hand" was the most popular topos through the potential range of gestures the image offers, its meaning in this line probably remains the most abstruse, if not to the point of requiring any of Hamburger's "reverse" procedures. Since "mit" always takes the dative, the preposition does not aid construal as directly as the earlier two-way prepositions did. Still, the fact that dative "dem" surfaces--in the masculine for the "-stab" segment of the grammatical object--as yet another definite article has to become significant. This vestige completes the central definite-dative section for the entire stanza in the reiterated "im"/"vor dem"/"mit dem" that leads directly into the "opposition."

The definite article thus continues to provide a crucial Iconic link, especially for this bulky compound, which at first glance is as impenetrable as the "opposition" itself. Indeed, the "Gitterstab" constitutes a *poetic neologism* and as such bears no validated Legisign engendering an indented Icon with an Indexical periphery. That is to say, the word as compound does not exist outside of this intextual frame; it has no part in the latent oppositional system of shared signitive convolutions and would thus be starred (*) were it not for its *derived* significance within this immediate context. The segments of the compound, to be sure, are Legisigns and thus aided my tanslation of the tripartite "grid-iron stave." For "Gitter" denotes generally something like an "iron grid" composed of "bars" or "railings" that suggest a "barrier." Since neuter "Gitter·," like the "Zimmer" in the Brecht poem, has a null plural morpheme, number was no help either. Lastly, the "·stab," translated as "·stave," may signify a ceremonial "staff" or a "crosier."

How can this abstruse object be brought together with the "Hand" in such a marked asyntactic setting? What does "with" imply here? Somehow, one may be reminded of a Marcel Marceau mime, the one which has flattened palms (though of both hands) with fingers uppermost touch unseen bars as if to assess bounds and the limited space left within them. Is the "Gitterstab" with its "Hand" a type of barrier conveying that mortals remain incarcerated in their own limitations? Then that lying "metaphorical" reality has turned into a "cage" enveloped by the "opposition." Though inscrutable, the grid-iron stave also implies an "intimacy" evoked by the closeness "with" suggests. Does this mean that the "Hand" is indelibly marked by this stave as though bearing it as a "wound"? If so, the Icons interlock to release something equivalent to a "stain"··perhaps the stigmata of Christ!

Although Celan was Jewish, this construal would not be that farfetched for his poetic idiolect. The cycle (1970, p. 58) containing this poem includes another entry whose very title, "Die feste Burg," trades on one of Luther's hymns of the strong or mighty fortress. Also, I am reminded of Celan's poem "Psalm," which obviously refers to the Old Testament but also bears an allusion to the (bloodstained?) Crown of Thorns in the imagery of a "corolla red" (in the bilingual Michael Hamburger edition of 1976, pp. 304-307). Similarly, a Christian type of "epiphany" may well apply to this poem's bilateral "confrontation" between the "Diesseits" and "Jenseits" already discussed, even if some of the connotations are secularized to impart human suffering through a sense of total inadequacy.

The radius of significance weighting this line may well illustrate Ingarden's idea (1965, pp. 149-151, 270) of semantic "opalescence" (Opalisierung), leaving *all* of the implications valid and oscillating in their ramified if not univocally conclusive import. Furthermore, my resorting to Celan's poetic diction in terms of a Judaic-Christian tradition may be defined as an "extrinsic" aid. Such recourse is justified and often vital, but must never outweigh the "intrinsic" dimensions obtained from the text's own Qualisign ground. This ground certainly displays also a Christian type of dichotomy between light and dark, the latter reinforced by the obscurity of the "Gitterstab" for contributing more of that "nebulous" opposition.

One remaining item of the first stanza's concluding line is the punctuation mark: the *colon* reflects the usual kind of "juncture" which gathers the serialized lines into an "aforesaid," leading from there into an "opening" of what follows. However, even this colon, like the dashes in Dickinson's text, has been nominalized into a structural metaphor, lending its meaning to the intextual meaning. Very concrete is its Qualisign disposition of two dots, creating a type of cylindrical "tunnel" or "channel" that lets the voice through to the imperatives. The colon thus accomplishes at a more degenerate level what the titular elements began: through it, the first half of this text concludes with yet another foregrounded "passageway." The voice, which first reached the text via the accusative and "·horn," is now relayed to the text's second stanza via the colon. No matter how automatic the operative role of a colon under normal syntactic conditions, here this vestige shapes a lyric ego through Rhemic backgrounding and foregrounding. To do justice to the colon's role as "juncture" between the stanzas, I cite the entire text once more.

<blockquote>
Ins Nebelhorn
Mund im verborgenen Spiegel,
Knie vor der Säule des Hochmuts,
Hand mit dem Gitterstab:

reicht euch das Dunkel,
nennt meinen Namen,
führt mich vor ihn.

Into the foghorn
mouth in the concealed mirror,
knee before the pillar of disdain,
hand with the grid-iron stave:

pass on the darkness to one another,
call my name,
lead me before him.
</blockquote>

Käte Hamburger (1968, p. 203; 1973, p. 253) has some fruitful comments on the role of this colon as a unique point of transition that affects especially the imperatives: it "indicates that the second person plural imperatives comprising the three lines of the second stanza refer to the parts of the body previously named." This type of plural is the "familiar" in contrast to the formal or polite use. The "reference" Hamburger mentions creates semantic interlacing, which is fitting for the *tercines* of these stanzas, though at the Iconic level the original order has been disrupted: "pass" obviously belongs to the "hand," "call" to the initiating "mouth," and the ability to get up and "lead" to the "knee," the "middle" vocative that now closes the entire poem.

Although the concluding period at the end of this stanza adds a touch of finality that was conspicuously absent in Dickinson's poem, the Icons comprising noun vocatives and imperatives come to a natural halt as their respective material contents are exhausted, which is not to say that, thematically, an ultimate solution has been found. As for the *number* in which the imperatives are cast, the plural "t" morpheme is the Sinsign that carries the missing plural "you" subject, in German "ihr," something English cannot imitate. The "t" Sinsign thus unites all the imperatives in their "finitude"··and provides the evidence which caused Ingarden, used to inflected languages, to ascribe a greater functionality to the direction-factor of verbs than nouns, even if the "nominalized" imperatives are structurally nouns as well and thus possess the intensified potency of a nominal direction-factor. The nominalized "t" Sinsign thus gathers up also *all* the vocatives of the preceding stanza, even as each imperative Icon takes its cue from a particular noun. Aiding the general significance is this stanza's "central" portion: where the definite-dative appeared before, a *personalization* has taken over, with an almost perfect vertical alignment between "euch," "meinen," and "mich." The first of these pronouns is a reciprocal type that as Index interlocks with the "t" Sinsign of the verbs by bearing also the familiar plural. Everything else should emerge with the detail, here starting with the *first* line,

reicht euch das Dunkel,
(pass on the darkness to one another,)

The hand is challenged in its capacity at least to reach out and share "communally" that "dark" fate, as the collective "t" plural underscores, together with the reciprocal "euch." One might Iconize the gist loosely in the proverb Chomsky cited for his selectional violation, "Misery loves company," or one might verbalize it as "There is compensation in commiseration." In a sense "misery" does return with the somber "das Dunkel," still clad in the definite to match recursively the right-sided opposition. Although the hyletic inventory of German also owns an adjectival "dunkel," the noun matters for the addition of the definite article and for continuing the nuance of "obstacle" a definitive "thing" can convey more readily. Of course, the dark is grammatically also an object, though this time of a verb rather than preposition. Actually, this verb takes two objects, where "thing" such as the darkness is direct, accusative object, and where "persons" such as the "euch" constitute an indirect, dative alternative--ready to become "receiver(s)" of this action. Thus Indexicalized, the darkness "changes hands."

As Sinsign composite, the "Dunkel" returns all the way to the fog of the instrument and to the visual concealment of the mirror, indeed reflecting the "-gel" of "Spiegel" by reverberating in mute sound and visual sign the "-kel" of "Dunkel," while the vocalic-nasal "un" then reaches diagonally across to the "Mund." Although thus crossing sides, the "Dunkel" may do so, in the sense that the mouth led to the first opposition on the other side while the dark on that side now lifts, or, more specifically, is made to lift through the Indexical return of the mouth in the Icon of naming.

Before I reach that point in the text, however, a word about possible choices omitted from my translation of this line. In comparison to the original, the English seems unwieldy and detracts from the indigenous symmetry. Certainly, "darkness" could have been changed to the substantive "dark," but at the time I preferred this Icon. I might have omitted also the verbal complement in "pass *on*," allowing the Index to become absorbed sufficiently by the final "to one another," regrettable as it is that the pronoun "euch" simply has to be shifted and extended this way. In addition, the English inventory does possess the verb Icon "reach" as a closer Sinsign to "reicht," but does not Indexicalize into a matching import. Then English also bears a verbal cognate for "hand" which, when used, would forge an unnatural pleonasm between the vocative and imperative, particulary since nouns are not capitalized in this language. The translator is then pounding in where an author stays subtle by making the "hand . . . hand on . . . ." With these possibilities at least entertained, I turn to the stanza's *second* line,

nennt meinen Namen,
(call my name,)

The M-base really comes into its own in the foregrounded Qualisign nazalization, which appears immediately with "nennt" and horizontally weaves in and out of the entire line as shown with my italicised "*nennt meinen Namen.*" The closest nasal profusion, especially in matching capitalization, the title bears with "Ins Nebelhorn." Gone, too, is the "dark" back-vowel "/u/" in "Dunkel," replaced instead by the recurring front vowel "e" of title and text. The "Mund" straddles positive and negative imagery with its strong nasalization and matching dark "u" vowel. But instead of its concealment, "Mund" goes into action through the imperative, removing the last "dark" cloud of opposition on that side. Accordingly, the "voice" attains yet another "voice" through the mouth's capacity to speak . . . out. The positive sound begun with "-horn" has finally conquered the negative, obfuscating vision of "Nebel-."

Added to the affirmation is the progressive personalization, imparting renewed confidence through self-assertion: the plural, collective "euch" yields to a distinctive first-person possessive adjective, the "meinen" accompanying the name which, in its slot, has forced out the definite that went with the opposition. The "meinen Namen" as direct-accusative object, consisting of the masculine name and its possessive, retains a syntactic if not an overt Sinsign identity with the darkness that has lifted. Cast in the possessive and the naming, the voice attains enhanced self-identity. Hamburger (1968, p. 204; 1973, p. 254) thus has a point when she says that "name is person to a far greater degree than mouth, knee, or hand." The voice "through" the foghorn finally comes to the fore.

The concluding line and Hamburger's final comments will indicate, however, where this critic stays misled in her search for lyric identity at all cost. But first I see fit to question once more my own translation. As with the "hand," English owns a verbal, uncapitalized cognate that might have induced a pleonastic "name my name" in yet another overburdened stylization. That I avoided. But to enhance the symmetry through a use paralleling the verbal complement in "pass on," I might have added "call out," yet decided against such an extension.

In any case, the bilingual version demonstrates that the faculty of naming in speech, with which the "Mund" becomes empowered here, is of greater "mental" exertion than the "manual" vector of sharing carried out by the "Hand" in the passing on of the darkness. Next, the act of leading exemplifies a decidedly "physical" activity as the only remaining imperative lets the "Knie" finally come into its own in the *last* line:

führt mich vor ihn.
(lead me before him.)

The task of leading, exacted of the "Knie" vocative through the imperative, involves complete motion of the whole body. The movement as such evokes loosely the idea of life as a path to be trodden or traversed, with hurdles overcome on the way. Thus, in a wider Index, the connotations embody Christian salvation, going all the way back to the Patristic age of St. Augustine and reaching into the late Middle Ages with such works as *The Pilgrim's Progress* by John Bunyan (1628-1688), for example. In a more immediate and secularized construal, the knee's static, humble posture of the first stanza is to be traded in for confident advancement in this stanza. To Iconize this intextual connection, there is the same two-way preposition, the "vor" of the second line. But through the (transitive) verb of motion, the "führt," this preposition now acquires an accusative object.

As the line reads, the "vor" separates the two final accusative pronouns, "mich" and "ihn," with the former a direct object of the imperative and the other of the "activated" preposition, as explained. In concrete Iconization, the syntagma "mich vor ihn" projects the preposition as "intervening" between the two pronouns--a final barrier warding off a full approach to the right side, if far less bulky than the former objects on that side. These objects, in fact, mount in the final pronoun "ihn," robbed of all "definite" accouterments as befits such an operative sign. Schematic in its amorphous material content, this unobtrusive pronoun discloses mainly that it is cast in the masculine third person. Compared to this pronoun, the "mich" of the voice has at least solidified into greater independence when compared to the former "meinen" in the same first person, which was still a possessive *adjective*.

So the voice has come as far as it can go, facing this transmuted opposition, if more independently in its naming prowess and pronominal state than before. The "ihn" the voice faces is overtly just an operative sign but covertly constitutes an eidetic, because nominalized element bearing the brunt of the construal when aided by the recursive powers of live memory. Even if Celan never read the theories of Ingarden, he intuitively trades on the abstruse, schematic nature of this pronoun, much as Dickinson was shown to be keenly aware of her signitive convolutions, the indentations of English. Fused to its right-sided Rhemic space, this "ihn," like Atlas, implicitly carries the weight of the obstacles from that side, interlocking with all these elements and burgeoning accordingly at the level of the Index, no matter how narrow the material content of its Icon.

Ingarden (1965, pp. 159-160) actually explicates how the more functional direction-factor of a schematic pronoun gets set "identically" with a nominal antecedent in order to absorb nominal content while creating intersyntactic "connections" (Zusammenhänge). Since no concatenation of syntactic correlates applies to the Rheme, the coherence is more implicit, depending on Indexical interlocking, which then causes even this pronominal direction-factor to expand by pointing centripetally inward as a content vital to the fullest contextualization. Here, the "ihn" thus constitutes the immortal reflection of the mortal "mich" while it has literally "the last word." The imperatives carried the voice as the "mich" forward, but perlocutionary compliance does not have to follow a command, no matter how strong the illocutionary force of appeal. Thus there may be a dim hope of reaching the "ihn" held back by the "vor," yet no wish is necessarily fulfilled.

All elements as structural metaphors have thus done their work, exuding meaning from meanings and rendering a thematic whole through inner interlocking. Meteorological imagery became intertwined with a metaphysical predicament. Indestructible functional metaphors, no matter what their lexical denomination, transferred their own sense to the significance of the whole, conveying thematically a "metaphorical" state of human existence, complete with all the impenetrable barriers that amount to Nietzsche's extramoral lie. Yet "truth" rests ultimately in the disclosure of a new world through these words; a tiny verbal vortex of human creativity came to the fore as the esthetic unhiddenness or symbolic synthesis of Heidegger's and Cassirer's notions of truth. As contents tied to their context, these functional metaphors cannot die. They are guaranteed to last in their thetic I-M-0 constitution as long as the language to which they belong preserves its M-0-I incline of generation.

By implication--and certainly not in my translation--the "ihn" deserves the Iconized capitalization of a "Him," since it suggests the ineluctible counterforce to finite existence. There was such support for a masculine godhead from the subtle connotation of stigmata, as discussed with the hand of the grid-iron stave. Moreover, since my suggestion pertains only to an Index minus a denotative core, my readers as equal Recipients of this poem may or may not come to the same conclusion. What made me bring up this point at all is rather the didactic intent to stress for the last time that every such Qualisign change as capitalization affects some semantic nuance from the first trichotomy on, in M-0-I generation. That is why this issue surfaced while discussing the natural leaps of language, which, in capitalizing English "God," held this Icon at bay from the other side of "dog."

Whatever the construal in terms of content, my basic method has not deviated from previous procedures of construing the Rheme, since the structure as such is not affected. As already indicated, a backgrounded and foregrounded lyric ego surely disclosed itself as all the Icons hung connotationally together. However, Hamburger (1968, pp. 203-204; 1973, pp. 253-254) attempts a similar justification of the final masculine pronoun that Levin tried with his logical recovery. She relies on grammar in terms of a normal syntactic hierarchy by treating the "ihn" of this poem like a regular pronoun derived from one precise antecedent. First she searches for a "male person." Finding none, she probes the masculine nouns in turn, ignoring simultaneously the left-and-right differences that affect the significance of this poem. Listing mouth, mirror, and disdain (though for some reason not the "Gitterstab") for their equivalent masculine gender, she determines that the "Namen" in the masculine (-accusative) must be the antecedent, since it is also closest in syntagma to the "ihn." Not surprisingly, Hamburger then forms the conclusion that the text's cohering sense she calls "object-relation" remains "very uncertain" (sehr ungewiss), indeed "abstruse" or "hidden" (verborgen).

By coincidence, Hamburger's last word in parenthesis turns out to be the same past participle that accompanied the first textual "opposition," the concealment of the "verborgenen" mirror. To this critic, it is not "God"--in any form--but the Rheme which has not disclosed itself because it was sought with dubious criteria. Levin applied logic to linguistic gender in his recovery of a nonmasculine lion for a decidedly feminine Etna, and Hamburger similarly gives priority to syntactic rules to determine the masculine for a decidedly poetic constituent in the masculine. Her quest for syntax in what is by content and function an asyntactic setting subverts the very logic of her argument. How can the name, which so obviously belongs to the voice, equal the "him" only on the basis of the masculine? No wonder the poem stays devoid of full sense to her. Underlying the problem is her neglect to separate a lexical "lyric I," such as the voice in the Icons presented, from a functional "lyric I" which is endemic in poetic intext, no matter what the textual denominations. Celan thus managed to "conceal" his authorial intent so well that not only the mouth got lost in the mirror but also the critic in her determination.

Not insignificantly, it is actually right after her above quest for syntactic coherence that Hamburger goes on to describe the "lyric I" as part of the three nouns, the passage quoted at the outset of my analysis. Instead, the lyric ego should be a structural criterion which transcends content--again, analogous to the Kantian transcendental ego cited before. Thus, the lyric ego is equivalent to the basic connective on which all selected contents subsist, be they present as an Iconic "I," "him," or whatever. Much as all the contents in their construal release the backgrounded and foregrounded lyric ego, this ego determines their very essence and function in achieving that goal. Only thematically, therefore, in view of the final enigmatic "him," can the text be described as "open." From the aspect of the lyric ego as transcendent connective, the structure remains teleolically closed, whether or not a period is there. The riddle of finite existence encased in "definite" barriers may not be solved beyond a modicum of hope. But the structure determining semantic content as a specific instance of thetic I-M-0 generation through an extended transference should not be a riddle to those probing a work's nonlexical depth.

Had Hamburger discovered that fundamental "closure," she would not have correlated a decidedly lyric "statement" with a literal "saying," as her bipartite genre theory has it. To be sure, I also availed myself of the entire nomenclature marking syntactic divisions, yet stressed in the very first analysis that this is a descriptive means for naming decidedly Rhemic entries. Every particle of Celan's poem has to remain an object of expression geared to a totality of expression that has been pieced together through an extended transference lodged at I, hence the Interpretant of human consciousness, and not at M, where the lexicon abides, in thetic I-M-0 generation. Thus the concrete, disdainful pillar I invoked as possibly a neo-Aristotelian metaphor remains lodged only at M. Be a constituent the type of "filter" the colon offered or of the "filmy" essence of that final and tantalizing pronoun, the elements, beyond their description, are equalized through their participation in a function. Thus, the very "uncertainty" or "concealment" Hamburger raised uncannily begins to assume "precise" sense as import relevant to this intext. When non-adequated "denoting" is precipitated at zero-point and then compounded into nominalized meaning, connotations are engendered through a special mode of transference, aided by the faculty of live memory.

Function and not lexical abstruseness or deviance created these "metaphors" as nominalized meanings, including the last pronoun in its extended significance as the supernatural, literally situated on the other (right?) side of empiricial immanence. Function converted each participating element as micro-component into a metonymic part of a holistic macro-structure. This relation lent sharp contours to everything--the accusative of motion, the dative lack of motion, the singular of vocatives, the interspaces of a colon, and the "t" Sinsign of imperatives, to name just a few idiosyncrasies observed in one language. In my final diagnosis, Hamburger's quest for syntactic connections caused her to miss second stance, which recognizes the esthetic ought of a construct. When that content-insensitive imperative becomes subverted, literary language ceases to make sufficient sense in its non-adequated esthetic essence--the very "sense-nexus" Hamburger ascribed to lyric statements but did not follow through logically to ultimate conclusions. Well, here it is; *no* "reverse" procedure made this poem cohere.

A final esthetic-hermeneutic concretization then benefits from all the recursive links established, not least for that concluding pronoun in sequence which paradoxically lends "further" meaning to all the contents that preceded it. Polyphony in full concretization of what live memory has released lets the interlacing tercines ripple through their nominalized foregrounding in all their rhythmic implementation. In a last resort to conventional prosody, the meter appears dactylic, working toward a gradual diminution from two-and-a-half measures to one. This one measure descends upon the little pronoun in the closing line, as shown.

$$
\overset{\textstyle/}{\text{führt}} \quad \overset{-}{\text{mich}} \quad \overset{-}{\text{vor}} \quad \overset{\textstyle/}{\text{ihn.}}
$$

Blunt and abrupt, this foregrounded rhythm lands on the final "ihn," adding further weight to the focalization of its import. Although the period spells the end, fulfillment is left open to doubt, as indicated. The sparse left-sided content, drawn chiefly from the inner repertoire which permitted the material contents of nouns to become linked with the verb-imperatives, has exhausted itself.

The same applies to my three exhaustive analyses, which should have demonstrated how Referent and Recipient meet through an alert superreader. To be sure, in any literary work of art there is "more" to be culled from a text--but not anything. The Icons confront the Recipient and their penetration discloses the Referent. Both interlocutory partners trade on units *natural* to language and accordingly on a competence wrought by the indenting power of one language, as the diatribe against my own translation was supposed to have underscored. My non-Aristotelian theory has thus been proven through five applications to texts, three of which differed, while the lyric ego was substantiated three times as athematic connective for entities that are functional metaphors. The study is thus ready to move on to the neo-Aristotelian adjunct which, as promised, offers in brief the most crucial aspects of the lexical "metaphor."

PART III

The Neo-Aristotelian Metaphor Through the Ages

The Neo-Aristotelian Metaphor
through the Ages

The Founding Fathers

The Founding Fathers of the neo-Aristotelian tradition usher in this "adjunct." They come in a triumvirate that closes the historical gap between the progenitor Aristotle (384-322 B.C.) and the Latin rhetoricians, specifically Cicero (106-43 B.C.) and Quintilian (ca. A.D. 35-100), who lived a century apart. From a "retrospective" view of their relevance to the present, these three ancients will enable me to crystallize the salient aspects of the neo-Aristotelian tradition. Such a perspective, then, converts these three thinkers into the deserving "fathers" of this tradition. Where an immediate link with the contemporary scene is needed, I shall emphasize this connection by citing a few modern critics right away, although the majority of them have their say individually in the last part of the adjunct, after summarizing vital points that tie past to present.

Aristotle himself worked against a backdrop of the controversial dichotomy known as *thesei* and *physei* (Leroy, 1967, pp. 4-5). It revolved around the question of whether language was based on convention or on nature. "Analogists" upheld a "natural" order, while Democritan skeptics became the "anomalists," who visualized mainly the disorder in language (Ivić, 1971, pp. 12-13, Bruns, 1975, p. 30). Essentially, the neo-Aristotelian purview of metaphor draws on both these positions: analogist is the endorsement of meaning as a representational mode of reference and anomalist the belief that metaphor accounts for arepresentational pockets of lexical deviance through a function of transference.

Originally, even the word for "etymology," which goes back to Greek "Etymon," was expected to foster "right names" that were "true" and "real" by preserving an analogous relation between language and empirical nature (Porzig, 1975, pp. 13-49). Plato (427-347 B.C.), as Aristotle's immediate precursor, is also remembered today for touching on this issue in the *Cratylus* (1970, IV, Loeb ed., pp. 6-7). There the question is whether everything possesses its right name by "nature" or by "agreement." Instead of answering directly, Plato lets Socrates express his distrust of wily Sophists who twist words without any respect for their verisimilitude (pp. 14-15, 32-33). Such was the Eleatic resistance to anything in flux; it revealed Plato's undeserved discrimination against the well-educated

213

Sophists, who seemed to have apprehended the power of language (Freeman, 1946, pp. 341-353).

To be sure, Plato has also been praised for being one of the first thinkers to entertain sign relations in this very Dialogue. (See Leroy, 1967, p. 3, and of late Sebeok, 1979, pp. 6, 110). Plato certainly realized that the world, never directly accessible, is less so in language than in perception. He was greatly admired by Cassirer, who in his volume on language (1972, I, p. 63), commented on Plato's *Seventh Epistle* (1975, IX, Loeb ed., pp. 532-535; Orth, 1967, p. 6). In this work, Plato was fully aware that a circle, for example, may be cast in a linguistic name, the "onoma," and that roundness in sheer meaning differed from its theoretical definition as "logos," its concrete perception as "eidolon," and its mathematical cognition as "episteme." Human consciousness thus construes what is supposedly one entity as several "objects," as these arise in accordance with their specific functions--something the modern neo-Aristotelians still have to learn. Indeed, they will be shown to trade on the very example of a circle, for which reason I cite it here.

Nevertheless, it was Aristotle rather than Plato who in his *On Interpretation* took a firm stand in favor of the *conventional* base of language. The linguistic name or *onoma*, also translated as "noun" (1973, I, Loeb ed. pp. 116-117), is to Aristotle "a sound having meaning established by convention alone." No linguistic sound, he adds, is "by nature" a noun but becomes one through human synthesis and thus constitutes a "symbol." Although Greek "onoma" denotes "word," "meaning," and "noun," the translators above no doubt settled for the "noun" because Aristotle then introduces the verb, Greek "rhema" (ibid., pp. 118-119), which is still a linguistic name but differs from a noun by bearing a "time reference." At first glance, Aristotle seems to endorse the type of syntactic hierarchy this study developed with the aid of Ingarden. However, that connection disappears fast when Aristotle (ibid., pp. 116-117) claims next that the noun as discrete word possesses "no truth nor falsity" but *attains* truth simply by attachment of a verb: *predication* leads straight to the *proposition*.

Here is the crux of the problem: Ingarden had nominal-verbal unfolding and interlocking occur at the level of the pure referent. Only upon formation of a correlate could adequation take over and thus induce the objective referent as truth claim in carefully defined processing. No neo-Aristotelian to date has recognized this important distinction. All Aristotle does is to assert (ibid., pp. 120-121) that, "while every sentence has meaning, . . . not all can be called propositions. We call propositions those only that have truth or falsity in them." "Truth or falsity" to non-Aristotelian semantics is a matter of context, since function precipitates truth claims irrespective of the lexical content, be such claims met positively or negatively. Yet Aristotle affirms only what is self-evident, thus without delineating how sentences that solely bear meaning operate differently from those harboring propositions. Frege, too, got no further a couple of thousand years later, with his "sense" versus "reference." Fregeans no doubt would uphold Aristotle's example for "meaning," or their "sense": the *prayer*, he says, "neither has truth nor has falsity." Non-Aristotelian semantics, however, classes the prayer with adequated usage because, no matter how effusive in content, it is uttered in a reality-nexus and thus not by fictive speakers. A similar example which this study cited was the devotional cycle by Novalis: when included in a church service as prayer, its poems lose the essence of their esthetic ought and acquire instead a reality-nexus.

With these thorny issues of *meaning* and truth yet unresolved in that vital obverse and reverse order of approach, Aristotle's *metaphor* is likely to be flawed too. The immediate link with *On Interpretation*, moreover, is a work that ususally appears in the same volume--*The Categories* (ibid., pp. 2, 18-19, 24-25). This proximity hardly pertains to the content of the *Categories* but becomes relevant to Aristotle's later analysis of metaphor. In Greek, "category" denoted "predicate," though not in connection with language but logic: what can be predicated of a world in accordance with "what sort of thing" an entity is? *The Categories* is a work to be commended for making one of the earliest attempts to systematize empirical reality through human cognizance. Of special relevance to metaphor are the genus and species classes (ibid., pp. 28-31). They are entered under "Quality" and "Secondary Substances"--secondary because their status does not comprise individuations: neither a man nor a woman as such goes by the species human of the genus animal, for example.

Ironically, despite Aristotle's effort at "sorting out" the world, his later exposition of metaphor found him cross-sorting important ontological domains; the proponent of logical categories and of *thetic* (or "synthetic") convention then committed the first ontological category-mistake as he sought a linguistic metaphor in lexical pockets of violated logical categories. The problem was exacerbated by the fact that Aristotle dealt with literary language, the subject of his *Poetics*, as the title indicates. Chronologically, the *Poetics* trailed the arrangement of the "Traditional Order" covering Aristotle's works (according to the Berlin Bekker edition of 1831, in *Nicomachean Ethics*, 1975, XIX, Loeb ed.,pp. ix-xii). A considerable gap thus exists between the first volume bearing *The Categories* and *On Interpretation* discussed and the two final works relevant to my topic, the "*Art*" *of Rhetoric* (to be abbreviated to "Rhetoric") and the *Poetics*. Some of the content entailed in that large middle between the first and last Aristotelian volumes can be adumbrated only in its immediate relevance to this study: the *Topica* (139b, 1966, Loeb ed., pp. 564-5) refers to metaphor, but mainly to stress its "obscurity"; the *Physics* is worth a reminder that it precedes the *Metaphysics*, an issue discussed when I explained the "metaphysical" nature of language; the *Nicomachean Ethics* surfaced while I delved briefly into the "energetic" tradition of language theory because it bears the dichotomy of "ergon" and "energeia."

Aristotle's *Poetics* contains the major exposition of metaphor, while comparisons between metaphor and the comparison, the simile, are taken up in the *Rhetoric*. Aristotle alludes in the *Rhetoric* (1411a, 1959, Loeb ed., pp. 398-399) to "the four kinds of metaphor" he developed in the *Poetics*, leaving the impression that these works stayed closely connected. Through the *Poetics*, Aristotle became the "father of evaluation-through-the-genre," as one critic put it (Hirsch, 1976, pp. 114-115). His main interest in genre was tragedy in its proper "construction," said another critic (Fyfe, 1966, pp. xv, xix), while yet another (Gassner, 1951, p. xxxix) commends him generally for his "honestly exploratory" approach. Curiously, the Homeric epics that Aristotle held sufficiently in regard to cite while treating metaphor came second to tragedy, with lyric awareness as yet subsumed under music (Fyfe, ibid., pp. xxvii-xxix). Aspects of dramatic plot supposedly meant more to him than stylistic detail (ibid.), yet the exposition of metaphor leaves a different impression.

This exposition is covered in chapter 21 of the *Poetics*. It follows chapter 20 on "Diction," the Greek "Lexis." Translators express their reservations about these parts of the *Poetics*: Fyfe (1960,1960, Loeb ed., pp. 74-75) suggests that diction, with its emphasis on "grammar and philology," does not fit into a "literary use of words," adding that Aristotle's own diction stays "obscure"; Bywater (1966, p. 53) takes the chapter on diction to be an interpolation and calls the sections treating metaphor "indubitably disappointing," if still relevant, while they demonstrate further that Aristotle did "not appreciate poetry"; Grube (1958, p. 41) expresses similar views regarding the "linguistic" nature of the topic, the abstruse style as well as questionable authenticity. To these comments must be added the reservations of Else (1967, pp. ix, 567), who meticulously examines the concepts from the *Poetics* except for chapters 20 through 22, thus also the entire exposition of metaphor, for lacking lucidity and "bristling" instead with technical problems too complex for this author to classify.

Other inconsistencies arise because the *Poetics* comprised Aristotle's lectures copied down by students. Also, since this versatile thinker covered so many fields, the translations are bound to suffer wherever the experts of Classical Greek had to be sufficiently familiar with the subject to accurately apply their inference--Iconize Indexes in non-Aristotelian terms. For that reason, I shall frequently offer two translations, putting my own limited knowledge of Greek to use by attempting to arbitrate between them. What seems curious in all of this is that the neo-Aristotelians reflect none of the concerns of the Classical scholars above, apparently unaware of the shaky foundation of their concept. In my own case, the major identity of focus with Aristotle remains the presence of metaphor in *language*, and there particularly as *noun*. Yet it must be remembered that I applied the noun as phenomenological principle and that the Greek word for "noun" encompassed the variety of meanings already elucidated.

Aristotle thus commences by presenting his metaphor as one of the "noun" species (1457b, 1960, Loeb ed., pp. 78-81), along with "ordinary," "rare," "ornamental," and "invented" words, among others. The actual exposition of metaphor I divide as follows: (a) the "Preliminary Statement" defining "metaphora" as a whole; (b) the four "epiphoras" as modes of metaphorical transference. If (b) is divided further into the genus-species type versus proportionality, the latter kind becomes (c). Although the genus-species epiphora consists of three parts--genus-to-species, species-to-genus, species-to-species--I discuss the first two types together and omit the third because it remains too vague despite editorial efforts to make it "intelligible" (Fyfe, 1960, Loeb ed., pp. 80-81). The two genus and species epiphoras to be treated come in examples from Homer, the first from the *Odyssey* and the second from the *Iliad* (Kassel, 1965, p. 79). What is left of the exposition in the *Poetics* I shall subsume loosely under "addenda"; they extend to the end of chapter 22 (from 1457b, 1458a, 1458b to 1459b), going up to what I label the "Similarity Statement." The *Rhetoric* takes over from there in my discussion, specifically for evaluating Aristotle's contrastive analysis of metaphor and simile.

The *Preliminary Statement* reads as follows in two translated versions (Fyfe, 1960, pp. 80-81; Bywater 1966, p. 56):

Metaphor is the application of a strange term . . . Metaphor consists in giving the thing a name that belongs to something else . . .

This time *onoma* of the cryptic Aristotelian Greek becomes Iconized by inference as "term" and "name" instead of "noun." Since some of the examples involve verbs, this nomenclature would be more suitable. What is decidedly present, moreover, concerns metaphor as *proxy-tenet* substitution. The Greek *allotrios*, denoting lexical deviance, is the original Greek for the translated "strange term" in one version and the adverbial phrase "(to) something else" in the other. So, when an "alien" term has been sighted--or "spotsighted" as I put it before to describe that localized focus--it is considered to be present as an usurper of another term or meaning. From this broad definition of *metaphora* Aristotle moves to the specific "epiphoras" of metaphorical *transference*. The fact that he does so immediately, namely where the ellipsis points are entered, leaves the impression that the other noun species, "ordinary" or "ornate," do not partake of this function. Yet their taxonomy is so diffuse that one can well see why it discouraged the Classical experts from engaging in a detailed analysis.

The first genus-to-species epiphora is exemplified with "Here *stands* my ship," and the species-to-genus epiphora with "Indeed *ten thousand* noble things Odysseus did" (Fyfe, 1960, pp. 80-1, his italics). In typical spotsignting, the verb "stands" and the number "ten thousand" constitute the Iconized "alien" elements which thus manifest the epiphoric function of substitution. Since the language is Homeric and accordingly literary, Aristotle lands in what I shall call a "hop, skip, and jump" from a vocable in a highly language-bound context. He claims that the predicate "stands" has replaced the more narrow reference of being moored or at anchor, as ships at rest normally appear to be; thus the epiphora from a wider genus to a species. Conversely, a specific number is obviously more narrow than the idea of "many" or equivalent, and so he turns the epiphora around.

What Aristotle does is to recover norms based on *fact* from a linguistic form as though he (like Levin) owned a logical and *paraphrasable* blueprint that could bridge the assumed "anomaly," the *allotrios*, by a logical analogy. Ships are moored, he implies, and a number is a particular in relation to a loose quantative qualifier. Yet these alternatives are not there as Icons and their association has to be induced during constituion as relevant Index. When such an import obtains, it is still not a substitution for a denotative core which only Icons possess; they lay the foundation of every authorial will, no less so Homer's. And being thus willed, they cannot be replaced. Put another way, the moment an Index is Iconized, a "parallel phrase" arises, and thus the paraphrase, yielding another (pure) referent. So either the epiphora evaporates as idiosyncrasy by just pinpointing a relevant Index in any constitution or it is simply untenable by straddling two separate phrases. Clearly, because the use of meaning is not understood, no special metaphor can be posited successfully. Deviance located at the lexicon ironically leads away from the lexicon into logic. Aristotle plays a *hide-and-seek* game with the language in trying to find his suggested alternatives that the extant choices are supposed to cover up.

The lexicon matters in terms of the chosen Icons but not as the direct cause of a singular function, here the epiphora. No expert is needed to *detect* lexical deviance but should be much in demand to penetrate mere appearances. Deviance, of course, remains questionable here anyway, by forcing the critic into sheer interpretation of a language-bound surface. Instead of coming armed with norms in terms of contents, the critic has to assess the context *not* bound to contents and determine the function from there. Non-Aristotelian semantics can immediately identify the Homeric epics as *Dicent*. So the first task of these contents is to form correlates which in concatenation with other such correlates engender mimetic augmentation of a world that words have knit together. Whether a vestige such as the verb "stands" seems deviant or plain, it is one more Dicentic entry, here helping to characterize a schematic "my" speaker and "his" vessel in one more presentational aspect. No one can "tell" from such a fragment what evolves. "Stands" may well be a *reinforcing* aspect to endow the ship with an added "vertical" nuance of "height" that releases illocutionary pride on the part of its owner. A related "hyperbolic" connotation may obtain for the other epiphora and its specifically high number instead of some generic quantity. English already possesses an indented commonplace of scolding errant persons who have been told "ten thousand" times, perhaps, not to do this or that.

I am trying to say that the dynamics of contextualization may leave other analogies far more important for the contents than the logical proxies Aristotle offers like semantic marbles. Also, the fact that one language may contain such commonplaces indicates in itself that the determining powers of these alleged norms lie within each language. Neither does Aristotle's language-bound spotsighting entertain the vital distance of *epochal time*. Since Homer lived in the ninth century B.C., the time span between his and Aristotle's Greek roughly equals that of Elizabethan and modern American English. At the level of the linguistic strata, there may thus be a discrepancy between inception and reception, forcing Aristotle as Recipient to "return" to the signitive convolutions that prevailed at the time of inception. Perhaps "stands" for moored ships was then the current indented Icon, thus mitigating the *allotrios*, with the epiphora fast evaporating. It is this later Recipient, Aristotle, who becomes a "stranger" to the text when forcing reception upon an earlier inception. Such are the hazards of his lexical, content-sensitive approach; they spell swift demise for a "metaphor," whereas my structural kind, going exclusively by function, cannot "die."

From a lexical, rhetorical perspective, there may be evidence that Aristotle's epiphoras reinforce *metonymic* and/or *synecdochal* relations, as some critics have claimed (Kurz and Pelster, 1976, p. 16; Grube, 1958, p. 44). Species are of course by nature "parts" of a "whole," the genus. This issue returns with the final epiphora, which is that of *analogy* involving the *proportional metaphor*. If the first two epiphoras concentrated on a verb and adjective, the proportional kind below evolves through nouns, in their proxy-tenet juggling. Aristotle (Fyfe, 1960, Loeb ed., pp. 80-81) describes and then illustrates this metaphor:

> Metaphor by analogy means this: when B is to A as D is to C, then, *instead of* B the poet will say D and B *instead of* D. . . . For instance, a cup is to Dionysus what a shield is to Ares; so he will *call* the cup "Dionysus's shield" and the shield "Ares' (sic) cup."

This particular translator (Fyfe) supplied letters for the Greek numbers "second" and "fourth," which others (Grube, 1958, p. 45) chose. My own contribution is the italics, added to project the phrase "instead of" as typical *proxy-tenet* barter and additionally the verbs "is"/"say" and "is"/"call" as a very concrete instance of the *ontological category-mistake*. What language "says" or "calls" and what "is" or exists in empirical reality are two different "things." That is the difference between ontic heteronomy and ontic autonomy, realms which my circles first separated, permitting only an overlap through adequation, when language becomes functionally "literal." Aristotle naively posits a neat correspondence between analogies that *exist* in the *world* and four extant *words* or terms that *express* them as perfect stand-ins, to the point of letting words then stand proxy for one another by falling into slots that norms have conveniently vacated. Not even adequated usage permits such a direct relation; the pure and objective referents remain distinct when forming the overlap between the two circles marking ontic heteronomy as language and ontic autonomy (real or ideal) as an extralinguistic alternative.

So much for Aristotle's theoretical statement. His *example* renders *two gods*, the mythological deities of "wine" and "war," characterized by their names, Dionysus and Ares, as well as their respective objects, a "cup" and "shield." True, these gods are no more "real" empirically than satyrs or unicorns. Yet my study identified such entities, or "beings," as ontologically distinct from words: they bear an autonomous-real base and autonomous-ideal significance when perceived and recognized on canvases, tapestries, and related artifacts as distinctive figures with a mythological import. Since recognition in the visual arts does not hold speakers to words in a language, ontic heteronomy is not involved in identifying these bacchanalian and military deities.

Aristotle's proportional metaphor thus is not effective either at the level of semantic functioning. Where my ellipsis points occur in the citation, one of Aristotle's "least lucid sentences" appears (Fyfe, 1960, p. 80), and such a stylistic problem may well be a further indicator of difficulties facing this metaphor. Fortunately, the numbers or letters are succinct enough in their use to make evident the error of plying such constants. My theory permits number only for such universal constants as the three trichotomies in their triadic relation, or for the double-intentionality involving one act of meaning and a series of selected meanings that provide the explicit base and implicit relevance for that act. To be sure, speakers ordain "number" in the quantity of the Icons chosen for an entire unit(y). For example, a phrase ending with the oxymoron "pretty ugly" would evolve as antonym if the final Icon were missing. Then "pretty" would be an adjective rendering beauty instead of an adverbial intensifier spelling "number" in the accentuation of ugliness, as it is here.

Number couched in formulas nevertheless continues to preoccupy critics of metaphor. In Brooke-Rose's *A Grammar of Metaphor* (1958, pp. 206-208), number erupts in a hot controversy with an example from a petrified nautical figure. Instead of the ship that stands, it is the ship that ploughs the waves. Brooke-Rose cites Kenner, who in turn cites Aristotle as he insists the metaphor is made up of *four* instead of *two* "things"--so related that "A is to B as C is to D." Next enters Donald Davie; not content with Kenner's numbers, he insists on *six* coordinating factors. Arguing that the ship is not called a plough as such, Kenner claims that similarity revolves around a dissimilar action, since "the ship does to the waves what a plough does to the ground . . . ." Six items are then enumerated: plough, ship, ground, waves, and the "action of ploughing" versus the "action of sailing" (ibid.). Nowottny (1965) also seizes on this frozen rhetorical figure. Splitting meaning from the meant and thus Icon from its Index (M-0), Nowottny separates "ship" and "plough" as a "literal" from a "figurative" meaning, since the foregrounded ploughing of land yields to the backgrounded thrashing through water. Nowottny's literalizing parallels what I termed a "metalinguistic gesture." None of these content-oriented formulas affect I-M-0 generation of meaning under the conditions of the structures elucidated.

In further description, Aristotle's two gods of wine and war are *personalized* by their *proper names*, Dionysus and Ares, and *personified* by their respective objects, the cup and shield. Names have to be called or spelled out in words, even the ones that give gods or persons an identity, and anything cast in linguistic Qualisigns used by one language ties in with the oppositional value system of that language in the shared indentations of signitive convolutions. Although the objects can be displayed on canvas or taspestry, the same rule obtains for them as words. In yet another recourse to rhetorical devices, the specific objects that the gods possess identify their possessor in a type of *metonymic-synecdochal* relation, if somewhat differently applied when compared to the genus and species epiphoras. This connection, furthermore, may resemble the rhetorical standby of "antonomasy": cup and shield circuitously "name" their owners as the gods of wine and war, perhaps more significantly so than do their proper names, "Dionysus" and "Ares." A conspicuous phenomenon to be added is the *genitive link*, given in the prepositioned order of "Dionysus's shield" and "Ares' (sic) cup," while another translation (Bywater, 1966, p. 57) opts for the postpositioned as well as pleonastic "shield of Dionysus' " and "cup of Ares'." The general formula befitting the trinary genitive linkage is "A=B of C," according to Brooke-Rose (1958, pp. 146 ff.).

So here I have indulged in some content segmentation of my own. This approach was evident also in my analyses. But when I called Celan's "pillar of disdain" a genitive link, I was aware of the limits imposed on description and thus continued to treat this vestige as one more Rhemic, intextual composite which, when fully compounded, yielded the Index "God"--if hardly Aristotle's polytheistic deities. Yet where do Aristotle's epiphoras pinpoint structural differences? As for the issue of naming mythological figures, a monograph could be devoted to their various allegorizations of traits and dispositions.

Nor do any of the problems abate with what my synopsis classed as the *addenda* of the Poetics. The first of these finds Aristotle (Fyfe, 1960, pp. 80-81) *insisting* that the inherent proportionality between the two gods and their characteristic objects permits speakers to render metaphorical *negation*, such as calling Ares's shield the "wineless cup." Negation is the most individual and in that sense "subjective" aspect of a language, giving reign to human intervention by referring to what is "not" present. But the rules stay identical; words cannot dictate directly the presence or absence of things. That is stretching their power to areas where they do not belong. Where their power resides is in that "positive" form discussed with the first, hyletic trichotomy--beyond "aught" else, to loosely reiterate Peirce who was cited at the time. Linguistic Legisigns are as "positive" as they are "true"; even when they negate in content they lend their content to an authorial will, since they become the selected vehicles for actualizing speech. Beyond that task, they may reflect negatively an objective referent when brought into juxtaposition with a reality-nexus that turns out to be false. But without such elaborations Aristotle's metaphor of negation remains invalid, indeed "impotent" *qua* linguistic functioning.

Aristotle's next example presents a "negative" phenomenon of another kind, and that is the *homonymic* or *catachretic filler* (Gerber, 1873, II, pp. 81 ff.). Being nonstylistic, it is called also the *natural* or *necessary* metaphor. Nowadays such a metaphor is pitted as "radical" against a "poetical" kind because it is not "deliberately invented" (Max Müller, in Barfield, 1928, pp. 54-59). In current parlance, the radical kind is the "dead metaphor," where "death" of this nature remains a *diachronic* indicator. Since new and "deliberate" teleological fusion occurs from selected, synchronic states, it bars such demise. To non-Aristotelian semantics, no special metaphor is thus involved but only meaning in amplification; to neo-Aristotelians, however, augmenting vocables constitutes a negative instance of compensating for *semasiological paucity*. Such former examples as the personality and corporal metaphors mirror this phenomenon, from the "wooden" personality to the limb of that substance which took over from the human extremity in order to name the "(table) leg." If the analogy in the anomalous naming becomes as opaque as it did in the earlier "pen" serving the writing tool and enclosure, metaphor resembles the homonym--literally the "one" (homo-) "name" (-nymy) standing proxy for two different meanings.

My study, of course, has eschewed all "nymy" tenets for the level of structure. But Aristotle (ibid., Fyfe, 1960, pp. 80-83) discusses his catachretic filler in a total confusion of diachronic and synchronic planes. Clearly, he should be dealing with the latter, since he refers to a "phrase"--in another translation (Bywater,1966, p. 58) even a poetic expression. Yet he insists that the speaker in question has simply filled in meanings where there is as yet "no word for some of the terms of the analogy. . . . " "No word" pinpoints semantic paucity which in evolutionary stages extends Icons to other indentations, although when these are as far apart as in the "pen" example, each Icon keeps its separate Index and/or indentation well at bay, despite the mnemonic Sinsign tie which in punning forces identity into consciousness. In his example, Aristotle nevertheless claims that because there is similarity between the *actions* of sowing seeds and the sun's scattering of its "fire" or rays, the verb "sow" may fill in for its predicate object, "the god-created fire," as in "sowing the god-created fire." Generation of speech, however, is never a "filling in" of detectible identities but a "forming" of new analogies, engendered only when "action" involves an act of meaning (I) choosing its explicit and implicit meanings (M-0), which then become fused to their act--as mine have here.

Again, one detects the language-bound surface of Aristotle's example and thus the diachronic past which leaves his missing "analogies" hardly transparent to modern readers, just because their provenance is not things but signitive values current for the linguistic inventory of Aristotle's Greek. No wonder some of the Classical scholars doubt the authenticity of this exposition! With one leap Aristtotle jumps from set similarities of activities perceived in the empirical world into a new combination of words, possibly even of a poetic nature as indicated. Yet another "beautiful" example of ontological type-trespassing! Whether or not seeding and the sun's emission of rays are alike is not at issue and thus plays no direct part in semantic "issuance," as speech-act theoreticians would say.

From a religious perspective, the very content of "seeds" and the reference to "god-" evoked for me the famous parable of the Sower in Matthew 13:24-31 (*Interlinear Greek-English New Testament*, 1966, p. 55). In this parable, the scattering of seeds and their germination is compared to Christ's spreading the message of the Kingdom of Heaven. The parable from a rhetorical aspect is close to metaphor; its etymological root, the "paraboley," embodies a didactic device whose abstract gist is made concrete through a "parallel alignment" between words. Critics who analyze the parable (Gerber, 1873, II, pp. 111-4) use proxy-tenet jargon of a "res propria" forced into alignment with the "res aliena."

The last item of the "addendum" from the *Poetics* that is to be cited is the *Similarity* Statement. That is indeed all *it is*, a "statement" about "similarity," and thus a subject that has been exploded already for its narrow representational handling by Aristotle and followers. From the standpoint of its popularity, this Statement has enjoyed immense attention throughout the centuries, no less so today. That reverence in itself remains suspect, since, no matter how nicely phrased, the Similarity Statement amounts to little more than a bland generalization. It occurs almost at the end of Chapter 22 in the *Poetics*, a chapter (1458a, Fyfe, 1960, pp. 84-85) which treats the "merit of diction" as a need to balance what is "clear" with what is "not commonplace." To paraphrase Aristotle, too much metaphor leads to the "riddle"--which in foregrounded Greek becomes an "enigma"--while rare words tend toward jargon. After Aristotle proceeds to detail the species of "nouns" cited prior to the Preliminary Statement of his exposition, he projects metaphor positively by drawing on the Similarity Statement.

Metaphor, begins the Similarity Statement, cannot be learned but rather involves an "eye for resemblances" (1459a, Fyfe, 1960, pp. 88-91). A second translation (Bywater, 1966, p. 62) offers an "intuitive perception of the similarity in dissimilars," and a third (Grube, 1958, p. 49), an "inborn talent" in the "ability to observe similarities in things." All the translated, Iconized inferences, however, cannot transform the Similarity Statement from a loose observation on synthesizing faculties into a cogent definition of metpahorical function. Anyone even vaguely familiar with Greek may discover that in the *Rhetoric* Aristotle uses exactly the same verb, "theorein" (in my transliteration), while he discusses "philosophy" and notes that "sagacity" enables the generally "adept" to "perceive resemblances even in things that are far apart" (1412a, Freese, 1959, Loeb ed., pp. 406-407; Cooper, 1932, p. 207.). What the Similarity Statement seems to have accomplished unwittingly is a justification for the present "syncretism," as I term the pluralism of fields, which thrusts metaphor into every area of investigation before having any clearcut idea as to what it is doing in one of these, perhaps the most basic one, language.

Preoccupation with similarity also concerns the main topic of the *Rhetoric* I intend to take up, and that is Aristotle's dubious attempt to differentiate the presentation of analogy by a *metaphor* or *simile*. Derived from Greek "eikon," the simile indeed "Iconizes" or "pictures" the comparison it bears. The irrational and simplistic assumption of Aristotle and his followers is that a metaphor and simile, with their respective *implicit* and *explicit* comparisons, are somehow attached to one another like linguistic Siamese twins. In order to explore this relation before detailing the simile itself it is necessary to mention another metaphor Aristotle presents in the *Rhetoric* and then make some connections between all the metaphoric versions in order to see where the simile fits in. The *Rhetoric* (1413a, Freese, 1959, Loeb ed., pp. 414-415) finds Aristotle alluding also to a *simple* metaphor (Greek "aplous"), whose proxy-tenet substituion of bridging anomaly by analogy has been radicalized to the point of a total usurpation on the part of the alien replacing term. Through the agency of this metaphor, contends Aristotle, speakers may call Ares's shield just a "cup" (though the translator of the *Rhetoric* uses "goblet" for the same "fialey" of the *Poetics*). Modern critics such as Brooke-Rose (1958, pp. 9, 26-45, 46-67) have also adopted this tenet verbatim as "Simple Replacement." Recipients become "linguistic detectives" instead of decoders in a true hide-and-seek guessing game.

If I play the devil's advocate, the following numeric schemas arise: (1) a simple or *single* metaphor with an inherent comparison caught in one substituted term; (2) a *regular, dual* metaphor with two explicit constituents, one of which is replacing; (3) a *tetradic* or *proportional* metaphor aligning *four* terms through two implicit analogies, in the manner explicated by Aristotle. Now, numerically the *simile* belongs between the regular and proportional metaphor: the explicit comparison it harbors to "liken" entities to one another may involve two terms or possibly three, when a third combining factor, generally known as the *tertium comparationis*, is included. Unable to emulate experts on metaphorical formulas, I nevertheless make some heuristic attempt of guiding my readers through a neo-Aristotelian labyrinth of technicalities. In terms of constants, then, a simple metaphor just juxtaposes B on A; a regular metaphor goes by "A (is) B," and the proportional type by A/B/C/D, where B is to A what D is to C, as Aristotle had it, thus permitting an exchange between B and D. The triadic simile instead subsists on A/B/C for its relational base, as in "A is like C," or when the *tertium comparationis* becomes added, "A is (has) B like C"--formulas mostly inferred from Aristotle's presentation in the *Rhetoric* (1406b, 1411a, 1411b, 1413a, Freese, 1959, Loeb ed., pp. 366-371, 398-399, 404-405, 414-415).

However, Aristotle accompanies this part of his analysis with a marked *vacillation*. First, he repeatedly praises the proportional metaphor, not infrequently by reiterating the example *of the two* gods and their characterizing objects. From such a positive appraisal of metaphoric extension one might adduce a similar fondness for the simile, but that is not conclusively the case. One minute he declares that differences between metaphor and simile are but "slight" (mikron), since good metaphors also yield good similes; the next he contends that similes are "less pleasant" due to the extension of the Iconized analogy, replete with comparative segments; in still other instances he considers similes exchangeable with metaphors because they *are* "metaphors without details" (1406b, 1410b, 1413a, Freese, pp. 366-373, 396-397, 414-415). Discussions on use and abuse of similes with their connecting particles surround these comments (pp. 371, 373) and later (p. 399) end in criticism of the added length they induce.

Aristotle's ambivalence shows that he is not sure of what he is labeling, which comes as no surprise. In the first place, length or brevity in any suggested numeric determination of antecedent slots should not be an issue in linguistic semantics, least of all through the addition of a couple of little operative signs, in English "like"/"so"/"as" and in Greek "hos." In Ingarden's syntactic hierarchy, they would fall far behind eidetic nouns and verbs; in a non-Aristotelian Rhemic structure, the function equalizes them, converting them into structural "nouns." Whatever the case, the lexicon as such does not suffice--and yet it should matter precisely where it is neglected by Aristotle and followers: the Icons that compose one constitutional unit(y) have nothing to do with constitutents from other such unities. So there is no "comparison" possible between metaphor and the comparison, the simile. They would be two differently Iconized expressions; whether or not the comparative segments are present or absent is only an issue for the authorial will that selected whatever comprises a teleological unit(y), purposively grounded in "closure"--again, just as my sentences are here.

These reservations notwithstanding, even the Aristotelian vacillation seems to have been appropriated by some modern critics while discussing the simile. Today Wheelwright (1962, p. 71) still maintains that although a "metaphoric comparison" is better without the explicit "like," a negative result does not always follow in use of a simile, since grammatical form should not supersede the "quality of semantic transformation." Any "transformation," however, which is of substance should not revolve around the presence or absence of a couple of comparative segments in the first place, unless one merely wanted to *describe* overt *stylistic* differences between "metaphor" and "simile." Surprisingly, another vacillator who misses the substance of function on that score is the otherwise discerning poet-critic Benn (1965, p. 504); first he condemns similes for causing a fissure (Bruch) in poetic vision and then he concedes that great poets (like Rilke) also fashion penetrating imagery with the use of similes.

Now to Aristotle's own famous *example*, which is supposed to distinguish metaphor from simile. His illustration might be called somewhat facetiously a "human lionization" or a "leonine human," because it involves not merely an animation of things but an *animalization* of a man. The lion and the warrior Achilles, states Aristotle (1406b, Freese, 1959, pp. 366-367), have courage in common. Therefore one may say of Achilles, "he rushed on *like* a lion" (my ialics) in an open comparison as simile, or "a lion, he rushed on" in the rendering of metaphor. Here, the *tertium comparationis*, the idea of courage, is not made explicit in the simile either, but rather, as a logical pivot, it operates between two different expressions as though it motivated each version. Since I have already offered my non-Aristotelian correctives of where the focus should go, there is little more to add. The two separately Iconized expressions, no matter what their formula, stay telologically independent of one another. To be sure, from a purely rhetorical standpoint, this curious lionization of Achilles may equal *antonomasy*. The lion then becomes an epithet for naming the Greek warrior much as the names and/or particular objects of the two gods supplied characteristics close to types of epithets that personalized these deities, for which reason antonomasy was also mentioned during their discussion. Quintilian (Watson, trans., 1876, p. 131), the exponent of rhetorical taxonomy, actually seizes on his own Achilles version for antonomasy, though the warrior is clad in the epithet of "the Pelides," a naming based on his ancestry in reference to his father, Peleus. By coincidence, a nineteenth-century drama entitled *Penthesilea* (1808) by H. v. Kleist (1964, pp. 324, 327, 332, passim) exhibits Quintilian's antonomasy by rendering Achilles repeatedly as "der Pelide."

Playing the devil's advocate one more time for Aristotle's versions, I class: (1) metaphor as predicate noun, yielding "Achilles is a lion," hence "A *is* C" on the basis of the same link, courage, B; (2) simile with a *tertium comparationis* and comparative segment, as in "Achilles has *courage* (is courageous as or) *like* a lion," so that "A is/has B like C" consists of an Iconic center portion likening Achilles (A) explicitly to his leonine counterpart (C) via his braveness (B). Perhaps, too, Achilles could be supplied with a more "offensive" weapon than Ares'"defensive" shield and wrestle with the lethal claw of a lion. I could then conjure up a tetradic A,B,C,D link for a neat proportional metaphor of my own making:

A spear (B) is to Achilles (A) what a claw (D) is to the lion (C); thus one may call the spear "Achilles's claw" and the claw "the lion's spear."

A type of pseudo-author paralleling my former role of translator, I offer above in contextless conjectures what "may" be said through certain contents--which actually could be an inexhaustible enterprise. Supposing some person named Achilles were dressed as a lion in a play or at a masquerade ball, for instance. The context with all its situational and/or written contacts may then literalize the expression anyway, relativizing metaphor and/or simile since the person named is "really" a "lion." Any time "Achilles" appears in this leonine Iconic "outfit" I may skim the Icon in question and indicate in a metalinguistic gesture that Achilles is "literally" a lion; I may point to the Index and state that Achilles is "not meant" to be a real lion and is thus "metaphorically" this creature. Nor is there anything to prevent a circus trainer from dressing up his leonine charge in the garb (the Shakespearean "weeds"?) of Achilles. At this point, then, I offer the antonomasy in reverse: instead of the leonine human, there is the humanized lion, the fiercest beast of the circus its trainer has named "Achilles"! These possibilities wreak havoc with the simplistic determinants neo-Aristotelians apply to literal or figurative meaning, with the latter divided further into metaphor or simile.

Moreover, the connotation of movement with Aristotle's leonine Achilles who "rushes on" also touches on a stylistic trait Aristotle never ceased to admire. It is *liveliness* in conjunction with *animation*, which often still comes across in his favorite device, because to Aristotle this quality readily lends itself to the proportional metaphor. The Greek terms are "astea," which signifies "liveliness" or "smartness," and "pro ommaton," denoting "vividness" and, more literally, a "setting before the eyes" (*Rhetoric*, 1410b, 1411a, 1411b, 1412a, 1413a, pp. 396-399, 402-405, 408-409, 414-415). Here Aristotle displays his perceptive insight into the poetic imagery of Homer, much as he may have failed literary language in a theoretical analysis of its essence. He refers to the "energeia," or in a more Latinized (translated) form, to the "actuality" that Homer induced as he breathed life into inert "apsycha" by thus converting them into lively "empsycha" endowed with action and animation (ibid., 1412a, 1412b, pp. 404-407, 414-415). Citing mainly from the *Odyssey*, Aristotle almost revels in the Homeric prowess of letting stones "roll," arrows "fly," and points of spears "speed eagerly" to their target as they pierce someone's breast.

This imposing detail concludes the analysis of Aristotle and yet returns somewhat modified with the *Latin* rhetoricians, Cicero and Quintilian. Their basic premise of "oratory," the Latinized form of "rhetoric," is sufficiently similar to merit treating their works together: Cicero's *De Oratore* (II, Book III, Loeb. ed., 1960) and Quintilian's *Institutes of Oratory* (Watson, 1876), in a translation from the Latin *Institutio Oratoria* (Butler, Loeb ed., 1959).

Greek "metaphor," according to Quintilian (Butler, 1959, pp. 302-303), becomes in Latin the *translatio* but in essence stays true to the Aristotelian principle. Moreover, what both these Latin rhetoricians project clearly before detailing metaphor is *meaning as the verbum proprium*, leaving metaphor tacitly as the "improper" alternative. In foregrounded Latin, Cicero's Book III (xxxviii, pp. 118-119, 122-123) makes explicit the "alien" word, and thereby provides the mnemonic link with the Aristotelian *allotrios* of the latter's Preliminary Statement. Cicero certainly views semantic reference as a type of object-language; stand-ins *for* . . . must point *at* things in the world in a representational parallelism that came with a "definite designation for things." These "things" Cicero actually expresses with the Latin word "res" rather than a neuter ending, as can be done. So there is no misunderstanding on that score. Cicero's use of "definite" in this context evokes Kripke's "rigid designators." Any critic who espouses such a view of a set representational correspondence between worlds and words will not find a solution to linguistic meaning or metaphor. "Definite" and "positive" is only what language in a language has validated and then indented for use among interlocutory partners of one language. Instead, Cicero comes armed with norms while ignoring the normalization prowess of language.

This criticsm applies also to Quintilian. His Book VIII, whose last part (vi) details metaphor, first (ii) has quite a bit to say about basic semantic "propriety" (Butler, 1959, Loeb ed., pp. 196-202). A proper term, he says, must involve a full understanding of meaning; when there are "a number of things"--and here the reference to things is left implicit in the substantive of plurality--the proper term remains the "original" one. For instance, in my "leg" example, the human extremity becomes then the "proper" term and the furniture support the "improper" counterpart. That idea again undermines language and confuses diachronic changes with synchronic staples. Not the chronology of coinage, but only the effective indentation of the content as linguistic concept takes priority in synchronic states.

Although these two rhetoricians thus at least attempted to define "proper" or literal meaning before detailing metaphor, their premise of signitive "propriety" for the obverse factor, meaning, leads them straight into the erroneous proxy-barter for the reverse factor, metaphor, which arises wherever arepresentational lexical pockets are detectible. The term--or more closely the epithet used as metaphor--for the functioning of metaphor is a "borrowing." Cicero (ibid., pp. 122-125) employs the word "aliunde," which signifies literally "from some other direction," and Quintilian (ibid., pp. 302-303) "mutari," which denotes explicitly "to borrow." Quintilian believes that metaphorical borrowing aids semasiological "copiousness" in the "interchange of words" for building vocabulary. Still today, by none other than the eminent I. A. Richards (1936, p. 94), metaphor is expected to engage in a "borrowing" that involves an "intercourse of thoughts" and a "transaction between contexts" without being necessarily a "verbal" matter. Of even more recent vintage is Judith Schlanger's essay (1970) which has metaphor "borrow" meaning as it crosses over "zones" or "sectors of reality." Yet the only "crossers" of bounds here are the critics: thoughts, sectors, or whatever, must be indigenous to language and the only "endower" of meaning is the act of meaning as it "lends" (Ingarden's "Verleihen") relevance to its chosen meanings, irrespective of their "alien" or "improper" surface.

Cicero (pp. 120-123) and Quintilian (pp. 302-303) both differentiate a "necessary" or "natural" metaphor from a stylistic kind. Based, according to Cicero, on the "pressure of poverty and deficiency," this type of metaphor may still be pleasing to use. Quintilian illustrates this diachronic phenomenon with a "hard" human disposition and thus the kind of personality metaphor my study had occasion to invoke. Although I characterized such a "dead" metaphor as "catachretic," Quintilian (Book VII, ii and vi, pp. 198-199, 320-321) regards "catachresis" more pejoratively as a downright "abusio." Speaker complacency then affronts his idea of a fitting reference by selecting the "nearest" rather than the best term for the meaning which is wanting, a normative stance that is to be anticipated of the representational "propriety" Quintilian espouses.

These two Latin rhetoricians also delve into metaphorical "audaciousness," a word obtained when foregrounded from the Latin. The impact governing their notion of boldness or daring upon modern neo-Aristotelians will turn out to be considerable. Cicero (III, xxxviii-xxxix, pp. 120-125) posits a "bolder" stylistic metaphor that is not based on paucity because its use is deliberate and is planned to please. Real metaphorical daring, claims Cicero (p. 125), lies in the "leap", Latin *transilire*, hence in the ability "to jump over things that are obvious and choose other things that are far-fetched." Of course, what is "far" or "near" remains a moot point when one supports the type of unnatural object-language these ancient fathers of metaphor upheld. Cicero's "transilire" was mentioned when I first analyzed linguistic form and content through the natural "leaps of language," caused by an act of meaning in its use of meanings. Such leaps thrust a "fool" together with a "cuckoo" in one language and with a "donkey" in another; they artfully, if not deliberately, left "god" the other side of "dog," and upheld a "red herring" only to toss it together with a "phony issue."

Cicero's bold jump instead encourages dogmatic *dissimilarity* cults, actually by taking for granted what belongs together in meaning as similarity and is then torn asunder by metaphor as dissimilarity. That made him valuable to modern experimentalist trends. To non-Aristotelian semantics, both similarity and disparity when reified become rubrics for dogmatisms which literally serve no purpose in a purposive domain such as language. Tacitly, such cults embody *linguistic skepticism* by not granting language its full due as a combinatory force.

In the case of Quintilian (VIII, vi, Butler, 1959, pp. 300-303), metaphor is a species--though not of the noun, as it was with Aristotle, but--of the trope, actually one of its most "beautiful" variations. Etymologically, the trope is derived from Greek "trepo," meaning "to turn." One translation (Watson, 1876, p. 124) has Quintilian define a trope as "the conversion of a word or a phrase"; another (Butler, Loeb ed., 1959, pp. 300-301) cites its power of "artistic alteration." In any case, the trope as genus parallels its species, metaphor, by harboring the duality of a "proper" and an "alien" meaning. Aristotle's *allotrios* is made to "turn" instead of effecting a juxtaposition, and even that nonexistent function miraculously will surface today as a metaphorical "twist."

For Quintilian, boldness enters with his favorite metaphor. This tropical species, the *translatio*, is based on *four* shifts that revolve around *animation* (Watson, p. 126; Butler, pp. 304-305). Of these--animate-to-animate, inanimate-to-animate, animate-to-inanimate and inanimate-to-animate--it is the fourth shift which gives rise to a "bold and daring figure," capable of generating "energy and feeling" along with a touch of "extraordinary sublimity" (Watson, pp. 126-127). Again, as with Cicero, the Latin carries explicitly "audaciousness" for this metaphorical boldness (Butler, pp. 306-307). Yet the particular reference to energy harks back to Greek "energeia" or "actuality," which Aristotle was shown to identify with the imagery of Homer. Quintilian also demonstrates with examples how lifeless objects assume life and go into "action" through the fourth shift.

In a methodological parallel, while Aristotle trades on Homer, Quintilian looks to Vergil, also to Livy, Cato--and the very predecessor discussed here, Cicero--in order to illustrate his metaphorical shifts. Some of the language-bound examples are again too abstruse to aid the reader in understanding a specific metaphorical function. Like Aristotle, Quintilian merely takes refuge in the literary examples; odd as they seem, they still leave behind the question of their literal or literary status. And animation, of course, was revealed in this study as something so basic that to align it to any special semantic phenomenon has only a disquieting effect. The Latin *transilire* and *translatio* as designation of metaphor thus leave a lot to be desired.

Both these Latin rhetoricians became no less famous for their *metaphor-as-shrunken-simile* theory. Cicero (III, xxxix, pp. 122-123) views metaphor as "a short form of simile, contracted into one word." Quintilian (Watson, p. 127) follows suit by saying that "On the whole, metaphor is a short comparison," and, in another translation, that it constitutes "a shorter form of 'simile'" (Butler, pp. 304-305). The original preserves enough cognates to be construable from the Latin "metaphora brevior est similitudo." Even Aristotle's example has stayed partially intact with Quintilian: the "lion" is still there but "Achilles" becomes generically a "man"; as simile he is "like a lion" and as metaphor he "is a lion" (Watson, p.126; Butler, pp. 304-305). All the objections raised in connection with Aristotle, then, in the disregard for structure in full contextualization, apply here too. But the need to identify metaphor simplistically as a contracted counterpart of the simile has never abated (Lieb, 1964, Shibles, 1971). As late as 1963 a relatively discerning critic such as Landmann (pp. 119-120) cites Quintilian on the "brevior similitudo," and then goes on with great gusto, as though he had made the discovery of the century, to state: "Der Vergleich kontrastiert, die Metapher integriert." Since everything here is a cognate except for "Vergleich" denoting the "comparison" or "simile," there is little difficulty in understanding what is a stylistically neat but otherwise vacuous observation.

The neo-Aristotelian fetish of animation never seems to have died down either, replete with the leonine example. Demetrius's *On Style* in the first century B.C. had metaphor animate the inanimate; the *Opera* of Hermogenes and *Ars Grammatica* of Donatus of the second and fourth centuries A.D. continued in the same vein by focusing on animation. Meier's "Observation" (Betrachtung) on metaphor in all its linguistic idiosyncrasies (1963, pp. 150-152) also takes the Aristotelian "lion" through its paces with help from Quintilian and modern Teutonic followers.

Contemporary Anglo-Saxon criticism is not to be outdone either in joining the ranks; Mackey, Campbell, Stewart, and Paul enter into rather needless controversies over metaphor's presumed untranslatable, unparaphrasable, and irreversible qualities—all traits any meaning should harbor when properly understood. Revolving around these supposed idiosyncrasies is not infrequently the "lion." In Mackey's essay (1965, pp. 279, 282) only the human has changed, since Achilles is taken over by the fabled British warrior, Richard Lion-Heart, who is said to enter the "class" of "brave ones" when juggled in lexical content with this beast. Mackey (p. 275) stays in awe of metaphor for its capacity to remain "meaningful" despite its "alogical structure" and "recalcitrance to logic." Then he should be impressed equally with his basic linguistic competence! Campbell's essay (1969, p. 153) treats problems of reversibility in "this man is a lion"/"that lion is a man." My former example of the circus lion named Achilles certainly permits such a reversed contextualization under specific conditions.

In any case, a true critic of language grasps that every issuance in the telological fusion with a pure referent abides by an irreversible base; no one here may "reverse" the order of my Icons (M) without changing their import (0) and thus my authorial intent (I). These reservations apply also to Stewart (1971, pp. 115, 118, 120). Coming so quickly after the other two above, his article still sees fit to seize once more on the hapless "lion" to prove yet another attenuated, indeed, "emasculated" metaphor by content taxonomy. Then, just one year later, Paul (1972, pp. 145-146) asserts confidently that metaphor is unique because it cannot be "literally paraphrased" or translated without "loss of cognitive content." Paul leans heavily here on Black, who is always prone to take recourse in unidentified "insights" and/or "cognitions" while discussing metaphor. Such broad terms remain loose generalizations if not more closely specified, preferably by beginning with meaning. Otherwise they are the lay person's game, and I see one more occasion to invoke the Calder physicist who, in the capacity of a scientist, must part with observations of the lay perceiver.

In a further Teutonic development of the abused lion, I can at least supply a diverting example, though hardly with the result of saving the neo-Aristotelian metaphor. If lexical deviance is not to be reified in a semantic juggling of the wrong categories, then there is still the resort to "spheric blending" (Mooij, 1976, pp. 35, 73-80; Nieraad, 1977, pp. 112-124). The 1914 study on the "Psychology" and "Statistics" of metaphors by Stählin treated this issue, which was then perpetuated in the *Sprachtheorie* or "Linguistic Theory" of 1934 by Bühler. Here, metaphor is believed to blend, mix, and neutralize spheres. The only "sphere," however, that concerns a critic of language is one which is constituted by acts of meaning, whether or not couched in the terminology I applied. With their concrete example, enter the "lion" once more, if this time in the compound of the "Salonlöwe." Unlike the "saloon," German "Salon" signifies a civilized, possibly even elegant social setting.

What this "social" lion conveys as compounded and indented Legisign is none other than the English "ladies' man" (*New Cassell's*, n. d., p. 389), whose irreversible and untranslatable Sinsign surface seems to spell out a curious linguistic "hermaphrodite": a "man" consisting of "ladies"? No, just a "person" tied in the English oppositional system to the "lady killer" who is no "feminine murderer" and to the "skirt chaser" who is not "in" but "after" the "skirt" that serves as a nice sartorial metonym for the entire female population. Indeed, such is the "insight" and "cognition" on which linguistic meaning relies, and not just some dubious "metaphor"; such is the capacity of language at combining the seemingly inimical or perverse, providing only as evidence its indigenous activity and coercive validating prowess by overriding all apparent oddities in the process of normalization. Whether the "skirt" attributive will ever be overtaken by "trouser(s)" in the age of the so-called sexual revolution remains a moot question, much as there may be "*gentlemen killers" one day, in skirts or trousers. Not every fact becomes transparent in a linguistic form, but every extant form encapsulating an Icon with its Index must be known to be wielded. Most likely the sexist attributive in "ladies' man" will shortly become "improper" and as such starred (*) "non-sense." Yet even then the Icon continues as "epochal" vestige, which, in later years of reception, should not be adjudged "alien" metaphor if a commonplace at time of inception.

As for that German "salon lion," when implicitly "animalized" in English--it leaps to a "wolf" as closest Index! Species are no more at issue than spheres; leonine or canine will do as long as validation reigns, "alogical" as one choice may be over the other. What a "decadent" end for the lion that started in the exalted figure of the Greek warrior Achilles! That is about as far as Aristotle's and Quintilian's leonine example got as supposed evidence of metaphor and/or simile. I reached the point of "cross-breeding" the lion with the lecherous English "wolf," an image that recurs later with the famous Blackian "wolf-man," as I call "him," if not quite in the same context. Moreover, my "skirt" example above, given as singular noun for the collective female sex, has a certain relevance for other species of tropes related to metaphor that Quintilian analyzes, namely the "synecdoche" and "metonym" (Watson, 1876, pp. 128-130; Butler, 1959, pp. 310-317). Yet even two translated versions for his loose definitions do not lift the ambiguity entirely from his wording, in the suggestion that synecdoche and metonym carry out what metaphor does to a greater degree or with added "force." Quintilian then describes how the synecdoche may be recognized by making known plurality through the singular, the whole through its parts, and very Aristotelian is his admiration for this trope in its vivid effect of setting before the eyes. In a type of species-to-genus epiphora, Quintilian exemplifies this trope with a roof that constitutes part of a house, for instance.

On the metonym, Quintilian quotes Cicero who considered it coterminous with Greek "hypallagey" (in my transliteration). This is where Quintilian contends that a metonym indicates the "thing possessed by the possessor," a link on which I had traded in the case of Aristotle's gods of wine and war together with their identifying objects. Anyway, I have been using these tropes interchangeably because Quintilian himself says that synecdoche and metonym are "not very different" (Watson, p. 129). They certainly amount to nothing but loosely related content taxonomy, for which reason no doubt the tradition as a whole has been pretty liberal in their exchange.

One more trope to be mentioned which was also briefly invoked with the naming of Aristotle's gods is *allegory*. This rhetorical standby is yet another tenacious concept that stretches from the ancient Aesopian fables to Medieval morality plays, only to become synonymous with the symbol in nineteenth-century Romanticism (Sørensen 1963, pp. 119-130), and at other times with an extended metaphor. Quintilian (Watson, pp. 135-137; Butler, pp. 326-331) treats allegory as yet another species of the trope, Latin "inversio." Allegory touches on metaphor through its very etymology which suggests an alignment, and Quintilian supplies the parallel spheres with the petrified analogy comprising the nautical *ship* and political *state*. To him, allegory stays "pure" if the spheres of ship and state persist in their parallelism; it becomes "mixed" when the language refers in part only to one or the other context. Yet in effect, allegory as "inversion" (from the above foregrounded Latin) remains a radical form of the trope--not merely a "conversion" but a more extreme "controversion"; Quintilian has allegory say one thing in explicit words and convey another in sense, touching in this discrepancy between stated and intended meaning on standard definitions for *irony*. Non-Aristotelian semantics could not similarly free Icons from their Indexicalization.

Quintilian's pure allegory nevertheless kept alive popular notions of the *continued-metaphor-as-allegory* tenet and thus in essence the equivalent of an "elongated proxy-*tenet*," I might add. In Tuve's interesting study on Elizabethan and Metaphysical poetry (1965, pp. 105-106, 219-220), Quintilian's classes for allegory seem to be present; also in Brinkmann's *Metaphern* (1878, I, pp. 26 ff.) critics are mentioned who identified an extended use of metaphor as allegory, while this author was discerning enough to concede that bounds (Grenzen) for stabilizing either concept were still hard to isolate. The reason for that difficulty should be apparent from my various interpolations. There is nevertheless more to come as contemporary neo-Aristotelians take over where these ancient founders began.

The Syncretistic Circumference: A Museum of Metaphors

My non-Aristotelian theory began with the "leaps of language," and in this last part, the neo-Aristotelian adjunct, I undertake a historical leap by jumping from the pre-Christian age of antiquity into the immediate present. To effect a smooth temporal transition, this particular chapter of the adjunct serves as an interlude between the ancient fathers presented formerly in a triumvirate and their modern, very faithful followers, to be introduced later in subsections that cover briefly Anglo-Saxon, German, and French contingents, with linguists getting some extra if limited space. My synoptic view, aided by a retrospective focus that singles out the neo-Aristotelian connections, should be adequate. However, this chapter quite literally fills in some historical gaps by the means of a "museum," a showcase in essence that lists the myriads of epithets in which metaphor has been cast through the ages. The museum follows my immediate summary of persistent neo-Aristotelian problems.

Since my theory of non-Aristotelian semantics essentially dissociates itself from the neo-Aristotelian tradition, its negative "non-" prefix takes on greater negative significance in this adjunct than it did in the earlier part intent on laying down the foundation of my own thesis. Often the critics themselves play inadvertently the devil's advocate as they--at times reluctantly--acknowledge their complacency in a tone of defeatism. Certainly, the majority of my contemporaries have been unable to surmount the rhetorical tradition; theirs is the legacy of what might be tagged metaphor's "patristic" beginnings, to what extent I shall summarize right here.

There is to date no adequate methodological equivalent to my *obverse* and *reverse* order. Time and again claims of metaphorical idiosyncrasies *cannot be upheld* because any "literal" meaning possesses the traits when not *subjected to* a linguistic *skepticism* equaling that of the ancient analogists. To consider reference directly a representational surrogate of empirical nature is a subversion of the true "metaphysical" nature of meaning, confusing the realities non-Aristotelian semantics has separated as ontic heteronomy and autonomy with the aid of Ingarden. Accordingly, the supposed arepresentational or anomalous *reverse* to meaning, regarded as "metaphor," becomes essentially a *nonentity* as well.

Aristotle's own representational view surfaced in the lexical alienation, the *allotrios*, that characterized his metaphora in the Preliminary Statement, and was continued in the proxy-tenet *epiphoras* whose task of transference switched genus and species classes or fixed contents in set terms of logical proportionality. While the Similarity Statement, as I identified this final passage of the Aristotelian exposition, seemed to endorse unique synthesis, the observation was far too broad to isolate anything in language, be it meaning or metaphor. In addition, Aristotle projected his epiphoric transference in such a manner that he left the impression that "literal" semantic reference dispensed with it. After him, the representational outlook was perpetuated by the Latin fathers. Metaphor in the Latin patristic age stayed assessed through the concept of semantic "propriety." As the arepresentational reverse of that premise, metaphor became the "improper" alternative of "proper" meaning, considered capable of subverting normal reference on the basis of phenomena as shallow as shifts of animation.

Naive as some of these ideas seem, they have been retained, even if some modern, specifically German, contingents like to trade on a dissimilarity cult, which remains just as dogmatic as stressing similarity when there is no genuine conception of what identities and differences, entities and categories amount to in language. The underlying skepticism stays, whether linguists seek metaphor's anomaly in selectional violation and philosophers in either Rylean types of category-mistakes or Fregean nondenoting, lexical contents. Indeed, from the very beginning Aristotle himself was shown in my critical analysis to type-trespass domains and cross-sort categories, thus being the first to commit what I have termed the *ontological* category-mistake despite his interest in categories. The practice becomes a mistake because there is no systematic distinction between what exists and what is being expressed. Right up to the end of my study will this mistake persist, following in ancient footsteps, Greek or Latin, as so-called conceptual leaps are posited to characterize a nonexistent metaphor simply because the critics themselves leap from logic into language by not realizing where concepts differ in these domains.

To be sure, concepts "collide," as I have described it in my diagnosis, when the traditional metaphor occurs, betraying an ontological category-mistake in a manner of speaking: two forms of programming conflict momentarily because sheer *sensation* of oddity intrudes on linguistic *signation*, especially when redundance is still weak or becomes supervened by clever punning. But fundamentally, a phenomenon based on sheer sense impression cannot disrupt the "sense" which has become indented through years of linguistic activity in acquisition, forming signitive convolutions by the means of linguistic forms, the Icons in their wielding which then develop Indexes through Symbolic feedback and feedforward. Nor can sensation in a particular, new completion of language undo the teleological unit(y) which forges all "similarities" and "differences" as it binds every constituent to its constitution--not without splitting (M-O) meaning(s) from what an author (I) "meant." The very provenance, in fact, of linguistic concepts and categories resides in such constitution.

Yet Aristotle, the father of genre as well as of categories, was shown also to predate participants of the Ingendahl Experiment in the practice I termed *spotsighting.* He isolated deviant pockets from a teleological whole, additionally an authenticated Homeric epic, much as his modern counterparts rated single words for their "metaphorical" contribution. While these participants seized on a feuilletonistic extract in a "poetological" seminar, Aristotle long ago filled in a truly "poetic" content as though its meanings were marbles for logic or served perhaps some political oratory. Methodological corollaries of such spotsighting are what I called a *hide-and-seek* guessing game and a *hop, skip, and jump.* The game Iconizes Indexes not derived from a use but an assumption about static analogies; it transforms the critic, supposedly an analytic Recipient and genuine "superreader," into a pseudo-Referent. The jump arises from seizing on detail as though literal and literary applications were immaterial, thus ignoring what I specified as "structure," the mode of contextualizing contents which endows the elements with their sole reason for being.

Further detrimental consequences of remaining locked in explicit contents, which as "M" in I·M·0 thetic constitution present literally the most "language-bound" base, concerned a vital *epochal* defect. Aristotle treated Homeric Greek as part of his contemporary inventory while probing semantic alienation. Modern critics, too, neglect parallel epochal discrepancies of inception and reception between them and Shakespeare, for instance, whose "weed" image as female apparel was discussed in order to obviate such oversights. Epochal neglect additionally leads to confusing crucial *diachronic* and *synchronic* differences. Thus the catachretic, natural, or necessary "dead" metaphor that the patristic contingent visualized as a product of semantic paucity is, conversely, merely a meaning undergoing various stages of explicit and implicit amplification, extending coinage through gradual semantic redundancy.

A processing of this nature may be described loosely as a form of "literalization." But of greater importance is the understanding that diachronic flux becomes halted by teleological fusion, since constitution draws on developed synchronic states--for which reason the non-Aristotelian metaphor, lodged at context (I) rather than (M-0) content, cannot die or destruct. That is also why only a nonlexical and thus content-insensitive structure genuinely "literalizes" meaning through the attachment of a reality-nexus. Yet the lexical opposition the tradition seeks would disappear swiftly in the synchronic network of positive and privative opposition, rooted as it is in values indigenous to a language in use. Only the metalinguistic gestures of motioning to Icon or Index to label a respective "literal" and "metaphorical" designation remain content-sensitive, for which reason precisely they are mere gestures without having to account for the absence or presence of a reality-nexus. As such, they can enter my language here, despite its truly literal foundation. Describing something as "literal" or "metaphorical" in "plain or "prosaic" style is not going to affect the structure of how my language, as Argument, amalgamates under the guidelines of adequation previously elucidated.

Yet today the domain of language remains such a mystery that its literal or figurative determination must be supported representationally by so-called *literal spheres*. Neo-Aristotelians eagerly seek "spheres of reference" (Reddy, 1969, p. 247) or "heterocosms" (McCanles, 1976, p. 279), as well as "literal purity" (Yoos, 1968, p. 219), to cite a few examples among thousands. As was pointed out earlier with Kripke's "rigid" designators set to endorse vague worlds, no such vantage point succeeds--as some of the very proponents (Yoos, 1968, pp. 219, 226) ultimately concede when encountering the "difficulty" of devising "criteria" that in any "rigorous" manner isolate a "literal" from a "figurative" expression on the basis of spheric parallelisms. Returning to my analogy for the visual arts, there is nothing wrong with merely describing a style of painting as "realistic" because its execution appears representational of empirical nature. But to assume that nature has obligingly mapped out domains for an accurate determinant of such a style in so many tints and forms--perhaps the pinks and blues of a sunset?--is incredibly naive, and the same applies to any presumed relation with language.

The major issues relevant to the ensuing discussions have been cursorily identified. Certainly, the lack of success was not marred by the breadth of expository works dealing with the intricacies of metaphor, although only a better understanding of meaning can actually disclose them. "Circumference" in terms of "girth" (Umfang) is indeed contained in the title of a dissertation by Lieb, who struggles hard with a "historical" conception of metaphor (1964) without reaching a synthesis among the welter of material. As Lieb (p. 33) grapples with a voluminous quantity that will not cohere to the point of a fruitful analysis, he concedes that although the earliest definitions of "metaphor" stayed "unclear and conflicting," they were adopted readily enough by successors. He adds that ridiculing the repetitiousness may be easy, while bringing metaphor under one common critical denominator stays an "insurmountable task"--as he apparently discovered. Actually, Lieb inadvertently provides part of the clue to the problem: I wanted to translate his statement but opted for the paraphrase because transferring his embedded clauses to English proved too laborious. Indirectly, then, his critical or "literal" use announces itself in all its complex origin, "deviant" enough to equal any of the simple metaphorical "anomalies" critics seek in set "analogies" that are supposed to counter a figurative style or keep it interpretable.

An expository work which eludes Lieb's type of defeatism mainly by avoiding controversy is the much revered study by Ricoeur, *La métaphore vive*, on whose translation I have drawn also a few times. "Blistering refutations," says the author (1977, pp. 7-8), are not his style. Of course, that blister must first be diagnosed correctly as a symptom of erosion and, once found, a cure at this point should be highly desirable. With such a critical stance not in evidence, Ricoeur's endeavor is interesting mainly as a summary of current theories. Even at an expository level of assessment, the work would have benefited from not simply republishing old lectures with their redundancies intact, then going to the trouble of translating all of the excess. The resulting diffusiveness at least veils the missing synthesis, and how painstaking that task can be, I have certainly discovered in my study here.

Yet another interesting expositon that treats a time span similar to Ricoeur's is also the *Study of Metaphor* (1976) by Mooij. I cited Mooij on occasion, specifically on German theories of metaphorical spheric blending. In addition, a modest but intelligent treatise by Nieraad (1977) deserves a mention. Its title trades on the "Bild" or pictorial "image" that is essentially an emblem for sartorial gloss. The Germans will be shown to use it frequently as a designation for metaphor. Nieraad's title has this image "blessed" and "cursed." Indeed, blessed may be the interest in metaphor but cursed the critical impotence that fails to delineate what it is. Another critic, Yoos, in an essay taking a rather halfhearted "Phenomenological Look at Metaphor" (1971, pp. 82-83), terms this impotence going back to the many devices of ancient rhetoric a "parade of tropes" whose diffuse "taxonomy" remains "about as theoretically enlightening as . . . common names for garden weeds." Yet instead of "weeding out" the parade, Yoos unfortunately adds to it, since his "look" merely defends construable deviance by proposing a broader, phenomenological perspective, which is hardly necessary once linguistic meaning is understood in its signitive autotelism. What the "weeds" image perhaps exhibits also is the penchant of "modern theorists" to "shoot off into an endlessly interesting series of metaphors," as Wimsatt (1967, p. 128) put it. Wimsatt is then cited by Nemetz in a tribute to "Metaphor: The Deadalus of Discourse" (1958, p. 420). But the "Supreme Artificer" Nemetz equates with metaphor also becomes just one more metaphor if it is not realized that language as bearer of meaning has as its ground such very artifice.

To demonstrate this neo-Aristotelian proclivity of drawing on metaphor in order to describe metaphor, I offer next a "museum" marking the proliferation of epithets which have been plied through the ages. So here is my own "metaphor," giving at least an impression of the welter of material that is being "exhibited" as "metaphor" in all its facets. Nor was the figure entirely picked at random: I took the term from Bréal's chapter devoted to "Metaphor" in his work offering *Studies in the Science of Meaning* (1904, p. 130; 1964, trans., p. 128). Despite his intent, Bréal did not penetrate to any scientific approach to meaning. Yet Bréal has a point when he describes how various languages create their "museum of metaphors" (musée des métaphores), because from his diachronic, etymological perspective languages own nothing but "dead metaphors." Bréal's title, furthermore, is reiterated to underscore the same *historical lag* in the obverse and reverse order that accompanies neo-Aristotelian theories, when one considers that meaning as a discipline had to await roughly two millennia after the appearance of metaphor.

In recognition of the founder of "semantics," then, my listing of epithets designating metaphor will be called "A Museum of Metaphors"--a museum, however, that critics rather than speakers of language have created. The actual material, though, is taken from Warren Shibles's painstaking *Annotated Bibliography and History* (1971), which covers metaphor from its ancient beginnings to the present. Moreover, Shibles offered a synopsis of the bibliography as prefatory material to his *Essays on Metaphor* (1972). This material, already condensed by Shibles, had to be cut down further--wherever the ellipsis points appear.

METAPHOR IN A MUSEUM OF METAPHORS

To describe abstract by concrete, in actions, anagogic, as analogical, as antithesis, archetypical, artificial, as as-if, as basis of arts and sciences, . . . as catachresis, as catharsis, . . . as cliche, as collage, as comparison, as concealing, as concise, as concrete, in context, controversion theory of, and counterfactuals, in creativity, crisis, as representing a culture or age, . . . dead, . . . as delusion, as description, as deviation, diagrams of, as dialectic, as disclosure, as dissolving distinctions, as distance, . . . as ellipsis, as emblem, as constituting emotions, as expressing emotions, . . . as emotive, as empathetic, . . . as basis of etymology, as euphemism, excess of, expansion of, as experience, as expressing the inexpressible, as expressive, . . . as false, familiar, as fantasy, far-fetched, as fiction, in film, as filter, fixed, as formula, . . . as fusion, in games, of gender, of genitive link, as a work of genius, based on genus-species transference, good, grammatical, as harmony, hidden, . . . as humanizing, as humor, as hyperbole, as hypothesis, . . . as identity, as illogical, as illustrating, as image, as product of imagination and fancy, . . . as rendering immaterial by material, as immediate experience, indirect, as inexhaustible concept, representation of inner by outer, as giving insight, as intellectual, intentional, as interaction, as intuited, as irrational, as juxtaposition, as kenning, as source of knowledge, to express unknown by known, as likeness, as not based on likeness, linguistic theory of, as indistinguishable from literal, as irreducible to literal, as reducible to literal statement, taken literally, mediational process of, as metamorphosis, of metaphor, . . . as metaphysics, as metonymy, to describe mind, misuse of, mixed, as model, as montage, and multiple meanings, in music, as mystical, . . . as myth, as a naming, as natural, as necessary principle of language development, . . . as new, as nonsense, of omitting, in oratory, origin of, as ornamenting, in painting, as a parable, as paradigm, as paradox, parallelism, as parataxis, perceptual, as perspective, as persuasive, . . . as pictorial, plastic, as play, as pleasing, poetic, . . . as pretending, as primitive, . . . as puzzle, . . . as constituting reality, to describe reality, reciprocal, rejuvenated, as relation, as seeing-as, as a sentence, of silence, as simile, . . . as slang, as representing spiritual by sensual, as the sublime, as a substitution, as suggestive, as surprise, symbolic, synaesthetic, as synecdoche, as synthesis, as based on taboo, as tension, as a single term, test for, . . . as constituting thought, . . . as transfer, as true, as type-crossing, as unifying, as unity in difference, . . . non-verbal, . . . as rendering the invisible by the visible, visual.

Viewed negatively, metaphor emerges as cliche, false, far-fetched, illogical, irrational, leading to misuse, nonsense, slang; viewed positively, metaphor accounts for euphemism, the good, and harmony; it also stays grammatical, humanizing, pleasing, poetic, sublime, and so on. Obviously, these types of value statements are too broad to correspond to anything of substance. Other characteristics cancel one another out: metaphor becomes described "as inexhaustible concept, . . . as indistinguishable from literal, as irreducible to literal, as reducible to literal statement, taken literally," and so forth. Rhetorical devices are not lacking either, from the catachresis and emblem to the hyperbole, metonym, and synecdoche, some of which were treated along with the ancients. Quintilian had synecdoche and metonym listed as species of tropes in a taxonomy of content that applies to "roof" and "house" or to "possessor" and (objects) "possessed." Non-Aristotelian semantics drew on the "metonym" only to render a functional relation of parts to whole. Not content but structure stood behind this metonym, equalizing all components in accordance with their task, even such a vestige as a punctuation mark, specifically a dash or colon.

Symptomatic of this "sea" of metaphors is the *syncretistic* breadth of application to a plurality of fields. This critical eclecticism, as it may well be called, is much in evidence of late. Shibles's own collaborative volume (1972) of essays listing the condensed museum is no exception: the very titles indicate the ramified expertise, ranging from "Art and Human Form" (Aldrich, pp. 105 ff.) to "Scientific Models" (Hesse, pp. 169 ff.), and "Synectics" (Raudsepp, p. 141). Apparently synetics aids creative business ventures that trade on such metaphorical analogies as the identity between the wings of birds and planes, or the auricle of the ear that went into the shape of telephone receivers.

Metaphor in language thus may become totally submerged in such a plurality of fields, and since it is barely understood in this one sphere, excessive ramification does not help. What prevails is the "omnipresence" or "ubiquity" Richards ascribed to metaphor (1936, p. 90), on which point he was repeatedly quoted (O'Neill, 1956, p. 81; Mackey, 1965, p. 272). Yet a principle that is *everywhere*-ends up being nowhere, as the result from the Ingendahl Experiment proved. All the recent special issues on metaphor put out by journals nevertheless continue in a similar vein of thematic diversification. *New Literary History* (1974) and *Critical Inquiry* (1978), for example, treat metaphor in fields that run the gamut of philosophy, sociology, and psychology, to name a few. With the "inquiry" not "critically" contained within one area, the "Conceptual Leap" one editor (Sacks) serves up in the introduction as a kind of motto for metaphor gets no further than the Ciceronian "transilire," which at least confined itself to linguistic "oratory." As I started out to say, without defining "concept," a leap remains literally useless, or belongs already to the nature of meaning rather than a specific "metaphor."

No wonder that Ortony, editor of a collaborative study that appeared one year later under the title, *Metaphor and Thought* (1979), ushered in this subject with "Metaphor: A Multidimensional Problem" (pp. 1-18). There are just too many "multiple" dimensions before metaphor is successfully isolated in one sphere. The "Thought" that accompanies this "Metaphor" splits into a diversity of topics including linguistics, pragmatics, psychology, sociology (as "society"), science, and education. Coupled with the pervading syncretism appears to be the dire need for republishing material that, were it not for the general stagnation of the field, would long be on the discard pile. A case in point is the still more recent collaborative effort entitled *Philosophical Perspectives on Metaphor* (1981) which, after an interesting introduction, also elects to trade at least partially on vintage material.

Enough critics also concede that the modern era cannot emulate that of the ancients. Accordingly, they become "devil's advocates" for my own contention. In the 1960s Allemann (1966, trans., p. 103) admitted readily that definitions of metaphor by Aristotle and Quintilian are still being accepted verbatim; in the 1970s Gardner (1970, pp. 727 ff.) similarly concurred with a comment he cites from Henle, made back in 1958, that because of a persistent if "rough agreement" with the ancient precepts, "little new" had been discovered on the subject of metaphor. Other critics will be shown to acknowledge similar admissions of defeat.

In anticipation of dealing subsequently with the most prominent theoreticians, I conclude this part with what I shall label the "KP Chart," named after two authors, Kurz and Pelster, of a rather modest pedagogical treatise (1976, p. 13), even if my presentation is considerably modified from their schema. Thus, in order to demonstrate the *critical pleonasm* and *vicious circle* of the tautologous nomenclature neo-Aristotelians apply so nonchalantly to their *proxy-tenet*, I added the headings "MEANING" and "METAPHOR" and simultaneously omitted the many German terms the authors offer under the Latin pairs below.

THE KP CHART

MEANING

M E T A P H O R

S u b s t i t u t   S u b s t i t u e n t

proprie   improprie

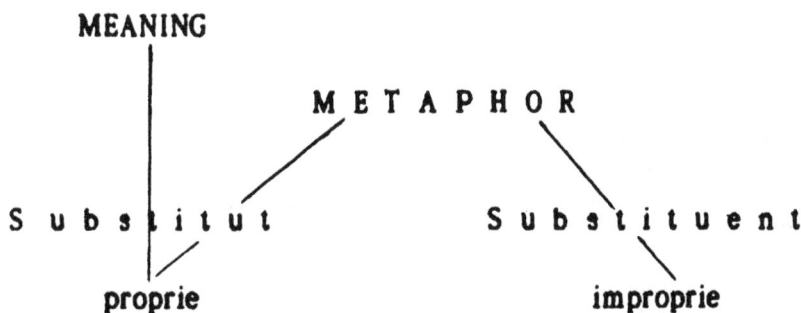

So here is the proxy-tenet dissected: dual "METAPHOR" consists of an ousted "proper" element, the replaced "Substitut," and a replacing "improper" agent, the "Substituent," that stands proxy for the Substitut. At the same time, univocal

"MEANING" as antonym of dual "METAPHOR" also is designated the "proper" alternative to "METAPHOR." Yet "MEANING" cannot share characteristics with the left segment that is decidedly a component of "METAPHOR." Similarly, the right segment of "METAPHOR" as the replacing agent cannot cover for complex "METAPHOR" as a whole, and to assert merely that metaphor also consists of a metaphoric component surely constitutes a tautology.

The authors of the original chart, who mainly present bipartite columns, also list "bildlich" and "übertragen" for that right side. The former is an adjective which contains that pictorial emblem, the "Bild" as noun; it played a part in past discussions on Nietzsche's idea of the combinatory prowess in art as well as Humboldt's imprint of the truly linguistic image. The "übertragen," which literalizes into a "carry-over" (here as verb or past participle), was also invoked with Nietzsche's all-pervading "metaphorical" reality. Since the term is listed here as a proxy-agent going into effect under "METAPHOR," it could present loosely the Aristotelian "epiphora" as well. In any case, even Kurz and Pelster (1976, pp. 14-15) realize that the substitution espoused by Aristotle and his followers should not occur at the level of the linear syntagma and that, accordingly, the substituting agent had to be drawn extrinsically from "elsewhere" (anderswo). Unwittingly, they express by that term a *critical* "allotrios" which imposes "alien" norms upon language while viewing language as having broken with norms, a theory so symptomatic of the ontological category-mistake.

The chart lends itself to the very example of Aristotle and Quintilian: the "courageous" male named "Achilles" either belongs to "MEANING" or to the left element of "METAPHOR," where it opposes the "lion" that becomes its deviant proxy on the right side of "METAPHOR." To make these semantic marbles complete, I add the *simile* to "METAPHOR": (1) "Achilles"; (2) "is courageous/has courage like/is as courageous as" (proper Substitut, with *tertium comparationis*); (3) "a lion" (improper Substituent). One can juggle these contents around as suggested by my alternatives, and critics who thrive on formulas may undoubtedly devise others. Since in non-Aristotelian semantics *every* Icon lays the denotative foundation (M) in order to release connotatively the relevant Index (0) through the intervention of an authorial will (I), formulas of this nature would alter the form of semantic generation, to the detriment of that signifying "nature" a language owns. The very transaction between reference and transference these jugglers wish to isolate and/or erroneously separate would then become disrupted.

If, moreover, there exists the parallel wish to study the ideas of a neo-Aristotelian correspondence between metaphor and simile, one can read on endlessly. Judging by the painstaking compilations of either Lieb or Shibles, metaphor emerges repeatedly as a contracted, abbreviated, or shrunken simile--and on and on. The idea is the same, but new terms take over in a colorful array, as if, in some magical incantation of never-ending epithets, metaphor might just disclose itself one day, or dutifully see fit to sever its relation with the simile. Optimism, though, has its bounds. If I have laid to rest one such ineffectual repetition, my final selective offering of neo-Aristotelian premises, complete with suggested correctives from the KP Chart, will have been worthwhile.

The Modern Followers

i. Anglo-Saxon Pairing.

I begin with the critic whom I quoted at the very outset of my theory--Richards. No doubt the most widely known concepts for the designation of metaphor are his *tenor* and *vehicle* from the *Philosophy of Rhetoric* of 1936. In this work Richards seems to have left behind the affectivism of earlier studies (Wimsatt and Beardsley, 1967, pp. 236-237, 243; Wimsatt and Brooks, 1967, pp. 610-656). For instance, his *Practical Criticism* of 1929 (1956, pp. 205-224) still concentrated on emotional appeal; the chapter "Sense and Feeling" treated an "emotive metaphor" whose "shift" is based on a "similarity" between "feelings" (p. 221). By comparison, the distinction of tenor and vehicle exhibits a more objective approach to metaphor, if not to the point of categorical isolation, as indicated (1936, pp. 97, 118-119):

> I am calling it (the tenor) the underlying idea or principal subject which the vehicle or figure means. . . . Whether . . . a word is being used literally or metaphorically is not always, or indeed as a rule, an easy matter to settle. . . . If we cannot distinguish tenor from vehicle then we may provisionally take the word to be literal; if we can distinguish at least two cooperating uses, then we have metaphor.

Richards himself becomes the arbitrator of whether his decision will land on meaning or metaphor. If linguistic constitution depended on "provisional" contingencies, no interlocutory partners could uphold intersubjectively the medium they share. The fact that the tenor is "underlying" immediately invokes the hide-and-seek game of proxy-tenet substitution. On the KP chart, tenor as the left, replaced Substitut would oppose vehicle as the right, replacing Substituent, with both appearing under "METAPHOR" when distinguishable from "MEANING." Richards's "two cooperating uses" also would need careful specification. Otherwise they apply broadly to double-intentionality, which initiates two such uses with *every* act of meaning (I) that becomes incorporated by an explicit and implicit reference (M-0), as meanings shift and "transfer" their contents in order to engender authorial intent--including my words here.

A "philosophy of rhetoric" Richards may offer, perhaps, but hardly the critical tools meeting the complexities of semantic functioning. To be sure, in the *Principles of Literary Criticism* (1925, pp. 128, 140) Richards demonstrates his acuity for detail that modern literary theory associated with the New Critic he was supposed to represent: his observations on natural and stylistic onomatopoeia as well as the "mnemonic power of verse" are well worth reading. In addition, his ideas of metaphoric "interanimation" or "interaction" had wide impact. Unfortunately, his definition of such a processing demonstrates also the ontological category-mistake. Richards (1936, p. 93) speaks about "two thoughts of different things active together and supported by a single word, or phrase, whose meaning is resultant of their interaction." "Thoughts" and "things" cannot be accepted without detailing their precise implementation for speech.

Nor does Richards (1936, p. 96) fail to exhibit in a larger historical context the legacy of British neo-Classicism as he approvingly cites Samuel Johnson

(1709-1784) for having devised a whole series of pairs in the "two ideas that any metaphor, at its simplest" is supposed to embody. Metaphor at its simplest, however, collapses with any ordinary meaning that harbors a functional duality; the semantic name as Icon is essentially the "vehicle" for a signitive act and its Index the "tenor" of relevant connotations that arise with every regulation by such an act. Metaphor at its most complex level then occurs in the Rheme, in accordance with functional guidelines that make explicit and implicit a poetic act of meaning.

Richards's interaction influenced Black's "filter" theory, a point of connection critics are certainly fond of making, with Mooij (1976, pp. 71-80) including also the spheric blending of the Germans. When I dealt with that issue, there were some comical demonstrations of the leonine "social" womanizer who in English is more likely to emerge as a "wolf." This Icon now becomes part of the canine satyr I term the "wolf-man"; it is the image Black chose to illustrate metaphorical filtering, if not with quite the same Index, or connotations. Indeed what Black's sentence, "Man is a wolf," signifies as contextless collocation is anyone's guess, yet it brought the essay "Metaphor" in which it occurred enough fame to become reprinted many times after its first appearance in the *Proceedings of the Aristotelian Society* (55, 1954-55, 273-294; Margolis, ed., 1962, p. 233; also *Models and Metaphors*, 1962). Black nevertheless seems confident that this sentence manifests an example of metaphor, which

selects, emphasizes, suppresses and organizes features of the principal subject by implying statements about it that normally apply to the subsidiary subject.

In that typical neglect of obverse and reverse priorities, Black at best describes what *always* obtains for the generation of meaning and not in some special "metaphorical" action. The lexical selection that has "man" and "wolf" conjoin in predication, however, is powerless to initiate a special function, potent though Icons remain for laying the denotative foundation of every speaker's meaning. Black's reference to a subsidiary "subject" in this context reflects Richards's formulation, of course. And, again, the proxy-tenet is at work, suggesting that this "subsidiary" canine image as vehicle becomes imposed on the human species, the tenor, through tacit replacement, filtered or otherwise.

Aside from the proxy-tenet formula, there is the parallel ontological cross-sorting: similar to Richard's "thought" or "idea" is Black's recourse to "normalcy." No critic of language, meaning, or metaphor can afford to cite such generalizations without systematically defining the terms. What are norms in language *qua* ordinary meaning? A language like English which can normalize a nonexistent "red herring" as "phony issue" and in certain contexts make this idiom either "literal" or "literary" obviously goes by its own categories, and these have to be critically delineated.

Nor are matters helped when Turbayne (1962, p. 15) comments on this example by insisting, "I do not pretend that man shares the properties of wolves, I intend it." Pretense, like borrowing and bartering, does not exist as linguistic activity, or does so only in a loose description of that quasi-mirror discussed along with Ingarden's ideas of non-adequated fiction. But that kind of "pretense" merely affirms that the explicit contents seem so "real"--for which reason they obviously delude so many of these experts on metaphor. "Properties," too, are extralinguistic unless their provenance is tied exclusively to linguistic activity. In language, properties come in Qualisign materiality, which leads to the contents and concepts indigenous--signitively indented--to language in a language. Another admirer of Black, Ricoeur (1977, pp. 87-88), cites the same passage and firmly believes that the "wolf-metaphor" actually "organizes" the "view of man," conferring on it an added perspective of "insight." All "sight," however, that permits a look "into" language commences with the functional processes of contextualizing contents; speakers share these as humans long before they may be named in contents to become juggled with canines in taxonomy.

Black's principal and subsidiary subjects thus constitute yet another duality built around localized relations which are not free of ontological type-trespassing, mainly because semantic faculties are not defined carefully enough. The same applies to Black's "model" and "metaphor," a pair that Ricoeur paraphrases obligingly as "epistemological" versus "poetic" counterparts (ibid., 1977, pp. 22, 85). Since no functional determinants keep these qualifiers apart, they cannot rise either to ontological levels. "Epistemology" belongs to encyclopedic cognition, is thus autonomous-ideal in essence and can have a bearing only on meaning, but not metaphor, when there is a valid explanation of how language acquires a reality-nexus.

The problems are sustained by Beardsley, another expert on metaphor who has enjoyed much acclaim. The expository contingent sees fit to label his approach "monistic" and "intuitionist" (Mooij, 1976 pp. 32-35, 81 ff.; Scheffler, 1979, pp. 82-83 ff.). To that assessment I cannot subscribe. Focal to Beardsley's theory is the "twist," made explicit in the title of the essay of 1961/1962, "The Metaphorical Twist." It was supposed to be a revision of what he had presented on metaphor in his *Aesthetics* of 1958, though whether this thesis is an improvement is open to doubt. Shibles (1971, p. 41), in his annotation of the vast material which was offered above as "museum," takes out time to laud Beardsley's ideas on metaphor. Well, let the reader be the judge!

Basically, the very term "twist" reminds of Quintilian's controversion tenet couched in the "trope." At first glance, however, Beardsley's aim appears sound enough. He wants to supplant a representational type of "object-language" with a more intrinsic, "verbal" or "metalinguistic" reference rooted in words. Accordingly, an "Object-comparison Theory" is to make way for an improved "Verbal-opposition Theory" (1961/1962, pp. 293-294). Wonderful! But the critical tools do not match the goal. Instead of positing anything that resembles the "oppositional" value system a linguistic inventory harbors intrinsically irrespective of lexical deviance, Beardsley plunges right into object-language in a naive ontological type-trespassing that treats meanings as marbles for things. By coincidence, Beardsley (p. 300) chooses "tree," the very word I used to demonstrate the natural leaps of language. Beardsley, however, endows his "tree" with natural "properties" such as "leafiness" and "shadiness." With such motivational attempts at a representational reference for meaning, there is little hope for a metaphor that is propelled by a twist, which he defines as follows (p. 294):

When a predicate is metaphorically adjoined to a subject, the predicate loses its ordinary extension, because it acquires a new intension--perhaps one that it has in no other context. And this twist of meaning is forced by inherent tensions, or oppositions, within the metaphor itself.

As was said of Black, at best the definition describes *any* generation of meaning. There is always an "ordinary extension" in centrifugal, nominal-verbal unfolding and concomitantly a centripetal, "new intension" with nominal-verbal interlocking at the very moment an act of meaning becomes materialized and embodied by chosen Icons, which then yield the relevant Indexical release. Thus one must ask once again what "ordinary" constitutes in meaning. That is the persistent problem paralleling Black's normalcy and Richards' recourse to thought. Certainly, there is nothing that "ordinary" about the intricate network of positive and privative opposition a linguistic inventory bears. All its values are signitively induced concepts, shared mental indentations. However, that Beardsley's "oppositions" remain localized in pockets of arepresentational lexical deviance, his illustrations should prove. Before I give these, I wonder also how original the "inherent tensions" are since they seem to have been preempted by Tate, as indicated where I cited Krieger.

In an attempt to categorize these tensive oppositions of the metaphorical twist, Beardsley distinguishes "Class I" and "Class II" (pp. 300-301). Two representative examples are "smiling sun" and "inconstant moon." So "opposition" means little more than two contents shown in a lexical deviance that is based on something as shallow as animation, tied to basic English commonplaces which also let the sun or moon "rise" in the sky, to cite examples mentioned in conjunction with Embler's "everyday metaphors." In a close historical connection, both classes qualify for Quintilian's "bold" fourth shift of metaphor by animating the inanimate, except that the former sounds more trite. A frozen figure of school rhetoric, "smiling sun" approximates the "laughing meadow," Latin "pratum ridet" (Curtius, 1963, pp. 128 ff.). When one turns the phrase around and gets a "sunny smile," sunshine and risibility have really lapsed into idiomatic redundance. Yet my study has underscored throughout that--and indeed how--structure revivifies any vestige when the language stays literary and thus non-adequated.

Clearly, such a resuscitation would relativize Beardsley's classes right away. But neo-Aristotelians never pay attention to structure. Instead, with his Class II metaphor, the "inconstant moon," Beardsley (p. 301) commits the *hop skip and jump* by landing right in literature, a problem typical of *seeking* a lexical, language-bound surface which, as such, looks the same everywhere. He himself confirms that these two contents stem from Shakespeare's *Romeo and Juliet*. So here he offers a contextualized content, to be sure, yet without considering at all *how* the language came together, only *what* its surface bears. Worse, Beardsley commits the *epochal* default by claiming deviance for a surface content that goes back to a much earlier inventory, similar to the time span separating Homer from Aristotle. How does Beardsley know whether or not the expression was then a commonplace? At least there should be an indication that he checked the inventory of Elizabethan English to prove that the animation was then as "alien" as it is to him now. Even if that were verifiable, nothing can be substantiated on the basis of only two contents picked like raisins out of a cake without knowing the dough of the pastry. Yet non-Aristotelian semantics immediately defines the structure as mimetic augmentation, Dicent, paralleling the Homeric epics. Then it is up to the critic to analyze the function of these contents, as I did in my first, triparite analysis.

The last individual in this group, Wheelwright, presents the pair *epiphor* and *diaphor*. According to Hawkes (1972, pp. 66-67), while Richards's tenor and *vehicle* describe *units*, Wheelwright's two terms render *modes* of "semantic transference." That focus is made explicit in the "-phora" suffix denoting movement, and the "epiphor" certainly appears close to Aristotle's *epiphora* of metaphorical transfer. Yet the nomenclature has been modified, as is made clear in Wheelwright's essay, "Semantics and Ontology" (Shibles, 1972, pp. 61-72). Going by etymology, Wheelwright (1972, p. 67) states that epiphor "connotes a semantic movement (phora) from something on to (epi-) something else," while "diaphor," with its changed prefix, conveys a "movement through" something. On the KP Chart bearing "METAPHOR," Wheelwright's epiphor would equal the substituted left and diaphor the replacing right component. Shibles, as one of Wheelwright's editors (1972), affirms this construal: the epiphor is based on the analogy of an "antecedent resemblance," which as proper term aids in grasping diaphor, the "novel, untranslatable, paradoxical, irreducible" counterpart. Wheelwright (1972, p. 63) himself also offers a type of Aristotelian "Preliminary Statement" when he says about his metaphor invested with these dualities that it possesses the "unique property of referring to something other than, or at least more than, itself."

To diagnose these comments together, nothing is described here that meaning cannot equal. Therefore, the "Ontology" of Wheelwright's supposed "Semantics" becomes a misnomer unless more carefully defined. Language itself creates all "antecedent resemblance" in a language, be that the "odd couple" marking the cuckoo-fool, or whatever. All these metalinguistic contiguities signitive acts have forged, though not in accordance with the way things *are* but rather how they have become *expressed* with *every* release of a speaker's meaning. Incorporating signitive acts becomes the primary means for all semantic contents to render something "else" or "other" or "more than" themselves.

The first of two examples I cite from Wheelwright certainly indicates how narrow his application is, reduced to a single and contextless vocabulary item, the "skycraper" (1972, p. 68). Its epiphor, notes Wheelwright, conveys height through touching the sky and its diaphor contributes the "novelty" that results from "combining the idea of sky with the mundane idea of scraping." Wheelwright should explain first that he is discussing a *diachronic* transparency of an original contact. He is thus dealing with a "dead metaphor" which is just semantic processing in flux, with the Iconic contact made conspicuous here. The compounded Legisign has then become sufficiently ingrained as synchronic state to yield an Icon and indented Index. To extend the example, the German compound is "Wolkenkratzer." When foregrounded, this Icon yields a "cloud(s)-scraper" (or "-scratcher"); only when backgrounded does the indented Index produce the English meaning. The suffix is close enough to the English, also bearing an onomatopoetic bruitism concomitant with the dissonance such an activity inflicts upon the ear. Yet the prefix "clouds" emerges as a nice "literal" transparency for the overcast skies of Europe.

Interesting as diachronic motivation of evolutionary stages is, neither compound is anything but what Wheelwright terms "epiphor" in its signitive provenance. Only synchronic states anchor a content functionally in new transference, causing the very (epochal) fusion Beardsley ignored in his literary vestige. As with some of the other compounds discussed, the syntagma may render a "scraper" "composed" of "sky" or "clouds." But this seeming nonsense or "non-sense" a full linguistic competence turns into sense, even if the sheer Iconic composition may play a role in punning just for being there, as did the components of Celan's foghorn, whose two segments effected a special unity between the meaning of title and text. Furthermore, the German renders a "*Himmelkratzer," denoting a "heavenly scraper" in a literalized translation. Why the religious connotations? They arise purely because the English inventory owns the two Icons "sky" and "heaven" and German only one "Himmel." *That* distinction is indeed an "opposition" speakers must know as interlocutory partners. But determining what is more "odd" than "even" only means running up against the Heideggerian "house" in which natives feel "at home."

To be sure, Wheelwright's two major works, *The Burning Fountain* (1954, pp. 25-29, 55-59) and *Metaphor and Reality* (1962, pp. 33-40, 45-46), contrast literal "steno-language" or "block-language" with a literary or "tensive" "plurisignation" based on semantic "plenitude." But no systematic distinction pinpoints these functions. The latter work (1962, pp. 79-80) also offers "pure diaphor," this time as a contextualized syntagma severed from Gertrude Stein: "Toasted Susie is my icecream." Wheelwright has now chosen a stylistic extreme which W. Steiner (1978, pp. 137, 145) labeled a "Literary Cubism" bordering on the bare "limits of analogy." Also, my work on Concrete Poetry (Gumpel, 1976, pp. 17-18, 39, 52, 100-102) drew attention to the impact of Stein's asyntactic serialization on postwar experimental literature. Yet even this "Cubist" vestige may be literalized, as when said Susie is a brand name for an ice cream or gets "toasty" brown while "roasting" in the sun and perhaps devouring a melted ice cream. English Iconic contiguities may put "Susie" commercially on water "skis" under blue "skies." The sky--and not "heaven"--is the limit for lexical deviance, but the critics who seek it without a structural anchor have not as yet come down to earth!

ii. Grammarians and Linguists

This topic has to stay brief because the subject has been discussed variously in connection with Chomsky and Levin. Brooke-Rose, in whom is vested the "grammarian" authority, also was quoted, mostly while I dealt with Aristotle's suggested constants of localized relations in order to preserve that direct neo-Aristotelian connection. Her grammatical approach followed largely the orientation of the nineteenth-century German critic, Brinkmann (1878); see Gläser, 1967, p. 259). Had I not wanted to maintain the parallelism which caused me to begin with Richards at the outset of my theory and again in this part of the adjunct, I would have commenced with Brooke-Rose, because the "semantic" definition of metaphor that precedes her grammatical taxonomy is a demonstration par excellence of the critical pleonasm which attenuates metaphor in a vicious circle of terminology (in my italics below). Confidently, she claims (1958, p. 9),

It seems to me perfectly obvious that a *metaphor* consists of two terms, the *metaphoric* term and the proper term which it replaces.

So "METAPHOR" as a duality that opposes univocal "MEANING" on the KP chart consists also of a "metaphoric term." How enlightening! This pleonastic definition, to which is added a conspicuous proxy-tenet "replacement" theory, bodes trouble for her grammatical formulas, even if some remain interesting. How arbitrary her notion of semantics is becomes apparent when she (p. 26) goes on to state that in a total or "Simple-Replacement" the substituted content is not "mentioned" and thus must be "guessed." Semantics reduced to sheer guesswork? No one would ever know when a "given word replaces another," as a critic (Henel, 1968, p. 117) has observed. That is indeed the problem of the hide-and-seek game neo-Aristotelians play with their proxy-tenet and tacit nondenoting premise in cases of lexical deviance. In my theory, "mentioning" is systematically assigned to denotative Icons which cannot be dislodged, while their full "meaning" produces connotative Indexes relevant to the teleology of the constitutional unit(y).

Another critic who as linguist shares Brooke-Rose's predilection for number and formula is Pelc. His essay, supposedly devoted to "Semantic Functions" while treating the "Concept of Metaphor" (1961), also bears critical misnomers since neither semantics nor functions surface. There is instead much interest in rhetorical devices, the very types Yoos was shown to have dismissed as overgrown garden weeds. Nor does Pelc shy away from blatant cross sorting, which makes evident that meanings to him appear as direct stand-ins for things and people in the world. Pelc is nevertheless hopeful that he can replace the standard duality with a "metaphoric triangle" (ibid., pp. 309-311, 315, 337). The evidence soon appears that this aim in itself is symptomatic of localized spotsighting. Pelc cites the genitive link, "hair of the sun," which supposedly stands for sun rays. His choice displays the very language-bound surface on which neo-Aristotelians are forced to draw for their lexical orientation: the phrase sounds as though it has beeen transported over into English from one of Pelc's Polish efforts.

Anyway, "hair of the sun" it shall be. Pelc (pp. 309-313) claims that this is a metaphoric expression (E) consisting of E(1) and E(2), in sum, three parts. In relation to the metaphorical expression, E, the "sun rays" constitute E(2) and, somewhat confusingly, in the same relation E(1) amounts to the "third term." Put another way, the reference to sun rays, E(2), is the replaced meaning because "rays" properly belong to "sun" but are not mentioned explicitly. Conversely, the reference to the "hair," E(1), is a replacing counterpart whose alien hirsute content glosses over the implicit solar emanation by making it explicit as "hair" in the rendering, "hair of the sun," E. The link between solar emissions, E(2), and hirsute strands, E(1), is implicit "isosemy"; the link between hirsute strands, E(1), and the actual rendering, E, "equiformity." All Pelc invokes here is the *homonymic* metaphor: the replacing vehicle, E(1), thrusts solar emissions and hirsute strands under "one" or "equal" name in the explicit rendering of the expression, E.

I rejected the catachretic, homonymic kind of filler for an "expression" that Pelc has here, because it is a diachronic phenomenon of semantic evolution, hence just "meaning" in different stages, as pointed out in discussing Aristotle's "solar seeding." Numerically, nothing is gained either; the implicit comparison prevails in this duality, lending itself readily to a *tertium comparationis*. Indeed, I can even add my own tetradic proportional type of metaphor to this example *à la* Aristotle: straggly hirsute strands (B) are to human hair (A) what rays (D) are to the sun (C).

Beyond the number, Pelc's example tacitly reinforces the critical pleonasm of Brook-Rose's definition: (E), the actual expression, constitutes "METAPHOR" and consists of a proper term, E(2), and an improper or "metaphorical" term, E(1). The "rays" of E(2), which Pelc so freely "counts in," must become relevant to the teleology of the constitution instead of being drawn from some static "isosemy" or analogy. Such a genitive link, too, can be literalized in an instant if rendered to extol a certain hair brightener as "hair of the sun." So, what does any noncontextual, lexical segmentation prove anyway in terms of "metaphor" or "meaning"?

This type of segmentation nevertheless is a popular method, largely based on Chomsky's *selectional* violation--the linguists' alternative to the philosophers' category-mistake that is already an ontological category-mistake. Indeed, all these attempts are "Ontological Arguments for the Existence of Language" that become superfluous once the indigenous nature of meaning and its categories are apprehended. For those interested in selection there is the lengthy article by Abraham and Braunmüller (1973, trans.), replete with the "sleepy wood" my study quoted while discussing Baumgärtner.

A unique regressive development is made evident in Matthews's article, "Concerning a 'Linguistic Theory' of Metaphor" (1971), where the special quotes refer to Bickerton's "Prolegomena to a Linguistic Theory of Metaphor" (1969). Now, Bickerton was on his way toward the grand discovery that language *marks* willfully, ordaining "bachelor girl" but not "*spinster boy." In a diachronic motivation, it is interesting to note the transparency which permits females to bear male attributives as in real life they may don male attire, but not the other way around for men. More importantly, Bickerton's marking stressed the validating prowess of language, but then he failed to know what to do with this discovery other than note that a language like English has norms and oddities side by side, which every lay speaker realizes. What makes that "odd" image shed its "*" disqualifier? *That* is the question he does not answer. Quite understandably, Matthews (1971) remains dissatisfied with Bickerton's marking, yet turns instead to those dissecting "markers" which featured also in Levin's analysis of poetic compression--a step in the wrong direction for resorting to an unwarranted "Atomization of Meaning" (Bolinger, 1965; Gumpel, 1974, pp. 183 ff.).

Levin, in fact, is to be reinvoked briefly, since his *Semantics of Metaphor* (1977) synthesizes the major theories of linguists. An eloquent reminder of their selectional focus is Chapter II, "Problems of Linguistically Deviant Expressions" (pp. 17-32). Levin treats some of the complicated appparatus linguists invent in their strenuous efforts of dealing with selectional anomaly. His analysis ranges from a "Selector" (Katz and Postal) to an "Extension Rule" (van Djik), as well as a "Calculator" and "Evaluator" (U. Weinreich), with the latter rules intended to serve a more flexible "Redistribution" than the lexicon of standard language would permit. The late U. Weinreich particularly is to be commended for trying in the mid-sixties to make logical strictures of selection more pliable and thus better suited to the dynamic essence of language. His lengthy article, "Explorations in Semantic Theory" (1966, pp. 395-400), manifests a courageous attempt to grapple with "lexicography" in the desire to incorporate in it the natural "intuitions" that transcend the narrow syntactic amalgamations linguists call "projection rules." Weinreich realized that some answer was needed to explain why certain apparent figurative anomalies stay consistently "interpretable."

Weinreich did not come up with the solution. Ironically, for once the neo-Aristotelian theory becomes more complex than non-Aristotelian semantics, since no special apparatus is needed once semantic provenance and signitive prowess are recognized. That is to say, linguistic competence is the very "Calculator" normalizing all "distribution," even when a syntagma releases an Iconic composite that at Indexical depth counters the apparent reference, as illustrated with those curious "hermaphroditic" womanizers, the English "ladies' man," "lady killer," and "skirt chaser" formerly induced by the Teutonic "salon lion." While dealing with Weinreich (et al.), Levin also (1977, pp. 20-22) provides an example involving a "questionable" male: instead of Bickerton's "*spinster boy," he cites the "*pretty boy." The expression should be starred because its attributive segment carries a "(-Male)" marker. Levin thus invokes the very marker he so eagerly foisted on Dickinson's feminine "Etna." Yet Levin admits that even in reference to a human male the adjective may render an "ad hoc" reading of a "sissyfied" or "unmanly" male.

Although this added flexibility is attributed to a Semantic Calculator, no such device is needed when language is grasped in its own sphere of ontic heteronomy, grounded in signitive acts. Nor is linguistic meaning ever ad hoc in application, as pointed out while dealing with Richards' "provisional" detection. Every semantic generation is authorially willed, as explained with the trichotomy of context. Without that will, there can be no teleological constitution and no interlocutory apprehension of speaker intent. Somehow, too, the "pretty boy" reminds one of a parrot's mindless shrieks. But, once Iconized as spoken or written words, these contents attain a "mind of their own" and exude meaning relevant to their contextualized relevance. Also, while discussing unwarranted number in conjunction with Aristotle's tetradic, proportional metaphor, I cited the English oxymoron "pretty ugly" to give a concrete instance of what a difference number makes as extra inclusion willed by an author. The point is that "pretty" in this case has its "(-Male)" suppressed anyway, releasing instead an adverbial intensifier--without the aid of any special Calculator. Such are the dynamics of meaning, and thus the linguistic activities which engender indigenous categories. The issue and example return shortly in reference to an "ironic" metaphor.

How strictly logical is gender anyway, with its diachronic personification and synchronic validation? What matters is its acceptance and potential revivification within non-adequated literary usage. As for the odd synchronic states of gender, German "neuterizes" a "girl" into "das Mädchen" while French "femininizes" a male soldier into "la sentinelle." True, philologists may point to the diachronics of grammar, since the suffixes "-chen" and "-elle" are cast in that gender. But this very reason should seem "odd" to skeptics, to think that sheer syntactic subcategorization rules supersede common sense and still make "common" this "sense." Language in a language asserts itself through speaker acceptance, at which point its entities become as "normal" as they are "absolute," since to ignore them leaves nothing but a star (*). To term such a perverse use of gender "nondenoting" is pointless. This is where the lexicon must be heeded; as long as there are Icons from validated Legisigns, they "denote."

In all fairness, apart from dealing with the above linguists in expository fashion, Levin's work (1977, pp. 104-113) proves that he is wary of Frege's nondenoting and Ryle's category-mistake as any satisfactory answers to the phenomenon of metaphor. Levin (pp. 127-139) thus makes an effort in the end to seek a better explanation while probing the "Poetic Metaphor." In circumlocution there is a hint that Levin gets the message. For this realization alone he no doubt deserves credit though he does little with it. Thus he states that "deviant sentences in poetry are to be taken literally" and, at their level, not only continue to possess meaning but even "express truth conditions" (p. 127). Precisely! But no systematic explanation follows; in the little space left, his awareness becomes literally (in skimming the Icons) an "after-thought." What is "truth" here? If he could answer that he would be able also to explain "literal" in this context. To reiterate, truth is first of all the intersubjectively validated Legisign and the structure under which it operates, while all selectional, lexical evidence stays content.

That point is lost again on Levin when next he gets to "nondeviant expression in poetry," where he invokes a "dual system of reference" (1977, pp. 128-129) for such lexical vestiges as geographic place names. All I can do is refer him to the poem of his own analysis, which uniquely intertwined "Etna" and "Naples," disregarding simultaneously certain geographic encyclopedic factors detailed at the time. Such factual knowledge Levin (ibid., pp. 95-99) leaves unsolved as a persistent "problem." While place names, like animal contents, may be more intrusive, these Icons function no differently from any other "poetic" constituent—did not do so even in Brecht's "prosaic" poem containing "Fin(n)land," where alliteration served the "Friends" and a host of images. So here Levin is misled by content again, while his nomenclature threatens to become circular for the want of a careful delineation: deviant poetry turns out to be "literal" and "true"; it simultaneously bears "nondeviant" elements invested with a dual reference which, however, as poetic constitutents must needs be "deviant." Since deviant is now "literal" anyway, though normally the "literal" is "nondeviant," why do these distinctions matter at all?

A set method which tackles obverse meaning before reverse metaphor clearly would have helped here. As a final resort, Levin (pp. 131-134) advocates submitting the poetic metaphor to a looser "phenomenalistic construal," which in theory parallels Yoos's "phenomenological look" cited before. Since the traditional metaphor actually is based only on a sensation of two forms of programming colliding that cannot hurt linguistic competence, such extended perspectives do not aid or hinder construal. Yet Levin assumes here that if deviance could be viewed more dynamically, it would perhaps go away and or explain a still construable semantic base. That argument Levin tried to press further in an essay bearing a "Proposal for a Literary Metaphor" (1979, pp. 131-135). But of course such a defense is not needed when language is assessed from its autotelic vantage point. Levin (1979, p. 132) does not even extend that autotelism to the text, since he seizes on yet another poem by Dickinson which has been bowdlerized. In the end, Levin (1979, p. 133) echoes the defeatism of others by admitting that he has no genuine proposal. So that leaves his argument where Chomsky kept the selection rules when their bounds would not separate semantics from syntax, as the latter was shown to concede.

Levin's entry nevertheless still compares favorably with others in the collaborative volume that contained his so-called proposal. This criticism applies particularly to Searle's effort (1979, pp. 92-123) immediately preceding Levin's, which in gross ontological type-trespassing aligns lexical compatibility with crude worlds that become even too much for Levin (pp. 124, 131). No wonder the editor, Ortony, was cited earlier for expressing his own misgivings at the "multidimensional problem" metaphor has come to present. Metaphor is not the culprit, but rather the critics who do not define semantics adequately before they plunge into a semantic idiosyncrasy.

iii. German Iconoclasm: The Absolute or Bold "Bild"

The "Bild" is a favorite designation Germans have used for centuries to describe metaphor (Lieb, 1964, pp. 44, 124-125). In this study, the term featured in Nietzsche's idea of the creative esthetic image as an antonym to the rational, equalizing "Begriff." To some extent, the "Bild" reflects the "Museum of Metaphors" because in this context it is itself an epithet, a type of metaphor. The term denotes "picture" and "image," and during the age of German national chauvinism it became stressed as the Teutonic counterpart to the Grecian "Metapher" (Pongs, 1965, I, pp. 1, 23, 67). But Greek "metaphora" of course suggested a form of movement and that equivalent "technical term" (Fachausdruck) is "Uebertragung" (Porzig, 1975, p. 70). Literalized into a "carry-over," this word was cited also with Nietzsche's idea of the ubiquitous metaphor as an extramoral, metaphysical predicament. According to Brinkmann (1878, I, pp. 24-26) "Uebertragung" additionally embodied vestiges of the Latin trope.

Contemporary critics of metaphor are still especially fond of the "Bild." The original KP chart (see p. 237) included it, though in the adjectival form of "bildlich." There it presented the substituting improper vehicle which in my diagram belonged to the dualistic "METAPHOR." What its reference to the pictorial insinuates right away is the sartorial gloss so typical of proxy-tenet substitution. Stählin and Bühler, for example, who were quoted before on spheric blending, have the "Bild" operate in a type of "exchange" (Austausch) with its "thing" or "Sache" on the basis of bartered and blended properties (Merkmale; in Mooij pp. 74 ff). Of late, however, the localized similarity cult has taken an interesting turn which appears to be the opposite focus but in its dogmatism registers no great change. That is the avant-garde dissonance cult or "icononoclasm," as it was called by Ortega Y Gasset in the *Dehumanization of Art* (1968, pp. 40-41). Ortega comments on the "loathing" this antiart movement felt toward traditional esthetics. In literature, gone was the lyric expression of sentiment, the type of "confessional poetry" Michael Hamburger describes as outpourings of the "empirical self" (1969, pp. 25, 28, 59, 142, passim). Language was to be challenged as an artifice capable of combining the uncombinable. But as this critic (ibid., p. 31) rightly observes, "Language itself guarantees that no poetry will be totally 'dehumanized' . . . ."

The arepresentational view of metaphor lent itself easily to radicalizing this iconoclasm: the Aristotelian Similarity Statement was ready to be converted into a neo-Aristotelian Dissimilarity Statement. Latin rhetoric, too, contributed to this idea with its metaphorical leaps and semantic appropriateness: the more distant the image from its content and thus the greater the gap between them, the more "absolute" in uniqueness the accomplishment of metaphorical transference. From the more immediate historical perspective, German Romanticism became the source and in turn influenced French Symbolism. These nineteenth-century tendencies aimed at breaking with the standard Classical verities of truth, beauty, and goodness, the "kalokagathia" (Käte Hamburger, 1966, pp. 82-128).

In poetics, Baudelaire's *Les Fleurs du Mal* (1857) auspiciously fostered new dissonance in imagery. His successor, Rimbaud, not only sought to evoke dissonant "flowers" through "evil" but also through disparate and mundane-"chairs." That was the message of his exhortation, "Trouve des fleurs qui soient des chaises!" (H. Weinrich, 1963, p. 339). Rimbaud was followed by Mallarmé, who insisted on a "de-objectified" imagery, which at times was to be implemented through negation in order to convey an "absolute nothingness" (Friedrich, 1965, pp. 94-95). Lastly, Breton (1896-1966), founder of twentieth-century Surrealism, advocated also keeping images and their objects "eloignés"--as far removed from one another as possible (H. Weinrich, 1963, p. 327). Another critic (Hocke, 1959, pp. 68-75) visualizes "Surrealist quintessence" as "neo-Asianic" excess, hence as the ultimate manneristic outcome of those "Asianic" roots that in pre-Christian times opposed "Attic" clarity.

Contemporary German critics as "absolutist" devotees have taken up those challenges with alacrity. Landmann's work entitled "Absolute Poetry" (Dichtung) includes a chapter treating "Absolute Metaphors" (1963, pp. 136-137) that in their uniqueness become the very "Organon of Philosophy." He thus echoes almost *verbatim* the nineteenth-century Romantic philosopher Schelling who put art on an ontological pedestal for reaching through the imagination where no scientific cognition could follow. However, the theorist who had most impact on postwar literary criticism is Friedrich, specifically his work, *Die Struktur der modernen Lyrik*. In Friedrich, the various strands discussed above coincide. He (1965, pp. 121-122) certainly makes evident Ortega's influence upon him by citing the latter's precepts of iconoclastic dehumanization. Michael Hamburger's (1969, pp. 28-30) appeal to a "humanized" art above occurred in discussing Friedrich. Both he and Friedrich also consider Baudelaire's work the turning point for the modern dissonance cult.

Friedrich's approach to modern "lyric" is excellent for observing the taxonomy of dissonant imagery but, again, any "structure" promised by the title then becomes a misnomer, since the work does not rise above content, leaving his presentation of an "absolute" metaphor in doubt. The topic occurs in a section of a chapter called "Einblendungstechnik" (pp. 151-152), which in foregrounded Icons becomes a "technique for inblending." Friedrich's precept thereby reinvokes the spheric blending discussed earlier, down to its components, the "Bild" and "Sache," except that "image" and "thing" must now effect "blending" at a distance. Friedrich begins by claiming that while the Classical tradition strove to designate metaphor through harmonious analogies such as "golden hair," the modern trend is to drive all congruities apart. Seizing essentially on a Ciceronian *transilire*, Friedrich then posits his "far jump" (Weitsprung): the image or "Bild" and its thing or "Sache" driven furthest apart in transfer (Uebertragung) cause metaphor to partake of a unique "supremacy" (Uebermacht) that results in an *absolute* "Bild" and as such counters an idolatrous, imitative surrogate called "Abbild."

However, Cassirer (1972, I, pp. 5 ff.) had already decried the naive realism of such an "Abbild" as unfit for linguistic synthesis. Cassirer thus rejects for meaning what Friedrich discards also for his absolute metaphor. Language is by its very nature "de-objectified," if not "dehumanized"; the "objects" it owns are indeed its "own," unique pure-intentional objects forged exclusively (and heteronomously) from acts of meaning. So critics of literature have to be more conversant with language, as Jakobson put it, to gain new ground for any type of metaphor that is not simply meaning. After I get to the next critic, I shall have a chance to show how oversimplified even Friedrich's periodization is here, just because a localized lexical coherence--in yet another "hirsute" example (à la Pelc)--proves nothing by itself.

These reservations notwithstanding, the modern critics reinvoked not only the Ciceronian leap but even Latin "audaciousness": the *absolute* image had to yield to the *bold* "Bild." Metaphorical boldness, too, constitutes an epithet that thrived in the last couple of centuries. Bouterwek, who had actually given the German Romantic movement its name in 1812 (Kluckhohn, 1966, p. 184), simply praised metaphor for being bolder than other tropes (*Aesthetik* (1825; 1969, pp. 49 ff.). In the late nineteenth century, Gottschall stressed boldness while describing the "metamorphosis of the imagination" which metaphor is capable of effecting (see Lieb, 1964, p. 126). However, since Humboldt's *Variations* (1963, p. 470) had already preempted boldness for the linguistic imagination or "Phantasie" that generates language, one wonders how idiosyncratic that quality can be for any valid type of "metaphor."

In this century, the bold "Bild" received special attention through a popular article entitled "Semantik der kühnen Metapher" (1963) by Harald Weinrich (not to be confused with Uriel Weinreich), where the only word that is not a cognate, "kühn," refers to boldness. One of Weinrich's earlier endeavors, "Münze und Wort" (1958), treats the "minting" of words that still exists in the English Iconic doubling of "coin" and "coinage." This essay also demonstrates Weinrich's neo-Humboldtian affiliation, specifically the field-theory semantics and content-related grammar discussed briefly with the "energetic" past. In addition, Weinrich's essay, "Semantik der Metapher" (1967, p. 3) begins by crediting Bréal, founder of the discipline of semantics, with the change that converted the rhetorical metaphor into a "semantic problem." It took history so long to get to this point in time, and still neo-Aristotelians do not seem able to solve the problem sufficiently to bring metaphor into the genuine fold of semantics.

Weinrich is no exception. Despite the neo-Humboldtian legacy and seeming awareness of semantics, this sphere will not surface. Boldness itself, after all, was shown to have a decidedly rhetorical foundation. As exclusive property of metaphor it is already in jeopardy from my brief survey of Weinreich's more recent precursors, including Humboldt, in the context of its value to meaning and not specifically metaphor. Undaunted, Weinrich (1963, pp. 325-337) posits a more daring incongruity than the jump marking Friedrich's absolute "far-metaphor" ("Fernmetapher"). That challenge is to be a "near" boldness, releasing a metaphor based on *counterfactuality*. Paralleling Friedrich's "image" and "thing" is Weinrich's (pp. 328-329, 336) "image-receiver" and "image-spender," between which operates an "image-span." When this span is close, counterfactuality arises and with it a "supra-concept." What Weinrich describes, again, *always* obtains except that the contents as such have no control; the acts make constituents "spend" their explicit and implicit contents in the transaction of reference with transference by "endowing" these entities with a specific purpose--terms that actually surfaced when I detailed these functions. As it stands, Weinrich's supra-concept becomes nothing more than a fixed rhetorical *tertium comparationis*, as he then makes explicit by invoking a "tertium commune."

Weinrich's bold, counterfactual ideal is the oxymoron, whose term is already a Greek oxymoron as "wise foolishness." Oxymora have held neo-Aristotelians in their sway through the ages and, among many others, they certainly preoccupied Beardsley (1961/1962, p. 306). One counterfactual oxymoron Weinrich (1963, pp. 335-336) offers is "square circle." He points out correctly that in logic such a circle remains a "contradictio in adiecto." Outside of logic, contends Weinrich, a bold metaphor with a narrow image-span obtains, since a supra-concept such as "geometric figure" readily presents itself. Henel (1968, p. 99) has rightly said about Weinrich's example that perhaps a well drawn "square circle" could signify just that, as it is common in English to speak of a "square meal" and mean a hearty repast. Henel adds that such a use has not been accepted as yet as a dictionary entry. That is to say, no such polysemous compound is as yet extant as Legisign.

Although the last point is open to debate, Henel indicates the fallacy of positing semantic antecedents for counterfactuality as though meanings were contextless marbles. What two or three contents come to engender depends on the authorial will, not the contents as such. "Geometry" in any form may not be a part of the context and the contacts that arise in the process. "Narrow" is mainly Weinrich's conception of language which thus needs some structural correctives: if "square circle" came adequated in a mathematical language-game it would possess a truth claim through the function, even when "false"; if it composed a quasi-mirror of (fictional) Dicent, perhaps involving a plot about an incompetent mathematician, "facts" will never be an issue, true or false. Instead, the first task is to "present" the character (à la Ingarden) in linguistic aspects traceable only to the given contents. Finally, the fact that a language like English has already surmounted mathematical incongruity in attaching "square" to (Henel's) "meal," for example, merely proves that any meaning is ever ready to jump such bounds. Indeed, English permits a "square circle" for rendering a staid group of friends--no less "miserable" than Chomsky's social "company"? Even for this staid "circle" structure comes first: are these people "in" a drama or novel as so many Legisigns or do they "exist" through an adequated reality-nexus?

Earlier I cited Plato on the "circle," because this ancient thinker realized that a linguistic name and a logical concept were two different things. Unaware of such ontological distinctions, Weinrich (1963, pp. 37-379) only makes matters worse when next committing that typical *hop, skip, and jump* that finds him picking an oxymoron from a poetic line. The poem, Celan's "Fugue of Death" (Todesfuge, 1970, pp. 37-39), appeared in the same cycle that contained the poem I analyzed and translated. In a published bilingual version (Michael Hamburger, 1964, pp. 318-321), the opening line renders the oxymoron in the genitive link, "Black milk of daybreak." Before seizing on this supposedly bold metaphor, Weinrich does not even point out that his oxymoron is not wholly Iconic, since the "white" opposing "black" is a relevant Index of "milk" minus a denotative core, a difference that must affect the M-base in Rhemic I-M-0 constitution of poetic intext.

That a holistic precept like context cannot be ignored finally dawns on Weinrich: in the end he admits that context determination can annihilate the boldness of even a narrow image-span (pp. 340-344). So he tacitly revokes what he has delineated in yet another one of those frustrating conclusions which end in contradiction. Indeed, the wider context of this Celan poem also offers a sequel to Friedrich's supposedly Classical "Abbild" opposing the modern "absolute" metaphor: it contains the image Friedrich quoted, "golden hair." Yet the contents serve as a sardonic comment on Nazi racism and stay in their setting as "absolute" as any other constituent!

The last critic to be cited in this iconoclastic group is the person after whom I have named *the* Experiment--Ingendahl. Judging by the dates of the essays given below, his input seems to have been strong around 1970. Ingendahl, too, makes known his neo-Humboldtian roots; one article (1970) promises to engage in an "energetic" investigation of literary processes while another (1970) suggests field-theory orientation of the content-related grammarians. Whereas Weinrich discusses the figurative minting of the word as "coinage," Ingendahl examines its implicit periphery in the metaphorical designation of a verbal "halo," the "Worthof." Since German possesses already the related compound for a lunar ring or halo, the Legisign "Mondhof," the analogy is easily bridged between the stellar and linguistic spheres. Aside from noting the transparency, however, I must reject this contextless "metaphor" as a purely diachronic phenomenon. The fact that Ingendahl had not come to terms with diachronic and synchronic differences was shown in another "lunar" example, where he examined juvenile use of the "moon" and "ball" in the very article containing the Experiment (1972, p. 268).

At the time I said that an analogy of roundness causing a child to Iconize the moon with the already extant "ball" does not constitute a truly linguistic metaphor. Speech does not originate until children have accepted the extant Legisign, the "moon," so that the Icon may be wielded and its Index indented in the development of shared metalinguistic contiguities. Ingendahl thus ignores the distinction between diachronic development and synchronic stabilization in meaning, a flaw which must affect any delineation of metaphor. In three more articles that appeared in 1970--"Metaphorical Processes" (p. 50), "Metaphorics of a Linguistic Poetics" (p. 128) and "Linguistic Fundamentals" (sprachliche Grundlagen) of "Ironie" (pp. 236, 239-241)--Ingendahl mainly relies on a metaphorical "outreach" (Ausgriff) which allegedly opposes the regular tool of semantic "disposal" (Zugriff), a neo-Humboldtian concept. The outreach becomes just another label for lexical deviance and in this translation was in fact borrowed from Wheelwright (1962, pp. 66-67). A metaphorical outreach applies essentially to the very "meta-physical" transcendence by language of "physis," as explicated, thus leaving the term yet another "museum" epithet for "metaphor."

Ingendahl nevertheless clings steadfastly to his outreach as he simultaneously tries to have it complement Weinrich's bold precept (1970, pp. 239-242) in the last of the three articles above devoted to an *ironic* metaphor. So dissonance is not only claimed as closest proximity but *turns* into its ironic opposite. That at least is the suggestion, recalling almost verbatim the "inversio" Quintilian examined with "allegory." Thus Ingendahl (1970, pp. 237-239) appears to repeat Quintilian's wording when he defines irony as a conflict between what is said and what is meant. Furthermore, Ingendahl's confusion between diachronics and synchronics surfaces as he tries to boost irony with "Is" and "Ought" discrepancies. My study relied on these values only as diachronic phenomena of flattening "dead metaphors" which, apart from their labels, are ordinary meanings anyway as they undergo the processing of linguistic activity through Symbolic feedforward and feedback. At synchronic levels meanings are always willed, with their Icons equal to stated "Is-factors" that anchor authorial intent, while Indexes serve "Ought-values" reaching their full relevance at the moment of constitution.

Unfortunately, Ingendahl (p. 237) takes refuge in sheer illustration, jumping from contextless offerings into a highly context-sensitive territory of no less complex a work than T. Mann's *Felix Krull*. This novel artfully contrives to exchange foregrounded cloying sentimentality with backgrounded craftiness in piecing together the very swindler the titular Krull really is. First, the structure needs to be identified, which is Dicent, thus demanding the presentation which corresponds to mimetic augmentation. Even the apparently "ironic" or "inverted" contents succumb to structure by depicting this character in all his devious fictive aspects. Yet armed with nothing but lexical aberrations, Ingendahl (ibid.,) lunges immediately into an interpretation of fragmented contents.

The ironic vestiges Ingendahl culls from the text which lend themselves best to English are "schön" and "schlimm," close to "beautiful" and "bad." As pointed out in discussing "pretty ugly," these adjectives may function as parallel "ironic" intensifiers, turning a seemingly positive Icon into a negative Index--in the most ordinary speech patterns, one of which calls to mind the "fine mess" that became a Laurel and Hardy staple. Ingendahl's "Linguistic Fundamentals," promised by this essay to serve the isolation of "Poetic Forms of Irony," are thus left in critical limbo. No mere construal of single contents can compensate for a systematic theory, which is the reason why mine began with the groundwork and then its application to textual analyses. In the spirit of the earlier-discussed English behabitive, which, though foregrounded as "stated" pleasantry has been indented into an automatized type of "intended" dismissal, I thus bid this critic "Good Day!"

iv. French Deconstruction and Reconstruction

The French have the final word, as they well deserve, considering their cultural lead throughout history and of late in the area of metaphor as well. Their "deconstruction" and "reconstruction" will be abbreviated also to the "de-" and "re-" prefixes. Since the terms are for the most part Latin cognates, they foreground well into English. My selection falls first on the major critics involved--Derrida, Ricoeur, and Riffaterre. Basically, of course, the proxy-tenet thrives on re- and de- factors, from "*deviance*" to "replacement," in the very idea that when the language registers lexical (de) oddity, a *parasitic* (re) element stands proxy for the "proper" norm in an "improper" denomination. The de-factor also featured in early twentieth-century Russian Formalism. Derived from "ostranenie," the Russian concept for alienation, the term becomes Anglicized as "*defamiliarization*" and "*deautomatization*" (Bruns, 1975, pp. 75-79; Hawkes, 1977, pp. 62-63, 66-69; Scholes, 1978, pp. 83-4; Stankiewicz 1974, pp. 634-6). There was also an allusion to "Re-Distribution" while discussing the linguists in search of more dynamic selection rules that could respond to metaphor rather than to plain meaning.

Related through principle in a wider "Gallic" connection are the "mu" and "me" Sinsigns of the Belgian (Liège) school. These are drawn from the Greek equivalent of "m" and yield in French the "métabole," a concept that in essence embodies a "de-" and "re-" dichotomy around which revolves all lexical "anomaly" as deviance in a figurative redescription. The resulting taxonomy of tropes, designed to aid the modern use of advertisement, outrivals the attempts of the ancients that Yoos had already reduced to "garden weeds." Closely allied in precept is Todorov's "Sa" and "Se" dichotomy, which stands for syntactic and semantic anomalies. The final critic to be included is deMan, who was not only influenced by

Derrida's deconstructionist precepts but complements Todorov's type of linguistic symbolism which I intend to analyze briefly.

Derrida's *deconstructive semantics* is certainly accompanied by a prodigious output, but in my selective approach I pick his long essay entitled, "La mythologie blanche: le métaphore dans le texte philosophique" (1971). The essay appeared in translation as the lead article (pp. 5-74) in one of those special journal issues on metaphor, this one from *New Literary History* (1974). In that syncretistic setting, Derrida's entry contributed the "philosophical" approach, as its title suggests. All the words of the above title are recognizable enough, even "blanche," denoting "white." What is this "white mythology"? Essentially, it is a symbol for Derrida's idea of linguistic *self-effacement*, and in the text (1974, p. 11) is caught also in the figure of the "palimpsest," whose invisible "white" ink leaves behind an indelible blank spot that carries the origin of language as the "myth" of its own creation. These figures are brought together with the philosophical perspective of Hegelian *sublation*, the German "Aufhebung" (ibid., pp. 9, 25, 73).

Hegelian sublation is an interesting concept which certainly has validity for language. Sublation resides in all latent "op-po-sit-ion" which, when thus syllabified, brings out the negative and positive "de-" and "re-" aspects. Indeed Symbolic feedback and feedforward is the cornerstone of linguistic sublation by preserving the past contextualization in contents while suspending the immediate transaction between reference and transference which can occur only at the trichotomy of context. The question is, where does a stable "metaphor" fit into this diachronic processing? In the way of an answer, I cite a definition from Derrida (1974, p. 71), where he posits that it is because

the metaphorical does not reduce syntax, but sets out in syntax its deviations, that it carries itself away, can only be what it is by obliterating itself, endlessly constructs its own deconstruction.

One key word is "syntax," which indicates new contextualization, and the only means for "constructing" it is generation through a specific authorial intent, "destroying" perhaps those implications not relevant to the constitution. Certainly, syntax is not "endless" but "finite," as this finitude pertains to the teleological fusion accompanying all semantic integration. The second key word in Derrida's phrasing is, predictably, "deviations," a term which insinuates that he, too, still clings to localized lexical incompatibility. In sum, Derrida's approach is "deconstructive diachronics," which does not extend to what he terms "syntax" but to evolutionary stages in flux. My diagnosis is borne out by his frequent references to a "detour"--also "de-tour"--and "return" (pp. 66, 68-69). Syntax grants no fluid detours, is in fact bound to its own "epochal" era of inception, to which later reception must "return" in order to avoid any subversion of the (fixed) authorial will. One of Derrida's examples (1974, p. 24) is typically that diachronic standby of the manual-mental "grasp" in physical or spiritual "apprehension," which he cites in German. All Derrida has are dead metaphors and thus meanings that have undergone developmental growth since their deictic, gestural origin.

Cassirer (1972, I, p. 129), too, traded on the very example Derrida quotes, though not to affirm a special metaphor but rather to confirm the unique linguistic progress of semiotic-semantic synthesis, experiencing an ever greater symbolic distance between itself and the immediate environment. Another is Barfield (1967, p. 53-59), who looks to the "grasp" example while pointing to changes that reach from "material" to "mental processes." Barfield then gets into those wasted polemics over which came first, the figurative or literal meaning and concludes that "nonfigurative language" was a "late arrival" (ibid.). That idea seems to correspond to Derrida's metaphorical detours and returns. In the Gallic preoccupation with diachronics, Bréal may be another link; Barfield (1928, pp. 54-59) refers to him while discussing how the development is to be taken "backwards through the history of language." There is no such "backward" reappropriation possible for a new integration of meaning.

Clever wordplay, of course, on the order of the former cartoons, may Indexicalize the manual-mental "grasp" singly or simultaneously, but only as long the Icons and their indented uses stay contemporaneous with the authorial will choosing them as solidified synchronic states. As to whether metaphor really came before meaning all depends on knowing what one is labeling. The early concrete immediacy in a closeness to nature, which simultaneously consists of a yet narrow, "degenerate" indentation where language is concerned, would seem "metaphorical" to Romantics, including the Rousseauan Primitivsts. To others, the "generate" expansion of Indexes in their full connotative potential would be deemed to merit this qualifier, despite the increased "abstract" mediacy caused by a greater distance between empirical nature and language.

None of these issues, however, is clearly defined by Derrida, and his figurative, somewhat rhapsodic style helps mainly to prove that the "deviations" involved in his own "syntax" may provide a lexical "metaphor" but no direct clue to the deeper, nonliterary function that belongs to his critical writing. For those interested, Derrida's sublation is well detailed by Ricoeur (1977, pp. 284-295), if not sufficiently synthesized in the way of a critical analysis. Ricoeur's own redescriptive tenet certainly demonstrates the influence of Derrida's deconstruction, though combined further with Ryle's ideas of the category-mistake, which he never tires of citing in the *Rule of Metaphor* (ibid., pp. 21-22, 170-171, 197, 235, 252-253, passim). Ricoeur's definition of redescription (ibid., p. 22) thus affirms that

the category-mistake is the de-constructive intermediary phase between description and redescription.

So the category-mistake becomes in essence the proxy-tenet catalyst which has (proper) description replaced by the (improper) redescribing agent, in keeping with the bilateral presentation of "METAPHOR" on the KP Chart. Metaphor, though, comes last and not first here, as it would for the diachronic dead metaphor which flattens into meaning. That is to say, the "re-" factor assumes parasitic overtones by drawing on "-description" once this has been destandardized through deconstruction. In an article of yet another collaborative journal issue, *Critical Inquiry*, Ricoeur's own deconstructionist focus lapses tacitly into Fregean nondenoting as he attempts to deal with a "metaphorical process." That is of course always the last resort and in this case may be symptomatic of the faculties the title of the article lists for such a process: "cognition, imagination, and feeling"--mean nothing unless systematically delineated as capacities that implement linguistic activity. The content of the article (1978, pp. 146, 152-154) has instead as its main thesis a linguistic self-effacement paralleling Derrida's; it is offered in a series of epithets ranging from a "self-abolition" and "collapse" to a "suspension" that the regular or literal meaning undergoes when, ceasing to denote, a (redescribing) metaphor takes over.

Close in idea to Ricoeur's redescription is Riffaterre's "rewriting" (1978, p. 54). Riffaterre assumes that language becomes relieved of its "arbitrariness in the extreme" when it

substitutes for these symbols icons or 'ideograms' that seem to explain or legitimate the relationships they symbolize by rewriting them in the code of the words linked by these relationships.

As has been pointed out all along, language is always "absolute" instead of "arbitrary," is always willed and never accidental. Riffaterre's "re-" factor also becomes parasitic here as it relies on a pronounced sartorial gloss of "icons" and "ideograms." My analyses proved, however, that function alone creates all "relationships" which in turn make "iconic" or "ideogrammatic" the most unobtrusive operative traits, able to convert capitalization and punctuation into types of "poetic hieroglyphs" on the basis of their Rhemic deployment.

There seems to be a further rhetorical influence affecting the re-theories of Ricoeur and Riffaterre, and this link involves yet another Aristotelian concept - "mimesis." Both these critics were well schooled in rhetoric, and they allude to mimesis often enough (Riffaterre, ibid., pp. 19, 37-38; Ricoeur, 1974, pp. 105-110; 1977, p. 7). In Latinized form, this Greek concept emerges as a "representation of reality," which is the translation for the subtitle of Auerbach's *Mimesis* (1957, trans., Trask). The original had "darstellen," which by coincidence is also Ingarden's choice for the "presenting" function of the literary strata, although I dropped the "re-" prefix in my translation in order to elude all nuances of parasitism. A similar afterthought must have occurred to Curtius (1963, p. 398), who first defined mimesis as a "refashioning" and then a "new fashioning."

A second influence, particularly upon Ricoeur, is Nelson Goodman, whom he cites close to offering his redescription (1977, pp. 6, 238-239). Indeed, Goodman's *Languages of Art* (1968) opens auspiciously with a reference to "Reality Remade," and continues on to describe metaphor as a "calculated" category-mistake based on "a migration of concepts, an alienation of categories" (p. 73), which should meet with Ricoeur's approval. Yet Goodman was one of the first critics I quoted to clarify that those esthetic "languages" do not necessarily depend on the word. Consequently, any meaning or metaphor arising from other media would need to be differentiated further.

An ancillary connection in areas of deviationist or deconstructive premises, which Ricoeur also cites intermittently (1977, pp. 158-161, 166-167, 248), is no doubt the Belgian Liège School, or "mu" group, devoted to a modern taxonomy of rhetorical devices. Led by Dubois, Edeline, and Klinkenberg, this group published a *Rhétorique générale* in 1970 where metaphor, under "métasémèmes," has its place among numerous classes dividing various aspects of an anomalous "métabole." Similar endeavors in somewhat less elaborate fashion pertain to Todorov's studies of lexical anomalies, and his essay, "Les anomalies sémantiques" (1966, pp. 100-123), not accidentally cites Chomsky's selection rule. Todorov also went in for "Sa-Se" tables detailing respective breaches in syntax and semantics, in a work entitled, *Littérature et signification* (1967, p. 114; Kloepfer, 1975, pp. 62-64, 68-73; Plett, 1975, pp. 144-147).

Moreover, of special interest is Todorov's article "On Linguistic Symbolism," presented in the same issue on metaphor that commenced with Derrida's white mythology (1974). Todorov aims to differentiate a "propositional symbolism" from a "lexical symbolism"--terms that are gradually whittled down to "discursive" versus "symbolic" usage (1974, pp. 112-118). If "symbolism" paralleled a pure referent that always forms first, while the "propositional" qualifier then applied to an adequated and the "lexical" alternative to a non-adequated usage proceeding from the word (Todorov, p. 112), the dichotomy would have had a systematic base. But although Todorov has an inkling of the purely "verbal" state involved in his lexical symbolism, he gets confused where he adds (ibid.) that some "initial proposition" has to be canceled when such a use takes over.

Tacitly, Todorov's position then equals that of the Fregeans and their skeptical notion that something is missing from literary language. Thus Todorov should realize that "initial" is the pure or his "lexical" referent, as explained with my linguistic *doppelganger* comprising a "propositional" adequation. Not surprisingly, Todorov (pp. 126-127) treats poetic "condensation" as did Levin his poetic "compression," by sensing a prosaic "omission" of reference where Levin tried to recover logical "deletion." Like Levin, Todorov (pp. 113, 127) also invokes "encyclopedic" knowledge, in conjunction with a vague "collective memory" that is insufficiently developed for the complexities of signation.

Paralleling Todorov's linguistic symbolism is deMan's dichotomy of "schematic language" versus "symbolic language" in the last part of his article, "The Epistemology of Metaphor" (1978, pp. 26-30), that appeared also in *Critical Inquiry*. Here "language" is the base, as was Todorov's "symbolism" above, with the "schematic" attributive paralleling Todorov's "propositional" factor and the "symbolic" alternative the latter's "lexical" qualifier. The schematic factor is adapted from the Kantian "schema." In Kant's *First Critique* (1914, Cassirer ed., III, pp. 141-147), this schema constituted the representational content of the otherwise empty categories; in the *Third Critique* (1914, Cassirer ed., V, section 59, pp. 428 ff.), it was pitted as logical judgment against the "symbolic" imagination embodied in esthetic judgment. Although an interesting adaptation, this Kantian dichotomy is not explicated sufficiently in its impact on language. At one point deMan (ibid., pp. 26-27) cites Kant in wondering how a mere "denominative noun" such as a lexical "triangle," for instance, can be "representational" of an abstraction by a "substitutive figure," to the point of becoming fully "adjusted" (angemessen) to it. Well, that type of "adjustment," precisely, Ingarden provided categorically. "Denomination" is the province of meaning and "symbolic" reference is language at its purest; to become "schematic," language must undergo special processing. But deMan (ibid., p. 27), adhering to Kant, stresses that symbolic language is epistemologically "not reliable" and thus gives rise to a metaphorical "translation" (Uebertragung).

No part of language, however, is epistemologically reliable without the adequation process. Yet neither are the epistemological categories "reliable" when determining language, for which reason neo-Aristelians are so unsuccessful in their search for a substantive "metaphor." That is why I also castigated the "motto" for metaphor as "Conceptual Leap," which is quoted from the *Critical*

Inquiry where deMan's essay appeared. Harries (1978, p. 167), who with this leap initiates one entry on "The Many Uses of Metaphor," certainly has jumped into the wrong domain as, in another effort, he turns to "collisions" and "struggles" which are supposedly the lot of "Metaphor and Transcendence" (1978, pp. 73-75, 77, 78, 79, 89). To Harries Metaphor is transcendent because it does not fit into the pattern of logic. Thus he has a need to boost his argument with a poetic line, MacLeash's "A poem should not mean/but be" (p. 77). The line has long been a favorite among critics of language (Burckhardt, 1956, p. 280, Michael Hamburger, 1969, p. 34). Stankiewicz (1974, pp. 636-637), who also cited it, rightly came to the conclusion that it expresses a too narrow view of reference if taken at face value. Indeed, the sole purpose of Legisign validation is to give meanings their "being" without which no act of meaning can become actualized either.

To cite Jeremy Bentham (1748-1832), "Error is never so difficult to be destroyed as when it has its root in language." Amen! Bentham's statement was quoted in the *The Meaning of Meaning* by Ogden and Richards. Language, analyzed theoretically by the neo-Aristotelians' meaning of meaning, has indeed remained a "red herring" unleashing a good many "phony issues." When will critics, like that Calder scientist in the age of Einstein, penetrate to the equivalent of the cool red, no matter what their sensation tells them?

Let me give Nelson Goodman the last word since he had the first: a page he includes in his *Languages of Art* (1968) projects the word "red" in all the colors of the rainbow. Admittedly, the schematic material content, in Ingarden's understanding of the term, does not "give" speakers the real color, and yet this semantic "color" preserves its meaning in all the chromatic changes. Skeptics of language who type-trespass from ontic heteronomy into ontic autonomy may seize on the chromatic hybrid, perhaps "red" in shades of green or blue. But critics of language who probe their native competence introspectively know that the power of speech is glued to the sonorous and visual Qualisigns in "r-e-d." No real color can eradicate these signs. As long as the language lives in full generation, Sinsign composites and validated Legisigns take shape, leading from them to Icons and their indentations, the Indexes. These critics know that "red" first establishes positive-privative contiguities with other words in one language, and not merely with the colors of the spectrum.

With "things" and their classes I cannot speak, nor can I express my thoughts before I have grappled with the "thought" which is rooted exclusively in the words of my choice. These vehicles I specified and analyzed from every aspect and use; they alone brought my own work together in adequated sentences, "literalizing" forms through their function, be their surface plain or poetic. Non-Aristotelian semantics has met its goal, in the hope that "post-Aristotelians" of the new millennium will be able to continue on from there.

Bibliography

Books, Published and Unpublished Dissertations, Master Theses

Ades, Dawn. *Dada and Surrealism*. London: Thames and Hudson, 1974.

Adler, Emil. *Herder und die deutsche Aufklärung*. Wien, Frankfurt: Europa, 1968.

Adler, Mortimer J. *Dialectic*. New York: Harcourt, Brace and Company, 1927.

Anscombe, G. E. M., and P. T. Geach. *Three Philosophers*. Ithaca, New York: Cornell University Press, 1961.

Anshen, Ruth Nanda, ed. *Language: An Enquiry into its Meaning and Function*. Port Washington, New York, London: Kennikat Press, 1971.

Aristotle. *Aristotle In Twenty-Three Volumes*. Vol. I: *The Categories, On Interpretation*. Trans. Harold P. Cooke. The Loeb Classical Library. Cambridge: Harvard University Press; London: William Heinemann, 1973.

——. *Aristotle In Twenty-Three Volumes*. Vol. XIX: *The Nicomachean Ethics*. Trans. H. Rackham. Ed. Loeb. Cambridge: Harvard University Press; London: William Heinemann, 1975.

——. *Aristotle In Twenty-Three Volumes*. Vol. XVII: *The Metaphysics, Books I-IX*. Trans. Hugh Tredennick. Ed. Loeb. Cambridge: Harvard University Press; London: William Heinemann, 1975.

——. (Poetics):

——. *Aristotelis: De Arte Poetica Liber*. Ed. and trans. Rudolf Kassel. Oxford: The Clarendon Press, 1965.

——. *Aristotle, On the Art of Poetry*. Trans. Ingram Bywater. Oxford: The Clarendon Press, 1909.

——. *Aristotle: On Poetry and Style*. Ed. and trans. G. M. A. Grube. New York: Liberal Arts Press, 1958.

——. *Aristotle's Art of Poetry: A Greek View of Poetry and Drama*. Trans. Ingram Bywater. Ed. W. Hamilton Fyfe. Oxford: The Clarendon Press, 1966.

——. *Aristotle's Theory of Poetry and Fine Art: With a Critical Text and Translation of the Poetics*. Ed. and trans. S. H. Butcher. New York: Dover Publications, 1951.

——. *The Poetics*. Trans. W. Hamilton Fyfe. Ed. Loeb. London: William Heinemann; Cambridge: Harvard University Press, 1960.

——. (Rhetoric):

——. *The "Art" of Rhetoric*. Trans. John Henry Freese. Ed. Loeb. London: William Heinemann; Cambridge: Harvard University Press, 1959.

——. *The Rhetoric of Aristotle*. Ed. Lane Cooper. New York, London: Appleton-Century, 1932.

————. *Topica*. Trans. E. S. Forster. Ed. Loeb. London: William Heinemann; Cambridge: Harvard University Press, 1966.

Auerbach, Erich. *Mimesis: The Representation of Reality in Western Literature*. Trans. Willard Trask. Garden City, New York: Doubleday, 1957.

Austin, J. L. *How to Do Things with Words: The William James Lectures delivered at Harvard University*. Cambridge: Harvard University Press, 1975.

Baeumler, Alfred. *Kants Kritik der Urteilskraft—Ihre Geschichte und Systematik*. Halle-Salle: Max Niemeyer, 1923.

Barfield, Owen. *Poetic Diction: A Study in Meaning*. London: Faber and Gwyer, 1928.

————. *Speaker's Meaning*. Middletown: Wesleyan University Press, 1967.

Beardsley, Monroe. *Aesthetics: Problems in the Philosophy of Criticism*. New York: Harcourt, Brace and World, 1958.

Benjamin, Walter. *Gesammelte Schriften*. Vol. I-II. Ed. Rolf Tiedemann and Hermann Schweppenhauser. Frankfurt a M: Suhrkamp, 1974.

Benn, Gottfried. *Gesammelte Werke in Vier Bänden*. Vol. I: *Essays, Reden, Vorträge*. Ed. Dieter Wellershoff. Wiesbaden: Limes, 1965.

Bentley, Eric, ed. *The Storm Over the Deputy*. New York: Grove Press, 1964.

Bense, Max. *Aesthetica: Einführung in die Neue Aesthetik*. Baden-Baden: Agis-Verlag, 1965.

————. *Zeichen und Design: Semiotische Aesthetik*. Baden-Baden: Agis-Verlag, 1971.

————, and Elisabeth Walthers, ed. *Wörterbuch der Semiotik*. Köln: Kiepenheuer and Witsch, 1973.

Berlin, Isaiah. *Vico and Herder: Two Studies in the History of Ideas*. New York: The Viking Press, 1976.

Black, Max. *Models and Metaphors: Studies in Language and Philosophy*. Ithaca: Cornell University Press, 1962.

Bloomfield, Leonard. *Language*. New York: Holt, Rinehart and Winston, 1962.

Blumensath, Heinz, ed. *Strukturalismus in der Literaturwissenschaft*. Köln: Kiepenheuer and Witsch, 1972.

Bolinger, Dwight. *Aspects of Language*. 2nd ed. New York: Harcourt, Brace, Jovanovich, 1968.

Borgis, Ilona. "Das semantische Problem der Metapher: Ursachen und Varianten eines Scheinproblems." Diss. Universität Hamburg 1972.

Bouterwek, Friedrich. *Aesthetik: Zweiter Theil*. Göttingen: Vandenhoeck und Ruprecht. 1825; rpt. Brussels: Culture et Civilization, 1969.

Bréal, Michel. *Essai de Sémantique: Science des Significations*. 3rd ed. Paris: Librairie Hachette, 1904.

Trans. Mrs. Henry Cust. *Semantics: Studies in the Science of Meaning*. New York: Dover Publications, 1964.

Brecht, Bertolt. *Gedichte: 1934-1941*. Vol. IV. Frankfurt a M: Suhrkamp, 1961.

————. *Hauspostille: Mit Anleitungen, Gesangsnoten und Einem Anhang*. Berlin, Frankfurt a M: Suhrkamp, 1963.

Brekle, Herbert E. *Semantik: Eine Einführung in die sprachwissenschaftliche Bedeutungslehre*. München: Wilhelm Fink, 1972.

Breuer, Dieter. *Einführung in die pragmatische Texttheorie*. München: Wilhelm Fink, 1974.

Brinkmann, Diedrich. *Die Metaphern: Studien über den Geist der modernen Sprachen.* Vol. I: *Die Thierbilder der Sprache.* Bonn: Adolph Marcus, 1878.

Brooke-Rose, Christine. *A Grammar of Metaphor.* London: Secker and Warburg, 1958.

Brooks, Cleanth. *The Well Wrought Urn: Studies in the Structure of Poetry.* New York: Harcourt, Brace and World, 1947.

Brown, Roger. *Words and Things.* Glencoe, Illinois: The Free Press, 1958.

Bruns, Gerald L. *Modern Poetry and the Idea of Language: A Critical and Historical Study.* New Haven, London: Yale University Press, 1975.

Bühler, Karl. *Sprachtheorie; die Darstellungsfunktion der Sprache.* Jena: Gustav Fischer, 1934.

Calder, Nigel. *Einstein's Universe.* New York: The Viking Press, 1979.

Cameron, Sharon. *Lyric Time: Dickinson and the Limits of Genre.* Baltimore, London: Johns Hopkins University Press, 1979.

Cassirer, Ernst. *Idee und Gestalt: Goethe-Schiller-Hölderlin-Kleist.* Darmstadt: Wissenschaftliche Buchgesellschaft, 1975.

———. *Immanuel Kants Werke.* Ed. Ernst Cassirer. Vol. XI: *Kants Leben und Lehre.* Berlin: Bruno Cassirer, 1918.

———. *The Philosophy of the Enlightenment.* Trans. Fritz C. A. Koelin and James P. Pettegrove. Boston: Beacon Press, 1965.

———. *Philosophie der symbolischen Formen, Erster Teil: Die Sprache.* Darmstadt: Wissenschaftliche Buchgesellschaft, 1972.

Trans. Ralph Manheim. *The Philosophy of Symbolic Forms. I. Volume One: Language.* New Haven: Yale University Press, 1961.

———. *Philosophie der symbolischen Formen. II. Zweiter Teil: Das mythische Denken.* Darmstadt: Wissenschaftliche Buchgesellschaft, 1969.

Trans. Ralph Manheim. *The Philosophy of Symbolic Forms. II. Volume Two: Mythical Thought.* New Haven: Yale University Press, 1960.

Celan, Paul. *Mohn und Gedächtnis.* Stuttgart: Deutsche Verlags-Anstalt, 1970.

Chafe, Wallace L. *Meaning and the Structure of Language.* Chicago: University of Chicago Press, 1970.

Chomsky, Noam. *Aspects of the Theory of Syntax.* Cambridge: The MIT Press, 1965.

———. *Cartesian Linguistics: A Chapter in the History of Rationalist Thought.* New York, London: Harper and Row, 1966.

———. *Language and Mind.* New York, Chicago: Harcourt, Brace and Jovanovich, 1972.

Church, Richard, ed. *Essays by Divers Hands: Being the Transactions of the Royal Society of Literature.* London, New York: Oxford University Press, 1965.

Cicero. *De Oratore: In Two Volumes.* Vol. II: *Book III.* Trans. H. Rackman. Ed. Loeb. London: William Heinemann; Cambridge: Harvard University Press, 1960.

Clark, Robert T. *Herder: His Life and Thought.* Berkeley, Los Angeles: University of California Press, 1969.

Corti, Maria. *An Introduction to Literary Semiotics.* Trans. Margherita Bogat and Allen Mandelbaum. Bloomington: Indiana University Press, 1978.

Crane, R. S., et al., eds. Critics and Criticism: Ancient and Modern. Chicago: University of Chicago Press, 1952.

Crystal, David. Linguistics. Harmondsworth, England: Penguin Books, 1971.

Culler, Jonathan. Structuralist Poetics: Structuralism, Linguistics and the Study of Literature. Ithaca: Cornell University Press, 1975.

Curtius, Ernst Robert. European Literature and the Latin Middle Ages. Trans. Willard R. Trask. New York, Evanston: Harper and Row, 1963.

Davis, Donald. Articulate Energy--An Inquiry into the Syntax of English Poetry. London: Routledge and Paul, 1955.

Davidson, Donald, and Gilbert Harman, eds. Semantics of Natural Language. 2nd ed. Dordrecht, Holland: D. Reidel Publishing Company, 1972.

Darmsteter, Arsène. La vie de mots: études dans leurs significations. Paris: 1950.

Demetz, Peter, ed. Brecht: A Collection of Critical Essays. New Jersey: Prentice-Hall, 1962.

―――, Thomas Greene, and Lowry Nelson, Jr., eds. The Disciplines of Criticism: Essays in Literary Theory, Interpretation, and History. New Haven, London: Yale University Press, 1968.

de Saussure, Ferdinand. Course in General Linguistics. Ed. Charles Bally, Albert Sechehaye, et al. Trans. Wade Baskin. New York, Toronto: McGraw Hill, 1966.

Dickinson, Emily. The Complete Poems of Emily Dickinson. Ed. Thomas H. Johnson. Boston, Toronto: Little, Brown and Company, 1960.

―――. The Complete Poems of Emily Dickinson. Ed. Thomas H. Johnson. London: Faber and Faber, 1975.

―――. The Poems of Emily Dickinson: Including Variant Readings Critically Compared with all Known Manuscripts. Volume II. Ed. Thomas H. Johnson. Cambridge: The Belknap Press, Harvard University Press, 1955.

Diels, Hermann. Die Fragmente der Vorsokratiker: Griechisch und Deutsch. 6th ed. Vol. I. Berlin, Grünewald: Weidmannsche Verlagsbuchhandlung, 1951.

Domin, Hilde. Wozu Lyrik heute: Dichtung und Leser in der gesteuerten Gesellschaft. München: R. Piper and Company, 1975.

Dressler, Wolfgang. Einführung in die Textlinguistik. Tübingen: Max Niemeyer, 1972.

Dubrow, Heather. Genre. London, New York: Methuen, 1982.

Eco, Umberto. Einführung in die Semiotik: Autorisierte deutsche Ausgabe von Jürgen Trabant. München: Wilhelm Fink, 1972.

Ehrmann, Jacques, ed. Structuralism. Garden City, New York: Doubleday and and Company, 1966.

Eliot, T. S. The Waste Land: A Fascimile and Transcript of the Original Drafts Including the Annotations of Ezra Pound. Ed. Valerie Eliot. New York: Harcourt, Brace and Jovanovich, 1971.

Else, Gerald F. Aristotle's Poetics: The Argument. Cambridge: Harvard University Press, 1967.

Embler, Weller. Metaphor and Meaning. DeLand, Florida: Everett Edwards, 1966.

Empson, William. Seven Types of Ambiguity. 2nd ed. Edinburgh: T. and A. Constable, 1947.

Ernst, Max. *Une semaine de bonté: A Surrealist Novel in College*. New York: Dover Publications, 1976.

Erwin, Edward. *The Concept of Meaningless*. Baltimore, London: Johns Hopkins Press, 1970.

Esper, Erwin A. *Mentalism and Objectivism in Linguistics: The Sources of Leonard Bloomfield's Psychology of Language*. New York: American Elsevier, 1968.

Essays on J. L. Austin. Ed. G. J. Warnock. Oxford: Clarendon Press, 1973.

Esslin, Martin. *Brecht: The Man and His Work*. New York: Anchor Books, Doubleday and Company, 1971.

————. *Jenseits des Absurden: Aufsätze zum modernen Drama*. Wien: Europaverlag, 1972.

Falk, Eugene H. *The Poetics of Roman Ingarden*. Chapel Hill: The University of North Carolina Press, 1981.

Feibleman, James K. *An Introduction to Peirce's Philosophy: Interpreted as a System*. London: George Allen and Unwin, 1960.

Fichte, Johann Gottlieb. *Erste und zweite Einleitung in die Wissenschaftslehre und Versuch einer neuen Darstellung der Wissenschaftslehre*. Ed. Fritz Medicus. Hamburg: Felix Meiner, 1961.

Fitzgerald, John J. *Peirce's Theory of Signs as Foundation for Pragmatism*. The Hague, Paris: Mouton, 1966.

Flew, Antony, ed. *Logic and Language*. 1st ser. Oxford: Basil Blackwell, 1963.

————, ed. *Logic and Language*. 2nd ser. Oxford: Basil Blackwell, 1961.

Fobes, Francis H. *Philosophical Greek: An Introduction*. Chicago, London: University of Chicago Press, 1966.

Foulkes, A. P., ed. *The Uses of Criticism*. Bern: Herbert Lang; Frankfurt a M: Peter Lang, 1976.

Fowler, Roger, ed. *Essays on Style and Language: Linguistic and Critical Approaches to Literary Style*. London: Routledge and Kegan Paul, 1966.

Freeman, Donald C., ed. *Linguistics and Literary Style*. New York, Chicago: Holt, Rinehart and Winston, 1976.

Freeman, Kathleen. *The Pre-Socratic Philosophers: A Companion to Diels, "Fragmente der Vorsokratiker."* Oxford: Basil Blackwell, 1946.

Friedrich, Hugo. *Die Struktur der modernen Lyrik: Von Baudelaire bis zur Gegenwart*. Hamburg: Rowohlt, 1965.

Frye, Northrop. *Anatomy of Criticism: Four Essays*. New York: Atheneum, 1967.

Furberg, Mats. *Saying and Meaning: A Main Theme in J. L. Austin's Philosophy*. Totowa, New Jersey: Rowman and Littlefield, 1971.

Gabriel, Gottfried. *Fiktion und Wahrheit: Eine semantische Theorie der Literatur*. Stuttgart-Bad Cannstatt: Friedrich Fromann, 1975.

Gadamer, Hans-Georg. *Wahrheit und Methode*. Tübingen: J. C. B. Mohr, 1960.

Garvin, Paul L., ed. *A Prague School Reader on Esthetics, Literary Structure, and Style*. Washington: Georgetown University Press, 1964.

Gasset, Jose Ortega Y. *The Dehumanization of Art and Other Essays on Art, Culture, and Literature*. Princeton: Princeton University Press, 1968.

Gauger, Hans-Martin. *Wort und Spache: Sprachwissenschaftliche Grundfragen*. Tübingen: Max Niemeyer, 1970.

Geach, Peter, and Max Black, eds. *Translations from the Philosophical Writings of Gottlob Frege.* Oxford: Basil Blackwell, 1960.

George, Stefan. *Werke: Ausgabe in Zwei Bänden.* München and Düsseldorf: Helmut Kupper, 1958.

Gerber, Gustav. *Sprache als Kunst.* Vol. I. Bromberg: Mittler'sche Buchhandlung, 1871.

————. *Sprache als Kunst.* Vol. II. Bromberg: Mittler'sche Buchhandlung, 1873.

————. *Sprache als Kunst.* Rpt. Hildescheim: Georg Olms, 1961.

Gerhardt, Marlis, ed. *Linguistik und Sprachphilosophie.* München: List, 1974.

Giannarás, Anastasios, ed. *Aesthetik heute: Sieben Vorträge.* München: Francke, 1974.

Gilson, Etienne. *History of Christian Philosophy in the Middle Ages.* New York: Random House, 1955.

————. *The Spirit of Medieval Philosophy: Gilford Lectures 1931-1932.* Trans. A. H. C. Downes. New York: Charles Scribner's Sons, 1936.

Goethe, Johann Wolfgang von. *Goethes Werke: Hamburger Ausgabe in vierzehn Bänden.* 7th ed. Vol. II. Ed. Erich Trunz. Hamburg: Christian Wegner, 1965.

Goodman, Nelson. *Languages of Art: An Approach to a Theory of Symbols.* Indianapolis, New York: The Bobbs-Merrill Company, 1968.

Goodman, Paul. *Speaking and Language: Defense of Poetry.* New York: Random House, 1971.

Gottschall, R. von. *Poetik: Die Dichtkunst und ihre Technik Vom Standpunkte der Neuzeit.* Breslau: 1882.

Grene, Marjorie. *A Portrait of Aristotle.* Chicago: The University of Chicago Press, 1963.

Gumpel, Liselotte. *"Concrete" Poetry from East and West Germany: The Language of Exemplarism and Experimentalism.* New Haven, London: Yale University Press, 1976.

————. *"Metaphor as Nominalized Meaning: A Phenomenological Analysis of the Lyrical Genre."* Diss. Stanford University 1971.

Gunzenhäuser, Rul, and Helmut Kreuzer. *Mathematik und Dichtung: Versuche zur Frage einer exakten Literaturwissenschaft.* München: Nymphenburger Verlagshandlung, 1965.

Habermas, Jürgen, and Miklas Luhmann. *Theorie-Diskussion: Theorie der Gesellschaft oder Sozialtechnologie--Was leistet die Systemforschung?* Frankfurt a M: Suhrkamp, 1971.

Hallett, Garth. *A Companion to Wittgenstein's "Philosophical Investigations."* Ithaca, London: Cornell University Press, 1977.

Hamburger, Käte. *Die Logik der Dichtung.* 2nd ed. Stuttgart: Ernst Klett, 1968. Trans. Marilynn J. Rose. *The Logic of Literature.* Bloomington, London: Indiana University Press, 1973.

————. *Philosophie der Dichter: Novalis, Schiller, Rilke.* Stuttgart: W. Kohlhammer, 1966.

————. *Wahrheit und aesthetische Wahrheit.* Stuttgart: Ernst Klett, 1979.

Hamburger, Michael. *The Truth of Poetry: Tensions in Modern Poetry from Baudelaire to the 1960's.* New York: Harcourt, and World, Brace 1969.

————, ed. and trans. *German Poetry 1910-1975.* New York: Urizen Books, 1976.

———, and Christopher Middleton, eds. and trans. *Modern German Poetry 1910-1960: An Anthology with Verse Translations.* New York: Grove Press, 1964.

Handke, Peter. *Stücke I.* Frankfurt a M: Suhrkamp, 1972.

Trans. Michael Roloff. *Kaspar and Other Plays.* New York: Farrar, Straus and Giroux, 1974.

Hardt, Manfred. *Poetik und Semiotik: Das Zeichensystem der Dichtung.* Tübingen: Max Niemeyer, 1976.

Hartmann, Nicolai. *Aesthetik.* Berlin: Walter DeGruyter, 1953.

Hawkes, Terence. *Metaphor.* London: Methuen, 1972.

———. *Structuralism and Semiotics.* London: Methuen, 1977.

Haym, Rudolf. *Die Romantische Schule: Ein Beitrag zur Geschichte des Deutschen Geistes.* Hildesheim: Georg Olms Verlagsbuchhandlung, 1961.

Hegel, Georg Wilhelm Friedrich. *Aesthetik.* Vol. I. Frankfurt a/M: Europäische Verlagsanstalt, 1955.

———. *Aesthetik.* Vol. II. Frankfurt a M: Europäische Verlagsanstalt, 1955.

Heidegger, Martin. *Holzwege.* Frankfurt a/M: Vittorio Klostermann, 1952.

———. *Kant and the Problem of Metaphysics.* Trans. James S. Churchill. Bloomington: Indiana University Press, 1962.

———. *Ueber den Humanismus.* Frankfurt a/M: Vittorio Klostermann, 1949.

———. *Unterwegs zur Sprache.* Pfullingen: Günther Neske, 1959.

Helbig, Gerhard. *Geschichte der neueren Sprachwissenschaft.* Reinbek bei Hamburg: Rowohlt, 1970.

Held, Karl. *Kommunikationsforschung—Wissenschaft oder Ideologie? Materialien zur Kritik einer neuen Wissenschaft.* München: Carl Hanser, 1973.

Hempfer, Klaus W. *Gattungstheorie: Information and Synthese.* München: Wilhelm Fink, 1973.

Hendel, Charles W. *The Philosophy of Kant and Our Modern World—Four Lectures Delivered at Yale University Commemorating the 150th Anniversary of the Death of Immanuel Kant.* New York: The Liberal Arts Press, 1957.

Henle, Paul, ed. *Language, Thought, and Culture.* Ann Arbor: University of Michigan Press, 1966.

Herder, Johann Gottfried von. *Abhandlung über den Ursprung der Sprache.* Berlin: Akademie-Verlag, 1959.

Hester, Marcus B. *The Meaning of Poetic Metaphor: An Analysis in the Light of Wittgenstein's Claim that Meaning is Use.* The Hague, Paris: Mouton, 1967.

Hirdt, Willi. *Studien zur Metaphorik Lamartines: Die Bedeutung der Innen Aussen-Vorstellung.* München: Wilhelm Fink, 1967.

Hirsch, E. D., Jr. *The Aims of Interpretation.* Chicago, London: The University of Chicago Press, 1976.

———. *Validity in Interpretation.* New Haven, London: Yale University Press, 1967.

Hochhuth, Rolf. *Der Stellvertreter: Ein christliches Trauerspiel.* Hamburg: Rowohlt, 1974.

Trans. Richard and Clara Winston. *The Deputy.* New York: Grove Press, 1978.

Hocke, Gustav René. *Manierismus in der Literatur: Sprach-Alchimie und esoterische Kombinationskunst.* Reinbeck bei Hamburg: Rowohlt, 1959.

Hook, Sidney, ed. *Language and Philosophy: A Symposium.* New York: New York University Press; London: University of London Press, 1969.

Humboldt, Wilhelm von. *Werke in fünf Bänden.* Vol. III: *Schriften zur Sprachphilosophie.* Ed. Andreas Flitner and Klaus Giel. Stuttgart: J. G. Buchhandlung, 1963.

Husserl, Edmund. *Cartesian Meditations: An Introduction to Phenomenology.* Trans. Dorion Cairns. The Hague, Paris: Martinus Nijhoff, 1960.

————. *Ideas:General Introduction to Pure Phenomenology.* Trans. W. R. Boyce Gibson. London: George Allen and Unwin; New York: The MacMillan Company, 1958.

————. *The Phenomenology of Internal Time-Consciousness.* Trans. James S. Churchill. Ed. Martin Heidegger. Bloomington, London: Indiana University Press, 1971.

————, ed. *Jahrbuch für Philosophie und phänomenologische Forschung.* Halle: Max Niemeyer, 1925.

Ingarden, Roman. "A Priori Knowledge in Kant vs. A Priori Knowledge in Husserl." Diss. Autumn, 1973.

————. *Gegenstand und Aufgaben der Literaturwissenschaft: Aufsätze und Diskussionsbeiträge 1937-1964.* Ed. Rolf Fieguth. Tübingen: Max Niemeyer, 1976.

————. *Das literarische Kunstwerk.* 3rd ed. Tübingen: Max Niemeyer, 1965. Trans. George C. Grabowicz. *The Literary Work of Art: An Investigation on the Borderlines of Ontology, Logic and Theory of Literature.* Evanston: Northwestern University Press, 1973.

————. *Vom Erkennen des literarischen Kunstwerks.* Tübingen: Max Niemeyer, 1968. Trans. Ruth Ann Crowley and Kenneth R. Olson. *The Cognition of the Literary Work of Art.* Evanston: Northwestern University Press, 1973.

The Interlinear Greek-English New Testament. Trans. Alfred Marshall. London: Samuel Bagster and Sons, 1966.

Ivić Milka. *Wege der Sprachwissenschaft.* Trans. Matthias Rammelmeyer. München: Max Hueber, 1971.

Jakobson, Roman. *Aufsätze zur Linguistik und Poetik.* Ed. Wolfgang Raible. München: Nymphenburger Verlagshandlung, 1974.

————, Gunnar M. Fant, and Morris Halle. *Preliminaries to Speech Analysis: The Distinctive Features and Their Correlates.* Cambridge: MIT Press, 1965.

————and Morris Halle. *Fundamentals of Language. Janua Linguarum.* Vol. 1. 'S-Gravenhage: Mouton, 1956.

Johnson, Mark, ed. *Philosophical Perspectives on Metaphor.* Minneapolis: University of Minnesota Press, 1981.

Jolles, Matthijs. *Deutsche Beiträge zur Geistigen Ueberlieferung.* Bern: Francke, 1957.

Jost, Leonhard. *Sprache als Werk und wirkende Kraft: Ein Beitrag zur Geschichte und Kritik der energetischen Sprachauffassung seit Wilhelm von Humboldt.* Sprache und Dichtung, 6. Bern: Paul Haupt, 1960.

Kant, Immanuel. *Immanuel Kants Werke.* Ed. Ernst Cassirer. Vol. III: *Kritik der reinen Vernunft.* Berlin: Bruno Cassirer, 1913.
Ed. Ingeborg Heidemann. *Kritik der reinen Vernunft.* Stuttgart: Philipp Reclam Jun., 1966.
———. *Immanuel Kants Werke.* Ed. Ernst Cassirer. Vol. IV: *Schriften von 1783-1788.* Berlin: Bruno Cassirer, 1913.
———. *Immanuel Kants Werke.* Ed. Ernst Cassirer. Vol. V: *Kritik der praktischen Vernunft, Erste Einleitung in die Kritik der Urteilskraft,* Kritik der Urteilskraft. Berlin: Bruno Cassirer, 1914.
Ed. Gerhard Lehmann. *Kritik der Urteilskraft.* Stuttgart: Philipp Reclam Jun., 1963.
Trans. James Creed Meredith. *The Critique of Judgement.* Oxford: Clarendon Press, 1961.
———. *Prolegomena: zu einer jeden künftigen Metaphysik, die als Wissenschaft wird auftreten können.* Ed. Karl Vorländer. Hamburg: Felix Meiner, 1965.
Katz, Jerrold J. *The Philosophy of Language.* New York, London: Harper and Row, 1966.
———. *The Underlying Reality of Language and Its Philosophical Import.* New York, Evanston: Harper and Row, 1971.
Kayser, Wolfgang. *Das Sprachliche Kunstwerk: Eine Einführung in die Literaturwissenschaft.* 9th ed. Bern, München: Francke, 1963.
Kermode, Frank. *Puzzles and Epiphanies: Essays and Reviews 1958-1961.* London: Routledge and Kegan Paul, 1963.
Kern, Iso. *Husserl und Kant: Eine Untersuchung über Husserls Verhältnis zu Kant and zum Neukantianismus.* Den Haag: Martinus Nijhoff, 1964.
Kevelson, Robert. *The Inverted Pyramid: An Introduction to a Semiotics of Language.* Studies in Semiotics. Bloomington: Indiana University Press; Lisse: The Peter DeRidder Press, 1977.
Kher, Inder Nath. *The Landscape of Absence: Emily Dickinson's Poetry.* New Haven, London: Yale University Press, 1974.
Kiefer, Howard E., and Milton K. Munitz, eds. *Language, Belief, and Metaphysics.* Albany: State University of New York Press, 1970.
Kleist, Heinrich von. *Sämtliche Werke und Briefe.* Vol. I. Ed. Helmut Sembdner. München: Carl Hanser, 1964.
Kloepfer, Rolf. *Poetik und Linguistik: Semiotische Instrumente.* München: Fink, 1975.
Kluckhohn, Paul. *Das Ideengut der Deutschen Romantik.* Tübingen: Max Niemeyer, 1966.
Knights, L. C., and Basil Cottle, eds. *Metaphor and Symbol.* London: Butterworths Scientific Publications, 1960.
Knörrich, Otto. *Die Deutsche Lyrik der Gegenwart: 1945-1970.* Stuttgart: Alfred Kröner, 1971.
Knox, Israel. *The Aesthetic Theories of Kant, Hegel, and Schopenhauer.* New York: The Humanities Press, 1958.
Kockelmans, Joseph J., ed. *Phenomenology: The Philosophy of Edmund Husserl and Its Interpretation.* Garden City, New York: Doubleday and Co., 1967.

Köller, Wilhelm. *Semiotik und Metapher: Untersuchungen zur grammatischen Struktur und kommunikativen Funktion von Metaphern.* Stuttgart: J. B. Metzler Verlagsbuchhandlung, 1975.

Koontz, Harold, and Cyril O'Donnell. *Essentials of Management.* 2nd ed. New York: McGraw Hill, 1978.

Körner, S. *Kant.* Harmondsworth, Middlesex, England: Penguin Books, 1967.

Kostelanetz, Richard, ed. *Visual Literature Criticism: A New Collection.* Carbondale and Edwardsville: Southern Illinois University Press; London, Amsterdam: Feffer and Simons, 1979.

Kraus, Werner. *Werk und Wort: Aufsätze zur Literaturwissenschaft und Wortgeschichte.* Berlin and Weimar: Aufbau-Verlag, 1972.

Krieger, Murray. *The New Apologists for Poetry.* Minneapolis: University of Minnesota Press, 1956.

Kristeva, Julia, Josette Rey-DeBove, et al., eds. *Essays in Semiotics/ Essais de sémiotique.* Approaches to Semiotics, 4. The Hague, Paris: Mouton, 1971.

Kurz, Gerhard, and Theodor Pelster. *Metapher: Theorie und Unterricht.* Düsseldorf: Pädagogischer Verlag Schwann, 1976.

Landmann, Michael. *Die absolute Dichtung: Essais zur philosophischen Poetik.* Stuttgart: Ernst Klett, 1963.

Langendoen, D. Terence, ed. *The London School of Linguistics: A Study of the Linguistic Theories of B. Malinowski and J. R. Firth.* Cambridge: MIT Press, 1968.

Langer, Susanne. *Philosophy in a New Key: A Study in the Symbolism of Reason, Rite, Art.* Cambridge: Harvard University Press, 1960.

Lausberg, Heinrich, ed. *Romanica: Festschrift für Gerhard Rohlfs.* Halle: Niemeyer, 1958.

Leroy, Maurice. *Main Trends in Modern Linguistics.* Trans. Glanville Price. Berkeley, Los Angeles: University of California Press, 1967.

Lessing, Gotthold Ephraim. *Lessings Werke in einem Band.* Ed. Gerhard Stenzel. Salzburg, Stuttgart: Das Bergland Buch, n.d.

Levin, Samuel R. *The Semantics of Metaphor.* Baltimore, London: Johns Hopkins University Press, 1977.

Lieb, Hans-Heinrich. *Sprachstadium und Sprachsystem: Umrisse einer Sprachtheorie.* Stuttgart, Berlin: W. Kohlhammer, 1970.

———. "Der Umfang des historischen Metaphernbegriffs." Diss. Köln 1964.

Lindsay, A. D. *Kant.* Westport, Connecticut: Greenwood Press, 1970.

Link, Jürgen. *Literaturwissenschaftliche Grundbegriffe: Eine Programmierte Einführung auf strukturalistischer Basis.* München: Wilhelm Fink, 1974.

Lohner, Edgar. *Schiller und die moderne Lyrik.* Göttingen: Sachse and Pohl, 1964.

Luther, Martin. *Luthers Werke.* Vol. III. Ed. Arnold Berger. Leipzig, Wien: Bibliographisches Institut, n.d.

———. Trans. Theodore G. Tappert. *Selected Writings of Martin Luther.* Vol. IV: *1529-1546.* Philadelphia: Fortress Press, 1967.

Lyons, John. *Noam Chomsky.* New York: The Viking Press, 1970.

Magliola, Robert R. *Phenomenology and Literature: An Introduction.* Lafayette, Indiana: Purdue University Press, 1977.

Marc-Wogau, Konrad. *Vier Studien zu Kants Kritik der Urteilskraft.* Uppsala: Lundequistska Bokhandeln; Leipzig: Otto Harrassowitz, 1938.

Martinet, André. *Grundzüge der allgemeinen Sprachwissenschaft*. Trans. Anna Fuchs. Stuttgart, Berlin: W. Kohlhammer, 1970.

McNeill, David. *The Acquisition of Language: The Study of Developmental Psycholinguistics*. New York, Evanston: Harper and Row, 1970.

McKeon, Richard, ed. and trans. *Selections from Medieval Philosophers*. Vol. II: *Roger Bacon to William of Ockham*. New York, Chicago: Charles Scribner's Sons, 1930.

Meier, Hugo. *Die Metapher: Versuch einer zusammenfassenden Betrachtung ihrer linguistischen Merkmale*. Winterthur: P. G. Keller, 1963.

Mews, Siegfried, ed. *Studies in German Literature of the Nineteenth and Twentieth Centuries*. Festschrift for Frederic E. Coenen. 2nd ed. Chapel Hill: Univ. of North Carolina Press, 1972.

Mohanty, J. N. *Edmund Husserl's Theory of Meaning*. 2nd ed. Phaenomenologica, 14. The Hague: Martinus Nijhoff, 1969.

Mooij, J. J. A. *A Study of Metaphor: On the Nature of Metaphorical Expressions, with Special Reference to Their Reference*. Amsterdam, New York: North-Holland Publishing Company, 1976.

Morris, Charles W. *Foundations of the Theory of Signs*. International Encyclopedia of Unified Science. Vol. I, No. 2. Chicago: University of Chicago Press, 1938.

Müller-Vollmer, Kurt. *Poesie und Einbildungskraft: Zur Dichtungstheorie Wilhelm von Humboldts*. Stuttgart: J. B. Metzlersche Verlagsbuchhandlung, 1967.

———. *Towards A Phenomenological Theory of Literature: A Study of Wilhelm Dilthey's Poetik*. The Hague, Paris: Mouton, 1963.

Murray, Michael, ed. *Heidegger and Modern Philosophy: Critical Essays*. New Haven, London: Yale University Press, 1978.

New Cassell's German Dictionary: German-English, English-German. New York: Funk and Wagnalls, n.d.

Nieraad, Jürgen. *,Bildgesegnet und Bildverflucht': Forschungen zur sprachlichen Metaphorik*. Darmstadt: Wissenschaftliche Buchgesellschaft, 1977.

Nowottny, Winifred. *The Language Poets Use*. London: The Athlone Press, 1965.

Ockham (Occam), William of. *Ockham's Theory of Terms: Part I of the Summa Logicae*. Ed. and trans. Michael J. Loux. Notre Dame, London: University of Notre Dame Press, 1974.

———. *Philosophical Writings: A Selection*. Ed. and trans. Philotheus Boehner. Edingburgh, London: Thomas Nelson, 1957.

Ogden, C. K., and I. A. Richards. *The Meaning of Meaning: A Study of the Influence of Language upon Thought and of the Science of Symbolism*. 8th ed. New York: Harcourt, Brace and World, 1946.

Orth, Ernst Wolfgang. *Bedeutung, Sinn, Gegenstand: Studien zur Sprachphilosophie Edmund Husserls und Richard Honigswalds*. Conscienta, Studien zur Bewusstseinsphilosophie, 3. Bonn: H. Bouvier, 1967.

Ortony, Andrew, ed. *Metaphor and Thought*. Cambridge, London: Cambridge University Press, 1979.

Paul, Hermann. *Prinzipien der Sprachgeschichte*. 9th ed. Tübingen: Max Niemeyer, 1975.

Pederson, Anna. "The Romanticism of Emily Dickinson." M. A. Thesis University of Minnesota 1944.

Peirce, Charles Sanders. *Collected Papers of Charles Sanders Peirce, Vol. I: Principles of Philosophy, and Vol. II: Elements of Logic.* Ed. Charles Hartshorne and Paul Weiss. Cambridge: The Belknap Press of Harvard University Press, 1960.

―――. *Collected Papers of Charles Sanders Peirce, Vol. III: Exact Logic (Published Papers), and Vol. IV: The Simplest Mathematics.* Ed. Charles Hartshorne and Paul Weiss. Cambridge: Belknap Press of Harvard University Press, 1960.

―――. *Collected Papers of Charles Sanders Peirce, Vol. VIII: Reviews, Correspondence, and Bibliography.* Ed. Arthur W. Burks. Cambridge: Harvard University Press, 1958.

―――. *Philosophical Writings of Peirce.* Ed. Justus Buchler. New York: Dover Publications, 1955.

―――. *Studies in the Philosophy of Charles Sanders Pierce.* Ed. Philip P. Wiener and Frederic H. Young. Cambridge: Harvard University Press, 1952.

Pitcher, George, ed. *Wittgenstein: The Philosophical Investigations: A Collection of Critical Essays.* Ed. George Pitcher. New York: Anchor Books, Doubleday, 1966.

Plato. *Plato in Twelve Volumes.* Vol. IV. Trans. H. N. Fowler. Ed. Loeb. London: William Heinemann; Cambridge: Harvard University Press, 1970.

―――. *Plato in Twelve Volumes.* Vol. IX. Trans. R. G. Bury. Ed. Loeb. Cambridge: Harvard University Press; London: William Heinemann, 1975.

Plett, Heinrich F. *Textwissenschaft und Textanalyse: Semiotik, Linguistik, Rhetorik.* Heidelberg: Quelle und Meyer, 1975.

Pongs, Hermann. *Das Bild in der Dichtung. Vol. I: Versuch einer Morphologie der metaphorischen Formen.* Marburg: N. G. Elwert, 1965.

Porzig, Walter. *Das Wunder der Sprache: Probleme, Methoden und Erebnisse der Sprachwissenschaft.* 6th ed. Ed. Andreas Jecklin and Heinz Rupp. München: Francke, 1975.

Pratt, William, ed. *Modern Poetry in Miniature: The Imagist Poem.* New York: E.P. Dutton, 1963.

Quine, Willard Van Orman. *From a Logical Point of View: Logico-Philosophical Essays.* 2nd ed. Cambridge: Harvard University Press, 1964.

Quintilian. *Quintilian's Institutes of Oratory.* Vol. II. Trans. John Selby Watson. London: George Bell and Sons, 1876.

Trans. H. E. Butler. Ed. *Loeb. Quintilian, In Four Volumes.* Vol. III: *The Institutio Oratoria of Quintilian.* London: William Heinemann; Cambridge: Harvard University Press, 1959.

Randall, John Herman, Jr. *Aristotle.* New York: Columbia University Press, 1960.

Richards, Ivor A. *New and Selected Poems.* Manchester: Carcanet New Press, 1978.

―――. *The Philosophy of Rhetoric.* New York, London: Oxford University Press, 1936.

―――. *Practical Criticism: A Study of Literary Judgment.* 10th ed. London: Routledge and Kegan Paul, 1956.

―――. *Principles of Literary Criticism.* New York: Harcourt, Brace and World, 1925.

Ricoeur, Paul. *Husserl: An Analysis of His Phenomenology.* Trans. Edward G. Ballard and Lester E. Embree. Evanston: Northwestern University Press, 1967.
———. *La métaphore vive.* Paris: Editions du Seuil, 1975.
Trans. Robert Czerny, Kathleen McLaughlin, *et al. The Rule of Metaphor: Multi-disciplinary Studies of the Creation of Meaning in Language.* Toronto, Buffalo: University of Toronto Press, 1977.
Riffaterre, Michael. *Semiotics of Poetry.* Bloomington, London: Indiana University Press, 1978.
Roberts, W. Rhys. *Longinus on the Sublime.* Cambridge: Cambridge University Press, 1935.
Rosenbaum, S. P., ed. *A Concordance to the Poems of Emily Dickinson.* New York: Cornell University Press, 1967.
Ruttkowski, Wolfgang Victor. *Die literarischen Gattungen: Reflexionen über eine modifizierte Fundamentalpoetik.* Bern, München: Franke, 1968.
Ryle, Gilbert. *Collected Papers. Vol. I: Critical Essays.* New York: Barnes and Noble, 1971.
———. *Collected Papers.* Vol. II: *Collected Essays, 1929-1968.* New York: Barnes and Noble, 1971.
———. *The Concept of Mind.* London: Hutchinson and Co., 1949; New York: Barnes and Noble, 1963.
Saussure, Ferdinand de. See: *de* Saussure, Ferdinand.
Schaff, Adam. *Sprache und Erkenntnis und Essays über die Philosophie der Sprache.* Trans. Elida Maria Szarota. Reinbek bei Hamburg: Rowohlt Taschenbuch, 1974.
Scheffler, Israel. *Beyond the Letter: A Philosophical Inquiry Into Ambiguity, Vagueness and Metaphor in Language.* London, Boston: Routledge and Kegan Paul, 1979.
Schelling, Friedrich W. J., von. *Friedrich Wilhelm Joseph von Schellings sämmtliche Werke.* Vol. III: *1799-1800.* Stuttgart, Augsburg: J. G. Cotta'scher Verlag, 1858.
———. *Friedrich Wilhelm Joseph von Schellings sämmtliche Werke.* Vol. VII: *1805-1810.* Stuttgart, Augsburg: J. G. Cotta'scher Verlag, 1860.
Schick, Edgar B. *Metaphorical Organicism in Herder's Early Works: A Study of the Relation of Herder's Literary Idiom to His World-View.* The Hague, Paris: Mouton, 1971.
Schlapp, Otto. *Kants Lehre vom Genie und die Entstehung der Kritik der Urteilskraft.* Göttingen: Vandenhoeck and Ruprecht, 1901.
Schlegel, August Wilhelm. *Kritische Schriften Und Briefe.* Vol. II: *Die Kunstlehre.* Ed. Edgar Lohner. Stuttgart: W. Kohlhammer, 1963.
Schlegel, Friedrich. *Friedrich Schlegel: Kritische Schriften.* Ed. Wolfdietrich Rasch. München: Carl Hanser, 1964.
Schleiermacher, Friedrich. *Hermeneutik.* Ed. Hans Kimmerle and Hans Gadamer. Heidelberg: Carl Winter, 1959.
———. *Ueber die Religion: Reden an die Gebildeten unter ihren Verächtern.* Hamburg: Felix Meiner, 1958.
Schmidt, S. J., ed. *Text Bedeutung Aesthetik.* München: Bayerisches Schulbuch, 1970.

Schnebli-Schwegler, Brigitte. *Johann Gottfried Herders Abhandlung über den Ursprung der Sprache und die Goethe-Zeit*. Winterthur: P. G. Keller, 1965.

Scholes, Robert. *Structuralism in Literature: An Introduction*. New Haven, London: Yale University Press, 1978.

Schon, Donald A. *Displacement of Concepts*. London: Tavistock Publications, 1963.

Schweisthal, Klaus Günther, ed. *Grammatik Kybernetik Kommunikation*. Festschrift für Alfred Hoppe. Bonn: Ferd. Dummlers, 1971.

Searle, John R. *Speech Acts: An Essay in the Philosophy of Language*. Cambridge: Cambridge University Press, 1970.

Sebeok, Thomas A. *Contributions to the Doctrine of Signs*. Studies in Semiotics, 5. Bloomington: Indiana University Press; Lisse: The Peter de Ridder Press, 1976.

―――. *The Sign and Its Masters*. Austin, London: University of Texas Press, 1979.

―――, ed. *Current Trends in Linguistics: Theoretical Foundations*. The Hague, Paris: Mouton, 1966.

―――, ed. *Myth: A Symposium*. Bloomington, London: Indiana University Press, 1955.

―――, ed. *A Perfusion of Signs*. Bloomington, London: Indiana University Press, 1977.

Seidler, Herbert. *Die Dichtung: Wesen, Form und Dasein*. Stuttgart: Alfred Kroner, 1959.

Shakespeare, William. *The Complete Works*. Ed. G. B. Harrison. New York, Burlingame: Harcourt Brace and World, 1952.

Shapiro, Michael, and Marianne Shapiro. *Hierarchy and the Structure of Tropes*. Studies in Semiotics. Ed. Thomas A. Sebeok, 8. Bloomington: Indiana University Press; Lisse: The Peter de Ridder Press, 1976.

Shibles, Warren. *Metaphor: An Annotated Bibliography and History*. Whitewater, Wisconsin: The Language Press, 1971.

―――, ed. *Essays on Metaphor*. Whitewater, Wisconsin: The Language Press, 1972.

Sørenson, Bengt Algot. *Symbol und Symbolismus in den ästhetischen Theorien des 18. Jahrhunderts und der deutschen Romantik*. Kopenhagen: Munksgard, 1963.

Spitzer, Leo. *Hugo Schuchardt-Brevier: Ein Vademekum der allgemeinen Sprachwissenschaft-Als Festgabe zum 80. Geburtstag des Meisters zusammengestellt und eingeleitet*. Halle (Salle): Max Niemeyer, 1922.

Staiger, Emil. *Grundbegriffe der Poetik*. Zürich: Atlantis, 1959.

Steiner, George. *After Babel: Aspects of Language and Translation*. London, Oxford: Oxford University Press, 1975.

―――. *Extra-Territorial: Papers on Literature and the Language Revolution*. New York: Atheneum, 1971.

Steiner, Wendy. *Exact Resemblance to Exact Resemblance: The Literary Portraiture of Gertrude Stein*. New Haven, London: Yale University Press, 1978.

Straus, Erwin W., ed. *Phenomenology: Pure and Applied*. The Lexington Conference. Pittsburgh: Duquesne University Press, 1964.

Tagiuri, Renato, and Luigi Petrullo, eds. *Person Perception and Interpersonal Behavior.* California: Stanford University Press, 1958.

Thiel, Christian. *Sinn und Bedeutung in der Logik Gottlob Freges.* Monographien zur philosophischen Forschung, 43. Meisenhein am Glan: Anton Hain, 1965.

Thomas, Owen. *Metaphor and Related Research.* New York: Random House, 1969.

Thompson, Manley. *The Pragmatic Philosophy of C. S. Peirce.* Chicago: University of Chicago Press, 1963.

Thüsen, Joachim von der. *Erzählbewusstsein und poetische Intelligenz: Beiträge zur Theorie des Romans.* Literaturwissenschaftliche Texte. Theorie und Kritik, No. 1. Ed. Edgar Lohner. Frankfurt a/M: Herbert Lang; Bern: Peter Lang, 1975.

Todorov, Tzvetan. *Littérature et signification.* Paris: Larousse, 1967.

Turbayne, Colin Murray. *The Myth of Metaphor.* New Haven, London: Yale University Press, 1962.

Tuve, Rosemond. *Elizabethan and Metaphysical Imagery: Renaissance Poetic and Twentieth-Century Critics.* Chicago, London: The University of Chicago Press, 1965.

Tymieniecka, Anna-Theresa. *Phenomenology and Science in Contemporary Thought.* New York: The Noonday Press, 1962.

————, ed. *Ingardiana: A Spectrum of Specialized Studies Establishing the Field of Research.* Dordrecht, Holland and Boston: D. Reidel Publishing Company, 1976.

———— and Lawrence Haworth, eds. *The Later Husserl and the Idea of Phenomenology: Idealism-Realism, Historicity and Nature.* Papers and Debate of the International Phenomenological Conference held at the University of Waterloo, Canada, 9-14, April 1969. Dordrecht, Holland: D. Reidel Publishing Co., 1969.

Uehling, Theodore Edward, Jr. *The Notion of Form in Kant's "Critique of Aesthetic Judgment."* The Hague, Paris: Mouton, 1971.

Ullmann, Stephen. *Semantics: An Introduction to the Science of Meaning.* Oxford: Basil Blackwell, 1970.

Vivas, Eliseo. *The Artistic Transaction and Essays on Theory of Literature.* Athens: Ohio State University Press, 1963.

Vygotsky, L. S. *Thought and Language.* Ed. and trans. Eugenia Haufmann and Gertrude Vakar. Cambridge: MIT Press, 1962.

Wackenroder, Wilhelm Heinrich. *Werke und Briefe.* Heidelberg: Lambert Schneider, 1967.

Wallace, Robert, and S. Toole. *Poems on Poetry.* New York: Button, 1965.

Walther, Elisabeth. *Allgemeine Zeichenlehre: Einführung in die Grundlagen der Semiotik.* Stuttgart: Deutsche Verlags-Anstalt, 1974.

Warning, Rainer, ed. *Rezeptionsästhetik: Theorie und Praxis.* München: Wilhelm Fink, 1975.

Waterman, John T. *A History of the German Language: With Special Reference to the Cultural and Social Forces that Shaped the Standard Literary Language.* Seattle, London: University of Washington Press, 1976.

————. *Perspectives in Linguistics.* Chicago, London: University of Chicago Press, 1970.

Watts, Emily Stipes. *The Poetry of American Women from 1932 to 1945*. Austin, London: University of Texas Press, 1977.

Wellek, René. *Concepts of Criticism*. Ed. Stephen G. Nichols, Jr. New Haven, London: Yale University Press, 1965.

Werner, Heinz, ed. *On Expressive Language: Papers Presented at the Clark University Conference on Expressive Language Behavior*. Worchester, Massachusetts: Clark University Press, 1955.

Wheelwright, Philip. *The Burning Fountain: A Study in the Language of Symbolism*. Bloomington: Indiana University Press, 1954.

————. *Metaphor and Reality*. Bloomington, London: Indiana University Press, 1962.

Whitehead, Alfred North. *Symbolism, Its Meaning and Effect*. New York: Macmillan, 1927.

Whitman, Walt. *Leaves of Grass and Selected Prose*. New York: Random House, 1950.

Whitney, George Tapley, and David F. Bowers, eds. *The Heritage of Kant*. New York: Russell and Russell, 1962.

Wienold, Götz. *Semiotik der Literatur*. Frankfurt a/M: Athenaum, 1972.

Willet, John. *The Theatre of Bertolt Brecht: A Study from Eight Aspects*. New York: New Directions, 1964.

Wilpert, Gero von. *Sachwörterbuch der Literatur*. 4th ed. Stuttgart: Alfred Kroner, 1964.

Wimsatt, W. K., and Monroe C. Beardsley. *The Verbal Icon*. Lexington: University of Kentucky Press, 1967.

————, and Cleanth Brooks. *Literary Criticism: A Short History*. New York: Random House, 1957.

Windelband, Wilhelm. *A History of Philosophy*. Vol. I: *Greek, Roman, and Medieval*. Trans. James H. Tufts. New York, Evanston: Harper and Row, 1958.

————. *A History of Philosophy*. Vol. II: *Renaissance, Enlightenment and Modern*. Trans. James H. Tufts. New York: Harper and Row, 1958.

Wittgenstein, Ludwig. *Philosophische Untersuchungen Philosophical Investigations*. Trans. G. E. M. Anscombe. New York: MacMillan, 1963.

————. *Tractatus Logico-Philosophicus*. London: Routledge and Kegan Paul, 1961.

The York Dictionary of English-French-German Literary Terms. York Press, n.p., n.d.

Essays and Articles

Abraham, Werner, and Kurt Braunmüller. "Stil, Metaphor und Pragmatik." *Lingua*, 28 (1971/1972), 19-47.

————. "Towards Theory of Style and Metaphor." *Poetics*, 7 (1973), 103-148.

Adams, E.W. "Metaphor, Simile and Analogy." *The London Quarterly and Holborn Review*, 164 (July 1939), 378-380.

Aldrich, Virgil C. "Pictorial Meaning, Picture-thinking, and Wittgenstein's Theory of Aspects." *Mind*, 67 (January 1958), 70-79.

Also in *Essays on Metaphor*. Ed. Warren Schibles. Whitewater, Wisconsin: The Language Press, 1972, pp. 93-104.

Allemann, Beda. "Die Metapher und das metaphorische Wesen der Sprache." *Weltgespräch*, 4 (1968), 29-43.

Trans. Gunther Rebing. "Metaphor and Antimetaphor." In *Interpretation: The Poetry of Meaning*. Ed. Stanley Romaine Hopper and David L. Miller. New York: Harcourt, Brace and World, 1966, pp. 103-123.

Anshen, Ruth Nanda. "Language as Idea." In *Language: An Enquiry into its Meaning and Function*. Ed. Ruth Nanda Anshen. Port Washington, New York, London: Kennikat Press, 1971, pp. 3-17.

Appel, Wilhelm. "Zeichen und System der Sprache." I. Veröffentlichung des I. Internationalen Symposiums. "Zeichen und System der Sprache." vom 28.9 bis 2.10.1959 in Erfurt. In *Schriften zur Phonetic, Sprachwissenschaft und Kommunikations-forschung*. Berlin: Akademie, 1961, n.p.

Asch, Solomon E. "The Metaphor: A Psychological Inquiry." In *Person Perception and Interpersonal Behavior*. California: Stanford University Press, 1958, pp. 87-94.

Austin, John. "Pretending." In *Essays in Philosophical Psychology*. Ed. Donald Gustafson. Garden City: Anchor Doubleday Books, 1964, pp. 99-116.

Babcock, Sister Mary "Cummings' Typography: An Ideogrammic Style." *Renascence: A Critical Journal of Letters*, 15 (1963), 115-123.

Baker, A. J. "Category Mistakes." *Australian Journal of Philosophy*, 34 (1956), 13-26.

Barthes, Roland. "From Work to Text." In *Textual Strategies: Perspectives in Post-Structuralist Criticism*. Ed. Josué V. Harari. Ithaca, New York: Cornell University Press, 1979, pp. 73-81.

Bateson, F. W. "Linguistics and Literary Criticism." In *The Disciplines of Criticism: Essays in Literary Theory, Interpretation, and History*. Ed. Peter Demetz, Thomas Green and Lowry Nelson, Jr. New Haven, London: Yale University Press, 1968, pp. 3-16.

Baumgärtner, Klaus. "Formale Erklärung poetischerTexte." In *Mathematik und Dichtung: Versuche zur Frage einer exakten Literaturwissenschaft*. Ed. Rul Gunzenhäuser and Helmut Kreuzer. München: Nymphenburger Verlagshandlung, 1965, pp. 67-84.

———. "Der Methodische Stand einer linguistischen Poetik." *Jahrbuch für Internationale Germanistik*, Heft 1 (1969), 15-43.

———. "Sprache, Technik und Dichtung." In *Linguistik und Sprachphilosophie*. Ed. Marlis Gerhardt. München: List, 1974, pp. 171-189.

Baym, Max I. "The Present State of Metaphor." *Books Abroad*, 35 (Summer 1961), 215-219.

Beach, John D. "Analogous Naming, Extrinsic Denomination, and the Real Order." *Modern Schoolman*, 42 (January 1965), 198-212.

Beardsley, Monroe C. "The MetaphoricalTwist." *Philosophy and Phenomenological Research*, 22 (1961-1962), 293-307.

Bentley, Eric. "Introduction." In *The Good Woman of Setzuan* by Bertolt Brecht. New York: Grove Press, 1978, pp. 5-14.

Berggren, Douglas. "The Use and Abuse of Metaphor, II." *Review of Metaphysics*, 16 (December 1962), 237-257.

Berry, Ralph. "The Frontier of Metaphor and Symbol." *British Journal of Aesthetics*, 7 (January 1967), 76-83.

Bezzel, Chris. "Grundprobleme einer poetischen Grammatik." *Linguistische Berichte*, 9 (1970), 1-17.

Bickerton, Derek. "Prolegomena to a Linguistic Theory of Metaphor." *Foundations of Language*, 5 (1969), 34-52.

Bierwisch, Manfred. Poetik und Linguistik." In *Mathematik und Dichtung: Versuche zur Frage einer exakten Literaturwissenschaft*. Ed. Rul Gunzenhäuser and Helmut Kreuzer. München: Nymphenberger Verlagshandlung, 1965, pp. 49-65.

Trans. "Poetics and Linguistics." In *Linguistics and Literary Style*. Ed. Donald C. Freeman. New York, Chicago: Holt, Rinehart and Winston, 1976, pp. 96-115.

Birch, Austin H. "The Abuse of Metaphor." *Hibbert Journal*, 45 (April 1947), 234-240.

Black, Max. "Metaphor." In *Philosophy Looks at the Arts*: Contemporary *Readings in Aesthetics*. Ed. Joseph Margolis. New York: Charles Scribner's Sons, 1962, pp. 218-235.

———. "More about Metaphor." In *Metaphor and Thought*. Ed. Andrew Ortony. Cambridge, London: Cambridge University Press, 1979, pp. 19-43.

Boas, George. "Symbols and History." In *Language: An Enquiry into its Meaning and Function*. New York: Kennikat Press, 1971, pp. 102-121.

Bolinger, Dwight. "The Atomization of Meaning." *Language*, 41 (1965), 555-573.

Bonsiepe, Gui. "Visual-Verbal Rhetoric." In *Essays on Metaphor*. Ed. Warren Shibles. Whitewater, Wisconsin: The Language Press, 1972, pp. 155-161.

Booth, Wayne C. "Ten Literal 'Theses.'" *Critical Inquiry*, 5, No. 1 (Autumn 1978), 175-176.

———. "Metaphor as Rhetoric: The Problem of Evaluation." *Critical Inquiry*, 5, No. 1 (Autumn 1978), 49-72.

Brand, Gerd. "Intentionality, Reduction and Intentional Analysis in Husserl's Later Manuscripts." In *Phenomenology: The Philosophy of Edmund Husserl and Its Interpretation*. Garden City, New York: Doubleday, 1977, pp. 197-217.

Bretall, R. W. "Kant's Theory of the Sublime." In *The Heritage of Kant*. Ed. George Tapley Whitney and David F. Bowers. New York: Russell and Russell, 1962, pp. 279-402.

Brooks, Cleanth. "New Criticism." In *Encyclopedia of Poetry and Poetics*. Ed. Alex Preminger. Princeton: Princeton University Press, 1965, pp. 567-568.

Bruzina, Ronald C. *"Heidegger on the Metaphor and Philosophy."* In *Heidegger and Modern Philosophy: Critical Essays*. Ed. Michael Murray. New Haven, London: Yale University Press, 1978, pp.184-200.

Burckhardt, Sigurd. "The Poet as Fool and Priest." *ELH: A Journal of English Literary History*, 25 (1956), 279-298.

Burke, Kenneth. "Four Master Tropes." *Kenyon Review*, 3 (1941), 421-38.

Campbell, Brenton. "Metaphor, Metonymy, and Literalness." *General Linguistics*, 9, No. 3 (1969), 149-166.

Campbell, Robin, and Roger Wales. "The Study of Language Acquisition." In *New Horizons in Linguistics*. New York: Penguin Press, 1970, pp. 242-260.

Carnap, Rudolf. "The Overcoming of Metaphysics through Logical Analysis of Language." Trans. Arthur Pap. In *Heidegger and Modern Philosophy: Critical Essays*. Ed. Michael Murray. New Haven, London: Yale University Press, 1978, pp. 23-34.

Chisholm, Roderick M. "Fallibilism and Belief." In *Studies in the Philosophy of Charles Sanders Pierce*. Ed. Philip P. Wiener and Frederick H. Young. Cambridge: Harvard University Press, 1952, pp. 93-110.

Cohen, L. Jonathan. "The Semantics of Metaphor." In *Metaphor and Thought*. Ed. Andrew Ortony. Cambridge, London: Cambridge University Press, 1979, pp. 64-77.

Cohen, Ted. "Metaphor and the Cultivation of Intimacy." *Critical Inquiry*, 5, No. 1. (Autumn 1978), 73-90.

Coleman, Elliott. "The Meaning of Metaphor." *The Gordon Review*, 8 (1965), 151-163.

Collins, Douglas C. "Kenning in Anglo-Saxon Poetry." *English Association Essays and Studies*, 12 (1959), 1-7.

Cross, R. C. "Category Differences." *Proceedings of the Aristotelian Society*, 59 (1959), 255-270.

Culler, Jonathan. "Commentary." *New Literary History*, 6, No. 1 (Autumn 1974), 219-29.

Daiches, David. "Myth, Metaphor, and Poetry." In *Essays by Divers Hands: Being the Transactions of the Royal Society of Literature*. Ed. Richard Church. London, New York: Oxford University Press, 1965, pp. 39-55.

Danto, Arthur. "Semantical Vehicles, Understanding, and Innate Ideas." In *Language and Philosophy: A Symposium*. Ed. Sidney Hook. New York: University Press, 1969, pp. 122-137

Davidson, Donald. "On Saying That." *Synthese*, 19 (1968/1969), 130-146.

―――. "Truth and Meaning." *Synthese*, 17 (1967), 304-323.

―――. "What Metaphors Mean." *Critical Inquiry*, 5, No. 1 (Autumn 1978), 31-48.

Davies, Cicely. "Ut Pictura Poesis." *Modern Language Review*, 30 (1935), 159-169.

deMan, Paul. "The Epistemology of Metaphor." *Critical Inquiry*, 5, No. 1 (Autumn 1978), 13-30.

―――. "Nietzsche's Theory of Rhetoric." *Symposium*, 28, No. 1 (1974), 33-51.

―――. "Semiology and Rhetoric." In *Textual Strategies: Perspectives in Post-Structuralist Criticism*. Ed. Josue V. Harari. Ithaca, New York: Cornell University Press, 1979, pp. 121-140.

Derrida, Jacques. "La mythologie blanche: la métaphore dans le texte philosophique." *Poétique*, 5 (1971), 1-52.

Trans. F. C. T. Moore. "White Mythology: Metaphor in the Text of Philosophy." *New Literary History*, 6, No. 1 (Autumn 1974), 5-74.

―――. "The Supplement of Copula: Philosophy Before Linguistics." In *Textual Strategies: Perspectives in Post-Structuralist Criticism*. Ed. Josué V. Harari. Ithaca, New York: Cornell University Press, 1979, pp. 82-120.

Dieckmann, Liselotte. "The Metaphor of Hieroglyphics in German Romanticism." *Comparative Literature*, 7 (Fall 1955), 306-312.

Djik, Teun A., van. "Neuere Entwicklungen in der literarischen Semantik." Trans. Jens Ihwe. In *Literaturwissenschaft und Linguistik*. Vol. III: *Zur linguistischen Basis der Literaturwissenschaft*, II. Ed. Jens Ihwe. Frankfurt a/M: Athenäum, 1972, pp. 153-175.

Dunham, Barrows. "Kant's Theory of Aesthetic Form." In *The Heritage of Kant*. Ed. George Tapley Whitney and David F. Bowers. New York: Russell and Russell, 1962, pp. 359-376.

Edie, James M. "Expression and Metaphor." *Philosophy and Phenomenological Research*, 23 (1963), 538-561.

————. "Vico and Existential Philosophy." In *Giambattista Vico: An International Symposium*. Ed. Giorgio Tagliacozzo. Baltimore: The Johns Hopkins University Press, 1969, pp. 483-495.

Einarsson, Stefan. "Skaldic Poetry." In *A History of Icelandic Literature*. New York: Johns Hopkins University Press, 1957, pp. 44-68.

Elliott, R. K. "Aesthetic Theory and the Experience of Art." *Proceedings of the Aristotelian Society*, 67 (1967), 111-126.

Esslin, Martin. "Brecht's Language and Its Sources." In *Brecht: A Collection of Critical Essays*. Ed. Peter Demetz. New Jersey: Prentice Hall, 1962, pp. 171-183.

Forguson, L. W. "Locutionary and Illocutionary Acts." In *Essays on J. L. Austin*. Oxford: The Clarendon Press, 1973, pp. 160-185.

Foster, Steven. "Eidetic Imagery and Imagiste Perception." *Journal of Aesthetics and Art Criticism*, 28 (Winter 1969), 133-145.

Foucault, Michael. "What is an Author?" In *Textual Strategies: Perspectives in Post-Structuralist Criticism*. Ed. Josué V. Harari. Ithaca, New York: Cornell University Press, 1979, pp. 141-160.

Fowler, Roger. "Linguistic Theory and the Study of Literature." In *Essays on Style and Language: Linguistic and Critical Approaches to Literary Style*. Ed. Roger Fowler. London: Routledge and Kegan Paul, 1966, pp. 1-28.

Frege, Gottlob. "On Sense and Reference." In *Translations from the Philosophical Writings of Gottlob Frege*. Ed. Peter Geach and Max Black. Oxford: Basil Blackwell, 1952, pp. 56-78.

Fruit, John P. "The Evolution of Figure of Speech." *Modern Language Notes*, 3 (1888), 251-253.

Fyfe, Hamilton. "Introduction." In *Aristotle's Art of Poetry: A Greek View of Poetry and Drama*. Ed. W. Hamilton Fyfe. Trans. Ingram Bywater. Oxford: Clarendon Press, 1966, pp. ix-xxxii.

Gadamer, Hans-Georg. "Wirkungsgeschichte und Applikation." In *Rezeptionsästhetik: Theorie und Praxis*. Ed. Rainer Warning. München: Wilhelm Fink, 1975, pp. 113-125.

Gardner, Thomas. "Zum Problem der Metapher." *Deutsche Vierteljahresschrift für Literaturwissenschaft und Geistesgeschichte* 44 (11970), 727-737.

Gassner, John. "Aristotelian Literary Criticism." In *Aristotle's Theory of Poetry and Fine Art*. 4th ed. Ed. S. H. Butcher. New York: Dover Publications, 1951, pp. xxxvii-Lxxvi.

Gerhardt, Marlis. "Wilhelm von Humboldt und die moderne Sprachtheorie." In *Linguistik und Sprachphilosophie*. Ed. Marlis Gerhardt. München: List, 1974, p. 11-27.

Gläser, Rosemarie. "A Structural Approach to Metaphor." *Actes Xe Congrès International des Linguistes Bucarest*, 10/3 (1967), 459-464.

Gray, James. "Abstact & Concrete Imagery." *Essays in Criticism*, 4 (1954), 198-206, 211-212.

Greene, Theodore M. "A Reassessment of Kant's Aesthetic Theory." In *The Heritage of Kant*. Ed. George Tapley Whitney and David F. Bowers. New York: Russell & Russell, 1962, pp. 323-356.

Greene, William C. "Aristotle on Metaphor." *The Classical Weekly*, 39 (January 1946), 94-95.

Greimas, Algirdas J. "La linguistique structurale et la poétique." *Revue des Sciences Sociales*, 19 (1967), 8-16.

Grube, G. M. A. "Aristotle as a Literary Critic." In *Aristotle on Poetry and Style*. Ed. and trans. G. M. A. Grube. New York: The Liberal Arts Press, 1958, pp. ix-xxx.

Gumpel, Liselotte. "The Essence of 'Reality' as a Construct of Language." *Foundations of Language*, 11 (1974), 167-185.

―――. "Metaphor as Nominalized Meaning: A Phenomenological Analysis of the Lyrical Genre." *Jahrbuch für Internationale Germanistik*, 2 (1975), 48-56.

―――. "The Structure of Idioms: A Phenomenological Approach." *Semiotica*, 12 (1974), 1-40.

Gurwitsch, Aron. "On the Intentionality of Consciousness." In *Phenomonology: The Philosophy of Edmund Husserl and Its Interpretation*. Ed. Joseph J. Kockelmans. Garden City, New York: Doubleday, 1967, pp. 118-137.

Hagopian, John V. "Symbol and Metaphor in the Transformation of Reality into Art." *Comparative Literature*, 20 (Winter 1968), 45-54.

Hampshire, Stuart. "The Anology of Feeling." *Mind*, 90, No. 241 (January 1952), 1-12.

Hamrick, William S. "Ingarden on Aesthetic Experience and Aesthetic Object." *Journal of the British Society for Phenomenology*, 5, No. 1 (January 1974), 71-80.

Harari, Josué V. "Critical Factions/Critical Fictions." In *Textual Strategies: Perspectives in Post-Structuralist Criticism*. Ed. Josué V. Harari. Ithaca, New York: Cornell University Press, 1979, pp. 17-72.

Harries, Karsten. "The Many Uses of Metaphor." *Critical Inquiry*, 5, No. 1 (Autumn 1978), 167-174.

―――. "Metaphor and Transcendence." *Critical Inquiry*, 5, No. 1 (Autumn 1978), 73-90.

Havranek, Bohuslav. "The Functional Differentiation of the Standard Language." In *A Prague School Reader on Esthetics, Literary Structure, and Style*. Ed. and trans. Paul L. Garvin. Washington D.C.: Georgetown University Press, 1964, pp. 8-16.

Hayes, Charles. "Symbol and Correlative." *Sprachkunst: Beiträge zur Literaturwissenschaft*, Jahrgang 1, Heft 3 (1970), 161-180.

Hendel, Charles W. "Introduction." In *The Philosophy of Symbolic Forms*. Vol. I: *Language*.
Trans. Ralph Manheim. New Haven: Yale University Press, 1961, pp. 1-65.

Hendricks, William O. "Three Models for the Description of Poetry." *Journal of Linguistics*, 5, No. 1 (April 1969), 1-22.

Henel, Heinrich. "Metaphor and Meaning." In *The Disciplines of Criticism: Essays in Literary Theory, Interpretation, and History.* Ed. Peter Demetz, Thomas Greene, *et al.* New Haven, London: Yale University Press, 1968, pp. 93-123.

Hesse, Mary. "Scientific Models." In *Essays on Metaphor.* Ed. Warren Schibles. Whitewater, Wisconsin: The Language Press, 1972, pp. 169-180.

Hester, Marcus B. "Metaphor and Aspect Seeing." *Journal of Aesthetics and Art Criticism,* 25 (Winter 1966), 205-211.

Hillman, Donald J. "On Grammars and Category Mistakes." *Mind* N.S., 72 (1963), 224-234.

Holz, Hans Heinz. "Das Wesen metaphorischen Sprechens." In *Festschrift für Ernst Bloch.* Ed. Rugard Otto Gropp. Berlin: Deutscher Verlag der Wissenschaften, 1955, pp. 101-120.

Husserl, Edmund. "Zur Logik der Zeichen (Semiotik)." In *Philosphie der Arithmetik.* Ed. Lothar Elegy. The Hague: Maritnus Nijhoff, 1970, pp. 340-372.

Ingarden, Roman. "Konkretisation und Rekonstruktion." In *Rezeptionsästhetik: Theorie und Praxis.* Ed. Rainer Warning. Munchen: Wilhelm Fink, 1975, pp. 42-70.

―――. "Künstlerische Funktionen der Sprache." *Sprachkunst,* I (1970), 20-31.

―――. "Poetics and Linguistics." In *Poetics, Poetyka.* Vol. I. Gravenhage: Mouton, 1961, pp. 3-10.

Ingendahl, Werner. "Leistung und Wirkung einer Metaphor, dargestellt am Terminus 'Worthof.'" *Muttersprache,* 80 (1970), 363-367.

―――. "Die Metaphorik und die sprachliche Objektivität: Brauchen wir noch den Begriff, ‚Metapher?'" *Wirkendes Wort,* 22 (1972), 268-274.

―――. "Sprachliche Grundlagen und poetische Formen der Ironie." *Sprachkunst,* 2 (1970), 228-241.

―――. "Versuch einer energetischen Betrachtung des dichterischen Prozesses." *Wirkendes Wort,* 20 (1970), 73-85.

―――. "Zur Metaphorik als Grundlage einer linguistischen Poetik: Zu Klaus Baumgärtners Beitrag." *Jahrbuch für Internationale Germanistik,* 2, Heft 1 (1970), 125-132.

―――. "Zur Systematisierung metaphorischer Prozesse." *Linguistische Berichte,* 2, Heft 8 (1970), 49-54.

Iseminger, Gary. "Roman Ingarden and the Aesthetic Object." *Philosophy and Phenomenological Research,* 33 (1973), 417-420.

―――. "The Work of Art as Artifact." *British Journal of Aesthetics.* 13 (1973), 3-16.

Isenberg, Arnold. "Symposium: Metaphor on Defining Metaphor." *Journal of Philosophy,* 60 (10 October 1963), 609-622.

Iser, Wolfgang. "Die Appellstruktur der Texte." In *Rezeptionsästhetik: Theorie und Praxis.* Ed. Rainer Warning. München:Wilhelm Fink, 1975, pp. 228-252.

―――. "Der Lesevorgang." In *Rezeptionsästhetik: Theorie und Praxis.* Ed. Rainer Warning. München: Wilhelm Fink, 1975, pp. 253-276.

Jakobson, Roman. "The Cardinal Dichotomy in Language." In *Language: An Enquiry into its Meaning and Function.* New York: Kennikat Press, 1971, 155.

―――. "Closing Statement: Linguistics and Poetics." In *Style in Language.* Ed. Thomas A. Sebeok. Cambridge: MIT Press, 1960, 347-358.

————. "Der Grammatische Bau des Gedichts von B. Brecht: 'Wir sind sie.'" In *Beiträge zur Sprachwissenschaft, Volkskunde und Literaturforschung.* Ed. Alexander V. Isacenko. Berlin: Akademie-Verlag, 1965, pp. 175-189. Also in *Strukturalismus in der Literaturwissenschaft.* Köln: Kiepenheuer and Witsch, 1972, pp. 169-183

————. "Poesie der Grammatik und Grammatik der Poesie." In *Mathematik und Dichtung: Versuche zur Frage einer exakten Literaturwissenschaft.* Ed. Rul Gunzenhäuser and Helmut Kreuzer. München: Nymphenburger Verlagshandlung, 1954, pp. 21-32.

————. "Poetry of Grammar and Grammar of Poetry." In *Poetics, Poetyka.* Vol. I. Gravenhage: Mouton, 1961, pp. 397-418.

————, and Claude Lévi-Strauss. "'Les Chats' von Charles Baudelaire." *Alternative,* (1962 63), 156-170.

Jauss, Hans Robert. "Literaturgeschichte als Provokation der Literaturwissenschaft." In *Rezeptionsästhetik: Theorie und Praxis.* Ed. Rainer Warning. München: Wilhelm Fink, 1975, pp. 126-162.

Johnson, Mark. "Introduction: Metaphor in the Philosophical Tradition." In *Philosophical Perspectives on Metaphor,* Mark Johnson, ed. Minneapolis: University of Minnesota Press, 1981, pp. 3-47.

Johnson, Thomas H. "Introduction." In *The Complete Poems of Emily Dickinson.* Boston, Toronto: Little, Brown and Company, 1960, pp. v-xi.

Juhl, Peter D. "The Doctrine of 'Verstehen' and the Objectivity of Literary Interpretations." *Deutsche Vierteljahrsschrift für Literaturwissenschaft und Geistesgeschichte,* 49, No. 3 (1975), 380-424.

Kant, Immanuel. "Beantwortung der Frage: Was ist Aufklärung?" In *Immanuel Kants Werke.* Vol. IV: *1Schriften von 1783-1788.* Ed. Artur Buchenau *and Ernst Cassirer.* Berlin: Bruno Cassirer, 1913, pp. 167-176.

————. "An *Answer to the Question:* 'What is Enlightenment?'." In *Kant's Political Writings.* Ed. Hans Reiss. Trans. H.B. Nisbet. Cambridge: Cambridge University Press, 1970, pp. 54-60.

Kaplan, Bernard. "Radical Metaphor, Aesthetic and the Origin of Language." *Review of Existential Psychology and Psychiatry,* 2 (Winter 1962), 75-84.

Katz, Jerrold J. "Analycity and Contradiction in Natural Language." In *The Structure of Language: Readings on the Philosophy of Language.* Englewood Cliffs, New Jersey: Prentice Hall, 1964, pp. 519-537.

————. "Recent Issues in Semantic Theory." *Foundations of Language,* 3 (1967), 124-194.

————. "The Theory of Language." In *The Philosophy of Language.* New York, London: Harper and Row, 1966, pp. 98-185.

————, and Jerry A. Fodor. "The Structure of a Semantic Theory." In *The Structure of Language: Readings on the Philosophy of Language.* Englewood Cliffs, New Jersey: Prentice Hall, 1964, pp. 479-518.

Ketner, Kenneth Laine, and Christian J. W. Kloesel. "The Semiotic of Charles Sanders Peirce and the Dictionary of Semiotics." *Semiotica,* 13, No. 4 (1975), 395-414.

Knapp, Robert H. "A Study of the Metaphor." *Journal of Projective Technique,* 24 (December 1960), 390-395.

Kreuzer, Helmut. "'Mathematik und Dichtung.' Zur Einführung." In *Mathematik und Dichtung: Versuche zur Frage einer exakten Literaturwissenschaft*. Ed. Rul Gunzenhäuser and Helmut Kreuzer. München: Nymphenburger Verlagshandlung, 1965, pp. 7-20.

Krieger, Murray. "Contextualism Was Ambitious." *Journal of Aesthetics and Art Criticism*, 21 (1962-1963), 81-88.

Kripke, Saul A. "Naming and Necessity." In *Semantics of Natural Language*. 2nd ed. Ed. Donald Davidson and Gilbert Harman. Holland, Boston: D. Reidel Publishing Company, 1972, pp. 253-355.

Kristeva, Julia. "Introduction: Le lieu sémiotique." In *Essays in Semiotics / essais de sémiotique*. Ed. Julia Kristeva, Josette Rey-Debove, et al. The Hague, Paris: Mouton, 1971, pp. 1-7.

———. "L'expansion de la sémiotique." In *Essays in Semiotics essais de sémiotique*. Ed. Julia Kristeva, Josette Rey-Debove, et al. The Hague, Paris. Mouton, 1971, pp. 31-41.

Kwant, Remy C. "Merleau-Ponty and Phenomonology." *In Phenomonology: The Philosophy of Edmund Husserl and Its Interpretation*. Ed. Joseph J. Kockelmans. Garden City, New York: Doubleday, 1967, pp. 375-392.

La Guardia, Eric. "Aesthetics of Analogy." *Diogenes*, 62 (Summer 1968), 49-61.

Lakoff, George, and Mark Johnson. "Conceptual Metaphor in Everyday Language." *The Journal of Philosopy*, 77, No. 8 (August 1980), 453-486.

Lee, Brian. "The New Criticism and the Language of Poetry." In *Essays on Style and Language: Linguistic and Critical Approaches to Literary Style*. Ed. Roger Fowler. London: Routledge and Kegan Paul, 1966, pp. 29-52.

Levin, Samuel R. "The Analysis of Compression in Poetry." *Foundations of Language*, 7 (1971), 38-55.

———. "Internal and External Deviation in Poetry." *Word*, 21 (1965), 225-237.

———. "Reply to Kintgen." *Foundations of Language*, 9 (1972), 105-112.

———. "Standard Approaches to Metaphor and a Proposal for Literary Metaphor." In *Metaphor and Thought*. Ed. Andrew Ortony. Cambridge, London: Cambridge University Press, 1979, pp. 124-135.

———. "Statistische und determinierte Abweichung in poetischer Sprache." In *Mathematik und Dichtung: Versuche zur Frage einer exakten Literaturwissenschaft*. Ed. Rul Gunzenhäuser and Helmut Kreuzer. München: Nymphenburger Verlagshandlung, 1965, pp. 33-48.

Lewis, Philip E. "Merleau-Ponty and the Phenomenology of Language." In *Structuralism*. Ed. Jacques Ehermann. Garden City, New York: Doubleday, 1966, pp. 9-31.

Lieb, Hans-Heinrich. "Probleme der sprachlichen Abweichung." *Linguistische Berichte*, 7 (1970), 13-23.

———. "Was bezeichnet der herkömmliche Begriff ‚Metapher'?" *Muttersprache*, 2 (1976), 43-52.

Lohner, Edgar. "The Intrinsic Method: Some Reconsiderations." In *The Disciplines of Criticism: Essays in Literary Theory, Interpretation, and History*. Ed. Peter Demetz, Thomas Greene and Lowry Nelson, Jr. New Haven, London: Yale University Press, 1968, pp. 147-171.

Lotman, J. M. "The Discrete Text and the Iconic Text: Remarks on the Structure of Narrative." *New Literary History: A Journal of Theory and Interpretation*, 6 (1974/75), 333-338.

Lucid, Daniel P. "Introduction." In *Soviet Semiotics: An Anthology*. Ed. and trans. Daniel P. Lucid. Baltimore: Johns Hopkins University Press, 1977, pp. 1-24.

Luther, Martin. "Sendbrief vom Dolmetschen" (1530). In *Luthers Werke*. Vol. III. Ed. Arnold E. Berger. Leipzig, Wien: Bibliographisches Institut, n.d., pp. 165-188.

MacCormac, R. Earl. "Metaphor and Literature." *Journal of Aesthetic Education*, 6 (July 1972), 57-70.

Mackey, Louis. "Aristotle and Feidelson on Metaphor: Toward a Reconciliation of Ancient and Modern." *Arion*, 4 (Summer 1965), 272-285.

Man, Paul de. See: de Man, Paul.

Marias, Julian. "Philosophic Truth and Metaphoric System." In *The Poetry of Meaning*. Eds. Stanley Romaine Hopper and David L. Miller. New York: Harcourt, Brace and World, 1966, pp. 41-102.

Marsch, Edgar. "Die Lyrische Chiffre: Ein Beitrag zur Poetik des modernen Gedichts." Sprachkunst: Beiträge zur Literaturwissenschaft, 1, No. 3 (1970), 208-240.

Martinet, André. "Structure and Language." In *Structuralism*. Ed. Jacques Ehrmann. Garden City, New York: Doubleday, 1966, pp. 1-8.

Maser, Siegfried. "Theorie und Praxis menschlicher Kommunikation." In *Linguistik und Sprachphilosophie*. Ed. Marlis Gerhardt. München: List, 1974, pp. 191-206.

Matthews, Robert J. "Concerning a 'Linguistic Theory' of Metaphor." *Foundations of Language*, 7 (1971), 413-425.

————, and Wilfried Ver Eecke. "Metaphoric-Metonymic Polarities: A Structural Analysis." *Linguistics: An International Review*, 67 (March 1971), 34-53.

Mazzeo, Joseph Anthony. "Critique of Some Modern Theories of Metaphysical Poetry." In *Modern Philology*, 50 (November 1952), 88-96.

McCanles, Michael. "The Literal and the Metaphorical: Dialectic of Interchange." *PMLA*, 91, No. 1 (March 1976), 279-290.

McKeen, Charles K. "Peirce's Scotistic Realism." In *Studies in the Philosophy of Charles Sanders Peirce*. Ed. Philip P. Wiener and Fredric H. Young. Cambridge: Harvard University Press, 1952, pp. 238-350.

McPherson, Thomas. "Assertion and Analogy." *Proceedings of the Aristotelian Society*, 60 (1959-60), 154-170.

Merleau-Ponty, Maurice. "What is Phenomenology?" In *Phenomonology: The Philosophy of Edmund Husserl and Its Interpretation*. Ed. Joseph J. Kockelmans. Garden City, New York: Doubleday, 1967, pp. 356-374.

Meszaros, Istvan. "Metaphor and Simile." *Proceedings of the Aristotelian Society*, 67 (1967), 127-144.

Morgan, Jerry L. "Observations on the Pragmatics of Metaphor." In *Metaphor and Thought*. Ed. Andrew Ortony. Cambridge, London: Cambridge University Press, 1979, pp. 136-147.

Müller-Vollmer, Kurt. "Von der Poetik zur Linguistik--Wilhelm von Humboldt und der romantische Sprachbegriff." In *Universalismus und Wissenschaft im Werk und Wirken der Brüder Humboldt.* Ed. Kurt Müller-Vollmer. Frankfurt a/M: Klostermann, 1976, pp. 224-240.

———. "Rezeption und Neuansatz: Phänomenologische Literaturwissenschaft in den Vereinigten Staaten." *LiLi,* Heft 17 (n.d.), 10-24.

Murray, Michael. "Introduction." In *Heidegger and Modern Philosophy: Critical Essays.* Ed. Michael Murray. New Haven, London: Yale University Press, 1978, pp. vii-xxiii.

Myers, Charles Mason. "The Circular Use of Metaphor." *Philosophy and Phenomenological Research,* 26 (March 1966), 391-402.

———. "Inexplicable Analogies." *Philosophy and Phenomenological Research,* 22 (March 1962), 326-333.

———. "Metaphors and Mediately Informative Expressions." *The Southern Journal of Philosophy,* 6 (Fall 1968), 159-166.

———. "Metaphors and the Intelligibility of Dreams." *Philosophy and Rhetoric,* 2 (Spring 1969), 91-99.

Nemetz, Anthony. "Metaphor: The Daedalus of Discourse." *Thought,* 33 (1958), 417-442.

Neumann, Gerhard. "Die 'Absolute' Metapher: Ein Abgrenzungsversuch am *Beispiel Stéphane Mallarmés und Paul Celans.*" "*Poetica: Zeitschrift für Sprach- und Literaturwissenschaft,* 3 (1970), 188-225.

Nietzsche, Friedrich. "Ueber Wahrheit und Lüge im aussermoralischen Sinne." In *Nietzsches Werke.* Vol. II. Salzburg: Das Bergland-Buch', n.d., pp. 1079-1092. Trans. "On Truth and Falsity in Their Extramoral Sense." In *Essays on Metaphor.* Ed. Warren Shibles. Whitewater, Wisconsin: The Language Press, 1972, pp. 1-14.

Ohmann, Richard. "Generative Grammars and the Concept of Literary Style." In *Linguistics and Literary Style.* Ed. Donald C. Freeman. New York, Chicago: Holt, Rinehart and Winston, 1976, pp. 258-259.

———. "Speech Acts and the Definition of Literature." *Philosophy and Rhetoric,* 4 (1971), 1-19.

O'Neill, John. "Time's Body: Vico on the Love of Language and Institution." In *Giambattista Vico's Science of Humanity.* Ed. Giorgio Tagliacozzo and Donald Phillip Verene. Baltimore, London: The Johns Hopkins University Press, 1976, pp. 333-339.

O'Neill, Joseph E. "The Metaphorical Mode: Image, Metaphor, Symbol." *Thought,* 31 (1956), 79-113.

Ong, Walter J. "Metaphor and the Twinned Vision." *The Sewanee Review,* 63 (April 1955), 193-201.

Ortony, Andrew. "Metaphor: A Multidimensional Problem." In *Metaphor and Thought.* Ed. Andrew Ortony. Cambridge, London: Cambridge University Press, 1979, pp. 1-18.

Paul, Anthony M. "Metaphor and the Bounds of Expression." *Philosophy and Rhetoric,* 5 (1972), 143-158.

Pausch, Holger A. "Die Metapher." *Wirkendes Wort,* 24 (1974), 56-69.

Peckham, Morse. "Metaphor: A Little Plain Speaking on a Weary Subject." *Connotation,* 1, No. 2 (1962), 29-46.

Pelc, Jerzy. "Semantic Functions as Applied to the Analysis of the Concept of Metaphor." In *Poetics, Poetyka.* Vol. I. Gravenhage: Mouton, 1961, pp. 305-339.

Pratt, William. "Introduction." In *Modern Poetry in Miniature: The Imagist Poem*. Ed. William Pratt. New York: E. P. Dutton, 1967, pp. 11-39.

Quine, W. V. "A Postscript on Metaphor." *Critical Inquiry*, 5, No. 1 (Autumn 1978), 161-162.

Ramsey, Ian T. "Models and Mystery." In *Essays on Metaphor*. Ed. Warren Shibles. Whitewater, Wisconsin: The Language Press, 1972, pp. 163-168.

Raudsepp, Eugene. "Synectics." In *Essays on Metaphor*. Ed. Warren Shibles. Whitewater, Wisconsin: The Language Press, 1972, pp. 141-154.

Reddy, Michael J. "A Semantic Approach to Metaphor." *Chicago Linguistic Society*, 5th Regional Meeting, University of Chicago Linguistics Dept. (18-19 April 1969), 240-251.

———. "The Conduit Metaphor--A Case of Frame Conflict in Our Language about Language." In *Metaphor and Thought*. Ed. Andrew Ortony. Cambridge, London: Cambridge University Press, 1979, pp. 284-324.

Reese, William. "Philosophic Realism: A Study in the Modality of Being in Peirce and Whitehead." In *Studies in the Philosophy of Charles Sanders Peirce*. Ed. Philip P. Wiener and Fredric H. Young. Cambridge: Harvard University Press, 1952, pp. 225-237.

Ricoeur, Paul. "Metaphor and the Main Problem of Hermeneutics." *New Literary History*, 6, No. 1 (Autumn 1974), 95-110.

———. "The Metaphorical Process as Cognition, Imagination, and Feeling." *Critical Inquiry*, 5, No. 1 (Autumn 1978), 143-160.

Riffaterre, Michael. "Describing Poetic Structures: Two Approaches to Baudelaire's *les Chats*." In *Structuralism*. Ed. Jacques Ehrmann. Garden City, New York: Doubleday, 1966, pp. 188-230.

———. "Generating Lautréamont's Text." In *Textual Strategies: Perspectives in Post-Structuralist Criticism*. Ed. Josué V. Harari. Ithaca, New York: Cornell University Press, 1979, pp. 404-420.

———. "Kriterien für die Stilanalyse." In *Rezeptionsästhetik: Theorie und Praxis*. Ed. Rainer Warning. München: Wilhelm Fink, 1975, pp. 163-195.

———. "Stylistic Context." *Word*, 16, No. 2 (1960), 207-218.

Robbe-Grillet, Alan, "Dehumanizing Nature." In *The Modern Tradition*. Eds. Richard Elmann and C. Fedelson, Jr. New York: Oxford University Press, 1965, pp. 362-378.

Roedig, Charles F. "Baudelaire and Synesthesia." *Kentucky Foreign Language Quarterly*. (Now called *Kentucky Romance Quarterly*) , 5 (1958), 128-135.

Rother, James. "Modernism and the Nonsense Style." *Contemporary Literature*, 15, No. 2 (Spring 1974), 187-202.

Rueckert, William. "Literary Criticism and History: The Endless Dialectic." *New Literary History: A Journal of Theory and Interpretation*, 6 (1974/75), 491-512.

Rumelhart, David E. "Some Problems with the Notion of Literal Meanings." In *Metaphor and Thought*. Ed. Andrew Ortony. Cambridge, London: Cambridge University Press, 1979, pp. 78-90.

Ryle, Gilbert. "Categories." *Proceedings of the Aristotelian Society*, 38 (1937-38), 189-206.
Also in *Logic and Language: Second Series*. Ed. Anthony Flew. Oxford: Basil Blackwell, 1961, pp. 65-81.

———. "Systematically Misleading Expressions." In *Logic and Language: Series*. Ed. Anthony Flew. Oxford: Basil Blackwell, 1963, pp. 11-36.

————. "The Theory of Meaning." In *Collected Papers. Vol. II: Collected Essays 1929-1968.* New York: Barnes and Noble, 1971, pp. 350-372.

Sacks, Sheldon. "The Psychological Implications of Generic Distinctions." *Genre,* 1 (1968), 106-123.

Sadock, Jerrold M. "Figurative Speech and Linguistics." In *Metaphor and Thought.* Ed. Andrew Ortony. Cambridge, London: Cambridge University Press, 1979, pp. 46-63.

Sambursky, S. "A Democritean Metaphor in Plato's Kratylos." *Phronesis,* 4 (1959), 1-4.

Sanner, Rolf. "Ueber das Verhältnis von Wort und Bild: Grenzen-Uebergänge-Spannungen." *Wirkendes Wort,* 13 (1963), 321-331.

Sarbin, Theodore R. "Anxiety: Reification of a Metaphor." In *Essays on Metaphor.* Ed. Warren Schibles. Whitewater, Wisconsin: The Language Press, 1972, pp. 125-140.

Schlanger, Judith E. "Metaphor and Invention." Trans. Yvonne Burne. *Diogenes,* 69 (Spring 1970), 12-27.

Schmidt, Siegfried J. "Alltagssprache und Gedichtsprache: Versuch einer Bestimmung von Differenzqualitäten." *Poetica: Zeitschrift für Sprach-und Literaturwissenschaft,* 2 (1968), 285-303.

Schneider, Herbert W. "Fourthness." In *Studies in the Philosophy of Charles Sanders Peirce.* Ed. Philip P. Wiener and Fredric H. Young. Cambridge: Harvard University Press, 1952, pp. 209-214.

Schwyzer, H. R. G. "Wittgenstein's Picture-Theory of Language." *Inquiry,* 5 (1962), 46-64.

Searle, John R. "Austin on Locutionary and Illocutionary Acts." In *Essays on J. L. Austin.* Oxford: The Clarendon Press, 1973, pp. 141-159.

————. "The Logical Status of Fictional Discourse." *New Literary History: A Journal of Theory and Interpretation,* 6 (1974-75), 319-332.

————. "Metaphor." In *Metaphor and Thought.* Ed. Andrew Ortony. Cambridge, London: Cambridge University Press, 1979, pp. 92-123.

Seidler, Herbert. "Der Begriff des Sprachstils in der Literaturwissenschaft." *Sprachkunst,* . No. 1 2 (1970), 1-19.

———— "Stilistik als Wissenschaft von der Sprachkunst." *Jahrbuch für Internationale Germanistik,* 1 (1969), 129-137.

Shipley, Elizabeth F., Carolota S. Smith, and Lila R. Gleitman. "A Study in the Acquisition of Language: Free Responses to Commands." *Language,* 45 (1969), 322-342.

Sparshott, F. E. "'As,' or the Limits of Metaphor." *New Literary History,* 6, No. 1 (Autumn 1974), 75-94.

Spitzer, Leo. "Language of Poetry." In *Language: An Enquiry Into Its Meaning and Function.* Ed. Ruth Nanda Anshen. Port Washington, New York, London: Kennikat Press, 1971. pp. 201-231.

Stählin, Wilhelm. "Zur Psychologie und Statistik der Metaphern. Eine methodologische Untersuchung." *Archiv für die gesammte Psychologie,* 31 (1914), 297-424.

Stanford, William Bedell. "Synaesthetic Metaphor." *Comparative Literature Studies,* 6-7 (1942), 26-30.

Stankiewicz, Edward. "Poetic and Non-Poetic Language in their Interrelation.' In
    Poetics, Poetyka, Vol. I. Gravenhage: Mouton, 1961, pp. 11-24.
————. "Poetics and Verbal Art." In A Perfusion of Signs. Ed. Thomas A. Sebeok.
    Bloomington, London: Indiana University Press, 1977, pp. 54-76.
————. "The Poetic Text as a Linguistic Structure." 'The Institute.' 1 September
    1971.
————. "Structural Poetics and Linguistics." In Current Trends in Linguistics.
    Vol. XII: Linguistics and Adjacent Arts and Sciences. Ed. Thomas A. Sebeok.
    The Hague, Paris: Mouton, 1974, pp. 629-658.
Starbuck, George. "Anacolouthon All Over Again: A Plea for Pedantry." In Poetic
    Theory Poetic Practice: Papers of the Midwest Modern Language Association,
    October, 1963. Ed. Robert Scholes. Iowa City: Midwest Modern Language
    Association, 1969, pp. 36-51.
Stearns, Isabel S. "Firstness, Secondness, and Thirdness." In Studies in the
    Philosophy of Charles Sanders Peirce. Ed. Philip P. Wiener and Fredric H.
    Young. Cambridge: Harvard University Press, 1952, pp. 195-208.
Stewart, Donald. "Metaphor and Paraphrase." Philosophy and Rhetoric, 4 (1971),
    111-123.
Strawson, P. F. "Austin and 'Locutionary Meaning.'" In Essays on J. L. Austin.
    Oxford: The Clarendon Press, 1973, pp. 46-68.
Sutton, Walter. "The Contextualist Dilemma--or Fallacy." Journal of Aesthetics
    and Art Criticism, 17 (1958-59), 219-229.
Tarski, Alfred. "The Semantic Conception of Truth and the Foundation of
    Semantics." Philosophy and Phenomenological Research, 4 (1944), 341-376.
Thompson, J. "Linguistic Structure and the Poetic Line." In Poetics, Poetyka, Vol.
    I. Gravenhage: Mouton, 1961, pp. 167-176.
Thorne, James Peter. "Stylistics and Generative Grammars." Journal of
    Linguistics, 1 (1965), 49-59.
Todorov, Tzvetan. "Les anomalies sémantiques." Languages, 1 (1966), 100-123.
————. "L'héritage méthodologique du Formalisme." L'Homme, 5 (1965), 64-83.
————. "On Linguistic Symbolism." Trans. Richard Klein, New Literary History,
    6, No. 1 (Autumn 1974), 111-134.
Tuve, Rosemond. "Imagery and Logic: Ramus and Metaphysical Poetics."
    Journal of the History of Ideas, 3 (October 1942), 366-400.
Uhlenbeck, E. M. "Language in Action." In To Honor Roman Jakobson: Essays
    on the Occasion of His 73rd Birthday, 11 October 1966. The Hague, Paris:
    Mouton, 1967, pp. 2060-2066.
————. "Some Further Remarks on Transformational Grammar." Lingua, 17
    (1967), 263-316.
Vianu, T. "The Poetic Metaphor." In Poetics, Poetyka, Vol. I. Gravenhage:
    Mouton, 1961, pp. 297-304.
Vonessen, von Franz. "Die Ontologische Struktur der Metapher." Zeitschrift für
    Philosophische Forschung, 13 (1959), 397-419.
Wackenroder, Wilhelm Heinrich. "Von zwei wunderbaren Sprachen und deren
    geheimnisvoller Kraft." In Werke und Briefe. Heidelberg: Lambert Schneider,
    1967, pp. 67-71.

Walther, Elisabeth. "Semiotische Analyse." In *Mathematik und Dichtung:* *Versuche zur Frage einer exakten Literaturwissenschaft.* Ed. Rul Gunzenhäuser and Helmut Kreuzer. München: Nymphenberger Verlagshandlung, 1965, pp. 143-158.

Webster, T. B. L. "Personification as a Mode of Greek Thought." *Journal of The Warburg and Wurtaubl Institute,* 17 (1954), 10-21.

Weinreich, Uriel. "Explorations in Semantic Theory." In *Current Trends in Linguistics.* Vol. III: *Theoretical Foundations.* Ed. Thomas A. Sebeok. The Hague, Paris: Mouton, 1966, pp. 395-477.

———. "Problems in the Analysis of Idioms." In *Substance and Structure of Language.* Ed. Jean Puhvel. Berkeley, Los Angeles: University of California Press, 1969, pp. 23-81.

Weinrich, Harald. "Münze und Wort: Untersuchungen an einem Bildfeld." In *Romanica: Festschrift für Gerhard Rohlfs.* Ed. Heinrich Lausberg. Halle: Niemeyer, 1958, pp. 508-521.

———. "Semantik der kühnen Metapher." *Deutsche Vierteljahrsschrift,* 37 (1963), 325-344.

———. "Semantik der Metapher." *Folia Linguistica,* 1 (1967), 3-17.

Wellek, René. "Aesthetics and Criticism." In *The Philosophy of Kant and Our Modern World: Four Lectures Delivered at Yale University Commemorating the 150th Anniversary of the Death of Immanuel Kant.* Ed. Charles W. Hendel. New York: The Liberal Arts Press, 1957, pp. 45-89.

Wells, Rulon. "Charles S. Peirce as an American." In *Perspectives on Peirce: Critical Essays on Charles Sanders Peirce.* Ed. Richard J. Bernstein. New Haven, London: Yale University Press, 1965, pp. 13-41.

———. "Distinctively Human Semiotic." In *Essays in Semiotics/essais de sémiotique.* Ed. Julia Kristeva, Josette Rey-Debove, et al. The Hague, Paris: Mouton, 1971, pp. 95-119.

———. "Nominal and Verbal Style." In *Linguistics and Literary Style.* Ed. Donald C. Freeman. New York, Chicago: Holt, Rinehart and Winston, 1976, pp. 297-306.

Welsh, Paul. "On Explication Metaphors." *Journal of Philosophy,* 60 (October 10, 1963), 622-623.

Wettstein, Howard K. "Can What is Asserted be a Sentence?" The *Philosophical Review,* 85, No. 2 (April 1976), 196-207.

Wescott, Roger W. "Linguistic Iconism." *Language,* 47, No. 2 (June 1971), 416-428.

Wheelwright, Philip. "Semantics and Ontology." In *Essays on Metaphor,* Ed. Warren Shibles. Whitewater, Wisconsin: The Language Press, 1972, pp. 61-72.

Wimsatt, William Kurtz, Jr. "The Chicago Critics: The Fallacy of the Neoclassic Species." In *The Verbal Icon: Studies in the Meaning of Poetry.* Ed. William Kurtz Wimsatt, Jr. Lexington: University of Kentucky Press, 1967, pp. 41-65.

———, and Monroe C. Beardsley. "The Intentional Fallacy." In *The Verbal Icon: Studies in the Meaning of Poetry.* Ed. William Kurtz Wimsatt, Jr. Lexington: University Press, 1967, pp. 3-18.

Wu, Joseph. "Chinese Language and Chinese Thought." *Philosophy East and West*, 19 (October 1969), 423-434.

Yoos, George E. "An Analysis of some Rhetorical Uses of Subjunctive Conditionals." *Philosophy and Rhetoric*, 8, No. 4 (1975), 203-212.

———. "A Phenomenological Look at Metaphor." *Philosophy and Phenomenological Research*, 32 (1971), 79-88.

———. "On Being Literally False." Philosophy and Rhetoric, 1, No. 4 (1968), 211-227.

Index

www.ingramcontent.com/pod-product-compliance
Lightning Source LLC
Chambersburg PA
CBHW020405100426
42812CB00001B/207